What some of the Reform contemporaries said about them:

"It is vain to talk of the good character of bishops. Bishops are not always the wisest of men; not always preferred for eminent virtues and talents, or for any good reason whatever known to the public." **Sydney Smith, Canon of St Paul's Cathedral**

"'Merit, indeed,' said Westmorland in surprise. "We are come to a pretty pass if they talk of merit for a bishopric." **Lord Westmorland's reaction to the Prime Minister's refusal to prefer one of his clerical protégés on the grounds that 'he had not sufficient merit for a bishopric'.**

"Parliamentary Interest, Family Connections or Party Gratitude, have in general filled up the vacancies as they have arisen, with the Sons, the Brothers and the Tutors of Ministers and of their adherents." **Lord Henley in his pamphlet *Church Reform* 1832**

"There is, in truth, no situation in which 'fitness' for the office has been less frequently consulted."
A.J. Johnes to Lord John Russell 1836

"Damn it, another bishop dead! . . . I believe they die to vex me!" **The Prime Minister, Lord Melbourne, who had to appoint three in 1840**

"Remember, remember
that God is the sender
of every good gift unto man;
but the devil, to spite us
sent fellows with mitres
who rob us of all that they can."
Bonfire procession in Crayford, Kent on 5 November 1831

"Good Lord! Put down aristocrats,
let Boroughmongers be abhorred;
and from all tithes and shovel hats
forthwith deliver us good Lord!"
The Poor Man's Guardian No 22. 19 November 1831

"The majority of the Bishops of the Church of England *always* are persons whose main object is to amass wealth, and to aggrandize their families." **R.M. Beverley in *A Letter to the Archbishop of York on the Present Corrupt State of the Church of England* 1831**

"A snivelling, snuffling, truckling set of rogues who followed the ministers of the Crown like well-trained pointers." **James Crow in *How to rise in the Church* 4th edition 1837**

"The qualities of a Bishop are, according to the long-established Tory creed, servility, decorum and recondite learning." **William Carpenter in *Peerage for the People* 1837**

The Reform Bishops
1828-1840

A Biographical Study

Trevor Park

*David

With thanks for your help and encouragement.

Trevor*

St Bega Publications

2016

With thanks for the life and ministry of Cyril Bulley (1907-1989),
Bishop of Penrith 1959-66 and then Bishop of Carlisle 1966-72,
who ordained me and was truly a father in God to me and my family.

And with heartfelt gratitude to my wife, Olaug Johanne Christiansen (1935-2015) from Stavanger in Norway, who shared in every way she could in my ministry after my ordination in 1966. Her goodness and love touched so many lives.

Copyright © Trevor Park 2016

The moral right of the author has been asserted.

All rights reserved. No part of this publication may be reproduced, stored in a retrieval system, or transmitted in any form or by any means, without the prior permission in writing of the author, nor be otherwise circulated in any form of binding or cover other than that in which it is published.

ISBN 978-0-9508325-6-2

Printed and bound in Great Britain by
CMP UK Ltd, 960 Capability Green, Luton, Bedfordshire LU1 3PE

Contents

Preface & Acknowledgements	6
Introduction	10
Chronological Table of Reform	12
Bishops of the Established Church 1828-1840	14
Childhood and Early Education	16
At Oxbridge	28
Climbing the Clerical Ladder	48
Patronage and Preferment	69
The Bishops as Legislators	99
Church Reform	140
The Bishops in their Dioceses	171
Their Visitation Charges 1828-40	220
Ministerial Training in the Dioceses	276
Episcopal Family Life	316
An Assessment	346
Appendix 1: Episcopal Stipends	366
Appendix 2: Population and Benefices of the Dioceses taken from the Returns of 1831	368
Appendix 3: *Address to the Parishioners of Alderley*	369
Bibliography	371
Index of People	387

Preface

It may be of interest to the reader to know how this book came to be written. The thought of it goes back more than twenty years to the time when I was a member of the General Synod of the Church of England and an elected Church Commissioner, which provided plentiful opportunity of observing and listening to members of the then bench of bishops. During the twenty-two years I served on the Synod, reports and measures galore were discussed and voted on, some of which were as important as any of those passed in the period under review in this book. I think especially of such measures as the Ordination of Women to the Priesthood, the Meissen and Porvoo Agreements, the creation of the Diocese in Europe, much liturgical reform, the equalisation of clergy stipends and such groundbreaking reports as *Faith in the City* which challenged both the Church itself, as well as the Government, to improve its care for people living in socially deprived conditions.

Memories of a few speeches given by bishops still remain with me decades later: in particular the passion and logic of John Austin Baker, the Bishop of Salisbury, arguing the case for unilateral nuclear disarmament, and Robert Williamson, the Bishop of Southwark, making a powerful plea for the ordination of women on the grounds of justice, and the theological intervention in other debates by such scholars as David Jenkins, the Bishop of Durham, and Stephen Sykes, the Bishop of Ely. There were also some rather dull episcopal contributions to debates, and occasionally, what seemed to me to be expressions of self-interest, for example when a motion on reducing differentials in the stipends of dignitaries and parish clergy was debated.

I saw, too, as the most junior member of the Synod's working party on 'Senior Church Appointments', chaired by a former Tory government minister, how such sensitive Church - State political issues are dealt with behind closed doors. The last quarter of the 20th century was, I believe, an era of reform which may well be seen by future historians as having been as important to the well-being of the Established Church and its ministry to the nation as were those reforms enacted between 1828 and 1840.

I occasionally wondered how like or different the members of the House of Bishops, whom I knew in the late twentieth century, were to their predecessors at the time of the Great Reform Act and of the subsequent church reforms. There was no General Synod in those days and the

Convocations of Canterbury and York no longer met to transact business but the bishops did have a high public profile then and a potentially influential voice in the House of Lords. Did that earlier generation of bishops include heavyweight theologians and persuasive orators, I wondered? Did they have a concern for social justice? Were they effective pastors and administrators who knew and cared for their clergy? So I made a tentative start on the essential background reading about the episcopate in the early nineteenth century.

I had already encountered, metaphorically speaking, seven of the men who appear in these pages when I was doing doctoral research into the theological education and professional training of the clergy of the Church of England during the first half of the nineteenth century. They were George Henry Law, Bishop of Chester, who founded St Bees Clerical Institution in West Cumberland in 1816, and Thomas Burgess, Bishop of St David's, who saw the need for a college in South Wales as early as 1805, though it did not open until 1827. These two men were pioneers in this respect. Bishop William Van Mildert's early direction and financial support for the founding of a university college in Durham in 1831 was essential to the success of that project. Archbishop Howley and Bishop Blomfield gave public support for King's College London in 1828 and for St Augustine's College Canterbury in 1845. William Otter took the initiative to found the first post-graduate theological college in Chichester in 1839. G.H. Law gave his blessing in 1840 to a second post-graduate institution at Wells though the impetus for its foundation came from others, including his son James who was Archdeacon. And lastly Bishop John Bird Sumner supported St Bees, was marginally involved in the founding of St Aidan's College Birkenhead in 1846, and, as Archbishop, dedicated St Augustine's College Canterbury. These were important and innovative episcopal actions at that time – signs of new life in the Church. Were their fellow bishops equally effective in other areas of the Church's life and ministry, I wanted to find out.

My research for this book, however, had to be put on hold in 1997 when I moved to Norway. The signing of the Porvoo Agreement a year earlier and my close family ties with Norway led me to accept a post there so that I could help implement the Agreement. At my Institution in St Edmund's Oslo by the Anglican Bishop in Europe I was also licensed by the Lutheran Bishop of Oslo for ministry in the Church of Norway. In the following eight years I was able to see and experience a different expression of episcopacy and of an established, folk church which, in some respects, is quite unlike the Church of England in its relations with the nation it serves. But being on the far side of the North Sea put a stop to my visiting record offices and cathedral and university libraries to read the letters, held in their archives, written by some of the bishops who appear in the following pages.

After retiring in 2005, I gave priority to producing a 2nd revised edition of my history of St Bees Theological College. I then completed the writing of my *Life* of Charles John Vaughan, who repeatedly refused offers of bishoprics in the late 19th century but who trained eighteen future bishops. So the subject of episcopacy as practised in the Established Church in that century was never far from my thoughts but by the time it came to writing this book personal family issues of age and infirmity had made it almost impossible for me to resume research into the primary manuscript sources on which I had started so long ago. Consequently it is the poorer for that omission which I regret. A bigger and better account must await the attention of a younger and more able historian. The result is that whilst this book is the product of wide reading it was limited very largely, though not entirely, to the reading of the available **printed** primary materials such as episcopal *Charges*, *Memoirs*, transcribed correspondence, newspaper articles and other contemporary writings, as well as of much later secondary material.

The events and politicians of the period continue to attract historians, and there is no end to new books on such issues as Catholic Emancipation in 1829 and the great Reform Act of 1832 but only four bishops of the reform period have been the subjects of substantial biographies published in the last twenty-five years. The most recent one is James Garrard's *Archbishop Howley 1828-48* which appeared in 2015. The others are Malcolm Johnson's *Bustling Intermeddler? The Life & Work of C.J. Blomfield* published in 2001, Nigel Scotland's *The Life & Work of John Bird Sumner* in 1995 and Elizabeth Varley's *The Last of the Prince Bishops: William Van Mildert* in 1992. In addition, Roger Lee Brown wrote a substantial Introduction to the life and ministry of Edward Copleston in his edited volume of the bishop's letters published in 2003. I hope this biographical study of all forty-five 'reform bishops' might inspire a few more in-depth accounts.

It was my good fortune that all the librarians and archivists I consulted were unfailingly helpful and I owe them a great debt of gratitude, in particular those at the Bodleian, the British Library, Cumbria Record Office, Lambeth Palace Library and the London Library. Full details of all quotations are given and sources are listed in the bibliography.

I am also deeply grateful to the many institutions which have given me permission to quote from papers deposited in their archives:
British Library - the Peel papers,
Cumbria Archives Centre Carlisle - Bishop Hugh Percy papers,
Durham University Library Archives & Special Collections - Thorp papers,
Lambeth Palace Library - the letters of Bishop Blomfield,
The Dean and Chapter of Landaff Cathedral - the letters of Bishop Copleston,
Balliol College Oxford - the Jenkyns' papers,
Bodleian Libraries Oxford - ms English letters,
Governors of Pusey House - the Ollard and Edward Coleridge papers,
the Keeper of the University Archives at Oxford - a Howley letter,
and to the Revd Canon Dr Roger Brown for permission to quote from his two books: *In Pursuit of a Welsh Episcopate* and the biographical introduction he wrote to the *Letters of Edward Copleston* which he edited.

The *Oxford Dictionary of National Biography* was a valuable secondary source and I acknowledge my debt to the writers whose articles I read and drew on in writing the chapter 'Climbing the Clerical Ladder'. The Bank of England's historical inflation tool proved useful in translating the purchasing power of early nineteenth century sums into twenty-first century ones. The map on p. 275 was drawn for me by a good friend, the late Dr John Todd, to illustrate an earlier piece of research I did; I use it again here as it provides a helpful introduction to the chapter on 'Ministerial Training in the Dioceses.'

Two retired diocesan bishops, who are both historians of the period, David Lunn and Geoffrey Rowell, read my draft manuscript critically and gave me much encouragement. David taught me theology when I was a student in the 1960s, and Geoffrey examined me on my doctoral thesis in 1991. I am so grateful to both of them for their helpful comments and suggestions. And lastly, a big Thank You to two other friends, Dorothy Warbrick and Jon Mellor, who proof read the final draft. Any remaining errors are, of course, entirely of my own making.

Trevor Park
St Bees
Easter 2016

Introduction

The years 1828 to 1840 saw radical changes in the Establishment as new civil and ecclesiastical laws were passed. Most famous was the Reform Act of 1832 which widened the electoral franchise and saw the creation of new constituencies. At long last industrial cities, such as Manchester and Birmingham, were given representation in Parliament. But that success was only achieved in the face of determined opposition over many years from the forces of conservatism and after repeated Bills had been rejected either in the House of Commons or in the Lords. Twenty-one bishops of the United Church of England and Ireland were among the majority who blocked it in the Lords in October 1831, sparking riots across the country. The bishops were so unpopular that on 5 November a mitred figure took the place of Guy Fawkes on bonfires. The Bill was only passed the following year because the Prime Minister, Earl Grey, persuaded the King to create enough new peers, if necessary, to force it through the Lords. At that point the opposition caved in.

In 1829 another landmark Bill had been passed which removed the last legal obstacles to Roman Catholics being elected to Parliament or holding high public office (with certain notable exceptions such as that of Lord Chancellor), but again that change was won in the face of bitter opposition, in particular, from Anglican Tories. Feelings ran very high. The Prime Minister, the Duke of Wellington, fought a duel over it with the Earl of Winchilsea who had accused him of treachery and of being in an alliance with Satan.

If there was need for electoral reform nationally and for radical change in local government and for new social legislation, there were other equally pressing needs for reform in the Church of England. John Wade's *Extraordinary Black Book* published in 1831 had documented a number of ills which were rife in the Established Church, among them the gross disparity in clerical stipends. The average curate earned at that time £81 a year (= £7,505 in 2014), but many had as little as £25, with no security of tenure, which was less than a coal face worker in a northern mine earned. At the other end of the financial spectrum were some of the bishops who were millionaires in today's terms. The Bishop of Durham, for example, received in 1831 £19,066 (= £1,766,666), just short of the Archbishop of Canterbury who had £19,182 (= £1,777,415). It was a situation more conducive to envy than to encouraging parish clergy to regard their bishop as a 'father in God'. And, as curates knew to their cost only too well, bishops, along with most other patrons, appointed their sons or other relatives and friends to the best endowed livings and ecclesiastical offices in their gift. Wade singled out Bishop Sparke of Ely who had appointed his two sons and a son-in-law to several livings in his diocese. He reckoned that between them they earned £39,942 a year (= £3,701,408). Worse still, some bishops exercised only perfunctory care in what should have been one of their most solemn responsibilities, that of ensuring that only men with a tested sense of vocation and some appropriate training were ordained to the sacred ministry.

The popular picture of an ecclesiastical prelate was of a privileged person totally out of touch with the lives and needs of the masses. Satirical prints from that period usually portray them as bloated, avaricious creatures. Whilst that is not a fair representation of the entire bench of bishops, there was more than enough truth in the charge for all of them to feel (had they so cared) besmirched and tarnished with the same brush.

This study seeks to provide a more measured account of the bishops in England and Wales during that decade: who they were, what their social background was, their education, how and by whose patronage they had come to be preferred to such high office and how they then carried out (or failed to carry out) its manifold duties and responsibilities both in their dioceses and at the national level, how they in turn exercised their patronage, and how supportive or resistant they were to reform in Church and State. It also includes some insight into their private family life. It provides a very mixed picture. Some of them deserved the derogatory comments of their contemporaries, quoted earlier; others were undoubtedly men of considerable ability and distinction.

As a preparatory aid to knowing the names and dates of bishops and the key events mentioned in the book, a short overview of reform legislation during the years 1828-40 and a list of all the bishops in England and Wales during that period follow. Bishops of the Established Church in Ireland are not included or listed in this study, though four 'representative' Irish bishops sat in the House of Lords from the time of the Act of Union passed in 1800. All four of them voted against the Reform Bill in October 1831. The Irish bishops and the problems of Ireland and of the Anglican minority there at that time deserve a separate volume.

Chronological Table of Reform

The Government and Prime Minister	Acts of Parliament	Church Reforms
1828 Tory: Wellington	Repeal of the Test and Corporation Acts.	
1829 Tory: Wellington	R.C. Emancipation.	
1830 Wellington resigns. Whig: Earl Grey	Bill for the Removal of Jewish Disabilities rejected by the House of Lords.	Ecclesiastical Courts Commission appointed.
1831 Grey resigns. General Election. Whig: Grey	Reform Bill rejected by the House of Lords in October.	Augmentation of Benefices Act.
1832 Whig: Grey	Reform Act. Poor Law Commission appointed.	
1833 Whig: Grey	Factories Regulation Act. 1st Grant for Education. Abolition of Slavery.	Irish Church Temporalities Act. Ecclesiastical Duties and Revenues Commission established.
1834 Grey resigns (July) Whig: Melbourne Tory: Peel (Nov)	Poor Law Amendment Act.	
1835 Peel resigns (April) Whig: Melbourne	Municipal Corporations Act. Prisons Act.	1st Report of the Ecclesiastical Commission published. Peel's Church Enquiry Commission established.

1836
Whig: Melbourne	Registration Act.	Established Church Act.
	Marriage Act.	Ecclesiastical Commissioners
		for England appointed.
		Tithe Commutation Act
		(England).

1837
Whig: Melbourne

1838
Whig: Melbourne		Pluralities Act.
		Parsonages Act.
		Irish Tithes Commutation
1839		Act.
Whig: Melbourne	Inspectors of
	Schools appointed.

1840
Whig: Melbourne		Ecclesiastical Duties and
		Revenues Act (Cathedrals
		Act).
		Clergy Discipline Act.

Bishops of the Established Church in England and Wales 1828-40

Province of Canterbury

Canterbury:	1805-28	Charles Manners Sutton (1755-1828)
	1828-48	William Howley (1766-1848)
London:	1828-56	Charles James Blomfield (1786-1857)
Winchester:	1827-69	Charles Richard Sumner (1790-1874)
Bath & Wells:	1824-45	George Henry Law (1761-1845)
Bristol:	1827-34	Robert Gray (1762-1834)
	1834-36	Joseph Allen (1770-1845) [Bristol was united with Gloucester in 1836]
Chichester:	1824-31	Robert James Carr (1774-1841)
	1831-36	Edward Maltby (1770-1859)
	1836-40	William Otter (1768-1840)
	1840-42	Philip Nicholas Shuttleworth (1782-1842)
Ely:	1812-36	Bowyer Edward Sparke (1759-1836)
	1836-45	Joseph Allen (1770-1845)
Exeter:	1820-30	William Carey (1769-1846)
	1830	Christopher Bethell (1773-1859)
	1830-69	Henry Phillpotts (1778-1869)
Gloucester:	1824-30	Christopher Bethell (1773-1859)
	1830-56	James Henry Monk (1784-1856)
Hereford:	1815-32	George Isaac Huntingford (1748-1832)
	1832-37	The Hon Edward Grey (1782-1837)
	1837-47	Thomas Musgrave (1788-1860)
Lichfield:	1824-36	Henry Ryder (1771-1835)
	1836-39	Samuel Butler (1774-1839)
Lincoln:	1827-53	John Kaye (1783-1853)
Norwich:	1805-37	Henry Bathurst (1744-1837)
	1837-49	Edward Stanley (1779-1849)
Oxford:	1827-29	Charles Lloyd (1784-1829)
	1829-45	Richard Bagot (1782-1854)
Peterborough:	1819-39	Herbert Marsh (1757-1839)
	1839-64	George Davys (1780-1864)
Rochester:	1828-60	George Murray (1784-1860)
Salisbury:	1825-37	Thomas Burgess (1756-1837)
	1837-54	Edward Denison (1801-1854)

Worcester: 1808-31 Folliott Herbert Walker Cornewall (1754-1831)
               1831-41 Robert James Carr (1774-1841)

Province of York
York: 1808-47 Edward Venables Vernon Harcourt (1757-1847)
Durham: 1826-36 William Van Mildert (1765-1836)
               1836-56 Edward Maltby (1770-1859)
Carlisle: 1827-56 Hugh Percy (1784-1856)
Chester: 1824-28 Charles James Blomfield (1786-1857)
               1828-48 John Bird Sumner (1780-1862)
Ripon: 1836-57 Charles Thomas Longley (1794-1868)
Sodor & Man: 1814-28 George Murray (1784-1860)
               1828-38 William Ward (1762-1838)
               1838-40 James Bowstead (1801-1843)
               1840-41 Henry Pepys (1783-1860)

Church of Wales (officially part of the Province of Canterbury)
Bangor: 1809-30 Henry William Majendie (1754-1830)
               1830-59 Christopher Bethell (1773-1859)
Llandaff: 1826-28 Charles Richard Sumner (1790-1874)
               1828-49 Edward Copleston (1776-1849)
St Asaph: 1815-30 John Luxmoore (1766-1830)
               1830-46 William Carey (1769-1846)
St David's: 1825-40 John Banks Jenkinson (1781-1840)
               1840-74 Connop Thirlwall (1797-1875)

Melbourne who is reputed to have once exclaimed "Damn it, another bishop dead!" had to appoint three bishops in 1840, i.e. in the last year of the period under review:
Henry Pepys 1783-1860 to Sodor and Man, consecrated 1 March 1840, Connop Thirlwall 1797-1875 to St David's, consecrated 9 August 1840, and Philip Nicholas Shuttleworth 1782-1842 to Chichester, consecrated 20 September 1840.

Childhood and Early Education

Preferment to the bench of bishops depended on who you knew rather than on what you knew or had achieved hitherto in life. It depended on your family connections and on the friends you had made at school or university who would later have influence in high places rather than on how many scholarships and university medals you had won in your early years, though becoming a Wrangler or a Chancellor's Medallist did undoubtedly mark you out as a man of ability and it was sometimes a route to finding a patron. Thomas Burgess benefited in this way.

It helped if you were born to the purple as was the case of George Henry Law whose father was Bishop of Carlisle and whose older brothers were Bishop John Law and Edward Law, 1st Baron Ellenborough. George Murray was another such son who followed in the episcopal footsteps of his father, the Rt Revd Lord George Murray, Bishop of St David's. It was even better if you happened to have a brother who was the Prime Minister as was the Hon. Edward Grey's good fortune. It was, after all, a common practice that individuals with the power to make senior appointments would look after members of their own family in preference to more able candidates who were unrelated. Lord North expressed this view as clearly as any nepotistic Prime Minister ever did when he appointed his younger brother at the age of 30 to the see of Coventry in 1771. When Fox challenged him about his brother's young age, North replied 'that his brother was no doubt young to be a bishop but when he was older he would not have a brother prime minister'. That eighteenth century attitude of mind still prevailed in the period under review.

Having served as a successful tutor to an aristocrat's son or to a future political leader was another route – Lloyd won preferment this way having tutored Sir Robert Peel at Oxford and formed a life-long friendship with him. Even better placed was George Davys who became Princess Victoria's tutor in 1827. Four years after his appointment he was made Dean of Chester and two years after her accession he became a bishop.

Forty-five men served as bishops in the Established Church in England and Wales at some time in the period under review 1828-1840. Of these, ten were born into titled families, nine were sons of land-owning 'gentlemen', eleven were sons of beneficed clergymen, two came from military families, three had fathers who were schoolmasters or ran a private school, and ten had fathers with less gentlemanly occupations, among them: three drapers (one of whom was also a wealthy tailor in Cambridge), a grocer, a gin distiller, a master weaver, a merchant, a brickmaker who subsequently became an innkeeper, a London silversmith and a dancing master! None came from the labouring class.

There are short articles about all of them with the exception of James Bowstead and Edward Grey in the Oxford Dictionary of National Biography. Biographies or memoirs have appeared in print of seventeen of them, and very short biographical chapters of four more. Charles James Blomfield, who was the very industrious Bishop of London for 28 years, tops the list with five accounts of his life including a two volume work edited by his son. In addition, he has been the subject of at least one doctoral thesis in recent years. Henry Bathurst has also had three substantial biographies written about him plus a brief chapter in a collection of East Anglian clerical biographies. Some, however, were so indolent or nepotistic that it was as well that no *Life* appeared. One such was John Luxmoore of whom it was said that he gained a reputation less for his intellect than as an example of eighteenth-century episcopal avarice. To D. R. Thomas, the historian of St Asaph diocese, Luxmoore was, quite simply, the worst offender in the matter of nepotism and plurality in its annals. [Quoted in the *Oxford Dictionary of National Biography*.]

Biographers tended to skip over their subject's early years presumably because there was so little of moment to note apart from a certain precocity or some other early signs of future greatness. It is claimed that at least two, whilst still a child, stated their intention of becoming a bishop. One was Shuttleworth. The other was Blomfield who showed great diligence from his earliest school days, rising at 5 a.m. to begin his work and is remembered as having said "I mean to be a Bishop." He was the eldest of a family of four sons and two daughters, and has been described as 'a small, delicate boy, full of high spirits and quick intelligence, adored by his brothers and sisters, full of invention and fancy'. [R. BLOMFIELD *A Memoir of Charles James Blomfield* p. 3] His father was described by a former pupil as 'on the Bench an upright magistrate, impartial, anxious not to punish the guilty, but rather to reclaim the sinner, not merely by good advice but often by pecuniary assistance when most needed.' This was the example of manhood young C.J. grew up with. 'A kindly, courteous and attractive old gentleman fond of riding, gardening and wasting his substance in altering his house' is another later description of him. [*Ibid.*, p. 2] Gardening would become one of C.J.'s fond pastimes.

George Denison, a younger brother of Edward who became Bishop of Salisbury at the early age of 36, gives a lovely picture in a single sentence in his memoirs of their childhood: 'We were brought up lovingly, tenderly, gently, wisely; never coddled, always cared for; in true subjection, but free from fear.' Their father was an MP and there were fifteen children in the family, nine boys and six girls; six of the boys went to Eton and Oxford. Edward was at Christ Church and took a First in Classics before becoming a Fellow of Merton. George was also awarded a First and became a Fellow of Oriel, and later an archdeacon.

The two Sumner brothers, whose father was the Vicar of Kenilworth and Stoneleigh, received their early education from him having first been taught to write by the old clerk of the church. He said of the younger boy that 'Master Charles was the inkspillingest boy I ever knew'. [COOMBS *Their Life and Times* p. 3] The boys were described 'as merry as grigs' and Charles 'as lively as a bird and as little troublesome as one can expect'. [*Ibid.*] Their father once wrote to his wife that a scold now and then does them good but they did not receive any 'flagellations'. It seems theirs was a gentle home upbringing. The father died in 1802 when Charles was just twelve, and a younger son, Humphrey, also died that year. One of their sisters kept a diary and she refers to her recollections of Charles in 1804 when he was at Eton:

> Charles was my delight and my admiration. Every holidays that he returned he appeared handsomer, improved in manners and in talents. He was very affectionate, especially to me, and always brought home some little present for me. To Mamma his behaviour was exemplary. He was domestic, studious – in short, in all respects, the most lovely boy I ever saw.
> [G.H. SUMNER *Life of Charles Richard Sumner* p. 4f]

Between leaving Eton and entering Trinity College Cambridge, Charles spent some months studying mathematics with a tutor in Sedbergh, and at its conclusion he went on a nine day hiking tour of the Lakes 'umbrella in my hand and fish-basket containing my clothes on my back', calling *en route* on Wordsworth and Coleridge in Grasmere. At the end of one particularly arduous day he wrote:

> Supped most voraciously on Ullswater trout, chickens, asparagus, and cucumber; with a good fire, which, after the heat of the last five miles had evaporated, was by no means unpleasant. This was a hard day's work of thirty-one miles, rather long at any time, but especially to one setting out at 9 o'clock, four hours after the proper time; however, I neither felt too much fatigued last night, or at all this morning. Draw an inference hence of my proper condition for walking. [*Ibid*. p. 10f]

Their mother, Hannah, survived her husband by forty-four years and became a strong influence on her children and grandchildren. She was a first cousin of William Wilberforce MP, who came to her aid as a widow. It is quite possible that he too was a significant influence on their spiritual development as both boys became Evangelicals.

Connop Thirlwall was a pupil at Charterhouse where he enjoyed no athletic or scholastic distinction. He was, however, a boy glued to his books who seldom mixed with other boys. His biographer writes, 'The only remembrance of Connop at Charterhouse is that of a diminutive child with an oversized head bending over a book during play-hours, while the other boys were out cricketing.' [THIRLWALL *Connop Thirlwall, Historian and Theologian* p. 8] But he did have a few close friends including George Grote who would later become an eminent historian and Julius Charles Hare an eminent archdeacon. They shared an interest in classical literature and it may have been in discussion with them that he thought of writing, one day, a history of Greece. He had no real desire to follow in his father's footsteps and be ordained, though ordination had one attraction if he could first win a fellowship at university: it would allow him the freedom to study and write and travel.

Henry Bathurst was the twenty-fifth of thirty-eight children his father sired (twenty-two by his first marriage and sixteen by his second) and was born prematurely. He was so tiny that he was not expected to live. He did, however, and died still in office as Bishop of Norwich at the age of ninety-three! Most of his childhood was spent in the household of a family friend who was a Whig, unlike the Bathursts who were High Tory Jacobites, but that didn't stop his uncle Benjamin from serving as MP for Gloucester. Henry asked his father one day, "How can you justify taking the oath to the present government, Sir, when I know you wish for the restoration of the Stuarts?" For which he earned the rebuke, "Hold your tongue, you bastard." Charles Linnell, one of his biographers, comments 'But this, and other crude expressions were received with that affability and tolerance which from the very earliest period of his life was always the way with him.' [LINNELL *Some East Anglian Clergy* p. 131f] He certainly didn't grow up sharing his father's political views and he became for many years the only liberal minded man on the bench of bishops.

One of the most famous future members of the bench was happily saved as a boy from a life as a tradesman. William Van Mildert, the third son of a London gin-distiller was baptized by the Rector of Newington, Samuel Horsley, who later became Bishop of St Asaph. William's father proposed him as an apprentice to a certain chemist, whom the boy admired. Fortunately the chemist was planning to retire and said No. The boy then said he would prefer to pursue his studies and become a clergyman; the Rector's advice was sought and he recommended young William should go to trade. The boy persisted and got his desire. He was sent to Merchant Taylor's School at the age of fourteen where he did well under the tuition of the Revd. Samuel Bishop. Five years later he was entered at Queen's College where his Tutor was Dr Septimus Collinson, later to become Provost of the College.

A few were educated at home by their father - a not uncommon practice particularly among the poorer clergy – and were sufficiently literate in Latin and Greek by their mid to late teens to gain admission to an Oxbridge college. Copleston was one such and won a scholarship to Oxford at the age of fifteen. Most had attended one of the great public schools: Eton produced eleven bishops, Winchester eight, Charterhouse five, Harrow three, Rugby, Merchant Taylor's and Westminster two each, and several grammar schools had provided the basis of their classical knowledge, among them the 'Free Grammar School in Manchester', and two small Grammar Schools in Cumberland (Bampton and Hawkshead). Gloucester Cathedral School's Master, the Revd Arthur Evans, taught the diligent, young Henry Phillpotts so well that he entered Corpus Christi College Oxford at the age of thirteen where he won a scholarship and graduated a month after his 17th birthday and was almost immediately elected a Probationer Fellow of Magdalene College.

Some were fortunate enough to have close family connections with one of the great schools. In the case of the two Sumner brothers it was Eton. Their grandfather had been its Headmaster, a Canon of Windsor, and then Provost of King's College Cambridge, and their uncle Humphrey (nicknamed Bantam Sumner) was an Assistant Master at Eton when John Bird Sumner entered the school. By the time he left to go to King's in 1798, his uncle had also moved there as its Provost, and JB arrived having ended his school days as the first of his year and been awarded a scholarship. When Charles Sumner entered the school, his older brother had graduated and returned to Eton as an Assistant Master, so the family connection continued. Charles is remembered for the sensational novel he wrote whilst a pupil, *The White Nun, or the Black Bog of Dromore*, which he sold to a publisher for £5 equal to about £350 today.

Being at Eton was not an entirely desirable experience. Charles Grey (later 2nd Earl Grey and Prime Minister at the time of the Great Reform Act) who was there from the age of nine to seventeen (1773-81) refused to send any of his numerous sons to a public school because, in G.M.

Trevelyan's words. 'he himself had been taught nothing at the most famous of those establishments.' [TREVELYAN *Lord Grey of the Reform Bill* p. 4]. This criticism probably stems from the very narrow classical curriculum of such schools but also from the many negative aspects of social life at Eton – the bullying, fighting, excessive fagging, gambling and other vices. Things didn't get any better in the following two decades when Christopher Bethell and other future bishops were there. In 1789 Stephen Hawtrey was doubtful whether he could entrust a son to Eton or King's: 'The total neglect of discipline at each of these places is shocking.' The *Gentleman's Magazine* published an article in 1798 complaining of the appalling state of sexual morality in the school. Being there did, of course, have some social advantages: friendships were made with other boys who would be future leaders in the nation's life, and indirectly it provided some training in public speaking which came by attendance at and participation in the school's Speech Days. Oratorical skills and the ability to quote classical authors were highly esteemed in the two Houses of Parliament.

There was, however, a substantial social divide at Eton between the 'Oppidans' (sons of titled or wealthy families) who boarded in a Dame's House and enjoyed better living conditions in every respect, and the 'Collegers' who were herded together in the rat infested dormitory known as the Long Chamber where they were locked in at night and left to their own devices. The room was 172 feet long and 15 feet high and was unheated until 1784 when at last two fireplaces were put in. There were not enough bedsteads so some of the boys had to sleep on the floor between the beds. As there was no running water, the boys had to wash down at the pump or carry water up. No breakfast was provided and the evening meal was always mutton and mash. Some Oppidans, by contrast to this, arrived at their Dame's House with one or two personal servants and sometimes a private tutor as well, all of whom needed rooms. The Collegers were able to attend the great school thanks to scholarships which paid for all their essential needs but their social status was daily made manifest by the coarse gowns they wore. Some of the wealthier Collegers rented a room in a Dame's House in order to be able to entertain their friends to a meal, and some Oppidans near the end of their school career changed to life in the College in order to qualify for automatic admission to King's College Cambridge.

One historian of Eton who spent his life there from boyhood to retirement as Vice-Provost claims 'The fundamental weakness of eighteenth-century Eton lay in the low quality of so many of the Fellows and

Masters, and this was attributable to the stranglehold of King's [King's College Cambridge] which only recruited from uncompetitive Eton Collegers and had no graduation requirements.' [CARD *Eton Established* p.102f]

A boy could, however, be fortunate and have a tutor who was both caring and competent to provide a decent training in the Classics, and there were many boys who looked back on their days there with affection despite the not-infrequent floggings which most of them suffered at one time or another. Charles Metcalfe was such a boy. He was an Oppidan who later became one of the greatest administrators of British India. He began a diary in 1800 at the age of fifteen. In one long entry he compared education in public schools to that offered in smaller private ones, and was in no doubt about the superiority of the former. He did not deny the negative things said about Eton but wrote,

> Secondly, at a public school every vice and every virtue which we meet with in the world is practised, although in miniature, every deception is triflingly displayed which one would be open to in life; we learn to abhor vice, consequently shun it; we learn to admire virtue, consequently imitate it; we learn to beware of deception, consequently to avoid it; in short a public school is but a humble imitation of the theatre of the world; it is what one conceives of a drama acted by boys, where the actors are small. [*Ibid.*, p.104]

That is a noble view from a strong-willed boy and written from the comparative security of his social standing but hardly likely to have been shared by his poorer fellow pupils enduring the bullying and other hardships of the Long Chamber. The boy also claimed in defence of his own school that Westminster School was 'still more dissipated than Eton.' Despite the positive memories and appreciation of boys such as Metcalfe, the late 18th century and early 19th was not a good time to be at Eton – Card gave the title 'A Dark Time, but with Gleams of Light' to his chapter on that period. Christopher Hollis in his history of the school was harsher still, 'Barbaric anarchy reigned and at the same time a system of discipline which was both utterly savage and at the same time utterly ineffective.'

What did the boys learn and what was the shape of their week? Lessons on whole school days were from 8-9 a.m., 11-12, 3-4 p.m. and 4-5 with an additional half hour for younger boys from 7-7.30 a.m. In between lessons, they would have been reading a classical author in preparation for the next lesson, or translating a passage or composing an ode in Latin. On Wednesdays there were no lessons. In the Lower School pupils were taught Latin grammar and Latin composition and how to construe passages. As they moved up the school they were introduced to Greek and how to write epigrams. In the Upper School they began to read Caesar and Ovid, and then gradually extended their knowledge of classical authors to such as Horace and Virgil. The day was punctuated regularly with 'Absences', i.e. praeposters were appointed to call the roll in order to ensure boys were in fact present.

On Saturdays Chapel was from 2-3 p.m., and on Sundays at 10 a.m. and 3 p.m. They were also required to learn about twenty verses of the Greek N.T. on Sundays which they would be tested on during the first lesson on Monday morning. On Sundays boys were expected to keep to their houses. Saints days were also marked by two services in the Chapel. Whilst there was a goodly dose of formal religious worship, there was no encouragement to develop their spiritual life. Masters and tutors were not expected to influence their pupils religiously.

Charles Lloyd, later to become Bishop of Oxford, was a Colleger at Eton. He was the son of a poorly paid clergyman who augmented his income by tutoring private pupils in the rudiments of Latin and Greek, classical literature, mathematics and some history. Eventually his father ran a successful private school at Great Missenden. Lloyd's biographer felt that his lowly place as a scholarship boy and the experience of being made to feel so inferior by the Oppidans marked him for life with a sense of social inadequacy. That feeling of inferiority was exacerbated when he matriculated at Christ Church Oxford in 1803 where he discovered the Fellows regarded Westminster far more highly than they did Eton.

Lloyd did, however, have one lasting positive impression from his boyhood which was unrelated to Eton. Not far from Great Missenden there was a private school for young aristocratic refugees from France some of whose pupils he met and remembered with respect for their 'virtuous and religious' life. A consequence of which was he always defended the rights of Roman Catholics and as a bishop voted for their emancipation.

One boy who escaped being at Eton was Charles James Blomfield. He was educated to the age of eight in his father's school at Bury St Edmund's and then sent to the local Grammar School. In 1799, he was examined at Eton and admitted as a King's Scholar. Fortunately for him, his father did not like what he saw of the place and never sent him there. Instead, he stayed on at the Grammar School until he was eighteen when he went up to Trinity College Cambridge.

We turn more briefly now to William Wykeham's ancient foundation at Winchester, the oldest of all the great schools in the land. The original purpose of the school in 1382 was to train seventy poor scholars who would move on to Wykeham's other foundation, New College Oxford, and then be ordained but by the 18th century it had simply become a desirable place to which the sons of the wealthy were sent. And, as at Eton, there were two categories of pupils: 'Scholars' and the wealthier ones known as 'Commoners' who lived in Houses run by the Masters for profit. Eight of the bishops being studied went to Winchester: Vernon Harcourt, Henry Bathurst, John Banks Jenkinson, William Howley, Philip Shuttleworth, Edward Maltby, Thomas Burgess, and George Isaac Huntingford.

One anecdote from his school days remains about the gentle William Howley who would later become Archbishop of Canterbury. He was at Winchester with the witty Sydney Smith who was five years his junior but who defeated him in a game of chess much to Howley's annoyance. What then happened Smith never forgot as he recalled the incident in his *Letters to Archdeacon Singleton* written in 1837 when he was defending his cathedral endowments at St Paul's which were under threat: 'I was at school and college with the Archbishop of Canterbury; fifty-three years ago he knocked me down with a chess-board for check-mating him – and now he is attempting to take away my patronage. I believe these are the only two acts of violence he ever committed in his life.'

We don't have Howley's views on his years at school but we do have Smith's – for him it was a rough and cruel place. His daughter recalled how he used to 'speak with horror of the wretchedness of the years he spent there; the whole system was then, he used to say, one of abuse, neglect and vice.' He loathed the place. In an article about public schools published in the *Edinburgh Review* in 1810 and obviously coloured by his own experience at Winchester, he criticized 'the prodigious honour in which Latin verses are held in public schools' and the wastefulness and irrelevance of compulsory versifying. He hated the practice of 'fagging' and the damaging effects it had on boys:

> In a public school . . . every boy is alternately tyrant and slave. The power which the elder part of these communities exercises over the younger is exceedingly great – very difficult to be controlled – and accompanied, not unfrequently, with cruelty and caprice. It is the common law of the place, that the young should be implicitly obedient to the elder boys; and his obedience resembles more the submission of a slave to his master, or of a sailor to his captain, than the common and natural deference which would always be shown by one boy to another a few years older than himself.

Thomas Burgess's biographer implied the same when he wrote that he 'passed through the dangerous ordeal of a public school . . . without being contaminated.' [HARFORD *Life of Thomas Burgess* p. 3] In contrast to that, Huntingford chose to spend most of his life at the school, from being a schoolboy to becoming an Assistant Master, then a Fellow and finally the Warden.

Thomas Arnold, who was to become the most famous headmaster in the 19th century, spent four years in the school 1807-11 and whilst there grew in his love of the classics. Wymer in his biography of Arnold gives a detailed account of the brutalities of schoolboy life at Winchester at that time along with an account of the academic demands made on the boys. The bullying was unbelievably cruel but it seems that no prefect or master ever tried to check it.

The boys were required to be up by 5.30 a.m. and in Chapel by 6. On four days a week they then endured three hours in 'School', i.e. crowded in the single schoolroom, 77 by 35 feet large, which housed every boy, with the Headmaster teaching his several classes at one end and the Second Master doing the same at the other end. The work being done was mostly exercises in Latin or Greek grammar. Half an hour was then allowed for a simple breakfast of bread and butter with beer or milk as the local water supply was often contaminated and unfit to drink. By 10.30 Scholars and Commoners alike were seated in the three rows of built-in wooden seats called 'books' at each end of the room ready to say their lessons, or at their 'scobs' (a kind of combined bookcase and desk), in the centre of the room, composing a number of Latin verses or *'vulguses'* on a theme set by their master. An hour's physical exercise followed outside up St Catherine's Hill. Then came lunch but not all younger boys were free to eat it as they were fagging for the older boys. Four more hours of work followed in the afternoon with just one short break in the middle. Arnold recorded having to learn two Latin poems by heart, read a lecture on the classics, and do a précis of about 40 pages of Adams's *Roman Antiquities* into six pages of good, grammatical prose – all within the space of one afternoon! The main meal of the day was at 6 p.m. More *vulguse*s took up the time before Evening Chapel which was at 8, and everyone was in bed by 9 p.m. What a day! Tuesdays and Thursdays were better in that the only organised academic work was 'Books' after breakfast. In theory most of the day was at a boy's own disposal but in reality the fagging duties for the younger were unending. [WYMER *Dr Arnold of Rugby* pp. 27-31]

Henry Bathurst admitted that he was never studious at Winchester but he discovered he had a remarkable memory and was able to recite the whole of Homer's *Iliad* in the original Greek. He appears to have enjoyed his years at the school where he made some lifelong friends, and he sent his sons there.

Tuckwell records that Shuttleworth made his mark as a writer of burlesques in his schooldays at Winchester. [TUCKWELL *Pre-Tractarian Oxford* p.173f] One of them has the title the 'Progress of Learning' and tells the tale of a boy from the time of his leaving home blubbering and carries him through school, college, country living to a Deanery. It ends with the predictive lines:

> As erst to him, O heavenly Maid,
> Learning to me impart thy aid;
> O teach my feet like his to stray
> Along Preferment's flowery way.
>
> And, if thy hallowed shrine before
> I still thy ready aid implore,
> Make me, O Sphere-descended Queen,
> A Bishop, or at least, a Dean.

He was reputed to have been a remarkable composer of Latin verses too.

We have looked at just the two main public schools where nearly half of those who were bishops during the years 1828-40 were educated but life would have been equally harsh at any of the other boarding schools which some of the others went to, and the curriculum equally narrow. Pupil rebellions broke out at one time or another in almost all of them which were put down violently and with much consequent flogging and birching. Being a day pupil at a local grammar school must have had its attractions even if it did not confer the status of attending one of the great public schools.

The only one of the forty-five future bishops not to have been educated in England or gone on to university after school was an Irishman called William Ward who attended school at Ballynakinch a dozen miles south of Belfast. A *Life* written by his granddaughter in 1931 describes William's father as a 'Gentleman' but presumably one not affluent enough to pay for his son's years at a university. Instead the young man at the age of twenty moved to London where he obtained a post as an Usher at a school run by a Frenchman. Fortune was with him as one of the pupils, a son of Lt General Samuel Townsend, took a liking to him and asked his father to employ Ward as his private tutor. He clearly fitted into the household well for it was from there that he was ordained Deacon 'as a Literate man' on 17 February 1788, and through that family he became known to Bishop Porteous of London who ordained him Priest. In 1787 he registered as a 'Ten Year Man' at Cambridge University, and was admitted a sizar at Caius College where he graduated BD in 1798.

Another out-of-the-ordinary one was Edward Stanley, second son of Sir John Stanley, 6th Baronet of Alderley Park Cheshire, who was educated in the south of England by a variety of private tutors at home and by attending a succession of private schools, latterly in Windlesham, Surrey. The result of this mix of teachers was that when he matriculated as a 'pensioner' at St John's College Cambridge he was ill-prepared. His son, Arthur, who became Dean of Westminster, wrote of him, 'Of Greek he was entirely, of Latin almost entirely, ignorant; and of mathematics he knew only what he had acquired at one of the private schools where he had been placed when quite a child.' [A.P. STANLEY *Memoirs of Edward and Catherine Stanley* p 3] He found that he had to start on the classics again almost from the very foundation. As his greatest desire as a child had been to go to sea and pursue a career in the Navy, the classics would never have figured very highly in his thinking. He may not have known his *Heroditus* or *Tacitus* but he knew the name of every British warship and who commanded her. As a child he used to leave his bed and sleep on the shelf of a wardrobe, for the pleasure of imagining himself in a berth on board a man-of-war! That was never to be – a family living in Cheshire awaited him, and eventually a mitre and a palace.

At Oxbridge

All but one of the forty-five bishops in this study attended one or the other of the only two universities in England at that time but not all of them graduated, and for many of those who did the examination for the degree of Bachelor of Arts was perfunctory and in no sense a real test of their knowledge or abilities. 'A century of inactivity' is how Cardinal Newman described university life at Oxford in the 18th century. G.C. Brodrick, writing in 1886, called it 'the Dark Age of academical history.' Before 1802, the degree examination was not just minimal, it was farcical. Cambridge fared better as it had real examinations for the degree of Bachelor of Arts and proposals for reforms were made in the 1770s such as broadening the curriculum and introducing annual examinations for all undergraduates. There were plans for reforming the examination system at Oxford too about that time and making it 'a formidable ordeal' but nothing came of it. Real and much needed, wide-sweeping reforms in both universities did not come until later in the 19th century.

Why then did men go to university? For many, it was an extension of the leisurely indulgent life they came from if their father was a country gentleman or a country parson in a well-endowed living – a privileged transitional period from boyhood to manhood. Baker has described the attractions of life at university at that time: 'Generously financed by their fathers and academically unchallenged by their tutors, young men apparently turned to the delights of hunting and shooting, tandem-driving, boating, hack-riding, smoking, drinking, whoring, betting and card-playing, rather than to the rigours of lectures and libraries.' [BAKER *Beyond Port and Prejudice* p. 13]

For those intending to make a career in the Church, there was a more serious reason - a university degree was a requirement the bishops made of almost all candidates for Holy Orders, and that affected about half of all those admitted to Oxford and Cambridge. But those men did not go there for any kind of professional clerical training – that was simply not available. For all students, it was to receive a grounding in the intellectual culture common to all gentlemen of the time, not more. Such intellectual exercise as existed at Oxford lay in deepening one's knowledge of classical languages and literature, and, at Cambridge, of mathematics. A smattering of knowledge of the NT and of the *39 Articles of Religion* of the Church of England and of Paley's *Evidences of Christianity* was also imparted and would eventually be tested. Commitment to the Christian

Faith was assumed – most Fellows were ordained and daily attendance at Chapel was mandatory. All students at Oxford had signed the *Thirty-nine Articles* at matriculation, and all who wished to graduate at Cambridge were required to sign but they could study there without first having subscribed. In effect dissenters were allowed to attend the university but not to graduate.

Bishop John Kaye, who had been the most brilliant man of his graduation year (1804) at Cambridge, stated in his *Charge* to the clergy of the Diocese of Lincoln in 1833, that he would ordain only graduates but he did not wish to see any changes in undergraduate studies. Kaye, at the time, still held the post of Regius Professor of Divinity at Cambridge. He said,

> I should deeply regret any change which gave to the studies of our Universities more of a professional character. My view, which was also the view of those wise and learned men who prescribed the course of academical studies – my view of those studies is that they are designed to discipline the mind of the student; to form in him habits of patient and persevering attention, and of accurate reasoning; to communicate to him those general principles, without the knowledge of which it is scarcely possible successfully to engage in any literary pursuit; to lay, in a word, the foundation on which the structure of professional training is afterwards to be raised. A strictly professional education, commenced at too early a period, has, for the most part, a tendency to cramp the mind, to narrow its view. [KAYE *Charge* 1831 pp. 68f]

Copleston at Oxford held a similar view: 'To exercise the mind of a student is the business of education.'

It is worth noting that both universities at this time and all the individual colleges and halls were numerically tiny entities in comparison with today's institutions. The annual average of matriculations between 1790 and 1799 was 245 at Oxford and 162 at Cambridge, though numbers began to rise in the early 19th century. St John's, the largest college in Cambridge, admitted on average just 47 men a year between 1781 and 1790. [JACOB *The Clerical Profession in the Long Eighteenth Century* p. 46] A man could make a name for himself here and be known by all, be he an academic high-flyer or a wastrel.

All students were required to be members of a college or hall in order to matriculate and be eligible for degrees in the university. But there was no preliminary examination common to all the colleges, each did what it wished. This weakness in the system was commented on by Richard Whately, who had been a pupil of Copleston's at Oriel and then a Fellow of that college before becoming Principal of St Alban's Hall in 1825 until Grey appointed him Archbishop of Dublin in 1831. He had tried in his Oxford days as a Head to get the system changed but failed:

> Very many persons come to the University so very ill-prepared for such a course of study as properly belongs to a University, that most of their undergraduate period is occupied in learning what they ought to have learnt at school. And the standard of examination for the degree of B.A. is in consequence so much lowered, that to have merely passed it at the end of three years, will never be regarded as a credit, but rather the reverse.
>
> The obvious and only remedy for this (and a very easy and complete remedy too), would be to establish a preliminary examination by the University, to test the fitness of each candidate for Matriculation. At present there is none. It is left entirely to the Governors of each College to examine a candidate either strictly or slightly, or (as often happens) not at all. And I need not enlarge on the various temptations some of them are exposed to, to receive ill prepared candidates.
>
> [WHATELY *Remains of the late Edward Copleston* p. 5 in the 2012 reprint]

There was another notable weakness in the two universities – there were plenty of professors but hardly any of them ever gave a public lecture. In 1800 Cambridge had twenty-one professors, among them three in Divinity and one in Moral Philosophy plus the four Regius Professors of Civil Law, Physic, Hebrew and Greek. Oxford had nineteen professors, one praelector and one reader – all equally inactive as far as the undergraduates could see. There were, however, some stirrings of new life on this front, and they came from one of the future bishops in this study.

When Herbert Marsh was appointed Lady Margaret Professor of Divinity at Cambridge in 1807, he marked it in a novel way by giving a course of public lectures in English and not in Latin. So unusual was this that the Divinity School could not hold the number of students wishing to attend and the lectures were delivered in Great St Mary's Church. Unfortunately Dr Marsh was not consistent in well-doing, lecturing only intermittently and not at all after he became Bishop of Peterborough in 1819, though he did continue to work on the published editions of his lectures well into the 1820s. He retained his professorship worth £1,000 p.a. [about £82,000 today] until his death twenty years later. In the 32 years he held the chair, he delivered only 30 lectures. Oxford had to wait longer for such professorial innovation and when it did come it was from another future bishop: Charles Lloyd.

It was in the separate colleges that the actual tuition took place. Cambridge had sixteen colleges in the late 18th century with one new one, Downing, added in 1800. Oxford had twenty at that time. Most of them were pre-Reformation foundations. Some colleges had exceptional rights. New College, for example, had the power until 1834 to bring forward its men for graduation without them having to submit to the normal university exercises. It was, in effect, 'an independent university' as one writer remarked in 1826. Very many of the fellowships were restricted to men from a given locality, or to those who had attended particular schools. Students who came from Cumberland or Westmorland, for example, had a monopoly of the fellowships at Queen's Oxford, and the Fellows of King's Cambridge were all required to be Etonians, and there were frequent complaints of venality and favouritism in the making of appointments.

A fellowship entitled its holder to a share in the income derived from property belonging to the college as a charitable institution. It was generally tenable for life subject to certain conditions being fulfilled such as getting ordained within a stated number of years, remaining celibate and not holding a church living or other income over a certain amount. Less than 10% of the Fellows were directly involved in the academic and administrative life of their respective colleges as tutors, lecturers, deans, bursars etc. Being elected a Fellow was, therefore, an invitation to an idle life if one was so-minded. In practice, a small number had private pupils and/or made a contribution to academic literature but most moved on to become parish clergy or to join the staff of a major school. Engel has commented: 'the fellowship and teaching duties in Oxford were not a career for life; they were a prize and a rung on a ladder leading to a career in the Church.' [ENGEL p. 308 in *The University in Society* ed. L. Stone Vol. 1] The colleges owned many advowsons, i.e. the right to appoint clergymen to livings, and these were offered, when a vacancy occurred, to Fellows in order of seniority but you could wait several years before a desirable one came up. Trinity was the wealthiest college in Cambridge, supporting the Master, sixty Fellows, seventy-two Scholars, sixteen Sizars and six Minor Scholars. It also controlled three headmasterships, forty-eight vicarages, ten rectories and nine perpetual curacies.

Such instruction as was on offer in the university was largely in the hands of the comparatively small number of recent graduates who had been elected Fellows and subsequently been appointed by the Head of their college to the post of lecturer, tutor or assistant tutor, for which they received a modest stipend in addition to their annual share in the college's income. Educational standards and expectations varied from college to college.

Whilst many colleges slept, new life was stirring in a few of them. Dean Cyril Jackson when appointed Head of Christ Church Oxford in 1763 determined to make his men work; John Parsons on becoming Master of Balliol in 1798 threw Balliol scholarships open to competition thereby ensuring some of the brightest new men entered his college; and Dr John Eveleigh, the Provost of Oriel, who was elected in 1781, had scholars of outstanding ability chosen for the unrestricted fellowships of his college. Edward Copleston, a brilliant young graduate, was one such candidate who was invited to join the senior common room at Oriel and eventually became Provost before accepting a bishopric. Other exceptional men who joined him at Oriel included John Keble, Richard Whately, Edward Hawkins, and Thomas Arnold.

It was Eveleigh who persuaded his fellow Heads to pass the 'Public Examination Statute' in 1800 which came into effect two years later and further reforms came in 1807. Not surprisingly, the final year of the old regime (1801) saw a surge in the number of candidates for the degree of BA. Aspects of the old system continued in that *viva voce* examinations were retained but now they were to be real public disputations, not mock ones. What had previously been a formal ritual was on the way to becoming a genuine competitive test. The main reform was the introduction of written papers though the actual questions were read aloud by an examiner, and knowledge of particular classical authors would now be tested in addition to the earlier requirements in the rudiments of the Christian Religion, grammar, logic, moral philosophy, etc. And candidates could now offer themselves either for a 'pass' degree or for Honours, and the Honours list was to be divided into two classes, in which the names of candidates were placed in order of merit. Here was an incentive to make one's name known, though initially very few ventured to do so.

Despite these reforms, academic life at the university was heavily criticised in a series of articles which appeared in the *Edinburgh Review* in 1808-10. Copleston, who was a Fellow and Tutor at Oriel by then, made a robust defence of the university and its collegiate system, and thereby marked himself out as a man worthy of future preferment. He argued that the system of collegiate lectures, as opposed to 'solemn public lectures' by professors, was more effective as a means of instruction since the student was given more individual attention and the instructor could gear his teaching to the capacities and previous knowledge of each of his students. That may have been true in Oriel College but it was not the norm in the university. Sir William Hamilton, who was a student at that time at Balliol (another of the best colleges) having already graduated at Glasgow, was not impressed by his lecturers. Years later, he wrote two articles, published in the *Edinburgh Review* in 1831, which attacked the Oxford system. His contention was that university education ought to be conducted by professors who taught one subject which they knew well, rather than by college tutors each of whom had to teach all subjects, though generally they were not qualified to teach any particular subject in depth. His memory of Oxford was not a flattering one - it was not really a public university but merely a collection of private schools!

Cambridge was similar to Oxford in so many ways in the late 18th century and early 19th but different in that the examination for the degree of BA was in mathematics, and the first Tripos list was published for the year 1747-48. Garland comments on the place of mathematics, 'It was generally viewed as the only really effective means of strengthening a man's intellectual capacities and academic self-discipline. At least in part out of respect for Newton and his memory the subject was endowed with a mystique which made it an object of near religious veneration.' [GARLAND *Cambridge before Darwin* p. 28]

Classics too were encouraged by the institution of the Chancellor's Medals, first given by the Duke of Newcastle in 1751. Candidates for these medals were, however, required to have passed the Mathematical Tripos and to have gained a high place either as a Wrangler, i.e. 1st Class Honours or as a Senior *Optime* = 2nd Class Honours. There were two prizes to the value of £25 each for the two students who had made the greatest progress in mathematics and natural philosophy. These were funded by a bequest of Robert Smith and were first awarded in 1769. For those not aspiring to honours and medals, such as E.D. Clarke, William Otter's friend and contemporary at Jesus College Cambridge in the late 1780s, the sum total of the classical lectures he attended during his three years of residence 'were confined to two little tracts of Tacitus, *De Moribus Germanorum* and *De Vita Agricolae*' [OTTER *The Life of Edward Daniel Clarke* Vol. 1. p.60]

A separate Classical Tripos was not introduced until 1824 but even then the mathematical papers had to be passed first. There were other prizes to be won for skill in composing Latin and Greek odes and epigrams, which encouraged classical studies; these were gold medals to the value of five guineas funded by the will of Sir William Browne in 1774.

In both Oxford and Cambridge attendance at Chapel services was compulsory and to be absent without permission a disciplinary offence –

the number of required attendances per week varied from college to college. The morning service was usually at 7 or 7.30 and the evening one at 5.30 or 6. Given that attendance was compulsory, behaviour and attention in chapel was not always what it should have been. Worse behaviour came later in the evening when heavy drinking was the common practice for many a student and Fellow, with the consequent hangover next morning.

Owen Chadwick provides an interesting, non-academic illustration of just how clerically dominated the two universities were:

> The first boat race between Oxford and Cambridge was rowed at Henley in 1829. Eight members of the Oxford crew became one bishop, two deans, one prebendary and four other clergymen. Only four members of the Cambridge crew were afterwards ordained, one bishop, one dean, one rector, one curate. [CHADWICK *The Victorian Church* Part 1. p. 90]

Another non-academic snapshot of undergraduate life appears in George Sumner's *Life* of his father Charles:

> It appears that in those days the undergraduates wore knee-breeches and white stockings, in summer the knee-breeches occasionally giving place, in the case of those who paid the greatest attention to dress, to nankeen trousers. Sumner, accordingly, was on one occasion met on the staircase leading from his college rooms by one of the Dons, who, seeing his nankeen trousers, and, indignant at the innovation, and knowing that as a further enormity he had a pet-dog, called out to him "young man, young man, you'll never come to any good. You wear nankeen trousers and keep a dog."
>
> [G.H. SUMNER *op. cit.* p. 12]

Politically, both universities were predominantly Tory. This was the mind set of most Anglican clergy at that time and of those contemplating ordination. A petition against the emancipation of Catholics was presented to Parliament from Oxford as early as 1810. Peel, who was an MP for the university, resigned his seat over the matter when he changed his views and supported the proposed legislation in 1829, and consequently lost his seat at the next election. The same conservative stance was taken against parliamentary reform in 1831 and against the Irish Church Temporalities Bill in 1833 and against the granting of a charter in 1834 to the new university in London. But when there was an election for a new Chancellor at Oxford in 1809, it was the pro-Catholic Emancipation politician, Lord Grenville, who won thanks to some successful canvassing on his part by Copleston. Cambridge too was similarly conservative except in the matter of the admission of dissenters to Oxbridge.

After that general introduction to Oxbridge we can now consider how our forty-five candidates fared and which colleges they attended. Twenty-six were admitted to Cambridge colleges, the four most favoured being Trinity College which had seven of them, St John's six, King's and Christ's three each. Eighteen went to Oxford: Christ Church was most favoured with eight followed by New College with four, and Corpus Christi three. Ward, as mentioned earlier, was a so-called 'Ten Year Man' at Caius College Cambridge and graduated long after his ordination.

It is easier to ascertain the relative abilities and achievements of Cambridge graduates thanks to the introduction of the Mathematics Tripos in 1774 and the system of grading which was, in effect, an Honours list. 'Wranglers' headed it, followed by 'Senior *Optimes*' and then 'Junior *Optimes*'. There were, in addition, more prizes to be won here for classical knowledge than at Oxford. An early indication in an undergraduate's life of future possible academic success was if he won one of the competitive scholarships available to members of his college or if he won an open university one such as the Bell and Craven Scholarships. Of the various awards he could win, a Chancellor's Medal for skill in the Classics was rated highest, then a Smith's Prize in Mathematics, and there were a number of medals for skill in Latin or Greek verse and lastly Member's Prizes, i.e. gifted by the MP for the university. Another prestigious one, the Porson Prize, for the best translation of an English poet into Greek verse, was started in 1816.

Of the twenty-six who matriculated at Cambridge, four were 'Fellow Commoners', i.e. aristocrats, who did not need to sit the BA examinations and could proceed directly to MA; three more were King's scholars and were likewise excused. Of the remaining nineteen, fourteen achieved Wrangler status and most of them were also awarded prizes for their classical scholarship. Kaye who was at Christ's won the highest honours in 1804 as Senior Wrangler, i.e. the top graduate of his year. In addition, he won the 1st Chancellor's Medal and the 2nd Smith's prize. Not surprisingly he went on to have a distinguished career at the university. Marsh in 1779, Law in 1781 and Bowstead in 1824 all had the distinction of being 2nd Wrangler as well as winning classical awards. Here is the full list in order of seniority as a wrangler:

Name   BA degree   Mathematical, Classical and other Awards
Kaye   Senior Wrangler 1804   Scholar, Tancred Student, 1st Chancellor's Medal, 2nd Smith's Prizeman

Law	2nd Wrangler	1781	Scholar, 1st Chancellor's Medal
Marsh	2nd Wrangler	1779	Scholar, 2nd Smith's Prize, Member's Prizes
Bowstead	2nd Wrangler	1824	Scholar, Prizeman
Blomfield	3rd Wrangler	1808	Scholar, Craven Scholarship, Browne Medals for Latin and Greek odes, Chancellor's Medal, Member's Prize for a Latin dissertation.
Otter	4th Wrangler	1790	Rustat Scholar
Sparke	7th Wrangler	1784	Browne's Medal, Chancellor's Medal, Member's Prizes
Monk	7th Wrangler	1804	Scholar, 2nd Chancellor's Medal
Allen	7th Wrangler	1792	Scholar, Prizeman
Maltby	8th Wrangler	1792	Scholar, Craven Scholarship, 1st Chancellor's Medal, Browne Medals
Davys	10th Wrangler	1803	Scholar
Musgrave	14th Wrangler	1810	Scholar, Member's Prize
Manners-Sutton	15th Wr	1777	Scholar
Stanley	16th Wrangler	1802	
Butler		1796	Scholar, 1st Chancellor's Medal, Browne Medals, Fellow of St John's
Thirlwall	22nd Senior Optime	1818	Scholar, Bell & Craven Scholarships, Chancellor's Medal

One immediate conclusion to be drawn is that most of the Cambridge men who went on to become bishops were not without intellectual ability and that they had shown a readiness to apply themselves to study. Many students fell short on the second score, preferring a life of leisure, and probably not a few on the first one also. Aristocratic undergraduates tended not to be 'reading men' whom they scorned. An exception was Henry Ryder who, after schooling at Harrow, spent two years at St John's College. He is reputed to have had a profound influence on his social equals because, unlike so many of them, he chose to attend lectures and to study seriously.

What about the Oxford men? Lloyd's biographer has described late 18th century Oxford as 'a haven of aristocratic privilege and academic lethargy.' [BAKER *op. cit.* p. xii] No college was more aristocratic than Christ Church, the largest, wealthiest and most prestigious of all the colleges as Lloyd was to discover. But under the determined headship of Dean Cyril Jackson the days of academic lethargy were over. Lloyd thrived under him and the Dean took a liking to the poor Etonian Colleger who heads the list of Oxford men. Lloyd felt acutely his comparative poverty as a student and later in life advised poorer men to avoid the most fashionable colleges and the temptations of mixing in the society of far wealthier men. 'A clergyman,' he wrote to Peel in 1825, 'who can only allow his son £100 a year, will hardly be persuaded to send him to a college where he might mix with noblemen and men of wealth, or, if he refuses to mix with them, must be exposed to a certain degree of humiliation and annoyance.'

For those who graduated prior to the reforms of 1800 and 1807, it is difficult to assess either their intellectual ability or their commitment to study. As Cornelius Ives put it diplomatically when writing about his illustrious relation William Van Mildert's years at Queen's, 'The examinations previous to degrees were not then of a public or discriminating kind; it is impossible, therefore, now to discover how he acquitted himself, or what were his relative attainments.' [IVES *Sermons on several Occasions* p. 9] But he adds respectfully, 'No doubt, however, he had made a becoming proficiency both in classical and other learning.'

Of the 'post reform' candidates Lloyd and Longley stand out; among the 'pre-reform' ones, Burgess and Copleston. The following list is in a rough order of achievement.

Name	BA degree	Awards and University Appointments
Lloyd	1806 1st Class	Christ Church Studentship, Tutor, Regius Professor of Divinity 1820
Longley	1815 1st Class	Tutor and Censor 1825-28, University Proctor 1827
Denison	1822 1st Class	Fellow of Merton College 1826
Copleston	1794	Scholar, Chancellor's Latin Prize, English Essay Prize, Fellow of Oriel 1795, Tutor '99, Professor of Poetry 1802, FSA 1804, Provost of Oriel 1814
Shuttleworth	1806	Chancellor's Latin Verse Prize, Tutor 1799, Proctor 1820, Warden of New College 1822
Burgess	1778	Tutor 1782, Fellow 1783, published a new edition of Burton's *Pentalogia* whilst still an undergraduate.
Howley	1787	Fellow and Tutor. Tutor to Prince William of Orange
Carey	1793	Tutor and Censor 1794-1800, Headmaster of Westminster School 1803
Phillpotts	1795	Fellow of Magdalen 1795 aged 17
Huntingford	1773	Fellow of New College, Tutor at Winchester whilst still at university, Fellow of Winchester 1775
Bagot	1803	Fellow of All Souls 1803
Gray	1784	Author of *A Key to the OT and Apocrypha* 1790 and Bampton Lecturer in 1796
Van Mildert	1787	Regius Professor of Divinity 1813, Bampton Lecturer in 1814
Carr	1796	
Grey	1803	

Jenkinson	1804	
Murray	1806	
Bathurst BCL	1768	[BCL was regarded as the degree for idle men]
Harcourt BCL	1783	Fellow of All Souls 1778-83

We can look now in a little more detail at a few of these men in their university years, beginning with those who went to Oxford.

Most fathers would have offered their sons some advice prior to starting on this new phase in their life. Henry Bathurst indirectly tells us how his father had advised him (and how he woefully ignored the advice when he entered New College as 'Founder's kin' in 1761 at the age of sixteen) in the letter he wrote to his own son, Robert, as the boy followed in his father's footsteps at Oxford.

> My dearest Robert,
> You will readily imagine, that when I took leave of you yesterday morning, the difficulty and danger of your new situation suggested to my mind ideas which (notwithstanding the confidence I have in your understanding and your heart) were not unattended with uneasiness; and the remembrance of the storms to which my own imprudence exposed me at your age, added to my apprehensions. At the same time, I readily allow, that your risk is less than mine was, because I was certainly far more idle then than you are now. There is, however, one rock on which most of us are equally liable to split – it is this: upon our first stepping into the world, the field before us appears, and indeed really is, wide and trackless; we naturally look round for some friendly guide to take us by the hand, or at least for some companion to accompany us on our road. Men of talents and of virtue are never obtrusive; so far from it, they rarely seek our acquaintance unless we are strongly recommended to them. On the contrary, the superficial, the frivolous, the vain, and the indolent, are to be met with at every corner of the street. Persons of this description, feeling themselves incapable of real distinction, wish to reduce others of superior abilities and more industrious, to their own level, and declaim incessantly upon the necessity 'eundi, non qua eundum, est, sed qua itur.' [literally; 'of not going where you go, but where you ought to go', a quotation from Seneca] Regardless of the difference, both of present circumstances and of future prospects, everybody, according to their creed, must do the same; a young man must implicitly adopt the opinions, customs, and prejudices of the herd. That all the world does so, is supposed to be a sufficient excuse for extravagance and for absurdity, not to say for vice. He who has not elevation of mind, and courage enough to think and to act for himself in defiance of such senseless and wicked maxims can never possibly arrive at any degree of excellence, either moral or intellectual.

One of the many advantages of a studious retirement is, that we are enabled by it, to acquire a manly strength of mind, a solidity of judgment, and a power of forming our characters after the purest models of better days; whereas the dissipation of the world and the bad examples which we meet with in mixed society, have a tendency not only to corrupt our principles, but to weaken both mind and body. When I first entered the University, a prudent and enlightened father gave me these hints: had I attended to them as I ought to have done, I should have escaped many a snare. I offer them to you with the same parental affection, and with the same anxiety for your welfare; but, 'melioribus, opto, auspiciis.' [literally 'I hope for better auspices', a quotation from Virgil]
Adieu, my dearest Robert! Believe me,
    Your most affectionate father and sincere friend,   H. Norwich

We turn to another Wykehamist, George Isaac Huntingford, who was admitted as a scholar at New College in 1768 and elected a Fellow in 1770 from where he graduated BA in 1773. While reading for his BA he returned to Winchester as tutor in commoners, a post in which he was paid directly by the Headmaster, Dr Joseph Warton. He was able to do this because the rules about attendance in college during term time were lax. At about this time he was ordained and became Curate of Compton, near Winchester, for which parish he must have held affection, for he was eventually buried there. In 1776 he was formally appointed sub-praeceptor at Winchester, and began to teach scholars as well as commoners. This dual position was resented by the scholars, who saw it as a breach of their privileges, and for a while Huntingford withdrew to London, from where he negotiated his return with Warton. He also began to publish. His *Short Introduction to the Writing of Greek* (1778) became Winchester's preferred textbook for sixty years, but his compositional style was not highly regarded. [ODNB]

  Thomas Burgess gained a Winchester scholarship to Corpus Christi College, Oxford, whence he matriculated on 14 March 1775. His tutor quickly discovered that this freshman was more knowledgeable in Greek than himself and excused him from attendance at lectures. His biographer and close friend J.S. Harford said that he devoted himself as an undergraduate 'to hard reading and to learned researches,' and he went on:

He studied some of the finest works of the Greek philosophers and poets, with critical attention; and being fond of the philosophy of language, applied its principles to the investigation of the origin and formation of that of Greece, with an acuteness which contributed much in its consequences to his future eminence. He delighted also in metaphysical reading and research and when he relaxed from these severer occupations, it was to cultivate a more intimate acquaintance with the finest productions of elegant literature, both classical and English. [HARFORD *op. cit.* p. 9]

The year before he graduated, Burgess produced a new edition of John Burton's *Pentalogia*, a textbook on five Greek tragedies; this was the first of his hundred and fourteen publications. Such a remarkable feat by an undergraduate brought him attention within and beyond the university, and led to a friendship with Thomas Tyrwhitt Esq., an Eton and Oxford educated former Clerk to the House of Commons. He had retained in old age a keen interest in classical scholarship and became a generous benefactor as well as a helpful critic and mentor, advising him on which Greek authors to devote time to. Burgess took his BA in 1778, and planned to take Orders and retire to a country curacy where he could pursue his research, as he did not have the means to stay on at Oxford. When Tyrwhitt heard of this, he immediately offered to support him financially, "You must on no account quit Oxford. You must be my Curate there for the next two years." An offer he gladly accepted. Tyrwhitt also provided him with numerous books and manuscripts. In 1780 he won one of the Chancellor's prizes for an essay on 'The Study of Antiquities'. The following year he won great scholarly praise for his edition of Richard Dawes's *Miscellanea Critica*. Having taken his MA he was made Tutor of his college in 1782 and Fellow in 1783 which made him financially independent and no longer in need of his friend's support. College life suited this quiet and shy man, described by a contemporary as 'having, in youth, been, in person and manner, more like what he was in advanced life, than is often the case'. After he was ordained Deacon and Priest in 1784 his scholarly interests turned to Hebrew and Theology. Late in life when a close friend asked him about his sense of vocation as a young man, he answered, 'At the time to which you refer, I was full of that ambition for literary distinction natural to a young scholar circumstanced as I was, but, after I had taken orders, and turned my attention to sacred studies, I gradually imbibed deep and serious views of Divine Truth.' [*Ibid.*, p. 73]

In 1791 when he was just fifteen years old, Edward Copleston, having been educated at home by his father, won a scholarship to Corpus Christi College, Oxford. Two years later he was the successful candidate for the Latin Verse Prize. The morning he got the good news he wrote to tell his father: 'One of the greatest sources of pleasure to me from so distinguished an honour, is the thought of the satisfaction you will feel, as well as all the family. I have just been to see Mr. Crowe, the public orator, who has paid me the most flattering compliments.' He had the honour of reciting his poem *Marius in Tugario ruinarum Carthaginiensium* at the installation of the Duke of Portland as Chancellor of the university.

An even greater honour was bestowed on him quite unexpectedly in 1795, the year he graduated. The Provost and Fellows of Oriel College invited him to join their select society. Other men had been examined for the vacant fellowship and all had been rejected. They wanted him. He proved their judgement right by winning the university's English Essay Prize during his probationary year as a Fellow. It was on *Agriculture*, and won him a unique compliment from Sir J. Sinclair, the President of the Agriculture Society who wrote to thank him on behalf of the Society. At the age of twenty-one he took on the responsible office of College Tutor, and as that was the year of the expected French invasion he used to lead his pupils from the lecture room to the parade ground to drill them in his capacity as captain in a regiment of volunteers! His diary for 1799 has an unusual entry for 12 January relating to perils of a different kind: 'Robbed by two mounted highwaymen, on my return to Oxford with Mr Woollcombe and Mr (afterwards Bishop) Mant, between Uxbridge and Beaconsfield.'

Copleston was destined for a career as an Oxford don, and eventually a wealthy one at that. He kept careful note of his finances and recorded on 1 January 1800: 'Upon settling accounts, found myself possessed of £21.' [= £1,571] His next step up the academic ladder was his appointment as Professor of Poetry in 1802, an office he held for ten years during which time he delivered thirty-five lectures. He had been ordained Priest in 1801 and instituted as Vicar of St Mary the Virgin (an Oriel living) and so climbed his first step up the clerical ladder. Years later as the Provost of Oriel he would become, in today's terms, a millionaire.

In the same year that Copleston joined the senior common room at Oriel, an even younger graduate was elected a probationer Fellow of Magdalene College on the Somerset Foundation. Henry Phillpotts was just seventeen years old, an age when most boys were still at school; in the same year he became university prizeman for his essay on 'The Influence of a Religious Principle'. He proceeded to the degree of MA in 1798 and two years later was elected Praelector of Moral Philosophy. Copleston and he became close friends and the two of them were among the first examiners of candidates for Honours in 1802 when the new regulations came into force. A few days later he was ordained Deacon by the Bishop of Oxford.

From the time of his election to Magdalene, Phillpotts came under the influence of the newly elected President of the college, Dr Martin Routh, and a lifelong friendship was begun with the older man whom he frequently turned to for advice. 'To him [Routh] it belonged to mould the mind of the youthful Fellow, and instil into it those sound principles of theology which qualified him in later years to become the uncompromising champion of the Faith.' [SHUTTE *Life, Times and Writings of Henry Phillpotts* p. 7] It looked as though he would pursue an academic career but in October 1804 he resigned his fellowship, having married. His bride was Deborah Maria, the daughter of William Surtees Esq. of Bath, and niece of Lady Eldon. He had been ordained Priest earlier that year by the Bishop of Chester. The Crown had appointed him to the vicarage of Kilmersdon near Bath which was worth £244 a year [= £21,809] – quite a wedding present! He never resided there, leaving the work to a Curate. Lord Eldon had been appointed Lord Chancellor in 1801 and so was in a position to advance the careers of conservative minded men he approved of – and Phillpotts certainly fitted that description as well as being a relative now by marriage.

Lloyd's path to preferment started with his good relationship with the Dean, Cyril Jackson. It was he who appointed him to a 'studentship', an honour peculiar to Christ Church – it has been described as 'something between a scholarship and a fellowship at other colleges.' 'After gaining first place in the Oxford BA honours list in 1806, Lloyd left Oxford to serve as private tutor to the children of Lord Elgin at Dunfermline, but within a year was summoned back to Oxford by Dean Jackson, who needed him to be a College Tutor. One of his first assignments was to prepare Robert Peel for his examinations; Peel attributed his double first to the teaching of Lloyd, who was in later life "a friend and counsellor"'. [ODNB] Others too reckoned him to be an extraordinarily attentive and effective tutor.

We will look now at the progress of half a dozen Cambridge men taking them in the chronological order of their graduation. Herbert Marsh, who would later make a name for himself as a Biblical scholar, had first shown his prowess as a mathematician, being placed 2nd Wrangler and 2nd Smith's prizeman in 1779. He went on to win the Member's Prize in both 1780 and 1781, having been appointed a Fellow of his college in the year he graduated. He quickly became a college official, being appointed Junior Bursar in 1801 and an academic career lay ahead. We shall hear much more about him and his time as a post-graduate student in Leipzig learning from German theologians in the next chapter.

Edward Maltby was the fourth son of a master-weaver who was a Presbyterian deacon in Norwich. He entered Pembroke College in 1787 where he won a string of awards and prizes including the 1st Chancellor's Medal in 1792, which marked him out as the top classical scholar of his year, having first graduated as 8th Wrangler. He was elected a Fellow of his college in 1792, and like Marsh, would go on to become a Professor of Divinity at the university.

John Bird Sumner's years at Cambridge were also marked by academic distinction: he was elected a scholar of King's in 1798 and a Fellow three years later. He won the Sir William Browne medal for a Latin ode in 1800, the subject being *Mysorei tyranni mors*. To this accolade he added the Hulsean Divinity Prize in 1802. These prizes are particularly significant in his case as an indication of his intellectual ability because, being an old Etonian and a King's man, he was not required to sit any degree examinations. Like many others of his generation Sumner was influenced by the Revd Charles Simeon (about whom more later), as was his brother Charles, and he left Cambridge a convinced evangelical.

Edward Stanley, the would-be naval officer, was sent in 1798 to St John's College ill-prepared, knowing nothing of Greek, almost equally ignorant of Latin, and possessing only a smattering of mathematics. He determined at once to apply himself to his studies and catch up with his contemporaries. His hard work paid off and in 1802 his name appears in the Mathematical Tripos as 16th Wrangler. Whilst not the most brilliant of these future bishops who were educated at Cambridge, he has left an appreciative account of his time there which his son included in the *Memoir* of his father's life:

> I can never be sufficiently grateful for the benefits I received within those college walls; and to the last hour of my life I shall feel a deep sense of thankfulness to those tutors and authorities for the effects of that discipline and invaluable course of study which rescued me from ignorance, and infused an abiding thirst for knowledge, the means of intellectual enjoyment, and those habits and principles which have not only been an enduring source of personal gratification, but tended much to qualify me, from the period of my taking orders to the present day, for performing the duties of an extensive parish. [A.P. STANLEY *op. cit.* p.3f]

John Kaye, the son of a linen-draper, did not have the privileged background of Stanley but he had the advantage of having been a pupil at Hammersmith School, Greenwich under a notable classicist, Dr Charles Burney. He entered Christ's College in 1800, aged seventeen, where he immediately won a scholarship and went on to become the top mathematician and classicist of his year, 1804. That was a formidable achievement. He was immediately elected a Fellow of his College and started on a distinguished academic career which would lead to him becoming Master of Christ's College, and Vice-Chancellor of the university, 1815-16, and succeeding Bishop Watson as Regius Professor of Divinity.

In 1804 Charles James Blomfield was admitted a pensioner at Trinity College. He had been a sickly child, and his efforts as an undergraduate left him with an enduring nervous condition. For years after, he suffered from disordered digestion and would experience nervous spasms when riding. His son tells how very hard his father had studied:

> During his first four months of residence at Cambridge, he read through Aristophanes, all the Greek tragedians, Heroditus, Thucydides, and a great part of Cicero; spending sometimes sixteen or eighteen hours out of the twenty-four over his books. He wrote everyday a piece of Greek or Latin composition, and a translation of a Greek or Latin author, which latter he translated back again some days after, and then compared his version with the original. He had no private tutor, but at the end of his first academical year he was fortunately introduced to Mr, afterwards Bishop Maltby, who was then residing at Buckden in Huntingdonshire, and taking pupils. Maltby, with much kindness, seeing in his young friend the promise of much classical eminence, took him into his house as one of his pupils, for six weeks, without payment, and gave him some good advice as to the method of reading he should pursue; his previous work had been too rapid; he had neglected commentaries, and had not written notes of his own.'
>   [A. BLOMFIELD *A Memoir of C.J. Blomfield* Vol. 1 p. 3f]

We are also told how this particular young man spent each day after taking Maltby's advice:

> His day was generally thus divided. Rising in time for the early chapel service, which he never missed during his undergraduate life, except when prevented by illness, he began reading at nine; at twelve, allowed himself two hours recreation, walking or rowing, or occasionally a game of billiards; dined at two, the college dinner hour, and, returning to his books at three, read without intermission till twelve at night, and occasionally till three in the morning. . . A Bury friend meeting him in the streets of Cambridge in a long vacation, exclaimed, "Why, Charles Blomfield, I believe if you were to drop from the sky, you would be found with a book in your hand."
>   [*Ibid*. p. 4f]

He gained a college scholarship in 1805 and won Browne's prize for a Latin ode, and the following year won a Craven scholarship for which he was examined by Porson and took Browne's prize for a Greek ode. When it came to the study of mathematics, he had the help of a friend who was a brilliant mathematician but a poor classicist, so they spent one long vacation helping each other. The result was that Blomfield graduated BA as third Wrangler in 1808, also winning the Chancellor's Medal and the Member's Prize for a Latin dissertation. Thanks to the scholarships and prizes that he won, he was able, almost from the start, to support himself financially. In 1809 he was elected a Fellow of Trinity and immediately started work on a new edition of Aeschylus with notes and glossary; he also started writing book reviews for the *Edinburgh Review*. The next step was almost inevitable and he gave the news to his sister on 3 March 1810:

> Before long you will have to direct to me, as the Rev.; for the Bishop of Bristol [William Lort Mansell who was also Master of Trinity College] has proposed to ordain me in the course of the present month. I began to fear that I should be obliged to go to Norwich or Buckden, for the former of which has no attraction for me just now; and I do not wish to be examined by the Bishop of Lincoln. [Pretyman] [*Ibid*. p. 10]

Mention has already been made of Charles Simeon. Many of the more serious minded students at Cambridge found spiritual support and sustenance outside the walls of their college chapels from his ministry at Holy Trinity Church. A Fellow of King's, Simeon had been exercising a special ministry among the student body since 1782 through his preaching and through the various 'Conversation Parties' which he hosted in his rooms. He began his 'Sermon Classes' in 1792 which were intended for future clergymen. Abner Brown attended them between 1827-30 by which time, he said, they had assumed the form of colloquial lectures to a small invited circle of fifteen or twenty gownsmen, held at eight o'clock on every alternate Friday evening.

> Whoever wished to attend waited on Mr Simeon, and at once received an invitation for that term, coupled with a request that he would attend regularly, and throughout the whole of the term, for each term had its own course of subjects. Towards the end of the allocated hour, Mr Simeon gave out a text, to be treated in some specific mode, and read on the next occasion; and each student who brought and read aloud his little written sketch received a few kind and pertinent criticisms on it, perhaps at times somewhat severe for young students, but always wound up with suggestions for a

more effective and simple mode of handling the subject. The writer has found the lucid and pointed remarks which he heard at those sermon parties of the greatest practical utility in his own ministry.

[A. BROWN *Recollections of Charles Simeon* p. 51]

Simeon had a succession of outstanding curates to assist him; among them were Thomas Thomason who was 5th Wrangler in 1796 and served with him until he went to Bengal as a Chaplain in the service of the East India Company in 1808, Thomas Sowerby Senior Wrangler and 1st Smith's Prizeman in 1798, Henry Martyn too was Senior Wrangler and 1st Smith's Prizeman in 1801, and became Simeon's closest friend; he had a short but brilliant career, first in India then in Persia where he died in 1812. Then there was the saintly Daniel Corrie, an Exhibitioner and Scholar of Trinity Hall who died in 1837 as Bishop of Madras. Another was James Scholefield, 1st Chancellor's Medallist in 1813, Fellow of Trinity and later Regius Professor of Greek. William Carus, Fellow and Dean of Trinity College 1832-50, was his last assistant who succeeded him at Holy Trinity. These young Evangelicals who were academic stars undoubtedly added to the lustre and attraction of Holy Trinity as a place for serious minded undergraduates to attend.

Simeon was a role model for future clergymen by the calibre and content of his preaching. Canon John Babington who heard him for the first time in 1810 when he went up to Cambridge could never forget the impression Simeon made on him, 'Never before or since have I heard a preacher who seemed so to take me by the hand, and lead me aside into close communion with himself as to the state of my own soul.' He gave them additional help in the 21 volumes of his *Horae Homileticae*, which contained 2,536 sermon outlines. He stated in the preface that the threefold object of his preaching was 'to humble the sinner, to exalt the Saviour, and to promote holiness.' He eschewed church politics and church conflicts, choosing rather to be an exemplary parish priest and a faithful Biblical preacher – 'My endeavour' he wrote 'is to bring out of Scripture what is there and not to thrust in what I think might be there.' His influence on the student body and on many of the resident Fellows may be judged by the enormous turn-out for his funeral. One of those who was at it, Francis Close, wrote 'More than 1500 gownsmen attended to honour a man who had [once] been greatly despised. When his venerable remains were deposited in that glorious building [King's College Chapel], every bell of the College chapels tolled for him.'

Among the many he had influenced were the two Sumner brothers but, it would appear, not Henry Ryder or Edward Stanley, though both proved to be diligent and effective parish priests and then bishops later in life. Simeon's example had a lasting effect on Sumner's care for the poor during his later years at Eton College and on his strategy as the bishop of a northern diocese.

In conclusion, what lasting benefit did the future clergyman who had graduated at Oxford or Cambridge leave with? He had had what might be termed a 'liberal education' which, as we have heard, John Kaye valued as a solid foundation on which to build. He would certainly have left with an improved knowledge of classical languages and literature, some ability in mathematics and a smattering of philosophy and theology, and possibly even have developed a love of literature. That, however, would be of little help to him in running a parish efficiently or equip him to be an effective pastor and preacher and worship leader even if he was going to minister in the less challenging setting of traditional village life or in a country town. On the other hand, if he was going to be a country parson he would have had the benefit of a shared experience with the likes of the local squires and landowners in his parish whose support he might need, and he would be able to mix with them socially with a degree of ease. That, however, would have been of far less value if he was going to minister in one of the rapidly expanding industrial towns with their alarming social problems where his social peers and the factory owners did not live and where masses of the people were becoming unchurched, not least because there were so few churches and with far too few seats in those that did exist for the number of parishioners. In such places he would be hopelessly ill-prepared and ill-equipped. Even the achievement of being a Wrangler or Chancellor's medallist was no preparation, and most curates were plunged into the deep end of ministerial life immediately upon ordination with few opportunities of learning from a more experienced clergyman.

If he was a Cambridge man and had attended Simeon's tea parties and sermon classes, he would, at least, have had some idea about how to write and deliver sermons, and he would have seen how a well-run parish was organised and the ministry shared with volunteer lay assistants who acted as district visitors. And for the one third of all the newly ordained who were the sons of clergymen and had grown up in a vicarage or rectory, they had lived, of course, for many years, for better or worse, with a clerical role model in their father.

Climbing the Clerical Ladder

In this chapter we will look in some detail at the early and middle years in the careers of fifteen of these future bishops, and just cursorily at six others. As we have already seen, some of our forty-five men started out professionally as College Fellows who had taken Orders, and lived on their fellowship plus a curacy in a local parish. For others there was a family living awaiting them or even some higher preferment.

Lord George Murray was immediately appointed Archdeacon of Sodor and Man which was in the gift of his family, and at the age of 29 was nominated by them as Bishop of that diocese though he had to wait till his 30th birthday to be consecrated. His was an exceptionally rapid ascent up the clerical ladder! He was eventually translated to Rochester, the second poorest diocese in the Church of England, but that was of little concern to a wealthy aristocrat. Being nearer London was much more important than the revenues of the diocese. The translation came about, incidentally when the Crown bought the right to nominate to Sodor and Man from the Duke of Atholl in 1827.

Murray was exceptional. The next man was also guaranteed a comfortable life thanks to his family having the right of presentation to a good living where he could have employed a curate or two to do the work and taken it easy but instead he chose to be a diligent parish priest.

Henry Ryder was ordained to the curacy of Sandon in 1800, which was a family living. A year later he was presented by the crown to the rectory of Lutterworth in Leicestershire, a living which from 1805 he held in plurality with the neighbouring vicarage of Claybrook. On 15 December 1802 he married Sophia Phillipps of Garendon Park, Leicestershire, with whom he had ten sons and three daughters, all of whom survived him except one son, Charles, who was drowned at sea in 1825.

While participating fully in the fashionable social life expected of a clergyman of his means and connections, Ryder seems, from the beginning, to have taken his pastoral charge at Lutterworth and Claybrook with great seriousness. His naturally amiable temperament facilitated relations with his parishioners, and he was notable for his attention to the poor and the sick and for the diligence with which he undertook the catechizing of the young. He took great care in the employment of his curates, choosing men whom he respected for their personal piety and pastoral abilities and conferring regularly with them about the spiritual condition of his parishioners. Ryder also took care to develop his own theological education, reading the early fathers and engaging in a critical study of the Bible. [ODNB] His connections and his attention to his duty guaranteed further preferment, and in 1808 he was presented to a canonry of Windsor

Ryder's initial reaction to the evangelical school in the church was one of suspicion, and he took the opportunity to attack evangelical principles when, in 1807, he preached a sermon at the archdeacon's visitation at Leicester in the presence of Thomas Robinson, vicar of St Mary's, the most prominent local evangelical. However, he was impressed by Robinson's forbearance in declining to reply to this attack when called upon to preach the visitation sermon in the following year, and the two clergymen developed a friendly acquaintance which may have been the catalyst for a gradual change in Ryder's religious views.

By 1811 Ryder was prepared not only to be identified as an evangelical but also to take the chair at a meeting of the Leicester branch of the most controversial of evangelical organizations, the Bible Society. His new theological convictions influenced Ryder's own practice of family worship, which became a daily event and featured Bible reading as well as prayer. They also led to an extension of his parochial ministry, as he introduced a cottage meeting at Claybrook and a weekly lecture in a factory at Lutterworth. His open avowal of evangelicalism made his appointment as Dean of Wells in 1812 a matter of some controversy among the local clergy. He also introduced an evening service into the parish church (regarded at that time as a sign of 'methodism') and preached at neighbouring churches. In 1814, he became the first dignitary to preach the annual sermon of the Church Missionary Society (CMS). During his years at Wells he became acquainted with the writer Hannah More, who was much impressed by him.

Charles Manners-Sutton with the advantage of aristocratic birth and family connections was assured of preferment but first he was appointed at the age of thirty to the family living of Averham with Kelham in Nottinghamshire, and to the rectory of Whitwell in Derbyshire. Six years later he was appointed Dean of Peterborough, and after just a year there was consecrated Bishop of Norwich.

Richard Bagot too was presented by his father to a living on his ordination in 1806: the rectory of Leigh in Staffordshire and a year later to that of Blithfield where his father had his country residence. He was also made a canon of Windsor that same year and ten years later appointed to a canonry of Worcester. When he was eventually appointed to the see of Oxford he was also made Dean of Canterbury.

Henry Bathurst's early career is one long list of livings and a couple of canonries thanks to family influence (his cousin was Lord Chancellor Bathurst) and then the patronage of the Hon. Shute Barrington, Bishop of Durham. 1776 was a profitable year for him when he was given a canonry at Christ Church Oxford. That came about because his cousin had first offered him the living of Bletchingly in Surrey worth about £500 a year, but a local family with influence wanted it for one of their own 'and begged Lord North to intercede with the Chancellor to offer Mr Bathurst in exchange a stall at Windsor, Durham or Westminster at the earliest opportunity or a canonry at Christ Church which was then vacant.' [LINNELL *op. cit.* p. 134] He stayed at Oxford for nearly twenty years, a curate and a friend looking after his parishes. 1795 proved to be an even more lucrative year. Bathurst had enabled a young friend of Bishop Barrington to be awarded a Studentship at Christ Church – the *quid pro quo* came some years later. The Bishop offered him the second best stall in Durham Cathedral which had become vacant on the death of the previous holder. The Bishop wrote on 2 March 1795 'Personal regard and public esteem induce me to give you this substantial proof of both in exchange for your Canonry at Christ Church.' For a man with four sons and three daughters to maintain, one of Durham's 'golden stalls' was a rich blessing even if it did require a move north.

Edward Stanley was made Deacon in June 1805 and ordained Priest in September and went to be Curate of Windlesham where he had attended school. He served there for three years before being appointed by his father to the family living of Alderley in Cheshire where his uncle, Baron John Stanley, was the major land owner. He was to live in and serve that parish for thirty-two years which would make him the most experienced parish priest on the bench of bishops. Even allowing for an element of uncritical adulation on the part of his son, Arthur, who wrote a *Memoir* of his parents, it is clear that Edward Stanley was an unusually diligent, caring and innovative parish priest with a particular concern for educating the children in his parish. He introduced into his schools gymnastic exercises, and subjects such as elementary botany, English history, and geography. He instituted twice-yearly examinations in which children were tested on a chapter of the NT, learned by heart, and on their knowledge of one or more books of the Bible. Medals and prize books were their reward. He visited all the homes in his parish systematically, not waiting to be called at times of sickness or approaching death. His son, who must have witnessed at first hand what he described later, wrote:

The Rectory became the 'home' of the parish. He sold daily at his house, to the honest and industrious poor, blanketing, clothing, and the like, at a cheaper rate than the cost price . . . In the winter evenings he lent out books to read; and generally, for anything that was wanted in the way of advice or relief, his house was the constant resort of all who were in difficulty. He established weekly cottage-lectures at different points in the parish for the old and infirm who were unable to walk to church. [A.P. STANLEY *op. cit.* p. 12]

Infant schools, temperance societies, mechanics' institutes, and statistical societies found in him a zealous patron. He was also instrumental in founding a clerical society among the neighbouring clergy. A keen ornithologist, he published a small book in 1836 entitled *A Familiar History of Birds: their Nature, Habits, and Instincts*. A Whig in politics, and by nature a reformer, he shared his views on questions of the day with his parishioners. Occasionally he would have one of his Sunday addresses printed which he delivered to every house in the parish, one such gave his thinking and reasoning about why Roman Catholic emancipation was a thoroughly just cause, but they were also on more general topics such as prayer and the proper observance of the Sabbath. When the new and unpopular Poor Law came into operation in 1834, he offered his services as chairman of the Board of Guardians in order to administer the Act in his union. He loved his parish so much that he returned to it every year after his move to Norwich, and, by his will, a copy of an *Address to the Parishioners of Alderley* was sent to every house in the parish after his death, and another one to each of his former school-children. [See Appendix 3 p. 369f.]

William Van Mildert's progress was similar to the previous two in that he had relatives to assist him but it was also very different, not least in the number of curacies and small livings he served in the first two years following ordination. It was his cousin Cornelius Ives who enabled him to set his feet on the next rung by nominating him to the small living of Bradden, Northamptonshire in 1805. His days of being a poorly paid assistant curate, which was the lot of most newly ordained deacons and priests, were over. There he married Jane Douglas, the daughter of a former *aide-de-camp* to George II. They never had children; Jane's nieces Mary and Helen Margaret became their foster-daughters.

In July 1796, sponsored by his uncle William Hill, Van Mildert became chaplain to the Grocers' Company and rector of St Mary-le-Bow, Cheapside, London. There was no habitable parsonage, so he rented a house just outside the parish boundary. In 1800 he was prosecuted for technical non-residence and, although Archbishop Moore of Canterbury spoke on his behalf and the court accepted that he was performing all his duties, Van Mildert was found guilty. An appeal was lodged but the Archbishop had paid the fine imposed by the court.

In London, Van Mildert became an active member of the high-church campaigning group known as the Hackney Phalanx. He was briefly editor of the *British Critic* which promoted the group's viewpoint. He served as Treasurer of the Society for Promoting Christian Knowledge from 1812 to 1815 and helped to found the National Society (1811) and the Church Building Society (1818).

In March 1807 Van Mildert became chaplain to his wife's kinsman the fourth Duke of Queensberry, an appointment which entitled him to hold two benefices in plurality. In April Archbishop Manners-Sutton made him vicar of Farningham, Kent. The parsonage was uninhabitable, and the building work ran dramatically over budget. In 1810 Van Mildert escaped bankruptcy only because his Hackney Phalanx associates paid his debts. He was appointed Preacher at Lincoln's Inn in 1812 which proved to be an important point in his career as it fell to him to preach on the death of Spencer Percival who had been assassinated in the House of Commons. A year later Lord Liverpool offered him the Regius Professorship of Divinity at Oxford, which he told him was worth 'at least a clear £2,000 per annum', and the rectory of Ewelme in Oxfordshire. As Regius Professor Van Mildert also became a canon of Christ Church. His Bampton Lectures delivered in 1814 brought him wider fame.

Then there were the academics who had stayed on at university and begun to climb the ladder of promotion as an officer of their college, starting with a tutorship and ending up as the Head of their college and a professorship, and sometimes with a deanery in addition.

Edward Copleston ordained in 1800 was one such, and the vicarage of St Mary the Virgin, Oxford, usually held by an Oriel Fellow, together with further college and university preferment followed. He became Professor of Poetry in 1802, and as Senior Treasurer of Oriel for six years from 1806 substantially improved the college's finances. He never married.

In his thirties Copleston entered a wider public stage. This was principally due to his successful support in 1809 for the candidacy for the office of University Chancellor of the pro-Catholic politician Lord Grenville. As a result, not only did he gain prominence in the university (he was elected unopposed Provost of Oriel in 1814) but also entry to the Liberal Tory political world. He became a frequent visitor to Dropmore, Grenville's country house, and to Althorp, the home of the second Earl

Spencer. In the 1820s he was consulted by Robert Peel and William Huskisson on financial questions.

Tuckwell in his reminiscences of Oxford described him during his time as Provost of Oriel as 'substantial, majestic . . . a man not without asperities of mind and manner – we recall his rudeness to J.H. Newman, dining in Hall as a newly-elected Fellow: - but as a man of the world, in London society, regular contributor to the *Quarterly Review*, author of widely-read and accepted pamphlets on currency and finance, he held absolute ascendancy amongst the higher class of University men, and filled his College with Fellows strangely alien to the port and prejudice, the clubable whist-playing somnolence, which Gibbon first, then Sydney Smith, found characteristic of Oxford society.' [TUCKWELL *Pre-Tractarian Oxford: a Reminiscence of the Oriel Noetics* p. 16f]

Copleston is remembered as a reforming spirit. Not only did he support the introduction of the new examination statute he also supported the abolition of closed scholarships and fellowships, and developed the tutorial system which made Oriel famous. He was the leader of the early Noetic school at Oxford, centred around Oriel College, and so called from the Greek *noesis*, meaning reason. This school was responsible to a large degree both for the intellectual revival of the university and a distinctive Anglican apologetic which, in the 1820s, combined a 'high' view of the church, as an externally visible, divinely appointed society, with a rational defence of the Christian creed. [ODNB] His main disciple was Richard Whately (1787–1863), who later became Archbishop of Dublin. Whately, commented on a rare honour bestowed on Copleston:

> As it is usual for the Head of a House to take a Doctor's Degree, the University, to mark their sense of the service done in his able reply to the attacks of the *Edinburgh Review* "spontaneously" conferred on him the degree of D.D. by diploma. This is the highest honour the University can confer, and it is accordingly a very rare one.' [WHATELY *op. cit.* p. 3 in 2012 reprint]

His rival at Oxford for episcopal preferment was **Charles Lloyd** who served for several years as Librarian and Censor of Christ Church, but his most important contribution was a pedagogical zeal which helped to extricate Oxford from the slough of 'port and prejudice' denounced by Gibbon. [ODNB] Ordained in 1808, Lloyd held the curacies of Drayton (1810) and Binsey (1818), both near Oxford. In June 1819 thanks to Peel's influence he was appointed to the Preachership of Lincoln's Inn, which he held until February 1822 when, on the nomination of Lord Liverpool, he was appointed to the Regius Professorship of Divinity at Oxford. On 15

August 1822 he married Mary Harriet Stapleton of Thorpe Lee, Surrey, and within four years they had a family of one son and three daughters.

As Regius Professor Lloyd revived theological studies in the university and infused a new and more energetic spirit into them. He supplemented his statutory public lectures with private classes attended by graduates, who included R. H. Froude, J. H. Newman, Edward Denison, Frederick Oakeley, and E. B. Pusey. Froude in a letter to his father said the class was made up of 'firsts and double firsts' and described Lloyd's unusual behaviour with the men:

> We, about twenty fellows, sit all about in his library, which is a very large room, and he walks up and down in the middle; sometimes taking his station before one fellow and sometimes before another asking them questions quite abruptly to catch them being inattentive, and amusing himself with kicking their shins. When any fellow happens to make a silly remark he laughs at him without scruple and exposes him in the most ludicrous way, but so very good naturedly that it is impossible to be the least offended. Sometimes he pulls the ears of the men he is very intimate with.
>
> [BAKER *op. cit.* p. 105]

Oakely claims that far from offending them by such liberties, they were received as the greatest of all possible compliments, as they were understood to be proof of his especial confidence and regard.

An Oxford academic of an earlier generation was **Thomas Burgess**. At Oxford he devoted most of his time to the study of Greek where his early scholarly publications won him a wealthy patron. Having taken his MA he was made Tutor of his college in 1782 and Fellow in 1783. College life suited this quiet and shy man.

In 1785 Burgess was appointed examining and domestic chaplain to Shute Barrington, Bishop of Salisbury, who became his principal patron. During summer vacations he lived at Salisbury, where he was treated as a member of the bishop's family and was appointed by Barrington to a prebendal stall in the cathedral. He refused the first stall offered to him because it was in too prominent a position in the choir but he later accepted a more secluded stall. He assisted the bishop in his scheme to increase the number of Sunday schools in the diocese, writing simple primers for Sunday scholars, and at Salisbury he met another promoter of Sunday schools, Hannah More. He also published, in 1789, a treatise advocating the abolition of slavery and the slave trade.

When Barrington was translated to Durham in 1791 Burgess chose to move north with him and to leave, with great regret, his academic work in Oxford. Barrington rewarded his chaplain for his loyalty by presenting him to the first vacant prebendal stall in Durham Cathedral and, shortly afterwards, to a more valuable stall there, which Burgess held until appointed Bishop of Salisbury. He gradually came to believe that he would be happier in the parochial ministry, and in 1795 the bishop appointed him rector of the 'sweet and delightful' rural parish of Winston in County Durham. On 1 October 1799 at St Mary-le-Bow, Durham, 'he relieved the solitude of his situation, effectually, by entering into the married state' [HARFORD *op. cit.* p. 197). His bride was Margery Bright of Pontefract, Yorkshire. There were no children of the marriage.

There were promising young academics at Cambridge too. Among them was **Herbert Marsh** who was admitted Fellow of St John's College on 23 March 1779 and was ordained Deacon by the Bishop of Ely on 16 May 1780. For the next five years he fulfilled his college teaching obligations. In 1785 he received permission to travel to Egypt and Arabia. *En route*, in 1786 he consulted the eminent biblical scholar Johann David Michaelis in Göttingen about learning Arabic. While wintering in Leipzig, his lifelong asthmatic condition worsened. He was confined to bed for the best part of the next three years, but was able to visit Christoph Martin Wieland in Weimar, a writer whom he held in awe. During his illness he became fascinated with Enlightenment authors, although his reading of Hermann Samuel Reimarus's writings shook his faith in biblical inspiration. Marsh was commissioned to translate the fourth edition of Michaelis's *Einleitung in die göttlichen Schriften des neuen Bundes*, his Introduction to the New Testament. He added extensive notes to Michaelis's text that primed his readers in continental biblical criticism. The first volume appeared in 1793.

With improving health, he returned to England in 1793 to take his delayed BD examination. In one of his two qualifying sermons he urged rigorous theological education for ordinands in the Church of England. Three more volumes followed in succession, the last in 1801. This appeared as a separate volume under the title of *The Origin and Composition of the Three First Canonical Gospels*. In 1806 he began canvassing covertly for election to the Lady Margaret Professorship of Divinity at Cambridge. In the event he was elected without opposition in 1807. He could now afford to marry Marianne Lecarriere, the daughter of a Leipzig merchant, to whom he had been engaged for eight years.

Following his professorial appointment, he published *The History of Sacred Criticism* (1809), *The Criticism of the Greek NT* (1810), *The Interpretation of the Bible* (1813), and *The Interpretation of Prophecy* (1816) –

all published in one volume in 1828. *The Authenticity of the NT* (1820), *The Credibility of the NT* (1822) and *The Authority of the OT* (1823) followed, and confirmed his reputation as a theologian.

He astutely cultivated politically sympathetic patrons, principally the Hardwicke family in Cambridgeshire. Marsh's attempts to build a political base were eclipsed by the Bible Society controversy that broke out in Cambridge in 1811. His public opposition to the society, an interdenominational and evangelically led society that distributed bibles at home and abroad, had been preceded by a successful campaign to promote Church of England educational provision for the poor. This came in response to the opening by Joseph Lancaster of a non-denominational school in Cambridge in 1808 and the gathering momentum of the Royal Lancastrian Society. Alarmed, Marsh used a charity schools sermon at St Paul's Cathedral, London, on 13 June 1811 to appeal for a parallel society to be founded that would be guided by the principles of the established church. In October he met with the Hackney Phalanx to plan the scheme. His sermon proved to be the catalyst for the formation that year of the National Society for Promoting the Education of the Poor in the Principles of the Established Church. The society mushroomed with support from Anglican churchmen of all persuasions. This success for Marsh was followed by public defeat in a cause he opposed, namely the Bible Society. His principal objection to that Society lay in his insistence that the Book of Common Prayer should be distributed together with the Bible – as SPCK did. His opposition drew responses from, among many others, William Otter, the future Bishop of Chichester in his *A Vindication of Churchmen who become Members of the British & Foreign Bible Society* published in 1812. Simeon reckoned that Marsh, by his public opposition, proved to be the Society's foremost promoter.

He had intended to lecture in three-year cycles but, because of the Bible Society dispute, the need to pursue his own research, and episcopal duties from 1816 onwards, he lectured only in 1809–10, 1813, 1816, 1822, and 1823. While he published thirty-six lectures, he delivered lectures on only three of the seven branches of divinity he planned to cover. He privately printed an abstract of the fourth branch for his Peterborough clergy in 1820 and a 46-page *History of Interpretation* in 1828. Thereafter his interest waned, due to his ill health and episcopal duties.

John Kaye studied under Richard Porson at Cambridge, forming a close lifetime association with C. J. Blomfield, afterwards Bishop of London, and J. H. Monk, afterwards Bishop of Gloucester. On 5 December 1804 he was elected to a Christ's fellowship. He served as college Tutor from

1804 until, on 5 September 1814, when still aged only thirty, he was elected Master of Christ's. During 1815-16 he was Vice-Chancellor of the University. On 18 July 1815 he married Eliza Mortlock, daughter of a Cambridge banker; they had one son and three daughters.

In 1808 he had been considered for the post of Regius Professor of Greek but withdrew in favour of Monk. Then in July 1816 a vacancy in the Regius Professorship of Divinity, which he desired, placed him in a delicate position because as Vice-Chancellor he was ineligible for any professorship. The appointment with the agreement of the other electors was deferred until November when he ceased to be Vice-Chancellor. The Regius Professor's public lectures had been suspended for over a century but Kaye, not wishing to be accused of indolence, reinstated them. He chose the Fathers as his subject, fostering the general revival in patristic studies. He published lectures on Tertullian and the ecclesiastical history of the second and third centuries (1825), Justin Martyr (1829), Clement of Alexandria (1835), and Athanasius and the Council of Nicaea (posthumously 1853). These books won him lasting esteem.

James Henry Monk was elected Fellow of Trinity in 1805 and became an Assistant Tutor in 1807 in which role he enjoyed considerable success, as his pupils carried off the greater part of the classical medals and honours. In January 1809 at the age of twenty-five he was elected Regius Professor of Greek in succession to Richard Porson. He was ordained Deacon in 1809 and Priest in 1810. Although he did not match his predecessor in scholarly distinction, Monk was an influential college Tutor and published several pamphlets advocating the establishment of a classical tripos, with public examinations and honours open only to those who had obtained a place in the mathematical tripos. His chief work, like Porson's, was on the text of *Euripides*. His editions of *Hippolytus* (1811) and *Alcestis* (1816) were regularly reprinted. The Latin notes are learned and appreciative of the work of earlier critics, especially Porson. He was one of the editors of Porson's *Adversaria* (1812) and of the short-lived but influential Cambridge journal *Museum Criticum*. His most important contribution to the history of classical scholarship was his Life of Richard Bentley, which appeared in 1830 and remains the fullest assessment of the greatest of English classical scholars. [ODNB]

In 1812 he was Whitehall preacher, and attracted the attention of the Prime Minister, Lord Liverpool, who appointed him to the deanery of Peterborough in 1822. He hoped to retain his professorship, but was unable to do so since he had become a Doctor of Divinity on his decanal appointment and the statutes of the university laid down that the Professor of Greek should not be a doctor. In right of his deanery, Monk nominated himself to the rectory of Fiskerton, Lincolnshire, in 1822, and afterwards held the rectory of Peakirk-cum-Glinton, Northamptonshire, from 1829. In 1823 he married Jane Smart Hughes of Hardwick Rectory Northamptonshire. They had three daughters and a son.

Being a successful schoolmaster proved to be another road to preferment for some. **John Bird Sumner** returned to Eton 1802, was made Deacon in 1803 and ordained Priest in 1805. He was secure in his post at the school for many years where he was very popular amongst the boys. Rees Gronow in his *Reminiscences of Regency and Victorian Life*, who was an old Etonian, said he was 'by far the most popular tutor . . . This most able and excellent man went by the name of "Crumpety Sumner," whether from some fancied resemblance in his fine open countenance to that farinaceous esculent, or from some episode of his more youthful days, I was never able to discover; but I can safely say that no one was more universally beloved throughout the precincts of the venerable college of Henry VI than he was.'

Two of Sumner's most significant published works belong to the Eton period of his life: *Apostolic Preaching Considered in an Examination of St Paul's Epistles* (1815) and *A Treatise of the Records of Creation and the Moral Attributes of the Creator* (1816). Both these works won immediate acclaim: *Apostolic Preaching* was revised and reprinted in 1817 and eventually reached a ninth edition in 1850, while the *Treatise* went through seven editions. The latter attracted more public attention, on account of its defence of a hierarchical class system and its view of Malthusian economic and social theories as acceptable Christian teaching.

These two works, published in successive years, brought Sumner into the public eye as a thoughtful writer and scholar. It came as no surprise, therefore, that in 1817 he was elected a Fellow at Eton College. The following year the valuable college living of Mapledurham fell vacant and was duly offered to Sumner; he was instituted on 20 November 1818. He retained his college fellowship until 1820, when Bishop Shute Barrington appointed him to the ninth prebendal stall in Durham Cathedral; in 1826 he succeeded to the more highly endowed fifth stall. From 1827 to 1848 he held the still more lucrative second stall. Apart from his periods of residence in Durham, Sumner lived out the life of a devoted evangelical pastor. He resided in his parish, held two services every Sunday, preached regularly, and attended himself to the occasional offices. His orthodox opinions, sound scholarship, and devotion to duty marked him out for elevation to the bench of bishops.

Samuel Butler was one of the most distinguished headmasters of his time. He had enjoyed exceptional distinction as an undergraduate and became a Fellow of St John's in 1797. A year later, aged only twenty-four, he was appointed by his college to the post of Headmaster of Shrewsbury School, a position which he held for thirty-eight years. In the same year, he married Harriet Apthorp, daughter of the Rector of St Mary-le-Bow in London. They had two daughters, Mary and Harriet, and a son, Thomas. The school was at its lowest point since its foundation in 1552 – one account says it was down to just a single pupil, so Butler was, in effect, facing the task of re-founding the school which he did successfully and by 1827 numbers had risen to 285. He proved to be an inspirational teacher and his pupils, emulating their Head's own earlier academic successes, won many distinctions at Oxbridge. Colman lists them as follows:

> At Cambridge Butler's pupils won 16 Browne Medals, 9 Chancellor's Medals and 19 University Scholarships. In the Classical Tripos, which was not established until 1824, 28 of his pupils were in the first class . . . At Oxford, where fewer of his boys were to be found, they had 11 first classes in *literis humanioribus* and 9 University Scholarships. Indeed, they won the Ireland in 1827, 1828, 1829, 1830, 1831 and 1833. The winner in 1831, Thomas Brancker, though on the books of Wadham College, was still in fact in the Sixth Form at Shrewsbury . . . among his competitors in that year were two Christ Church men, one of whom was William Ewart Gladstone and the other Brancker's old friend and schoolfellow Robert Scott, later Master of Balliol and joint author of Liddell and Scott.
>
> [COLMAN *Sabrinae Corolla. The Classics at Shrewsbury School* p. 5]

He must surely have been one of the greatest headmasters of the nineteenth century. Benjamin Hall Kennedy won the Porson prize while still a Shrewsbury schoolboy in 1823 and later succeeded Butler in 1836 on his retirement and appointment as Bishop of Lichfield. Butler had other clerical posts in addition to being Head of a great school. In 1802, he became Vicar of Kenilworth; in 1807 he was instituted to a prebend at Lichfield and in 1821 he was appointed Archdeacon of Derby. His published visitation *Charges* show how seriously he took this office, and that he had wide-ranging ideas for the reform of church administration.

Colman provides a lovely vignette of how important the classics were at that time in the lives of educated men:

> A MS letter of Butler to Robert Scott, then an undergraduate at Christ Church, is preserved in the School Library. "Let me entreat you for one more copy of your hexameters for my friend Mr Hawtrey of Eton. I heard nothing

but praises of them last week in London from the Bishops of London and Chichester – the latter lent them to the Lord Chancellor". That Lord Chancellor was Brougham, and the Bishops were Blomfield and Maltby, two of the most polished scholars and critics of their day. One catches a distant echo of another world in which dignitaries in Church and State had the time and inclination (as well as the capacity) to debate the neat handling of a hexameter. [*Ibid*. p. 13]

George Isaac Huntingford was another successful schoolmaster whose life, as boy and man, was given to Winchester College. In 1785, on the expiry of his Oxford fellowship, he was elected a Fellow of Winchester and seems to have resided in his rooms in Chamber Court, which was unusual for the period. Without any formal requirement to teach at Winchester, he planned to spend three years as a private tutor in Salisbury, but in 1787 the death of his brother Thomas, Master of Warminster School, Wiltshire, left him with responsibility for Thomas's pregnant widow, Mary, and her six children. He applied to the patron at Warminster, Thomas Thynne, third Viscount Weymouth, and was appointed Master there. He ran the school with diligence—'sound education and morals will be my objects' he told Henry Addington. He was devoted to his brother's children: he sent four of his five nieces to school and married them into prominent families associated with Winchester College, and energetically supported his nephews' careers in the Church of England.

One of his early pupils at Winchester was Henry Addington, speaker of the House of Commons from June 1789. Huntingford wrote over 600 letters to Addington over the course of his career. It was perhaps through Addington's influence that he was elected Warden of Winchester College by the Fellows of New College, Oxford, on 5 December 1789, although he later credited another former pupil, Gilbert Heathcote, with having brought him the post. Huntingford moved into the Warden's lodgings at Winchester with his sister-in-law and her young family, and set out to be an active Warden, attempting to restore discipline among the boys and ensure adherence to the statutes of William of Wykeham.

Charles James Blomfield's father had been a successful schoolmaster running a private establishment and he followed in his father's footsteps in that he took private pupils who resided with him. His rise, however, was via a succession of livings, some of which he held in plurality – a practice he would later condemn as a bishop. In 1809 he was elected a Fellow of Trinity. Blomfield was ordained Deacon in March 1810 and Priest in June by the Master of Trinity, who was also Bishop of Bristol, and, having declined the position of tutor to Lord Chesterfield's sons, accepted a curacy at Chesterford, Essex. In October 1810 he was presented to Quarrington, Lincolnshire, by Lord Bristol (a former pupil of Blomfield's grandfather and friend of his father). There being no parsonage at Quarrington, he continued to reside at Chesterford. In November 1810 Blomfield married Anna Maria Heath of Hemblington, Norfolk. The couple had six children, of whom only one survived infancy.

In December 1811 Blomfield resigned Chesterford (retaining Quarrington until 1820) when the second Earl Spencer, impressed by his edition of *Prometheus vinctus* (1810), presented him to the rectory of Dunton, Buckinghamshire, where he resided until 1817. A parish of only seventy-two inhabitants, with only one non-communicant male, this, like his previous livings, afforded Blomfield the opportunity to take in pupils (including George Spencer and Lord Hervey) and pursue his classical studies. He soon established a considerable reputation, being among the most important of a group of scholars, including Maltby, Monk, and Peter Paul Dobree, who were pupils of Richard Porson and adopted his editorial principles. Blomfield's editions of *Septem contra Thebas* (1812), the *Persæ* (1814), *Agamemnon* (1820), and the *Choephoroe* (1824) were accurate and critical, if prosaic, and displayed his extensive learning. His 1815 edition of *Callimachus* was for some time the standard text; he also produced an edition of *Euripides* (1821), and contributed editions of fragments of *Sappho, Alcaeus*, and *Stesichorus* to Thomas Gaisford's *Poetæ minores Græci* (1823). When his brother, Edward, died in 1816 Charles completed his translation of Matthiae's Greek grammar. [ODNB]

If clerical life at Dunton was relaxed, Blomfield was not simply a gentleman scholar. In 1813 he was appointed a JP. He was reading in patristics, and in 1817 and 1819 published on Jewish tradition and the understanding of scripture. More practically, he established a district depot at Aylesbury for the Society for Promoting Christian Knowledge (SPCK). In a visitation sermon for Bishop George Pretyman he called the clergy to pastoral responsibility and doctrinal orthodoxy, condemning both Calvinism and Socinianism. While in his preaching he was emerging as a high-church man, he was widely regarded as a liberal politically on account of his support for Roman Catholic relief.

A new phase of Blomfield's life began a few years before 1820. His first wife died in 1818 and in the following year he married a widow, Dorothy Kent. The eleven offspring of this marriage proved healthier than those of Blomfield's first, only one dying in infancy. His clerical career now advanced rapidly. In 1817 Lord Bristol presented Blomfield to the rectory and vicarage of Great and Little Chesterford and to the rectory of Tuddenham, Suffolk (resigned 1820); he was also appointed Chaplain to Bishop Howley of London. In 1819, shortly after Bristol brought Blomfield to the attention of his brother-in-law Lord Liverpool, Howley presented him to St Botolph without Bishopsgate. With his new parish yielding some £1600 per annum net, Blomfield's financial position was secured. St Botolph's was a fashionable living. It further contrasted with Blomfield's previous cures in having a population of over 10,000; Chesterford, which he retained and where he spent three months annually, became literally a rest-cure. During the rest of the year when he was in London, the curate resident in Chesterford sent him a weekly report in a basket of fresh vegetables.

St Botolph's presented Blomfield with the pastoral challenge of the city. He reorganized the parish finances, visited his flock, promoted infant schools, and preached regularly in his straightforward style, expounding basic doctrines. His classical publications were now supplemented by a catechism, sermons, occasional essays in church defence, an abandoned plan for a simplified Old Testament, and, perhaps surprisingly for a high-churchman, a *Manual of Family Prayers* in 1824. Pastoral experience softened his attitude to evangelicalism, for he gradually permitted the SPCK to distribute more evangelical tracts, and even proposed Charles Simeon as a member. As an associate of Howley in London he was at the heart of the network of charitable and auxiliary societies of the orthodox high-church circle of the Hackney Phalanx, and his activity in both the SPCK and the National Society probably confirmed him in his own high-churchmanship. The year 1822 brought further preferment when Howley appointed him Archdeacon of Colchester.

We turn now from Blomfield, the most active and influential of all the bishops under review, to another very able man but of a very different nature who would later frequently oppose Blomfield's efforts to reform church structures and finances – **Henry Phillpotts**. As noted earlier, the most significant relationship to emerge from his Magdalen years was the friendship formed with the president, Martin Routh, who helped shape his religious views and remained one of his most trusted counsellors until his death in 1854. He resigned his fellowship on his marriage on 27 October 1804 to Deborah Maria Surtees of Bath. The couple had eighteen children, of whom no fewer than seven followed their father into holy orders.

Phillpotts's first preferment was the crown living of Kilmersdon, near Bath, which he received (probably through Lord Eldon's influence) in 1804. He seems never to have resided there or at Stainton-le-Street, co.

Durham, another crown living received the following year. Resigning Kilmersdon in 1806, Phillpotts was presented to the crown living of Bishop Middleham, where he resided for two years, Routh's recommendation having secured him a chaplaincy to Shute Barrington, Bishop of Durham. It was to support Barrington in a controversy with the Roman Catholic John Lingard in 1806 that Phillpotts made the first of his innumerable sallies into pamphlet controversies. This may have led the Bishop to reward him with the important living of Gateshead in 1808 and in 1809 the ninth prebendal stall at Durham. Middleham was given up in 1810 on Phillpotts's collation by the Dean and Chapter to St Margaret's Chapel, Durham, and the remainder of his Durham career was punctuated by further lucrative preferment: promotion to the second stall in 1815, and in 1820 (on resigning it) appointment to another episcopal living, Stanhope, one of the richest livings in England. Barrington insisted on residence (and counselled the renunciation of cards) as a condition of this last piece of largess, and Phillpotts spent £12,000 on the construction of a new parsonage. Both in Durham and at Stanhope Phillpotts was a conscientious pastor, and in the latter instance an active magistrate. It was his prolific activity as a controversialist, however, that brought both wider recognition of Phillpotts's considerable talents and notoriety.

Phillpotts entered the lists in defence of both Anglicanism and the social and political order, to the preservation of which he believed the establishment essential. In 1819 he attacked proposals for reform of the law of settlement and for the abolition of the Test Act, but it was his resolute defence of the authorities in the wake of Peterloo, singling out J. G. Lambton (later Lord Durham) for censure, that provoked a bitter attack on Phillpotts in the *Edinburgh Review* and a controversy in which he was widely judged to have emerged victorious. His Tory credentials were confirmed in the following year when he promoted a clerical address in support of the government in the Queen Caroline affair, accusing Earl Grey of opportunism in championing her cause. This resulted in a foretaste of Phillpotts's other great passion beside pamphleteering—litigation—when whig lawyers sought unsuccessfully to prove a libel. In the article 'Durham clergy—clerical abuses', published in November 1822, the *Edinburgh Review* once more singled him out, and further controversy ensued. By 1823 his growing reputation led Liverpool to contemplate his promotion to the Irish see of Clogher, a preferment Phillpotts spurned. From 1825 the Catholic question became the dominant theme in Phillpotts's writings and won him national prominence, reflected in his elevation to the deanery of Chester in May 1828. His *Letters to Charles Butler*

(1825) set out key doctrinal differences between the Anglican and Roman Catholic churches; they were followed in 1827 by two Letters to Canning, arguing that current schemes for emancipation offered inadequate securities, and proposing an alternative test in which Catholics would accept the possibility of salvation within the Church of England and renounce any intention of harming it. Public perception of Phillpotts as a leading opponent of emancipation was confirmed by *A Letter to an English Layman on the Coronation Oath* (1828). Phillpotts also engaged in extensive (if one-sided) private correspondence with Wellington, Eldon, and others, in which he discussed the developing political situation and proposed possible securities. As early as 1812 Phillpotts had told Barrington that, given adequate safeguards, he had no objection to relief, and a letter to Eldon demonstrates that by October 1828 he felt that now inevitable concessions should be enacted, while the government still had control of the situation. This conviction, combined with a belief that Peel had behaved honourably, led Phillpotts to support Peel in the Oxford election of 1829, even though emancipation had been enacted without some of his specified precautions. Public opinion, however, interpreted this vote as evidence that Phillpotts ('the great rat') was an unprincipled careerist, *The Times* commenting that he had 'wheeled to the right and about as if by military command' (3 February 1829). The accusation dogged Phillpotts throughout his career. It didn't stop his advancement, however, to a seat in the House of Lords.

There was another aspect to Phillpotts which added to the bad impression many had of clergy as rich and greedy. Some clergy managed to negotiate tithe on mineral production as was the case at Stanhope. The new rector was not satisfied with the financial agreement reached in 1799 which was an annual payment of £1,500. Jacob tells the story:

> In 1820, the new incumbent, Henry Phillpotts was offered £3,000 a year, but counterclaimed for 250 tons of lead a year or £5,000 a year. The company threatened to reduce work in the mines, bringing out the mining community against Phillpotts, but settled at £4,500. However legally and morally justified Phillpotts was in enforcing his claims, the publicity reinforced an impression created by caricatures and satires, of a grasping clergy growing fat on others' hard work and initiative. [JACOB *op. cit.* p. 129]

In contrast to careerist clerics such as Phillpotts, there were some who had not really wished to be ordained. Stanley, whom we have already noted, belongs in this class. As does his fellow liberal **Connop Thirlwall**, who was called to the Bar in 1825, after eating the requisite number of dinners at Lincoln's Inn, and practised for two years on the home circuit. In October of 1818 he was elected Fellow of Trinity College Cambridge and was now able to realize what he called 'the most enchanting of my daydreams'. He spent several months on the continent in the company of Julius Hare, strengthening his familiarity with the German language and with German theology and philosophy.. The winter of 1818–19 was passed in Rome, where he formed a close friendship with Bunsen, then secretary to the Prussian legation, at the head of which was Niebuhr. In 1824 he translated two tales by Tieck, and began his work on Schleiermacher's *Critical Essay on the Gospel of St Luke*. Both of these were published (anonymously) in the following year, the second with a critical introduction, remarkable not only for thoroughness, but for acquaintance with modern German theology, then a field of research virtually untrodden by English students. In October 1827 Thirlwall abandoned law and returned to Cambridge at the invitation of his friend Whewell to become an Assistant Tutor at his old college. The prospect of the loss of his fellowship at Trinity, which would have expired in 1828, probably determined the precise moment for taking a step which he had long meditated. He was ordained Deacon before the end of 1827, and Priest in 1828; his motivation seems to have been the opportunity for literary study.

At Cambridge Thirlwall at once undertook his full share of college and university work. In 1828 the first volume of the translation of Niebuhr's history of Rome appeared, the joint work of himself and Julius Charles Hare. In 1831 the publication of the journal *The Philological Museum* was started with the object of promoting 'the knowledge and the love of ancient literature'. Hare and Thirlwall were the editors, and the latter contributed to it several masterly essays. It ceased in 1833. In 1829 Thirlwall held for a short time the Vicarage of Over, and in 1832, when Hare left college, he was appointed Assistant Tutor.

In 1834 Thirlwall's connection with the educational staff of Trinity College was rudely severed when—true to his liberalism—he supported the admission of dissenters to Cambridge degrees. He replied to a pamphlet by Thomas Turton in *a Letter on the Admission of Dissenters to Academical Degrees*; it argued that 'Cambridge colleges are not theological seminaries' or even 'schools of religious instruction' and he attacked college divinity lectures and compulsory chapel. This publication is dated 21 May 1834, and five days later Christopher Wordsworth, the Master, wrote to the author, calling upon him to resign his appointment as Assistant Tutor. Thirlwall immediately obeyed.

On Thirlwall's return, in November 1834, from a continental visit Lord Brougham offered him the valuable living of Kirby Underdale in Yorkshire. He accepted without hesitation, and went into residence in July 1835. He had had little experience of parochial work, but he proved himself both energetic and successful in this new field; he was sometimes helped by W. H. Thompson, a future Master of Trinity. At Kirby Underdale Thirlwall completed his *History of Greece* (8 vols. 1835–44). This work entailed prodigious labour. At Cambridge, where the first volume was written, he used to work all day until half-past three, when he left his rooms for a rapid walk before dinner, at that time served in hall at four; in Yorkshire he is said to have worked sixteen hours a day in his study. [ODNB]

We can look more briefly now at four more of the worthier men:

George Henry Law Elected fellow of Queens' College in 1781, he proceeded MA in 1784, DD in 1804. He was also a Fellow of the Royal Society and of the Society of Antiquaries. In July 1784 Law vacated his college fellowship on his marriage to Jane Adeane of Cambridgeshire. In 1785 he was collated to a prebendal stall in Carlisle Cathedral by his father, who also, a few days before his death in 1787, presented him to the vicarage of Torpenhow, Cumberland which he held until Bishop Yorke of Ely presented him to the Rectory of Kelshall, Hertfordshire, in 1791, and of Willingham, Cambridgeshire, in 1804.

Charles Richard Sumner On 5 June 1814 he was ordained Deacon by Bishop Bathurst. He did not have what is technically called a 'title' for holy orders, i.e. a particular cure of souls to go to, but the bishop was a family friend and did not regard technicalities as an insuperable obstacle. Shortly after his ordination Sumner accompanied, as their tutor, Lord Mount-Charles (who had been a fellow undergraduate at Trinity College) and Lord Francis Nathaniel Conyngham, the eldest and second sons of Marquess Conyngham, through Flanders and by the Rhine to Switzerland. In Geneva he unexpectedly met John Taylor Coleridge, who introduced them to J. P. Maunoir, a Professor of Surgery. The Professor's wife was an English woman, and Sumner became engaged in January 1815 to the eldest of their three daughters, Jennie .

During the winter of 1814–15 he obtained a building for an English congregation at Geneva and ministered to them over that winter and the next. On 24 January 1816 he married his fiancée at the English chapel; they had four sons and three daughters. From September 1816 to 1821 Sumner served as curate of Highclere, Hampshire, and took pupils, Lord Albert Conyngham and Frederick Oakeley being among them.

In 1820 Sumner was introduced by the Conynghams to George IV at Brighton, where he dined with the king and talked with him afterwards for three hours. He made a favourable impression and in April of the following year George, without waiting for the approval of Lord Liverpool, the prime minister, announced to Sumner that he intended to promote him to a vacant canonry at Windsor. Liverpool refused to sanction the appointment, even threatening to resign his office, and an angry correspondence took place between king and minister, which ended in a compromise. The canonry was given to Dr James Stanier Clarke, and Sumner succeeded to all Clarke's appointments, which included the posts of historiographer to the crown, chaplain to the household at Carlton House, and librarian to the king. George IV also made him his private chaplain at Windsor, with a salary of £300 a year 'and a capital house ... opposite the park gate'. Other promotions followed in quick succession. From September 1821 to March 1822 Sumner was vicar of St Helen's, Abingdon; he held the second canonry in Worcester Cathedral from 11 March 1822 to 27 June 1825, and was then the second canon at Canterbury until 16 June 1827. He became Chaplain-in-Ordinary to the king on 8 January 1823, and Deputy Clerk of the Closet on 25 March 1824.

William Otter was elected a Fellow of his college in 1796 and subsequently served as a Tutor. He had been ordained Deacon in 1791 and served as Curate of Helston, Cornwall and Master of the Grammar School 1791-96. In 1799 he travelled in Northern Europe with his friend from university days, Malthus. Otter resigned his fellowship on his marriage in 1804 to Nancy Sadleir Bruere of Leatherhead. The couple had three sons and five daughters. Shortly before his marriage Otter was presented by his prospective father-in-law to the rectory of Colmworth, Bedfordshire. He resigned this living along with that of Sturmer, Essex, which he had held for only one year, on his appointment as rector of Chetwynd, Shropshire, in 1811, to which he added the vicarage of Kinlet in 1814. Otter supplemented his income through tutoring, numbering among his pupils sons of Sir Samuel Romilly, Sir John St Aubin, and Sir Roger Newdigate. In 1822 he moved his family to Oxford and acted as private tutor to the third Lord Ongley. In 1825 Otter acquired a third benefice, the Vicarage of St Mark's, Kennington, through the patronage of George D'Oyly, the husband of his wife's sister. Possibly through his association with D'Oyly, Otter was chosen as first Principal of King's College, London (after John Lonsdale declined the post), in June 1831, and resigned Kennington on his appointment. He was simultaneously appointed Divinity Lecturer, delivering weekly sermons and Monday discourses on Theology throughout his tenure.

William Howley graduated BA in 1787 and MA in 1791, and was elected Fellow and Tutor. While at New College he served as tutor to the Prince of Orange, later William II of the Netherlands. In 1792 he became Domestic Chaplain to the Marquess of Abercorn, who played a vital role in forwarding his career. In 1794 he was elected Fellow of Winchester College, and was appointed Vicar of Bishop's Sutton in 1796 in succession to his late father. He became Vicar of Andover on 22 January 1802, and on 23 May 1811 vicar of Bradford Peverell, both Winchester College livings. Howley married Mary Frances Belli of Southampton. They had two sons and three daughters. In 1804 he had been made Canon of Christ Church, Oxford, and in 1809 was appointed Regius Professor of Divinity there – but he never gave a lecture or wrote a theological book.

The route for many of the others was by way of accumulating livings in the gift of family and friends – in some cases, being an absentee incumbent employing a curate to do the work – then enjoying the income, but with minimal duties, of a prebendal stall or two or even three! Two Bishops of Carlisle illustrate this: **Edward Venables Vernon Harcourt** and **Hugh Percy**. After ordination Vernon was instituted in 1782 to the family living of Sudbury; in October 1785 he was installed a Canon of Christ Church Oxford and a month later a Canon of Gloucester Cathedral. On appointment at the age of thirty-four to the see of Carlisle in November 1791, he resigned the latter canonry but kept his other preferments to supplement the income of his bishopric which he held for sixteen years.

Percy, who was a grandson of the first Duke of Northumberland, married the eldest daughter of the Archbishop of Canterbury in 1806, by whom he was ordained Deacon in December 1808 and Priest a month later. He was immediately appointed a chaplain to the Archbishop and collated to two livings, Bishopsbourne worth about £1,500 a year and Ivy worth about £460. In 1810, at the age of twenty-six, he was appointed Chancellor and a prebendary of Exeter worth over £3,000, and two years later Chancellor of Salisbury. In 1816 he was collated by his father-in-law to a prebendal stall in Canterbury Cathedral, and in the same year was given another very rich stall, this time at St Paul's Cathedral, which he held till his death. His annual income was reckoned to be £6,000 which is over half a million in today's terms. In 1822 he was made Archdeacon of Canterbury and three years later Dean. The bishopric of Rochester followed in 1827 with the expectation of promotion as soon as possible. It clearly paid to marry an Archbishop's daughter in those days!

Patronage and Preferment

Richard Whately, the Archbishop of Dublin, published some reminiscences of Edward Copleston, his friend from Oxford days. He wrote:

> All the most remarkable steps of his elevation in life took place without any application whatsoever on his part. He was elected Fellow of Oriel College, Provost of the same, Doctor of Divinity by Diploma, Dean of Chester, and Bishop of Llandaff (and at the same time Dean of St Paul's), all without his having offered himself for any of these appointments.
>
> Now as for what relates to the deaneries and bishoprics, this is not, it is to be hoped, anything uncommon. It does, indeed, undoubtedly sometimes occur that applications for such appointments are made, and sometimes, it is supposed, with success; at least, although no one can be certain that an applicant has been successful in consequence of his application, this has certainly not proved in every instance a bar to success. But doubtless the great majority of cases, and those in which the promotion has been the best deserved, have been those of persons who never did, and never would, use solicitation for themselves. [WHATELY *op. cit.* p. 2].

Whately describes this as 'a remarkable circumstance'. It was, indeed, remarkable because that is not how things normally happened. Most men had received preferment to the bench of bishops because they had the right connections, and in many cases had in fact asked their patron to use his influence on their behalf. Charles Lloyd, Regius Professor of Divinity at Oxford and a contemporary of both Copleston and Whateley, is a case in point. Here is an extract from a letter to Sir Robert Peel, one of his former students, dated 28 February 1826 and marked 'Most Private', in which he set out his arguments for why he (and not Copleston who was a likely candidate) should be given the See of Oxford. He claimed for himself, truthfully if immodestly:

> I am working day and night in my Professorship, no man ever did what I am doing, or the tenth part of it . . . I will conclude by telling you my own real wishes about myself. My anxious desire is to make myself a great Divine and to be accounted the best in England. My second wish is to become the Founder of a School of Theology at Oxford. For the accomplishment of these purposes, I must remain some years longer here, say ten years from the time of my appointment to the Professorship. I shall by that time working as I do now, have laid a strong foundation, upon which any man may build a lasting superstructure. Now, no Bishopric will enable me to do this, except

the See of Oxford. Any other will carry me gradually away from the University. [BL Add MS 40342, ff. 328-9]

Lloyd was successful.

Charles Sumner became a bishop at the direction of the King because he was one of his favourite clergymen, and his preferment happened despite opposition from Lambeth and from Westminster where suspicion lingered over any candidate's name if he was an Evangelical. That is not to deny, as we have seen, that Sumner was a conscientious and able priest, and he turned out to be an equally conscientious and effective bishop but he got there because George IV liked his company. There were others too who were appointed to canonries, deaneries and bishoprics because they had come to the personal notice and favour of the sovereign, e.g. the man who had been their tutor when they were children: Henry William Majendie to Prince William (later King William IV) and George Davys to the Princess Victoria.

Looking at all 45 bishops in the period under review, it seems that their promotion came about for one (or more) of the following reasons:
As noted already, they were a favourite of the sovereign, e.g. Charles Manners Sutton, or they were related by blood or by marriage to one of most influential officers of State, e.g. Edward Grey and Henry Phillpotts; or they had been the tutor or schoolmaster of one or more sons of an aristocratic family with influence at court or with the Cabinet, e.g. George Isaac Huntingford and Charles Lloyd; or they had come to note because of some scholarly or apologetic work written early on in their career, e.g. Thomas Burgess and Herbert Marsh; or they were men of genuine ability who, coincidentally, shared the political beliefs of the party in power; e.g. Charles James Blomfield. Some appointments were, of course, blatantly political and served as a reward or compensation to a 'deserving' supporter of the party in power – Edward Maltby was such a one, as was Connop Thirlwall.

Lord Liverpool who was Prime Minister from 1812 to 1827 made twenty-one appointments, four of them translations – so seventeen new bishops in all. He is credited with choosing bishops on the basis of personal distinction and ability – 'ability' to him included editing a Greek play whilst doing a decent job as a priest! His biographer, Norman Gash, has this to say about his episcopal appointments:

> Like Pitt he had a certain partiality for men of good family, but he was more insistent than his illustrious predecessor on high standards of scholarship, impeccable moral responsibility, and a conscientious performance of past-

oral duties. Not all his cabinet colleagues were troubled by such scruples. Arbuthnot had a story about a clerical protégé for whom Lord Westmorland made repeated applications for preferment. In the end Liverpool sent Arbuthnot as patronage secretary to tell him that the clergyman in question had not sufficient merit for a bishopric. 'Merit, indeed,' said Westmorland in surprise. 'We are come to a pretty pass if they talk of merit for a bishopric.' Liverpool, however, persisted with his peculiar notion that certain standards were demanded of the episcopacy. . .
To find suitable men in an age of unrest and in the face of the King's express wish for bishops of political and theological orthodoxy, preferably connected with the aristocracy, was not a light task. [GASH *Lord Liverpool* p. 202]

In the late Victorian era there was much mention of so-called 'Greek-Play Bishops' as though excellence in classics and the publication of an edited version of a Greek play had been the main cause of preferment earlier that century. The three bishops most frequently mentioned were Maltby, Monk and Blomfield, though Maltby never published a critical edition of a Greek play, and there were others, such as Samuel Butler, who had. Classical scholarship was simply one indicator of ability and not the main reason or sole reason for preferment. [See BURNS & STRAY *The Greek-Play Bishop* in *The Historical Journal* vol. 54 pp. 1013-1038]

There were, inevitably some appointments made under pressure from political allies, such as that of the reactionary Huntingford for Hereford in 1815. And there was nepotism in the appointment of his cousin, J.B. Jenkinson, to St David's in 1825. Gash comments on that appointment:

It was not a disreputable appointment; and in the field of education for the poor, at any rate, Bishop Jenkinson, whatever his theological shortcomings, ranked with the more progressive members of the episcopate. For the rest the Prime Minister had nothing to be ashamed of in a list of bishops which included the active, pious Law, the reforming administrator Kaye, the evangelical Ryder, the able and scholarly Bethell, the learned energetic Marsh, the gentle, liberal-minded Howley, the serious devout Burgess, and the respected Van Mildert. 'The world will at least give me credit,' Liverpool wrote with a touch of complacency to Hobhouse in 1825, 'for my ecclesiastical promotions, whatever they may say or think of me in other respects.'
[*Ibid*. p. 203]

Lord Holland, Chancellor of the Duchy of Lancaster, recorded in his diary how the appointment process worked when Melbourne was in power in the late 1830s, and the part that politicking played in it.

Melbourne was more harassed in selecting his Bishops. There was a great push on the part of the Prelates to get Lincoln [KAYE] advanced to Durham and some Tories and Churchmen talked of the claims of Bishop Grey of Hereford in the hopes that, so doing, they should either get an intolerant narrow minded Man in an elevated situation, or breed some discontent in Lord Grey's mind at the pretensions of a brother being overlooked. Grey was however quite satisfied at the preference given to Maltby, and every Man who loves liberality of sentiment on civil and religious matters, respects great learning, and esteems modest worth was rejoiced at his advancement. The new Bishopricks were not filled with such entire satisfaction to the Reformers. Melbourne hesitated too long. I had once hoped, and indeed Melbourne told me, that one of the vacant Mitres might fall on Dr Shuttleworth's head, but when the choice was talked of either in the Cabinet or in Whig Societies, it was soon clear that his offence in signing in [18]35 the address to Peel to remain in office could not be overlooked and, in truth, that circumstance and his conduct, though he voted right, on Hampden's business thoroughly persuaded me that, with all his integrity and disinterestedness, and he has both, he lacks the nerve, the spirit, and the energy which would render him a useful friend in the hour of need. His conscientiousness, tho' sincere, has the gait of indecision and his conciliation and ingenuity assume the appearance and perhaps in some degree the reality, of timidity and compromise. The earnestness with which his name was caught at by the Archbishop of Canterbury, and with which Melbourne was exhorted to prefer him, did not sharpen my pangs at his disappointment. I hardly know how to account for Longley [appointed to Ripon in 1837], who has never voted with us and declared at the outset that he could not support the appropriation. Butler [Lichfield & Coventry in 1836] had claims of long standing; it was an appointment gratifying to many old and steady adherents, though his health and age have hitherto prevented him from giving any active support. The merits of Otter [Chichester in 1836] are said to be firmness and liberality. But the clamour raised about Hampden deterred Melbourne, I think, from taking the marked men on the side of Liberalism such as Thirlwall, Sedgwick, Arnold, and Sydney Smith or even those approved and suggested by the Archbishop of Dublin [Whately], who wrote several sensible, candid, manly and confidential letters on the subject and, though perhaps the whole correspondence was tinctured with a little Oriel predilection, was as just and impartial as he was acute and discriminating in his estimation of Men.

[KRIEGEL ed. *The Holland House Diaries 1831-1840* p. 344]

It was an issue that troubled Chancellor Holland for he notes elsewhere

Melbourne was much harassed with rumours of more Bishops dropping, but I fear that he will still neglect to prepare himself for that event by making up his mind in the interim what stout Clergyman to prefer, and shutting his ears after the vacancy to all the objections which should be considered and overruled before he absolutely designates a Man for the Bench. [*Ibid*. p. 359]

He also reveals that the offer of a bishopric was occasionally declined by a man of aristocratic birth with a brother in the Cabinet.

> 1839 December. Dr Butler, Bishop of Lichfield, died; the bishoprick was offered and even pressed on Lord Wriothesley Russell, who modestly, unaffectedly, but steadfastly declined it, alledging (*sic*) that he felt himself every way unqualified for a station of this importance. I believe he is sincere and I am sure he is disinterested in this determination, for neither his present circumstances nor his prospects are very prosperous and I should think those most nearly connected with him will lament and even disapprove of his determination. [*Ibid*. p. 415]

Russell was the fourth son of the sixth Duke of Bedford and brother of the Home Secretary, Lord John Russell. He had been rector of the parish of Cheneys in Buckinghamshire since 1829. Other preferment came his way a year later when he was made a canon of Windsor and appointed a chaplain to Prince Albert.

We can look now at each one in more detail, and see how their contemporary, William Carpenter judged them in his critical two-volume work *A Peerage for the People*, published in 1837 and revised four years later. Carpenter, the son of a London tradesman, was a self-educated man who made a name for himself as a political journalist supporting reform. A friend of Cobbett, he was a strong proponent of the Chartist Movement; he also wrote widely on Biblical matters.

Province of Canterbury
Canterbury: 1805-28 Charles Manners Sutton (1755-1828)
As the grandson of the 3rd Duke of Rutland, preferment was assured. He was made Dean of Peterborough at the age of 37, Bishop of Norwich at 38 and because the diocese, though large and expensive to run, was poorly endowed he was made Dean of Windsor two years later which post he held *in commendam*. That same year he was also offered the Archbishopric of Armagh which he declined. He and his wife became great favourites of George III who personally intervened with Pitt in 1805 to have him translated to Canterbury. The Prime Minister had wished to appoint his former college tutor, Bishop Pretyman-Tomline of Lincoln, but the King prevailed. Charles's younger brother, Thomas, was also helped by the family connections and became Lord Chancellor of Ireland;

and the Archbishop's son, also called Charles, became Speaker of the House of Commons.

1828-48 William Howley   (1766-1848)

While at New College Oxford he served as Tutor to the Prince of Orange, later William II of the Netherlands, which led to him becoming a favourite with the royal family. He was at the same time domestic chaplain to the Marquess of Abercorn who played a vital role in forwarding his career. In 1809 he was appointed Regius Professor of Divinity, and four years later was offered the see of London by Lord Liverpool, and on Sutton's death was translated to Canterbury. In 1820 when the Bill for divorcing George IV from Queen Caroline was going through Parliament, Howley argued in the Lords that the King could do no wrong – despite knowing of his scandalous behaviour! Later historians have described the King rather differently, e.g. 'a wayward and capricious monarch, whose vices and extravagance had confirmed his unpopularity'. [DERRY *Reaction and Reform* p. 100] The King never forgot Howley's loyal support and rewarded him when Canterbury became vacant.

Carpenter wrote about him: 'He was violent in his opposition to the Catholic claims, and it is said, that it was to this circumstance, more than to any other, that he owed the archiepiscopal chair; although it happened, singularly enough, that he was ultimately placed in opposition to the Government who conferred upon him the dignity, but who had changed their own policy on that question.' [CARPENTER *A Peerage* . . . p. 116]

London: 1828-56 Charles James Blomfield (1786-1857)

His early parish appointments, as noted earlier, had come with the help of Lord Bristol, a friend of his father's. It was Lord Bristol who recommended him to his brother-in-law, Lord Liverpool, and he also had the support of Howley whose opinions were always respected by the King. The offer of Chester duly followed. Although a vast diocese geographically and in terms of its population, it was poorly endowed. One of his patrons, Lady Spencer, fearing he might decline it urged him to accept, 'remember it is the step you must tread on to a richer one.' She already foresaw a likely move to London when Howley would probably succeed Sutton, and she proved to be correct. The press welcomed his appointment and paid tribute to his character, learning and commitment to the Establishment.

Carpenter wrote, 'It is said that Dr Blomfield owes his elevation to the episcopal chair, to his classical attainments; but this is no discredit to him . . . he is at least entitled to the praise of thorough independence of mind and action. This has ever been his great characteristic, and it was this that gave him favour with Mr Cobbett – no very lenient censor upon the character of the clergy.' [*Ibid.* p. 462]

Winchester: 1827-69 Charles Richard Sumner (1790-1874)

It has been claimed that whilst on the continental trip in 1814 with two of Lord Conyngham's sons, he spared the noble father some embarrassment by marrying Jennie de Maunoir in Geneva whom the elder of the two Conyngham boys, Lord Mount-Charles, had become attached to and wanted to marry. That story is roundly condemned as untrue by Joyce Coombs in her biography of Charles's son George. She quotes from contemporary family correspondence which does certainly show theirs was truly a love match, and not one of convenience. Sumner came to the King's notice through his two former pupils, who stood high in the King's favour and spoke warmly of their former tutor to him. He was invited to Brighton and made such a favourable impression that preferment of various kinds quickly followed. He was the focus of a row, mentioned earlier (p. 68), between the King and his Prime Minister. Greville recorded in his diary that in May 1821 a canonry at Windsor became vacant and Lady Conyngham asked the King to give it to Sumner:

> The King agreed; the man was sent for, and kissed hands at Brighton. A letter was written to Lord Liverpool to announce the appointment. In the meantime Lord Liverpool had sent a list of persons, one of whom he should recommend to succeed to the vacancy, and the letters crossed. As soon as Lord Liverpool received the letter from Brighton he got into his carriage and went down to the King, to state that unless he was allowed to have the distribution of this patronage without interference, he could not carry on the Government, and would resign his office if Sumner was appointed. The man was only a curate, and had never held a living at all.
>
> [GREVILLE MEMOIRS Part 1 p. 45f]

A compromise candidate was appointed so that neither monarch nor his chief minister lost face, but George never forgot nor forgave Liverpool. In January 1824 the new see of Jamaica was offered to Sumner at a salary of £4,000 a year but the King refused to sanction his leaving England. In December that same year, at the King's request, he attended the deathbed of Lord Mount-Charles in Nice. Five months later he was consecrated Bishop of Llandaff which he held with the Deanery of St Paul's and the prebendal stall of Portpoole *in commendam*. In December 1827, he took possession of the third wealthiest see in the country, Winchester. However, he forfeited the affection of George IV when he voted in favour of the Catholic Emancipation Bill in 1829 to which the King was opposed.

Greville added a footnote to the above entry about Sumner: 'Afterwards Bishop of Winchester. This was the beginning of the fortune of that amiable prelate, of whom it must be said that if he owed his early advancement to a questionable influence, no man has filled the episcopal office with more unaffected piety, dignity, and goodness.' [*Ibid.*]

His older brother, John Bird, wrote a gracious congratulatory letter,

> . . . most heartily I am glad for your own sake that you are safely seated on the bench. You have so conducted yourself in every situation that you have filled, that I feel a certain confidence for the future. The girls are already pleasing themselves with the phrase "my uncle the Bishop".
>
> [COOMBS *op. cit.* p. 8]

He was even more generous in his words of praise when Charles was translated to Winchester and would soon be living near him.

> I have been trying but cannot recollect any event which I consider more beneficial to the great interests of the Church of Christ than your promotion to Winchester . . . . Besides which it is impossible not to feel gratification at the enjoyable value of the diocese and residence and its nearness to Mapledurham and to every other seat of civilisation, and of fixing you without fear of change till you become Archbishop of Canterbury. [*Ibid.*]

Carpenter, whilst not critical of him personally, used the dismissive term 'a Courtier Bishop' to describe him.

Bath & Wells: 1824-45 George Henry Law   (1761-1845)

The son and the brother of bishops, elevation to the purple was always a likelihood. His father started him on the road to episcopal preferment by collating him to a prebendal stall in Carlisle Cathedral. His father-in-law's influential Cambridgeshire connections provided him with two livings there in the gift of the Bishop of Ely. His preferment to the see of Chester came as a result of the powerful influence of his brother, the Lord Chief Justice, as well as through the personal favour of the Prince Regent.

Bristol: 1827-34 Robert Gray (1762-1834)

He was one of the few theologians to serve on the bench of bishops. His first book, published in 1790, *A Key to the Old Testament and Apocrypha* became a text book at both universities. In 1791-2 he took part in a Grand Tour in the company of Sir Thomas Clarges, the nephew of Shute Barrington, Bishop of Durham, who later appointed him to valuable livings in his gift as well as to a prebendal stall in Durham Cathedral. He also had the backing of the King who supported his preferment to a bishopric.

On his appointment in 1827 to the see of Bristol, which was worth just £1,700 a year, he had to give up the living of Bishopwearmouth worth £3,000 p.a. but was allowed to keep his Durham stall *in commendam*. A member of the Hackney Phalanx, he was regarded as an efficient bishop.

1834-36 Joseph Allen (1770-1845)

He enjoyed rapid preferment thanks to the patronage of the 2nd Earl Spencer whose Private Secretary he was. Lord Spencer appointed him to two important livings in his gift, first to Battersea and then to St Bride's, London. He also served as tutor to Lord Althorp (later 3rd Earl Spencer) 1830-34 who secured his appointment to Bristol in 1834 and two years later his translation to Ely. Le Marchant (Lord Brougham's Principal Private Secretary) noted in his diary on 10 March 1832, a national day of fasting, that he had attended a service in the Abbey 'where Maltby preached an excellent sermon . . . Dr Allen was not equally successful before the House of Commons at St Margaret's. His sermon lasted 3 quarters of an hour and was proportionately dull. It must be confessed that he is a very dull man. I hope and trust his pupil, Lord Althorp, will never raise him to the bench.' [ASPINALL ed. *Three Early Nineteenth Century Diaries* p. 212] He did. But to his credit Allen was one of the few bishops to have had first-hand experience of ministering in an urban living prior to his preferment.

Lord Holland approved of Allen's preferment describing him in his diary as 'a Clergyman of respectable character . . . Dr Allen if not a warm is a good Whig, and an honourable man.' [KRIEGEL ed. *op. cit.* p. 265] Greville records that William IV when receiving Allen's homage on his preferment to Ely expressed this hope: 'My Lord, I do not mean to interfere in any way with your vote in Parliament except on one subject, the *Jews*, and I trust I may depend upon your always voting against them.' [quoted in TURBERVILLE *The Episcopal Bench 1783-1837* in *CQR* 1937 p. 282]

Carpenter wrote, 'His claim to the distinction he now enjoys appears to have rested upon his having been tutor to Lord Spencer (then Viscount Althorp); for we are not aware that he has ever distinguished himself by any extraordinary display of erudition, or of that peculiar description of learning more especially called for in a Bishop. Dr Allen was a pluralist of some distinction, and his promotion excited on this account some notice, and called forth strong animadversion.' [CARPENTER *op. cit.* p. 70]

Chichester: 1824-31 Robert James Carr (1774-1841)

Preferment came his way because during his years as Vicar of Brighton he became friends with the Prince Regent who acted as his patron and had him appointed to various cathedral posts after he became King. In

1824 he was offered the see of Chichester at the King's initiative, who regarded him as 'an excellent and exemplary man'. That is not how some of his clergy regarded him; E.B. Ellman, who was confirmed by him in 1829 and later given *Letters Dimissory* by him, wrote, 'Carr had for many years been Vicar of Brighton and was a boon companion of George IV, when Prince Regent. He was raised to the Bishopric by him when he came to the throne, to enable Carr to pay his debts. . . He certainly did not make a good Bishop.' [ELLMAN *Recollections of a Sussex Parson* p. 177] Translation to Worcester followed in 1831.

Carpenter appears not to have known of Carr's royal connections but he is dismissive of him as a bishop, 'The Right Reverend Peer is not, so far as we are informed, "a burning and shining light" in any sense of the phrase. . . His Parliamentary conduct is not so obnoxious to popular censure, as that of some members of the Right Reverend Bench; but it is only so many degrees removed from the most illiberal, as to make that appear most odious, without reconciling us to this.' [CARPENTER *op. cit.* p. 775]

1831-36 Edward Maltby (1770-1859)

His cousin Elizabeth Maltby married George Pretyman who later became Bishop of Lincoln and appointed him as a domestic chaplain soon after his ordination, along with a prebendal stall in Lincoln Cathedral and two livings in his gift. His *Illustrations of the Truth of the Christian Religion* published in 1802 marked him out as a man of scholastic ability but, given his Whig opinions in a Tory dominated age, he had to wait for preferment until Grey came to power. He was appointed quickly as his vote in support of the Reform Bill was needed in the House of Lords! Four years later he was translated to Durham, and in 1847 was considered for York by his friend Lord John Russell but he declined. Ellman was only a little less dismissive of him on his appointment to Chichester 'His only qualification (as far as I could understand) being that he had edited a Greek lexicon.' [ELLMAN *op. cit.* p. 177]

Carpenter approved highly of Maltby's liberal views and wished all bishops might imitate his conduct – 'if learning, virtue and unremitting attention to clerical duties furnish a title to promotion in the Church, that of Dr Maltby was made with good reason and propriety.' [CARPENTER *op. cit.* p. 128]

1836-40 William Otter (1768-1840)

George D'Oyly, the Vicar of Lambeth, married Otter's wife's sister and it was through his patronage that Otter acquired fairly late on in life the important benefice of St Mark's Kennington and in 1831 his appointment as the first Principal of King's College, London. Otter was a known Whig, and Melbourne rewarded him with the see of Chichester in 1836. Ellman approved of him and his 'establishing various works for the good of the Diocese. He was a most lovable man, but I doubt whether, if he had been spared long, he could have effectually and well carried out the various schemes he had originated.' [ELLMAN *op. cit.* p. 177]

1840-42 Philip Nicholas Shuttleworth (1782-1842)

After graduation he became tutor to the Hon. Algernon Herbert and later to Lord Holland's son, Charles Richard Fox. He visited the continent in 1814-15 with Lord and Lady Holland who became his patrons. A strong Whig who supported Catholic emancipation and the relaxation of the religious tests which excluded Dissenters from studying at Oxford, he would have expected promotion from a Whig ministry but lost favour with them when he signed an address in 1835 urging Peel to remain in office. As Warden of New College he was a vigorous opponent of the Oxford movement. Melbourne, who appears to have taken appointments to the episcopate seriously, promoted him to the see of Chichester in 1840 but only with reluctance as he did not think the man had much merit. He remarked in a letter to Russell that Holland 'did not care a damn for Shuttleworth but my lady's vanity and love of meddling would be pleased by his being made.' [quoted in BRENT *Liberal Anglican Politics* p.113] He died just fifteen months after his appointment which Pusey interpreted as a 'token of God's presence in the Church of England'!

Ely: 1812-36 Bowyer Edward Sparke (1759-1836)

He had shown his mathematical and classical knowledge and ability by winning a string of prizes at Cambridge including the Chancellor's Medal in 1782 but preferment lay via his having served as tutor to John Manners, the 5th Duke of Rutland.

Carpenter wrote, 'Dr Sparke had the good fortune to become tutor to the Duke of Rutland; and from his Grace's mansion the road was straight and easy to the episcopal chair. . . We are not aware that his Lordship has ever been conspicuous for anything but the sedulous care with which he has tended the interests of his family, and the negligent manner in which he has discharged some of his most important episcopal functions. [CARPENTER *op. cit.* p. 284]

Exeter: 1820-30 William Carey (1769-1846)

His earliest patron was Cyril Jackson, President of Christ Church, Oxford who appointed him to the headmastership of Westminster School in 1803 and thereby brought him to the notice of many influential parents. He had already by then been given stalls in York Minster as well as being appointed preacher at Whitehall Chapel. A prebendal stall at Westminster followed in 1809 and the Duke of York, another patron, placed him in charge of the Royal Military Asylum at Chelsea, and of arrangements for the education of soldiers' children. Lord Liverpool appointed him, as a safe Tory, to Exeter in 1820 and the Duke of Wellington to the more lucrative see of St Asaph ten years later. The old DNB says of him in his Exeter days: 'The administration of the diocese by the former occupant of the see had not been marked by an excess of zeal, and the energy with which Carey threw himself into his new labours was much praised.'

Carpenter admits to knowing little about Carey, but nonetheless says he 'is in no way distinguished, except for some three or four good books on Latin prosody.' [CARPENTER *op. cit.* p. 640]

1830-69 Henry Phillpotts (1778-1869)

Martin Routh, the President of Magdalen College, Oxford was his first patron who secured him a chaplaincy with Shute Barrington, the Bishop of Durham, who in turn rewarded him with dignities in his gift. Secondly, by marrying a niece of Lady Eldon, he became related to Lord Chancellor Eldon, many of whose ultra-conservative views he shared. His undoubted ability as a polemical writer and defender of the Establishment marked him out for promotion by a Tory government. He supported Wellington when political expediency required the Prime Minister to do an about-turn in his views on Catholic emancipation, thereby earning the Duke's gratitude who appointed him to Exeter, though Wellington explicitly stated it was not done as a reward. Phillpotts wrote to his secretary on 18 November 1830 'Oh! That I had known what a clatter my unhappy promotion would cause! But I sought it not; it came unsolicited, and therefore I had no scruple in taking it. As matters are, I must go on, or submit to be extinguished.' Phillpotts had made his appointment even more unpalatable to the incoming Whig government by insisting on retaining his wealthy living of Stanhope *in commendam*. An acceptable compromise was reached when Van Mildert gave him a Durham canonry.

To Carpenter, Phillpotts was a 'political adventurer' and a 'political Judas' distinguished by his 'violent and virulent Toryism'. He started his article on the Bishop of Exeter with this judgemental blast, 'The history of the Anglican Church records many extraordinary and discreditable facts relative to ecclesiastical promotion, and the character and claims of those upon whom its highest and most lucrative honours have been conferred; but we much question whether it records a case parallel in disgrace and infamy, to that pertaining to the elevation of Dr Phillpott (*sic*) to the see of Exeter.' [*Ibid*. p. 304]   He then proceeded to justify his judgement.

Gloucester: 1824-30 Christopher Bethell (1773-1859)

He was another high-church Tory with an academic background who had published a few theological works, notably *A General Review of the Doctrine of Regeneration* (1821) which went through four editions. More importantly he was tutor to the politically influential Duke of Northumberland. His episcopal progression seems to have been related to the relative wealth of the three dioceses he was appointed to: Gloucester in 1824 on the nomination of Lord Liverpool, followed by Exeter on 8 April 1830 by Wellington who less than seven months later moved him on to the still more lucrative see of Bangor.

Carpenter regarded Bethell as a servile creature, always ready to support his political masters however illiberal and intolerant their measures might be, and a perfect illustration of how such appointments were made. 'The way of a Bishop to his see is a most curious path. An examination of the claims of the existing Lords Spiritual will show the workings of this part of the machinery. The end to be answered by the Bench of Bishops is to ensure a certain number of servile votes, where service is of use; and to have a class of men on the bench, who, by preserving a solemn aspect, and professing an obscure learning, be it Greek or Hebrew, shall give the people to understand that they are a peculiar order, devoted to something mystical, and beyond vulgar apprehension, while at the same time is cultivated for the general good, - a good, it is true, which arrives to them by remote channels, known only to the initiated. The qualities of a Bishop are, according to the long-established Tory creed, servility, decorum and recondite learning.' [*Ibid*. p. 33]

1830-56 James Henry Monk (1784-1856)

'Dr Monk is a Greek scholar and a Tory politician – the former qualified him, and the latter recommended him, to become a Bishop!' is how Carpenter introduced his short article on the Bishop. Monk was indeed a notable Greek scholar who at the age of twenty-five in 1809 had been elected Regius Professor in succession to the famous Richard Porson, and as Tutor at Trinity his pupils carried off most of the high classical honours at Cambridge. His elevation to the episcopate came from Lord Liverpool who had been impressed by the young cleric when he was Whitehall Preacher in 1812, just two years after his ordination as a priest. Liverpool appointed him Dean of Peterborough which was the stepping stone to a bishopric.

Hereford: 1815-32 George Isaac Huntingford (1748-1832)
Henry Addington, Speaker of the House of Commons from June 1789 and then Prime Minister in 1801, became a lifelong friend with his old Master from his days at Winchester. Addington tried to have him appointed Bishop of Bath and Wells but King George III preferred to have him at Gloucester so that he should not 'withdraw his attention to that excellent seminary at Winchester.' As a staunch defender of the Establishment and a strong opponent of Roman Catholic emancipation, Huntingford had found favour with the King.

1832-37 The Hon Edward Grey (1782-1837)
Politically poles apart from his older brother who badly needed episcopal support in the Lords, he was nonetheless appointed to the see of Hereford when Earl Grey was Prime Minister. Lord Holland, in a diary entry dated 4th May 1832, records that the appointment was made at the express desire of the King:

> The King insisted on making Grey's brother Bishop of Hereford, would take no refusal, likened this act of favour to one bestowed on Lord North's brother by his father, and accompanied by what he called this testimony of regard and gratitude with some equivocal phrases that had a sound of somewhat a valedictory nature . . . Whatever might happen, he said, he was anxious that a tribute of his affection and a record of the sense he entertained of the handsome manner in which Grey had come forward on the dissolution of his last Ministry should be preserved. [KRIEGEL *op. cit.* p. 174]

The Bishop absented himself from the vote on the Reform Bill and he later frequently voted against the Government in the Lords. His earlier preferment to the Deanery of Hereford and the wealthy London living of Bishopsgate had come from the Tories whom he supported. Carpenter commented, 'He has seldom opened his lips in Parliament, but he has never been absent when the Tory party wanted his aid.' This was just one of several acts of patronage that the Prime Minister made to members of his family. Brock reckons that they were receiving £18,000 per year of public money (worth about 1.6 million today) but comments that 'Wellington's relatives and connexions cost far more than this.' [BROCK *The Great Reform Act* p. 132] 'The "Grey List" of these appointments was later published in the newspapers and provided an agreeable reek of scandal to critics of the ministry.' [E.A.SMITH *Lord Grey* p. 261] It was clearly something that Grey felt he had to defend, and he did so in his last speech in the Lords on the day of his resignation as Prime Minister. All those members of his family and friends he had appointed, he said, had been given 'situations which have been laborious', and they had justified their appointments by their activities. How true that was of his brother Bishop is open to question.

1837-47 Thomas Musgrave (1788-1860)

His university distinctions and liberal politics marked him out for preferment from the Whigs, and Melbourne duly obliged by appointing him Dean of Bristol in March 1837 and then Bishop of Hereford five months later on the death of the Tory Edward Grey.

Lichfield: 1824-36 Henry Ryder (1771-1835)

An aristocrat with the right connections, preferment was always likely to happen except for his pronounced Evangelical views which were, at that time, a barrier to promotion. His elevation to the see of Gloucester in 1815 was opposed by, amongst others, Archbishop Manners Sutton but he had the support of his brother, the Earl of Harrowby, who was the President of the Council and an influential member of Lord Liverpool's administration. The Dean and Chapter tried to exclude him from the cathedral pulpit but his tact and personality weathered that storm.

He was translated to Lichfield and Coventry in 1824 where not a word of protest was heard, and he proved to be an effective diocesan administrator and a caring father in God to his clergy. William Wilberforce in his *Recollections* 'highly prized and loved Bishop Ryder' as a prelate after his own heart, 'who united to the zeal of an apostle the most amiable and endearing qualities, and the polished manners of the best society.' Dr Samuel Parr said that 'there is a halo of holiness about that man'. It was his winsome personality and piety and energy which won over those clergy who had been initially critical of his appointment.

1836-39 Samuel Butler (1774-1839)

Butler made his name at Shrewsbury as one of the great headmasters of the 19th century. He had also shown himself to be a diligent archdeacon (of Derby) whose *Charges* to the clergy in the 1830s were balanced and sensible when so many episcopal ones were not. Preferment to the bench of bishops came too late for him to show what he might have done had ill-health and his age not prevented it. He was appointed by Melbourne despite his not supporting the government on the Irish Church question.

His grandson, also called Samuel – the author of *Erewhon* – included some of the correspondence between his grandfather and Bishop Maltby of Chichester when his forebear was fishing for preferment. In October 1834 Maltby had to tell him the bad news he had learned from Lord Chancellor Brougham that the vacant bishopric of Bristol would be offered to Allen and not to him. When Butler replied three days later he gave vent to much unedifying disappointment and ambition:

> Look at the Bench – with the rare exception of yourself, can you find a man on it who owes his preferment to his actual merit? Can you name one other, not even excepting the Bishop of London, superlative as his merits are, who does not owe it to private tuition or family connection? . . . I will not pretend to say that I am not disappointed, but I should have been less so had the disappointment been softened by giving me something else *ad interim*. I confess to you what it would be very injurious to me to confess to the public, that I feel worn out by thirty-six years very laborious occupation, and I see Mrs Butler's health and activity impaired by it. I see Carey with his bishopric, Keate with his canonry of Windsor, Russell with his great living and his stall at Canterbury, Tate with his canonry (God bless him with it, dear, honest fellow!); I see Goodenough with his deanery, and my namesake of Harrow with his living; but I see myself without any of these good things. I do not grudge others their success, but I know that I have laboured as much as any, more than most, and longer than all . . .
> [BUTLER ed. *The Life and Letters of Dr Samuel Butler* Vol. 2 p. 95f]

The man was sixty years old, 'worn out' by his own admission and in poor health himself, yet he was still lusting after a seat on the bench of bishops and feeling hard done by! He got what he wanted two years later though he had to wait some weeks from the time that Melbourne submitted his name to the King and actually discovering which of the vacant bishoprics he would be given. He lobbied the Prime Minister to appoint him to Lichfield, part of which diocese he had served as archdeacon for sixteen years. He got his wish, and Maltby, who had pleaded his cause with Brougham and Melbourne, was one of his consecrators in Lambeth Palace chapel on 3 July 1836.

Lincoln: 1827-53 John Kaye (1783-1853)

Kaye was one of the few real scholars to be made a bishop and was enjoying a distinguished academic career at Cambridge when Lord Liverpool appointed him to Bristol in 1820. Because of the relative poverty of the see, he was allowed to retain both his university posts of Regius Professor of Divinity and Master of Christ's College. He was translated by Lord Liverpool to the much larger and wealthier diocese of Lincoln in 1827 where he brought reform and new life to the parishes.

Carpenter is particularly critical of him, seeing little worthy of note in him, but that is probably because Kaye, who had once held Whig views became a Tory supporter which was not surprising as he was at heart a conservative High-Churchman.

Norwich: 1805-37 Henry Bathurst (1744-1837)

Bathurst owed his early preferment to family influence and then to the goodwill of the Bishop of Durham. Episcopal preferment to Norwich in 1805 came from William Pitt whose patronage had been solicited by Bathurst's cousin and former pupil, the 3rd Earl Bathurst. He had been offered the Irish bishopric of Killala ten years earlier but declined it. He preferred the golden stall he had been offered in Durham. A convinced Whig, his was a lone liberal voice on a very conservative bench of bishops in the Lords in the 1820s. When the Whigs returned to power, he was offered, at the age of 87, the Archbishopric of Dublin in 1831 which he declined. Soloway comments about him, 'Though the most liberal prelate on the bench, he was also perhaps the worst diocesan administrator, and the neglect of his see was shocking to improving ecclesiastical sensibilities.' [SOLOWAY *Prelates and People* p. 247]

Bathurst recognized his limitations and unpreparedness for what lay ahead of him in his new role – on his journey south he wrote to his wife, 'Dearest Grace', back in Durham soon after the announcement of his appointment:

> Among other subjects which have exercised my thoughts, my new situation has had its full share. Whether this professional advancement will contribute to my real happiness or not, time alone can prove; at present I feel I have many duties to perform, and many objects to attend to, with which I am very little acquainted, and consequently may act my part less well than I could wish to do, on this untried stage. It is, however, some consolation to me when I reflect, that human affairs would go on still worse than they do, were not good intention and a moderate portion of industry sufficient in general for the management of them. Comforted with this idea, I lull to rest all my doubts, my fears, my anxieties; nor would these take even a temporary possession of me if you travelled with me. [THISTLETHWAYTE *Memoirs and Correspondence of Dr Henry Bathurst* p. 130f]

Carpenter praised him for his pro-reform and pro-Catholic views but turned a blind eye to his neglect of his diocesan responsibilities, and ends his article 'His Lordship is almost universally respected for his independence and amiable qualities; but he has no pretensions to eminence, either as an author or an orator.' [CARPENTER *op. cit.* p. 562]

1837-49 Edward Stanley (1779-1849)

At the time of his preferment, his brother was a rising star in the Whig party: MP for North Cheshire, patronage secretary to the Treasury and party whip, so Edward Stanley's name would have been known to the

Prime Minister. He was also an exemplary parish priest who held liberal, pro-reform views. He was sounded out by Melbourne for the new see of Manchester which he declined, but in 1837 he accepted the offer of Norwich, a diocese desperately in need of firm episcopal leadership and reform after so many years of decline under the aged Bishop Bathurst. King William much approved of the appointment, telling Melbourne that he attached great value to an exemplary discharge of the duty of parish priest, and that he rejoiced when a man like Stanley added to this virtue that of a good family, gentlemanly habits, and literary and scientific pursuits. [CHADWICK *op. cit.* Part 1. p. 125]

Stanley was approved of by the Whig grandee Lord Holland: 'Stanley, the brother of Sir John and the author of some very liberal letters on Ireland as well as of the only candid, correct, and full account of the Massacre at Manchester, which about 15 years ago made so deep an impression on the neighbourhood and country and was, in truth, a most unjustifiable proceeding' [KRIEGEL ed. *op. cit.* p. 359f].

The truth is that Stanley did not wish to be a bishop and did not want to leave Alderley. His son says that the decision to move 'for a time almost broke down his usual health and sanguine spirit' – he broke down emotionally at his first meeting with Melbourne after deciding to accept. He recorded his feelings in a private journal:

> It would be vain and useless to speak to others of what none could feel so deeply as myself. What it cost me to leave Alderley, it is for myself alone to feel – the utter absence of all selfish motives – my reluctance, not to say aversion, for an office for which, in many respects, I feel myself so peculiarly unfitted; and yet could I or ought I to have refused undertaking it, with a consciousness that I might possibly be an instrument, in the hands of a higher power, of working out views which I conceived to be essential to the extension of liberal sentiments in my profession, and yet tremblingly alive to the difficulties I had to encounter, and my incompetency to stem the current if it set strongly against me? Will the change be productive of good or evil – will it aid my progress, or fatally impede it? Time alone can show.
> [A.P. STANLEY *op. cit.* p.30]

Oxford: 1827-29 Charles Lloyd (1784-1829)

As mentioned earlier, Lloyd enjoyed the friendship and patronage of Sir Robert Peel who used his influence with Lord Liverpool to secure the preferment of his former tutor, first to the Regius Professsorship of Divinity at Oxford to which a canonry at Christ Church was attached, and later to the see of Oxford. Archbishop Manners-Sutton had also marked him out by appointing him as one of his chaplains in 1820. Given his teaching record and the renewal he brought to theological studies in the university, he was a worthy candidate for preferment but he did not live long enough to make his mark as a bishop.

Baker revealed in his biography of Lloyd, by quoting from the man's correspondence with Peel between February 1826 and February 1827, an unattractive side to this academic who repeatedly compared others unfavourably to himself. He regarded Copleston, who was a likely candidate for the see of Oxford and his equal in scholarship, as having inferior claims; Lloyd consider himself as high above his rival 'as the Andes are to a molehill.' And as for another favoured candidate, Robert Gray, a prebendary of Durham who was made Bishop of Bristol, 'he has turned out the most absolute twaddle that the Church ever produced.' When doubting he would ever get Oxford and weary of his academic work, he told Peel he was not averse to 'retirement with good provision in some easy Bishopric.' In an earlier letter he had admitted 'I want money [despite having a professorial stipend of £1,500] because I am poor & have children, and I desire character: for I cannot live without it.' Baker tells the story in all its sad detail and comments:

> Yet the event accurately reflected the ecclesiastical and political temper of the times. Undramatic as a whole, petty in its particulars, distinctly unheroic, this was the way in which offices were secured in the early years of the nineteenth century. If a man was not well-born, as Lloyd was not, he had to be supported by the well-placed. Shrewd manipulations and calculated risks were forever part of the game. [BAKER *op. cit.* p. 148f]

1829-45 Richard Bagot (1782-1854)

Bagot had the right family connections to ensure promotion to the purple but it seems that it was not an office he particularly sought, being of a modest and retiring disposition. The ODNB states that he 'utterly refused the bishopric of Oxford when it was first offered him by the Duke of Wellington, and accepted it only on the assurance of William Howley that the diocese would never give him trouble.' How mistaken that proved to be! He was, inevitably, caught up in the theological storm provoked by the Tractarians.

Carpenter wrote, 'This prelate is brother to Lord Bagot, to which circumstances, we assume, he is indebted for his promotion in the Church . . . In 1827 he was made Dean of Canterbury, and, in 1829, was elevated to the Bishoprick of Oxford, retaining his Deanery. He is not remarkable for anything, either as a Theologian or a Politician. He is an Ultra-Tory, and swells the ranks of that party in all its resistance to liberal legislation.' [CARPENTER *op. cit.* p. 576]

Peterborough: 1819-39 Herbert Marsh (1757-1839)

Despite his ability, he had to wait a long time for academic preferment. He was 50 years old when appointed Lady Margaret Professor of Divinity but it was a justly deserved promotion. He proved to be a conservative and pugnacious controversialist in such matters as the establishment and spread of the Bible Society and he was critical of the leading Cambridge Evangelicals, Charles Simeon and Isaac Milner. His learning and loyalty to the religious and political Establishment were eventually rewarded with the see of Llandaff in 1816 (financially a very poor reward) and three years later his translation to the wealthier diocese of Peterborough. His opposition to Calvinistic Evangelicalism persisted throughout his episcopate, making it difficult for incumbents to appoint Evangelical curates. His practice of sifting out such curates by means of an 87 question long investigation led to an appeal and debate in the House of Commons and to his being pilloried as a persecuting bishop in the pages of the *Edinburgh Review* by Sydney Smith in 1822.

Carpenter described him as 'one of the political Bishops' having obtained a pension of £514 a year from Pitt in 1804 for having written some political pamphlets in furtherance of the war with France. He saw him as a lifelong High-Church champion and a Tory partisan. 'At the same time, he is, perhaps, the most learned man on the Episcopal Bench, and has certainly published much more than any of his right reverend contemporaries. His Biblical works are of a very high character, and had he abstained from meddling with politics, and preserved a more meek and quiet spirit in his attempts to promote what he considered to be religious truth, he would have stood high among the theologians of his time. [*Ibid.* p. 580]

1839-64 George Davys (1780-1864)

Having made a name for himself as a simple, pious writer on the basic tenets of the Christian faith, the Duchess of Kent appointed him tutor to the Princess Victoria in 1827. Promotion followed from that – first a crown living in London in 1829, then the deanery of Chester in 1831, and finally the see of Peterborough in 1839 two years after Victoria became Queen. Lord Melbourne was reluctant to recommend this undistinguished Evangelical cleric whom he feared was a Tory to a bishopric even though it was customary for the tutor of the reigning monarch to be made a bishop but he gave in to pressure from the press and to save the Crown the necessity of paying Davys a pension. The *Nottingham Mercury* commented on 18 May that Davys' promotion was 'a reward for his long and valuable services in the education of our youthful sovereign', adding that it 'was a distinction totally unconnected with party politics', which it called 'something of a novelty in these times'. [CARNELL *The Bishops of Peterborough* p. 63]

Rochester: 1828-60 George Murray   (1784-1860)

Murray's path to a bishopric was the shortest and fastest of them all, having been nominated by his kinsman the Duke of Atholl to the see of Sodor and Man at the age of twenty-nine, i.e. below the minimum age for consecration as a Bishop, and consequently he had to wait.

Carpenter did not approve! 'His lordship, as it will have been seen, is one of the Aristocracy, and hence he is a Bishop. . . He is conspicuous for nothing but his ultra-Toryism, and the contemptuous tone in which he occasionally speaks of the people, from whom he and his connexions derive their wealth.' [CARPENTER *op. cit.* p. 626]

Salisbury: 1825-37 Thomas Burgess (1756-1837)

Burgess had gained a reputation as a classical scholar at Oxford and so came to the attention of the Bishop of Salisbury, Shute Barrington, who appointed him an examining and domestic chaplain in 1785. Burgess wisely chose to accompany Barrington north when he was translated to Durham in 1791. Advancement and financial security came his way in the form of a prebendal stall in Durham Cathedral and in 1803 promotion to the bench of bishops when his old school and university friend, Henry Addington, nominated him to the see of St David's. The text of the Prime Minister's letter, dated 3 June 1803, survives in Harford's *Life* of Burgess:

> Though we have been separated almost thirty years, I have not, let me assure you, been a stranger to the excellence of your private character, nor to your exertions for the interests of learning and of religion; and I have been anxious that your services should be still further noticed and distinguished, and your sphere of being useful enlarged. These considerations, alone, have led me to mention you to his Majesty as the successor of the late Lord George Murray, in the diocese of St David's, and I am happy to say that his Majesty has entirely approved of the recommendation. It will not be expected that you should relinquish your prebend in the cathedral church of Durham. [HARFORD *op. cit.* p. 198]

Burgess's greatest service to that diocese would be the raising of clerical standards culminating in the founding St David's College at Lampeter. At the age of 68, he accepted translation to Salisbury. He felt by then that he had achieved all that he could in St David's and the extensive travelling was becoming a problem for him. At an even more personal level, his wife who was plagued with rheumatism and almost an invalid blamed her condition on the dampness of Abergwilli. A move back to Salisbury where he had been Shute Barrington's chaplain was welcomed.

Carpenter commented favourably about Burgess as a Greek scholar but not so about him as a bishop.

> In Biblical erudition, Dr Burgess is one of the most learned men upon the Episcopal Bench and he has published many works belonging to that department of literature, of a very high character. We regret that we can say nothing commendatory of the Bishop of Salisbury's political opinions and conduct. He is an ultra-Church and King man, as was evinced by his appointment to the office of "Grand Chaplain" to the "Grand Lodge of the Orange Institution of Great Britain"; a society which called forth the censure, not only of the House of Commons, but also of the King. [CARPENTER *op. cit.* p. 646]

1837-54 Edward Denison (1801-1854)
An Oxford scholar of liberal Whig sympathies, he came to the notice of Lord Melbourne who nominated him to the see of Salisbury at the age of thirty-six. W.M. Jacob in his article about Denison in the ODNB says, 'Joseph Blanco White alleged he was appointed because, although learned, he never published, and was passive in theology, and it was difficult to find a sympathetic Oxford whig to prefer.' Hardly a ringing endorsement, yet Denison proved to be a diligent, effective, reforming bishop.

Worcester: 1808-31   Folliott Herbert Walker Cornwall   (1754-1831)
Family connections started him off on his road to episcopal preferment. In 1780, just two years after being ordained Priest, a second cousin who was Speaker of the House of Commons nominated him as Chaplain to the House. He could hardly have asked for a better introduction to men of influence, and preferment followed quickly, as we have seen. He was appointed to the see of Bristol in 1797, translated to Hereford in 1803 and to Worcester in 1808. Before his third move, the Prime Minister had told George III that his appointment was 'much wished for by the principal gentry as well as the clergy' and that his political opinions would help secure the diocese's loyalty to the administration. [ODNB]

Province of York
York: 1808-47 Edward Venables Vernon Harcourt (1757-1847)
His appointment to Carlisle at the age of thirty-four was probably due to the influence of his father-in-law, Earl Gower, who was Lord Privy Seal at the time. He maintained his contacts with and support for Pitt's admin-

istration, and, having proved himself a conscientious and moderately reforming bishop during his sixteen years at Carlisle, was translated to York in January 1808. He was at the same time made a privy counsellor and George III's lord high almoner. He was appointed one of the first members of the Ecclesiastical Commission in 1835, attended its meetings regularly and supported its proposals for reforming the Church.

Carpenter has, however, nothing good to say about him. 'His aristocratic connexions was no doubt the cause of his promotion in the church; at least, we shall look in vain for any other recommendation. . . We are not aware of anything which his Grace has done to distinguish him from the crowd of churchmen, and we shall not, therefore, uselessly occupy our space by further remarks.' [CARPENTER *op. cit.* p. 782]

Durham: 1826-36 William Van Mildert (1765-1836)
Van Mildert enjoyed the patronage of Archbishop Manners Sutton but it was a sermon, he delivered shortly after his appointment as Preacher of Lincoln's Inn in 1812, which gave his journey to promotion a significant boost. It was on the assassination of Spencer Percival and achieved wide circulation; Lord Liverpool was amongst those who heard it preached and he appreciated Van Mildert's talents. The following year, he appointed him to the Regius Professorship of Divinity at Oxford. In May 1819 he was consecrated Bishop of Llandaff, and the following year was offered the Archbishopric of Dublin which he declined. When offered Llandaff, Van Mildert hesitated about accepting the poorly endowed bishopric.

> Until, by your Lordship's unexpected patronage & recommendation, I was brought to my present station, my preferments had been very inconsiderable in point of emolument, & my private means scarcely sufficient to my station. Consequently, I am just beginning to reap the fruits of my improved condition: & I feel it incumbent upon me to weigh well the possibility of involving myself in any pecuniary difficulties by accepting a higher station. [VARLEY *The Last of the Prince Bishops* p. 89]

Liverpool allowed him to retain temporarily his two livings and the Regius Professorship until he became Dean of St Paul's which he held *in commendam* with Llandaff. In 1826 he accepted Liverpool's offer of Durham.

Carpenter wrote, 'The Bishop of Durham is, without doubt, a person of considerable erudition, and eminent literary attainments. He is, moreover, said to be a very able preacher; and, upon the whole, one of the most illustrious of the English Hierarchy. . . In politics, he is a Tory of the Liverpool school; and his name will be found in almost every division against liberal measures.' [CARPENTER *op. cit.* p. 250]

Carlisle: 1827-56 Hugh Percy (1784-1856)
With his own immediate family's patronage and political influence, a bishopric was always likely to come his way but it was his marriage to Archbishop Manners Sutton's daughter that clinched it.

When offered the See of Rochester in 1827, he asked Canning to allow him to retain the deanery of Canterbury. The Prime Minister refused and said he reckoned Percy would have £4,000 a year with his other various livings and prebends. Canning gave him the option of remaining Dean until 'some better Bishoprick than Rochester shall fall vacant' or to accept Rochester, having resigned his deanery, 'with the understanding that an early opportunity shall be taken of compensating him for his present loss of income, by promotion.' [Cumbria Record Office DX1398/15] He chose Rochester and was translated to Carlisle just months later.

Chester: 1828-48 John Bird Sumner (1780-1862)
Sumner's early books *Apostolic Preaching Considered in an Examination of St Paul's Epistles* and *A Treatise of the Records of Creation and the Moral Attributes of the Creator* had marked him out as a scholar and thoughtful writer. He also enjoyed the patronage of Shute Barrington, the Bishop of Durham, and his name was known at the highest level in the land thanks to his brother. In 1827 he declined the offer of Sodor & Man but accepted Chester the following year to which the Duke of Wellington had nominated him. He proved to be a hard-working leader who tackled the many demands and problems of his vast diocese with energy and enthusiasm, and who was a caring pastor to his clergy. Balleine describes him as 'A ripe scholar, a fluent writer, a kindly, simple-hearted man, he grappled with the task before him with tremendous energy.' [BALLEINE *A History of the Evangelical Party* p. 195]

In Carpenter's eyes, Sumner was a 'courtier Bishop' like his brother but he had some good things to say about him. 'Were the Bishops deprived of their political functions, which are as incompatible with the gospel as they are mischievous to the country, we are disposed to think that the elevation of such a man as Dr J. B. Sumner to the episcopal chair would be a most proper act. He is learned, and pious, and indefatigable, we believe, in the discharge of his spiritual duties. As it is, we can say nothing more of him.' [CARPENTER *op. cit.* p. 127]

Ripon: 1836-57 Charles Thomas Longley (1794-1868)
He had been appointed Headmaster of Harrow through the influence of Thomas Vowler Short, whose Curate he had been at Cowley. He was an ineffective head but fortunately for him his father-in-law was Paymaster General in Melbourne's administration. The offer of a bishopric eased his

exit from the school. In the space of a week, he was offered four different sees, and settled on the newly created one of Ripon. Melbourne made the appointment but later commented 'I hardly know how to account for Longley who has never voted with us.' Longley had advised Lord Radnor in the preparation of the Oxford University Bill in 1835, which enabled him to recommend Longley to the Whig government as that rare phenomenon, an Oxford man favourable to the abolition of subscription to the Thirty-nine Articles on matriculation at the university. One other famous Oxford man whom Radnor recommended for episcopal preferment, but without success, was Thomas Arnold.

Sodor & Man: 1828-38 William Ward (1762-1838)
Edith Wilson in *An Island Bishop,* the short biography she wrote of her grandfather, said that he owed his preferment to Viscount Goderich and Earl of Ripon who advised George IV in 1827 to exercise the right, recently acquired from the Duke of Atholl, to appoint a bishop for the diocese of Sodor and Man. Ward had been appointed, on the recommendation of Bishop Porteus, Goderich's tutor when he was an orphaned boy, and a lasting bond of affection developed between the two. Goderich revered him, she said. But it has to be said, Ward was his second choice – John Bird Sumner had been offered the post but declined it. Ward had initially been minded to decline the offer too as he was very happy in his present situation but was persuaded by a friend to accept. A letter has survived from Ward to his wife written in January 1828 from London when he was going through the costly legal process of becoming a bishop which shows just how very expensive it could be to accept a poorly endowed bishopric – see p. 97.

Goderich had a very brief premiership and Ward was his only episcopal appointment. He was said to be so utterly incompetent that the King expressed his determination to perform all the duties of the premiership himself. Lauderdale said that Goderich was not fit to manage a poultry yard! Nonetheless, Ward owed his elevation to him.

1838-40 James Bowstead (1801-1843)
Bowstead does not merit an entry in the ODNB and Venn's *Alumni Cantab* provides only the bare bones of his clerical career; Carpenter also ignored him. It is possible that Bishop Allen of Bristol and subsequently of Ely who had appointed him an examining chaplain in 1834 used his connexions with the Spencer family to further his protégé's advancement. A mark in his favour in Whig eyes was that as a Fellow of Corpus he had been closely associated with the Trinity Whigs in their campaigns to remove university restrictions on Nonconformists.

1840-41 Henry Pepys (1783-1860)
Pepys possibly owed his preferment to the influence of his brother, the Earl of Cottenham. His book *The Remains of the Late Lord Viscount Royston, with a Memoir of his Life*, published in 1838 brought him some publicity. More importantly, he was politically a liberal and Melbourne, who appointed him to Sodor and Man in 1840 and a year later to Worcester, could count on his support in the Lords which he duly gave. He was a resident, popular and conscientious prelate.

Church of Wales (part of the Province of Canterbury)
Bangor: 1809-30 Henry William Majendie   (1754-1830)   -
Majendie had been Prince William's preceptor since 1780 and an instructor before that, and had accompanied the Prince on board ship during and after the American War of Independence for which he was rewarded with a canonry at Windsor in 1785. He was appointed Bishop of Chester in 1800 and allowed to retain a valuable prebendal stall at St Paul's *in commendam* as well as the living of New Windsor. He resigned both of these extras when he was translated to Bangor in 1809.

1830-59 Christopher Bethell – see page 81.

Llandaff: 1827-49 Edward Copleston (1776-1849)
As one of the most prominent Oxford Heads of the time with a reputation for being a liberal reformer in education, and famed as the defender of the university against the attacks made on it in the *Edinburgh Review*, and having won the support of such men as Lord Grenville and Earl Spencer, his promotion to the bench of bishops seemed guaranteed but it was a long time in coming. He was passed over for the Bishopric of Oxford in 1826 which went to Lloyd who had a more influential patron in Peel. The poor diocese of Llandaff, to which the Deanery of St Paul's was attached *in commendam*, may have seemed a second-best offer in 1827.

Carpenter did not have a high opinion of Copleston's intellectual abilities or of him in the House of Lords where, he claimed, the Bishop 'seldom or never opens his mouth. . . His votes, however, are constantly given against liberal measures.' [CARPENTER *op. cit.* p. 461]

St Asaph: 1815-30 John Luxmoore (1766-1830)
He owed his preferment to his connections with the Duke of Buccleuch whom he had tutored when he was the Earl of Dalkeith. The *Gentleman's Magazine* wrote, '[he] was thus introduced into a rich career of preferment.' Valuable livings, a prebendal stall in Canterbury and the deanery of Gloucester lined his path to the see of Bristol in 1807, a move a year

later to Hereford and in 1815 to St Asaph. He was most distinguished for the great care he took in appointing members of his family to wealthy positions in his gift.

St David's: 1825-40 John Banks Jenkinson (1781-1840)

Preferment was inevitable when his cousin, the second Earl of Liverpool, was Prime Minister. His advancement followed the usual route of good livings, a prebendal stall and then a deanery before being elected Bishop of St David's in 1825. Initially he also held a stall in Durham *in commendam* which was replaced in 1827 by the even richer post of Dean of Durham worth £9,000 a year (about £850,000 today) which put him on a par financially with the Archbishops. He had the privilege of opening St David's College Lampeter (the fruit of Bishop Burgess's labours) in 1827 as well as being involved in the foundation of Durham University five years later.

Carpenter wrote, 'His Grace was consecrated to this See in 1825, and though not especially distinguished by any individual acts, either in the Church or in the literary world, he has generally given his vote in the House of Peers for liberal and reforming measures. It was, no doubt, his aristocratic connexions which raised him to a Bishopric; but it will be seen, from what we have said, that he is more endurable than most of his right reverend compeers.' [CARPENTER *op. cit.* p. 640]

1840-74 Connop Thirlwall (1797-1875)

Thirlwall's pamphlet in 1834 in favour of the admission of dissenters to degrees at Cambridge brought him to the notice of the Whig leaders, and his consequent sacking by Christopher Wordsworth, the Tory Master of Trinity College Cambridge, made him something of a martyr in their eyes. During his years at Kirby Underdale he became part of Yorkshire Whiggery society. Preferment followed in due course but not without some opposition from Archbishop Howley in 1837 when Melbourne had wished to appoint him to Norwich. Three years later, the Prime Minister secured Howley's agreement before offering Thirlwall St David's – the issue had been the preface Thirlwall had written to his translation of Schleiermacher's essay on St Luke's Gospel in which he appeared to share the German's unorthodox views. Melbourne had read it – the Archbishop had not! More importantly, from the Prime Minister's point of view, Thirlwall was known to be an excellent speaker who shared his political views and would prove to be a doughty opponent to Bishop Phillpotts in debates in the House of Lords. Jenkinson died on 7 July and the letter inviting Thirlwall to succeed him was sent on the 15th, thereby giving the proponents of a Welsh-speaking candidate (and there were some good ones, notably Archdeacon John Williams and Chancellor Bruce Knight, but all Tories) little time to organize opposition to his appointment. He did, however, meet with a deputation of Liverpool Welsh leaders wanting to press the need of a Welsh-born, Welsh-speaking bishop. Thirlwall answered on the 21st in these words:

> It would be impertinent to thank your Lordship, as for a personal favour, for the unsolicited preferment which you have given on no other than public grounds, to a stranger. I will only permit myself to say that my obligation to your Lordship will render me doubly anxious not to throw discredit – as far as depends on my own exertions – on your Lordship's recommendation.
> [quoted in BROWN *In Pursuit of a Welsh Episcopate* p. 52]

Melbourne did also interview Thirlwall. Lord Cecil describes the event.

> Dr. Thirlwall found Melbourne in bed surrounded by heaps of patristic folios. "Very glad to see you," said Melbourne. "Sit down, sit down; hope you are come to say you accept. I only wish you to understand that I don't intend if I know it to make a heterodox bishop. I don't like heterodox bishops. As men they may be very good anywhere else, but I think they have no business on the Bench. I take great interest in theological questions, and I have read a great deal of these old fellows" – pointing to the folio editions of the Fathers – "They are excellent reading and very amusing; sometime or other we must have a talk about them. I sent your edition of Schleiermacher to Lambeth, and asked the Primate to tell me candidly what he thought of it; and look, here are his notes in the margin; pretty copious, you see. He does not concur in all your opinions; but he says there is nothing heterodox in your book.
> [CECIL *Lord M* p. 139]

By this blatantly political appointment, Melbourne got what he wanted : a loyal and powerful spokesman for his party in the Upper House. Wales got a conscientious bishop who learned the language but, by his own admission, it was the language of the study not of the 'hearth and home.' He was never an effective, intelligible preacher in Welsh. Brown comments, 'The real tragedy of Thirlwall's elevation was not the fact of his appointment, but rather that the option presumably offered to Melbourne by the Liverpool deputation was never taken, namely to transfer the new bishop, if not Welsh speaking, to an English see when one became vacant. Thirlwall remained at Abergwili for thirty-three years, an alien on an inhospitable shore.' [BROWN *op. cit.* p. 60]

* * * *

It is clear from the above that the offer of an Irish bishopric or even an archbishopric was not always welcomed and nor did men necessarily accept the first see they were offered. The comparative poverty of certain dioceses, notably Llandaff at the bottom of the league, meant the holder needed to have other posts *in commendam* in order to pay his way as a bishop. Consequently, some, though not all, men appointed to the poorer sees saw them merely as a stepping stone to a better offer.

William Ward set out in a letter, written on 3 January 1828 from a London hotel to his wife, the price of some of the steps he had to take between accepting the offer of a bishopric and being consecrated:

> I have been busier all this day than you can tell, and have now but five minutes to tell you that the sun begins to shine on our path to the Isle of Man, without the appearance of a cloud the bulk of a man's hand. Dear Goderich will do everything that is kind in employing the powerful arm of Government in the article of tythes, leaving the Bishop nothing to do but preach the Gospel to the poor, and the Bishop's wife to supply their backs and bellies. Every report of the island is encouraging. Tell dear Uncle he must come to Bishop's Court next summer. . . . I must tell you that dear kind Goderich allows me to hold everything *in commendam*, it being uncertain how much old Mona will produce, and it being very clear to him that the station of Bp. of Sodor and Man will unavoidably entail more expense than that of Rector of Gt. Horkesley by the difference of a bare £2,500 a year and I sh^d think £500 to that. The first year's income will not cover the expense nor near it. £200 for one stamp! O the cormorants of Courts of Law and Courts of Kings! To kiss the King's hand will cost me £100! It cost the Bp. of Rochester the other day two years income of the See to take possession.
>
> [E.C WILSON *An Island Bishop* p. 92f]

Five days later Lord Goderich ceased to be Prime Minister, so Ward just made it in time.

Whether or not a bishop in a poorly endowed diocese was translated to a richer one depended in part on how loyal he had been to the party which had appointed him originally and what his voting record in the Lords was. It also depended on whether his face fitted with the sovereign! Tryphena Thistlethwayte in her biography of her father, Bishop Bathurst, records how his conduct was 'regarded with little favour' in high places.

> A friend of my father happened to mention, in the presence of Queen Charlotte, that the Bishop of Norwich ought to be removed to the see of St Asaph, as the emoluments were better and the duties less onerous. "No,"

said her Majesty quickly, "he voted against the King." In the course of the following year the bishopric of Bangor was vacant. In one of his letters to my brother James, my father says, "Randolph is the new Bishop of London. Had I been a good boy, it was hinted that I might have gone to Bangor, which would have suited me exactly; but I am very well pleased where I am, and meet with a great deal of attention and kindness. [THISTLETHWAYTE *op. cit.* p. 168]

Bathurst's faithfulness to the Whig cause was eventually noticed when Grey came to power and he was offered the Archbishopric of Dublin but by then he was far too old and inactive to be able to accept it.

There were, of course, men who felt they deserved preferment and were bitterly disappointed at being overlooked – Archdeacon Bathurst was just such a man. Others had to make do with a deanery – such as Hook, the famous Vicar of Leeds. Stranks, Hook's biographer, felt he was not offered the bishopric of Ripon when Longley was translated to Durham because he had always preferred to speak his mind and to act as he thought fit and that, in Hook's opinion, made promotion impossible. [STRANKS *Dean Hook* p. 107] Sidney Smith hoped for a mitre but only got a canonry at St Paul's. A similar fate to that of the great reforming schoolmaster Dr Thomas Arnold – deemed to be too outspoken, too prophetic to be a bishop but in the end given a Regius Professorship at Oxford which probably suited him better.

Men were not promoted to the bench of bishops for their piety and humility and 'servant' nature but that doesn't mean there were not genuinely pious, humble men amongst them, and some had a marked desire to serve and care for the poor. Such a one was Charles Sumner who wrote to his mother the day after his consecration:

> I cannot permit so solemn a day as yesterday to pass without requesting your prayers that the duties to which it devoted me may never be absent from my mind during my future life. The awful and devotional nature of the ceremony is well calculated to make an impression on the most unthinking heart, and I earnestly desire that its influence may be permanent on mine through the grace of Him to whose service I have been so solemnly devoted. John [his brother] exceeded himself on this occasion. He preached from 1 Tim. iv. 16, in a manner which is beyond all praise.
>
> [G.H. SUMNER *op. cit.* p. 110]

The Bishops as Legislators

In 1906 Joseph Clayton wrote an instant best-seller with the above title. It was a careful analysis of the voting record and speeches delivered by bishops in the House of Lords during the 19th century. One of the leading Christian Socialists of the day, the Revd Stewart Headlam, wrote the preface. His opening paragraph succinctly sums up what followed in the book:

> I have been engaged for some twenty years in endeavouring to get the people to understand that the Church is intended to be the great instrument for Social Reform. This little book explains why I have failed. The whole witness of the Church's sacraments of Equality and Brotherhood, of the Church's emancipating literature, of the Church itself as a divine Society for the promotion of Social Justice, is spoilt by the action or inaction of the chief officers of the Church in the exalted position in which they have been placed in the great Council of the Nation. They have had a splendid opportunity – "if they had known" – and missed it. [CLAYTON *The Bishops as Legislators* p. 7]

It needs to be said that Clayton was writing as a churchman with a manifest respect for the bench of bishops and an admiration for individual members of it, and that he stated his case with studied moderation. A few lines from his Introduction can illustrate this:

> These Bishops of the nineteenth century were all men of good character and of blameless private life. They were neither worldly nor ambitious above their fellows. They were not men who amassed fortunes out of the Church of England, or neglected to perform the work of the office they had accepted... Many of them were great scholars, a few were men of rare piety.
>
> And yet as legislators they were the despair, not only of politicians, but of the plain average citizen. These kindly prelates of the nineteenth century could not be got to see that it was wrong in a Christian country to hang starving people for stealing a few shillingsworth of drapery, and unwise to exclude from all political power great masses of law-abiding people keenly interested in politics. Tolerant and far from fanatical in religion, the Bishops still held that persons who shut themselves out from the ample fold of the Established Church did not deserve to sit in Parliament, to vote, or to enjoy the educational advantages of our ancient universities.
>
> One conception of their duties as legislators filled the minds of these Bishops – they were in the House of Lords to maintain the rights and privileges of the Established Church and to resist every innovation that might threaten these rights and privileges, or endanger the constitution of which

> the Established Church was an integral part. Erastian, and unashamed, the Episcopal Bench never admitted that the constitution could be improved or the Church of England strengthened by any relaxing of the bonds of Church and State. [*Ibid.* p 11f]

Clayton dealt with a whole century, we are focussing on just thirteen years of that century. He recorded the essential details of what transpired in the House of Lords, we shall also hear what some of their Lordships had to say in their *Charges* and letters to their clergy and in other episcopal publications. The issues we shall look at are: the civil rights of non-conformists, Roman Catholic emancipation, Jewish disabilities, popular government at national and municipal level, the right of non-Anglicans to baptize, solemnise marriage and bury their dead, and an issue at the end of the period under review, namely national education.

1828 was a very significant year because it was then that the exclusive relationship of the Church of England with the State was breached when Parliament repealed sections of the Corporation and Test Acts. More particularly the 'sacramental test', which had applied to all who wished to hold public office as members of borough corporations, was abolished. On 15 March 1828, the two Archbishops, and the Bishops of London, Durham, Chester and Llandaff, met with Peel, the Home Secretary, and agreed the terms of a Bill. A full meeting of the bishops on the 21st approved this but they did it with misgivings on the part of some of them, and at the Committee stage of the Bill the Bishop of Llandaff introduced an amendment, which was accepted, that the words "on the true faith of a Christian" should be included in the declaration to be made by elected councillors. He later claimed that it had not been his intention to disenfranchise anyone by that amendment but that is exactly what it did to the Jews and certain other minorities. That same declaration included the promise not 'to injure or weaken the Protestant Church as it is by law established in England, or to disturb the said Church, or the bishops and clergy of the said Church, in the possession of any rights or privileges to which such Church, or the said bishops and clergy, are, or may be by law entitled.'

Despite the wording of the declaration, not all the bishops were happy with the Bill when it emerged in an amended form from the Committee stage, thirteen of them voted in favour of the new defences but eight voted against them as being inadequate. Among these was Van Mildert who regarded the amended Bill as 'anything but satisfactory.' His fear was of further encroachment on the Church's relationship with the State 'which may hereafter be grounded upon this measure, and which I have no doubt we shall have to encounter session after session, until all our ascendancy is done away.' On the opposite side, Canterbury, York, Chester and Lincoln, all supported it. Kaye of Lincoln declared that the Church could have no better security than 'the hold which it possesses on the esteem and affection of the people.' True enough but it did not sufficiently recognize just how important the repeal of that Act was. Lord John Russell did when he wrote, 'It is really a gratifying thing to force the enemy to give up his first line, that none but churchmen are worthy to serve the state, and I trust we shall soon make him give up the second, that none but protestants are.'[quoted in HALEVY *History of England in the 19th Century* Vol. ii. p. 266] E.R. Norman commented on the Act's significance, 'The change in constitutional theory was very considerable: the Legislature now became, in theory as well as in practice, a body of mixed religious membership – it no longer consisted solely of the laity of the Establishment.'[NORMAN *Church and Society in England 1770-1970* p. 77f]

The wedge between the Church of England and the State was driven in deeper when Catholic Emancipation was passed in 1829. This had been a bitter and drawn-out political issue in Parliament for three decades. Following an abortive rebellion in Ireland in 1798, a Union Act was passed in 1800. Irish Roman Catholics had not opposed the Act at the time as they believed emancipation was more likely to be granted by the new united Parliament in Westminster than the old Irish one. Pitt had hoped to bring this about but George III blocked it on the grounds that it would violate his Coronation Oath when he had sworn to uphold Protestant ascendancy. Pitt resigned in 1801 but the Irish Catholics were left believing they had been duped. It was an issue that was to simmer and re-surface again and again in Parliament but George III had set his face resolutely against it. Canning brought it back in 1812, Gratton in 1813, and Sir Francis Burdett in 1825 – on the last occasion the Relief Bill was passed in the Commons but thrown out in the Lords. Van Mildert was an uncompromising opponent of all measures to relieve Roman Catholics of their civil disabilities. In a speech in the Lords in 1825 he set out the grounds of his opposition. It was 'not for their religious errors or corruptions, but because they are "Papists"; advocates, i.e. of the Pope's arrogated supremacy, and authority over the whole Christian Church.' In a letter dated 21 January 1829 he wrote,

> My own views are simple enough. Only keep the Papists out of Parliament,

and I care little what else is done for them. But once bring them into Parliament, and what security will there be for our securities, be they what they may? "*Quis custodiat custodes*?" [IVES *op. cit.* p. 101]

Opposition to the *status quo*, however, grew ever stronger on the ground in Ireland. The victory of the Irish Catholic barrister and agitator for reform, Daniel O'Connell, at the bye-election in County Mayo in 1829, even though the voters knew he could not take his seat in Parliament, was the decisive event which persuaded Wellington, the Prime Minister, that emancipation had to happen. The alternative, he feared, was further civil unrest leading to war in Ireland.

In the end emancipation was granted not because the justice of their cause had been acknowledged and civil equality recognized as a natural right, it came as an act of political expediency. But first Wellington had to persuade members of the Government and the King and, if possible, the bishops who formed a sizeable block of votes in the Lords, to support it.

The issue had been before the Lords, yet again, in 1828 when a resolution was introduced for 'the consideration of Catholic Disabilities' with a view to a final and conciliatory adjustment. It was opposed by the Archbishop of Canterbury, and the Bishops of Durham, Lincoln, Llandaff, Bath and Wells, and was lost by 182:137. That would prove to be the last and a short-lived victory for the ultra-conservatives among them. Wellington conferred with Archbishop Howley and the Bishops of London, Durham, Winchester, Lincoln and Chester in November 1828, trying to win over these leading bishops but without success. He met again in January 1829 with the Archbishop of Canterbury and the Bishops of London and Durham. All three declared their decided hostility to any concessions to the Catholics. Bishop Burgess wrote two agitated letters to Wellington in February and March condemning what was proposed. In the first, he claimed that the admission of Papists into Parliament was contrary to the fundamental laws of our Protestant Constitution in Church and State. 'Should subjection to a foreign Church and Sovereign be recognized as compatible with our public institutions; should Popery be thus exalted, and Protestantism degraded; even the immortal and matchless victory of Waterloo would not compensate for such reverse of national character, and infringement of national independence.' [BURGESS *Letter to the Duke of Wellington on the Catholic Question* p. 5] In his second letter a fortnight later, he argued that 'Protestants and papists can never be fellow subjects in this our Protestant country. Though they may be nominally united in office, they must ever be divided by principle, and by many irreconcilable interests.' He went on to express the hope that if the Bill did pass in both Houses, the King would refuse to consent to it. And even if that failed, the voters would show their Protestant faith and 'make such a selection of representatives, as will do justice to their constituents, and restore the Protestant constitution of their country.' [BURGESS *Second Letter on the Catholic Question* p.7] His hopes were not fulfilled.

Copleston took the opposite view. 'The notion of a Protestant Parliament being essential to the Constitution,' he wrote. 'in such a sense that the admission of a single Catholic member vitiates it & militates against the Constitution I hold to be utterly unfounded.' Bishop Murray of Rochester, likewise, voted in favour and argued in the Lords that his belief in Protestant supremacy did not require his concurrence in oppression of the Catholics.

The Government's intention to introduce a Bill to repeal Catholic disabilities was made public in the King's Speech on 5 February, and the Bill was given its first reading on 10 March. Peel moved the third reading on 30 March and the Government majority in the end was 178, thanks to support from the Whigs and from pro-Catholic Tories. A higher hurdle lay ahead in the Lords, and, as expected, some of the bishops attacked it, but not all. The Archbishop called a meeting of the bishops to see if there was any chance of their acting with unanimity. Finding this was not possible, they resolved that each should take his own line.

One of those who spoke and voted in favour was Lloyd of Oxford on the grounds of 'cogent necessity' created by recent events in Ireland. At the second reading of the Bill, he tactlessly condemned the views of the Archbishops of Canterbury, York and Armagh, and the Bishops of London and Durham for opposing the Bill. He claimed 'the rising talent of the country' now favoured emancipation, while those who still oppose it had 'reached that time of life when most men have seceded from the busy scene of human life – when far the greater part, indeed, have been called away, altogether, from this sublunary scheme of things.' He had even foolishly dared to suggest that his own views merited greater notice as a Regius Professor of Divinity. Van Mildert, who was known for his great courtesy, attacked him personally in a speech the following day, reminding the House that three other bishops who had been Regius Professors of Divinity took the opposing view. He challenged Lloyd to produce his evidence that the rising talents of the country favoured emancipation, and poured scorn on the notion that passing the Bill would end all dissatisfaction among Irish Roman Catholics. Lloyd won praise for his speech in some newspapers but met with bitter hostility in others. The Bill had its third reading on 14 April and was carried 217 to 112; eight bishops voted in favour (among them Sumner of Winchester who thereby fell out of the King's favour) and sixteen against. At a levee in St James's Palace later that month, George IV showed his favour to those lords who had opposed emancipation but literally turned his back on those who had supported it and refused to speak with them. Lloyd felt he had been publicly humiliated and sank into depression. A few days later he caught a cold which developed into a cough and was soon on the verge of pneumonia. On Sunday 31 May he died. Newman, who owed much to Lloyd's teaching, suggested afterwards that vexation and anxiety had much to do with his illness.

The passing of the Bill failed to put an end to Irish discontent, as Van Mildert had correctly predicted – in that respect Wellington had totally miscalculated the outcome. It didn't help his cause that the financial qualification to be a voter in Ireland was raised which effectively disenfranchised the mass of Irish Catholic peasants, and in the election of 1830 only eight Irish Catholics were elected to parliament.

As in the 1828 Act relating to Dissenters, the newly enfranchised Roman Catholics had to swear not to harm the Established Church in any way: 'and I do hereby disclaim, disavow, and solemnly abjure any intention to subvert the present Church Establishment as settled by law within this realm: and I do solemnly swear, that I never will exercise any privilege to which I am or may become entitled, to disturb or weaken the Protestant religion or Protestant Government in the United Kingdom. . . '

Emancipation had moved the State further from its confessional character. Opponents of the Bill rightly claimed that a precedent was now on the statute book which opened the way for further changes in the very foundations of political society, that no paper guarantees could protect the Church. And the Church, with no government of its own (as the Convocations were no longer allowed to debate and transact business) was controlled by Parliament. [NORMAN *op. cit.* p. 83]

Fifteen years later, Bishop Charles Sumner, who had supported the Bill, wrote:

> As a political measure, it has hitherto been a signal failure. It has not restored tranquillity to the country – it has not lightened the difficulty in the councils of the state – it has not contributed to the safety of the branch of our church in Ireland – it has not opened up the way to converts from Popery . . . if I could have read that measure by the light of the fifteen years which have elapsed since its enactment, I could not have given, in 1845, the vote I gave in 1829. [G.H. SUMNER *op. cit.* p.163n]

An American historian, Clyde J. Lewis, drew the same conclusion from the passing of this Bill: 'the Irish Catholics were not placated; they were only betrayed; and their resentment was to plague English statesmen during the rest of the nineteenth century.' [LEWIS *The Disintegration of the Tory-Anglican Alliance in the struggle for Catholic Emancipation* p. 41] And he added a second: it also 'destroyed that formidable Tory fortress which had protected the Church for so long, and it supplied new vigour for the liberal movement.' [*Ibid*. p. 40]

In the following decade three attempts were made to add to these civil liberties for Catholics but all were defeated in the Lords. In 1835 a Bill to allow Roman Catholics to be married according to the rites of their own Church and to relieve them from compulsory attendance at Church of England services was rejected – the Bishops of London and Exeter spoke against the motion. A similar Bill was introduced in 1836 relating exclusively to Ireland where four-fifths of the population were Catholics: the Roman Catholic Marriages (Ireland) Bill, but again without success or even much interest on the part of their Lordships, the voting was 39:19. In 1839 the Lords rejected a clause in the Prisons Bill, sanctioning the appointment of Roman Catholic chaplains. The Bishops of London, Lincoln and Exeter spoke against the clause, the Bishop of Durham (Maltby who had been translated from Chichester) in favour. He, alone, of the bishops voted in favour, eight voted against.

Smarting under the political defeat of 1829, the bishops were not going to support any government reforms which might further change and endanger the existing relationship between Church and State. They knew that their assailants hoped the days of the Established Church were numbered, and a reformed House of Commons with more middle class Dissenters among its members was more likely to ensure that it happened. The various Reform Bills which came before the Lords in the following three years were doomed to be resisted by all ultra-Tories and by the bench of bishops with few exceptions. Copleston said in a letter to J.M. Traherne on 16 September 1831, 'As soon as the Reform Bill reaches the Lords for Debate. I swear to be at my post – anxious as I am to strike out some of its noxious ingredients.' [BROWN ed. *The Letters of Edward Copleston* p.81] A sentiment shared by almost all episcopal brethren except Bathurst of Norwich who had been a lifelong supporter of liberal causes but his was a lone voice until the appointment of Maltby to Chichester in 1831.

A brief outline of events leading up to the great Reform Act of 1832 could be helpful at this point in our story and with some explanation of why it was needed and yet why it is was so passionately opposed, not least by the bishops. There were a number of reasons why the old unreformed system of elections had to change but let it suffice to note two of them. Most obvious was the unjust allocation of seats, e.g. 'in 1831 the cities of Manchester (population 182,000), Birmingham (144,000), Leeds (123,000) and Sheffield (92,000) had not a single MP between them. . . Cornwall with a population of 192,000 sent 44 members to parliament. Lancashire sent a mere 14. The southern bias was most notable.' [EVANS *The Great Reform Act* p. 6] And then there were the 'rotten boroughs', in some cases not even hamlets, where a tiny number of electors returned one or two members to Parliament. Dunwich, for example, a former seaport in Suffolk had only 44 houses in 1831 with 32 electors yet it elected two MPs, and Gatton in Surrey had just seven electors who, nonetheless, sent one member to Westminster. Even hardened anti-reformers recognized this was wrong.

Another reason was that the system favoured landowning patrons who determined in large measure how the small number of electors would cast their vote. Again, to quote Professor Eric Evans:

> Roughly half of Britain's MPs sat in Westminster because a patron had put them there. Since voting was an open declaration of allegiance and not a secret ballot, landowners could easily check whether electors defied them. It is not surprising that about one-fifth of all MPs were the sons of peers; their fathers feathered the family nest. Nor is it surprising that fewer than one-third of parliamentary seats were contested in the century before the Reform Act. [*Ibid*. p. 8]

Parliament was not representative of the people, and a growing number of literate working class people were becoming interested in politics, reading broadsheets, attending meetings and joining political unions. These people now wanted to have a say in what happened at Westminster. Tom Paine's *The Rights of Man* first published in two parts in 1791-1792, which stated that universal manhood suffrage was the only legitimate basis for government, had quickly become a best-seller. A Constitutional Society was founded late in 1791 in Sheffield, and over the next two years a string of radical societies of working men were founded in most of Britain's larger towns. The French Revolution and the overthrow of the aristocracy there caused many to hope that England too might soon have a more broadly based elected body. Aristocratic Whig leaders who favoured a small measure of reform formed their own organisation called the Association of the Friends of the People. One of its members was the young Charles Grey who introduced a motion in the House of Commons in 1793 urging the need to look at the principle for reform. It was given little support. From 1797 to 1815 during the years of the war with France, the question of reform was almost forgotten but it returned after the end of the war. By then there were other factors too. The post-war years saw much economic hardship, unemployment and bad harvests in 1829 and 1830. All this added to popular agitation and a widespread feeling that the unreformed Parliament cared little about the sufferings of the poor.

In 1830 the Birmingham Political Union was set up at the instigation of Thomas Attwood, a banker, 'to obtain by every just and legal means such a reform in the Commons House of Parliament as may ensure a real and effectual representation of the lower and middle classes in that House.' Similar unions were formed in other towns, and in some places there were unions just for working class men. A new generation of pro-reform activists was making itself known and noticed at Westminster. Many of those who joined the political unions wanted universal manhood suffrage, a secret ballot (as opposed to the current practice of casting one's vote in public) and annual parliaments but when the details of the Bill were made public they dropped those demands and gave their support to the Whig proposals for reform.

Not all those who opposed reform were illiberal men. Canning, for example, who was Prime Minister for a few months before his death in 1827 strongly supported removing political disabilities from Roman Catholics and was sympathetic towards the aspirations of industrial workers, yet he was a lifelong opponent of parliamentary reform. The revolutionary events across the Channel had convinced him and very many others of his class and generation that opposition to such reform in the early decades of the nineteenth century was 'a crusade for civilisation.'

Attempts to introduce legislation failed despite the growing support and agitation in the country. The coalition of the lower middle classes with the working classes resulted in some large scale demonstrations at which tub-thumping, radical orators such as Henry Hunt spoke. Political reform was the route to economic improvement was their message. One result was that hundreds of petitions were sent to Parliament. Sometimes these meetings were met with frightening violence as when the local yeomanry was used to disperse a large crowd in St Peter's Fields in Manchester in August 1819, and did so by a sabre charge killing eleven people. These victims of what became known as the 'Peterloo Massacre' were regarded as the first martyrs of parliamentary reform, and many more people now came out in support of the cause as a result. The Government responded with heavy-handed penal legislation. That worked temporarily but by 1831 it would more likely have sparked off a full-scale rebellion and MPs had begun to recognize that political concessions could no longer be avoided. Reform was now expedient and necessary.

As long as the Tories remained in power, however, there was little likelihood of any substantial reform, and when Wellington, a known conservative, was asked to form a government in January 1828 no one expected to see any significant changes. Yet, they did. First, the repeal of the Test and Corporation Acts that same year, followed in 1829 by Catholic Emancipation, though both Wellington and Peel had previously been opposed to it. Having reneged on that major issue which had created division in the Tory ranks, neither man could afford politically to do the same again on parliamentary reform. In November 1830, Wellington made a speech which was to herald the end of his government. He told the Lords that he, as Prime Minister, was 'fully convinced that the country possessed at the present moment a legislature which answered all the good purposes of legislation, and this to a greater degree than any legislature ever had answered in any country whatever. He would go further and say that the legislature and the system of representation possessed the full and entire confidence of the country.'

That was manifestly untrue. Under pressure from pro-reformers in Parliament and because his own party was imploding, Wellington resigned a fortnight later and the Whigs, led by Lord Grey, who had been in favour of a moderate measure of reform all his political career, came to power. Hopes were high that real change would come about, at last, but that was unrealistic as the Whig grandees had no intention of undermining the power of the aristocracy and other land-owners. Grey's ministry was the most aristocratic of the century! He told the Lords in 1831 that the principle of his reform was to prevent revolution. 'There is no one more dedicated against annual parliaments, universal suffrage, and the ballot, [i.e. secret ballot] than I am.' Moderate reform, in his judgement, was the only secure route to political stability in the country, and, by attaching the growing numbers of middle class voters to the existing system, he meant to safeguard and retain the government of the country in the hands of men of property which was, in fact, what he achieved.

Grey had already indicated that whilst parliamentary reform was needed, other old ways of doing things such as nepotistic preferment could go on unchanged. Mrs Arbuthnot recorded in her journal on 29

November 'Ld Grey has given *good* places to his son, his three sons-in-law, three brothers-in-law, besides nephews . . . the Duke of Wellington did not crowd the offices with his sons and nephews.' [quoted in E.A. SMITH *Reform or Revolution* p.35] One of Grey's brothers-in-law, Dr Ponsonby, he appointed to the Irish see of Derry.

It is not necessary to look in any detail at all the political machinations of 1830-32, the changes of government and the King's obstructive attitude and his frequent changes of mind on the issue, or at the details of the various drafts of the three bills which were successively introduced in the Commons. Though it is worth noting that many ordinary clergy voted for pro-reform candidates in the 1830 election, and in Brock's judgement whilst 'Many of those who voted for Reform candidates wanted to see the Church reformed and the last disabilities removed from dissenters. . . the election provided no evidence of a serious attack on the English Church in the sense of an intention to disestablish and disendow it.' [BROCK *op. cit.* p. 199]

The bishops became directly concerned each time the bill was introduced in the House of Lords, and they could not be unaware of or ignore the huge public interest in reform and in how they would vote. By March 1831 the subject dominated the conversations of most thinking people. Greville noted in his diary on 7 March, 'Nothing talked of, thought of, dreamt of, but reform. Every creature one meets asks, What is said now? How will it go? What is the last news? What do *you* think? – and so it is from morning till night, in the streets, in the clubs and in private houses.'

Some of the bishops had been prophesying doom in their private correspondence and public visitation *Charges* and trying to justify their opposition. They were not alone in thinking this way. The ultra-Tory John Wilson Croker predicted, 'The Reform Bill is a stepping stone in England to a republic. The Bill, once passed, goodnight to the Monarchy, and the Lords, and the Church.' Wellington too feared the worst. In a letter to Lord Melville on 30 May 1831 at the time of the parliamentary election which would return a reform-minded Commons, he wrote:

> I don't in general take a gloomy view of things; but I confess that, knowing all that I do, I cannot see what is to save the Church, or property, or colonies, or union with Ireland, or eventually monarchy, if the Reform Bill passes. It will be what Mr Hume calls 'a bloodless revolution.' There will be, there can be, no resistance. But we shall be destroyed one after the other, very much in the order that I have mentioned, by due course of law.
>
> [quoted in E.A. SMITH *op. cit.* p. 72]

Van Mildert in his 1831 visitation *Charge* warned, 'we all ought to prepare ourselves for such a state of things as none of us yet have lived to witness. I pray God they may prove less disastrous than at present we are warranted in expecting.' Phillpotts thought the Bill would undermine the constitution and imperil the legal position of the Church. His words were full of foreboding, 'There is laid up a store of woes for England, the elements of a wider and more irreparable devastation, than any which the history of man has ever yet recorded.' He accordingly campaigned actively in the west country against Whig candidates in 1831.

Political leaders on both sides were concerned to win episcopal support. The Tory Lord Ellenborough noted in his diary on 12 September 'The Bishop of Gloucester [Monk] dined with me. He seems very well disposed, but shaken as to the second reading by the knowledge that the A.B. of Canterbury, the B. of London, and the B. of Lincoln, at present intend to vote for it – thinking it is dangerous to the Church, but less dangerous than rejection. I shall tell this to the Duke [Wellington] tomorrow.' A week later he met with Wellington who thought the Bishop of London would vote for – the Archbishop would not vote for but might stay away if he did not vote against.

The Times in its editorial on 29 September 1831 warned the bishops of the dangers they would be putting the Church in if they voted against the Bill. The Church, it predicted, would be 'exposed to a hurricane, the like of which has never blown', and that the people would blame the bishops for having crushed their liberties and destroyed them if the Bill were not passed. On the eve of the debate in the Lords, *The Times* tried again to put pressure on the bishops to support the Bill: 'If the Bishops love the Church, they will vote with those Peers who have a wise attachment to their order. To both we commit the nation's peace.' [*Times* Monday 3 October]

After a fiery debate in the Lords, the voting on the third reading of the Reform Bill in the early hours of 8 October 1831 was 158:199. The Archbishop of Canterbury spoke briefly late in the debate against the Bill on behalf of the bench. 'To a Reform synonymous with the extermination of abuses, and the restoration of the excellencies of the Constitution, he professed himself a sincere friend', he said, and his fellow members of the Bench concurred with him in that sentiment. But he ended with words, which sound contrary to that view, that he had opposed the Bill because he thought it was 'mischievous in its tendency, and would be extremely dangerous to the fabric of the Constitution.'

Twenty-one bishops voted against it. Beverley later listed them in his *Second Letter to the Archbishop of York* as:

Wm Howley Archbishop of Canterbury, P. le Poer Trench Archbishop of Tuam, G.H. Law Bath & Wells, R. Gray Bristol, C. Bethell Bangor, H. Percy Carlisle, J. Brinkley Cloyne, T. Lawrence Cork & Ross, Wm van Mildert Durham, H. Phillpotts Exeter, J.H. Monk Gloucester, E. Copleston Llandaff, J. Kaye Lincoln, H. Ryder Lichfield & Coventry, T. Elrington Leighlin & Ferns, R. Bagot Oxford, G. Murray Rochester, T. Burgess Salisbury, W. Carey St Asaph, H. Marsh Peterborough and C.R. Sumner Winchester.

Had those same twenty-one bishops voted for it, the Bill would have had a majority of one. It brought the wrath of the people down on their heads with tumultuous attacks in some places. Riots broke out that same day in Derby and Nottingham, and spread to towns, large and small, across the country. Bristol, in particular, witnessed much destruction, the Bishop's Palace being burnt to the ground, though that happened three weeks after the vote when the first rage at the Bill's defeat had had time to subside. The riots in Bristol were caused by the visit of the ultra-Tory Recorder Sir Charles Wetherell who had gone there to attend the Assizes. Wetherell's arrival resulted in three days of rioting which included mobs storming the Mansion House, Customs House and a number of private dwellings in addition to the Bishop's Palace. [qv LOPATIN *Political Unions, Popular Politics and the Great Reform Act 1832* pp. 93-97] The Bishop retreated to the safety of his son-in-law's vicarage ten miles away at Almondsbury but kept a preaching engagement in the city.

In Canterbury the Archbishop's carriage was attacked and a dead cat thrown at him in it which (fortunately for him) struck his Chaplain in the face. "Be glad it wasn't a live one!" Howley is reputed to have said to the poor man. Bishop Ryder was hooted in church in Coventry. Farnham Castle was barricaded, and at the bishop's palace at Worcester twenty-five special constables drove away a mob. 'Judas Iscariot, Bishop of Worcester' was chalked on the walls of that cathedral city.

It was the same in the far north, Van Mildert wrote to his nephew, Henry Douglas, 'We have had our share of turmoil, & the compliment has been paid me of burning me in effigy in sight of my Castle gates, with threats of demolishing windows, & so forth.' He received many gross insults and believed that it was planned to do him personal violence. The Archbishop of York had not been present for the vote in October but having voted for an amendment postponing the disfranchisement of the pocket boroughs, he was regarded as an opponent of reform. 'Consequently the citizens of York regarded him as an enemy, paraded his effigy through the streets, and then marched on Bishopthorpe Palace, where they smashed the fence, broke the windows and burnt the effigy in front of the house.' [TINDALL HART *Ebor* p. 156] Bishop Percy was likewise burned in effigy by a huge crowd in Carlisle.

The Bishop of Exeter had his palace defended by coast guards, and on one occasion by yeomanry. Phillpotts wrote to the Duke of Wellington on 5 November about the threatening mood in the west country:

> At Plymouth and the neighbouring towns, including a population of more than 100,000, the spirit is tremendously bad. The shopkeepers are almost all Dissenters, and such is the rage on the question of Reform at Plymouth, that I have received from several quarters (the soberest and most respectable) the most earnest entreaties that I will not come there to consecrate a church, as I had engaged to do. They assure me that my own person, and the security of the public peace, would be in the greatest danger.
> [E.A. SMITH *op. cit.* p. 107]

Elsewhere in the southwest, Bishop Law's carriage was stoned and he took a house at Torquay in order to be away from his see city of Wells. Copleston stayed in London for a few days and told Bruce Knight on 13 October, 'No Welsh Bishops but myself is in town. I should be glad to be anywhere else – not that I have met with, or that I apprehend any personal insult or outrage – but it is an uncomfortable state of things - & I have nothing particular to do here after this week. It is a satisfaction to me to have been at my post & to have acted as I have done.' [BROWN ed. *op. cit.* p. 83] But the public mood worsened and in another letter to Knight written eleven days later he described his experiences since returning to Wales:

> I found the country (or rather the towns) in a state of angry excitement about the Reform Bill. At Wotton under Edge & at Chepstow a few loose fellows collected hooting and yelling as I drove off. At Abergavenny I understood the spirit is still worse & more violent – insomuch that I am advised by several people not to go there for some time. They have insulted and mobbed every member of Parl*t*. that voted against the Bill, on his way thro' the town – and Bishops, as you know, are particularly obnoxious. [*Ibid*. p.84]

Copleston now felt it necessary to have a shovel hat and a 'long brown coat' available to use as a disguise if he had to flee his residence through the back door and across the fields. By 5 November, he had begun to accept the Bill would have to be passed,

> I am grieved at heart, & tremble for my Church and my country.
> Of the Bill I will not say much. My opinion is strong that a measure substantially the same must pass & that quickly – the country will be in rebellion – what is perhaps as bad, indebted for peace to the Political Unions, which are fast taking to themselves the power of Government.
> I have been perfectly unmolested but I am still advised not to appear in Abergavenny. [*Ibid.* p. 86]

A mob took control of the town of Farnham and then marched up the castle hill but the heavy gates of the castle stopped their onward progress. They retreated back to town planning to burn the bishop in effigy on a bonfire but some tradesman paid them not to do it. It seems that Sumner was not concerned for his own safety – 'what happened here,' he wrote, 'was nothing, absolutely nothing, a mere handful of rabble - nothing to what might have been expected, and to what probably will be, ere matters are finished.' [G.H. SUMNER *op. cit.* p. 198] It wasn't just the bishops who suffered abuse and the threat of physical violence, many ordinary clergy did too, not least those who served as magistrates.

In the judgement of Eric Evans, 'Britain in modern times has never been closer to revolution than in the autumn of 1831.' [EVANS *op. cit.* p.54] Twenty-one bishops were responsible, in part, for that situation. The Press too shared some responsibility for the heightened atmosphere nationwide. The *Morning Chronicle* and the *Sun* were both printed with black borders on the day following the vote in the Lords. Greville commented on 14 October, 'The press strained every nerve to produce excitement, and *The Times* has begun an assault on the Bishops whom it has marked out for vengeance and deprivation for having voted against the Bill.' [GREVILLE *op. cit.* p. 83f] A Dublin newspaper *The Freeman's Journal* described the bishops as 'reverend vultures that pounce upon the vitals of the country and drive the nation into despair and death.' *The Times* shared the people's indignation at what had happened in the Lords and predicted Reform would come. 'In looking over the elements of which the fatal majority is composed, attention fixes first, and principally, on the Bishops. These reverend Lords have more to do with the people than the other Peers: their functions, and those of their less elevated brethren, are discharged with and among the people; and yet through them it is, that a bill for the establishment of the people's rights has been lost. . . ' [10 October 1831]

Whilst all this was going on, the north had been hit by a fresh outbreak of cholera which had started in Sunderland and Newcastle, and was spreading. The King in Privy Council duly ordered the Archbishop of

Canterbury to prepare forms of prayer to be read in all churches and chapels. Howley, assisted by the bench of bishops, produced two wordy prayers, which were read in every parish in the land on Sunday 6 November, beseeching the Almighty to put an end to the plague.

The previous evening, being Bonfire Night, Guy Fawkes had been replaced by effigies of a bishop on many a pyre. Phillpotts, in a letter, to Wellington written on 6 November was quite philosophical about it – the local magistrates had informed him that an effigy of him plus one of Lord Rolle had been made and he had expressed his '*wish* that the burning should take place, for it seemed to me quite plain, that it was much better the effigies, as they were prepared, should be got rid of, else the peace would be endangered on some other night, when the authorities were less ready to meet the mischief.' At the other end of the country, similar scenes were being played out. *The Poor Man's Guardian* carried an article on 19 November about what had happened in Huddersfield. It reported that 'Between fifteen and twenty thousand persons paraded the streets with an effigy of a Bishop (*as natural as life*) and no funeral was ever conducted with greater awe and solemnity. When the procession reached the spacious and open square in the Market Place, all formed around the *Right Reverend Father in God*, and a person in priestly habiliments then delivered, in an audible and impressive manner' a funeral oration which began;

> Here is a great, fat, bloated, blundering bishop, whom we have bartered for the poor, deluded, murdered Guy Faux! This is the last Fifth of November which shall constitute the anniversary of a bloody church and state conspiracy, in support of tithes, Easter offerings, oblations, obventions, (*sic*) and all the horrid and dreadful train of business, got up by the worse than devils, to deceive their dupes, for the purpose of rioting in luxury out of the *grindings* of our bones, to our utter ruin and past and present degradation.

This is stirring, revolutionary stuff touching on several popular perceptions or misperceptions about the Church and more particularly the bishops and their luxurious lifestyles.

Even Blomfield, who had been absent at the fateful vote (as he said he was still mourning his father's death}, did not escape obloquy. He had undertaken to preach at the re-opening service of St Ann's Soho on 23 October but the congregation let it be known that if he entered the pulpit, they would all walk out. He prudently excused himself from preaching but the press then interpreted his decision as one taken out of fear. The bishop was attacked by conservative and liberal papers alike.

'Such a proof', said *The Times* on the next Monday morning, 'of public antipathy towards the entire Order, whose conduct in the House of Lords was so conspicuous on the second reading of the Reform Bill, is without example in modern history, and is worth a whole library of comments. The Bishop of London did not vote against the Bill, but then he did not vote for it, and the nation will not be served by halves.'

[BIBER *Bishop Blomfield and his Times* p. 116]

Popular indignation was prolonged as well as fierce as the pamphleteer R.M. Beverley noted in his *Second Letter to the Archbishop of York* in January 1832, 'At this very moment there are new churches waiting till the bishop of the diocese can gain courage to consecrate them.'

Kitson Clark paints a dire picture of that time:

> For churchmen therefore the winter of 1831 was a time of crisis and fear. It looked as if the enemies of the Church were closing in for the kill. Besides the anger of the mob there was the more persistent hatred of the Protestant dissenters and the Roman Catholics. To the Radicals the Church seemed to be no more than a rabbit warren of aristocratic privilege and abuse. Great publicity had been given to the Church's corruptions, which had been exaggerated, and moderate men had learned to look askance at it as an institution not worth preserving. Lord Grey had told the bishops to put their house in order.
>
> [KITSON CLARK *Churchmen and the Condition of England 1832-1885*. p. 54]

Real fear was provoked among bishops and clergy that the established order of things was in mortal danger. Given their unpopularity and the pressure put on them to change their votes when the Bill was re-introduced in 1832, several showed courage in refusing to recant despite knowing that Earl Grey had persuaded the King to create, if necessary, enough new peers to force the Bill through the House of Lords. At the second reading, Van Mildert the elderly Bishop of Durham opposed it on the grounds that it would 'infuse a very large portion of the democratic influence into the legislature, tending to weaken the executive Government, the aristocracy, and eventually the Monarchy itself.' He also feared that the Bill would lead to 'the ascendancy of the House of Commons, and make it substantially the ruling power of the State.' Prophetic words! [quoted in CLAYTON *op. cit.* p. 50] At the second reading, which passed 184:175, twelve bishops, including the Archbishop of York, voted for the Bill but sixteen, including the Archbishop of Canterbury, voted against it.

Among the bishops who now recognized that it was politically expedient to give, and publicly express, their support were Blomfield of London and, as noted earlier, Copleston of Llandaff. The former had met with

Lord Grey in November 1831 and seems to have agreed to promote a modified Bill and to try and persuade some of his episcopal colleagues to do likewise. In the Lords he heartily commended the Bill as 'a measure which would improve the representation, conciliate the affections of the people, and, adding strength and perpetuity to whatever was valuable in the constitution, cherish religion and consolidate the best interests of the country.' The contrary view was expressed by Monk of Gloucester who believed the Bill was supported mainly by the rabble: 'persons incapable of forming an opinion on political subjects.' Bishop Murray of Rochester, grandson of the Duke of Atholl, adopted the same tone of social superiority. He claimed to respect the people 'so long as they maintained their respective and private stations.' For him that meant 'the lower classes should not be called into council; they should not be suffered to interfere with matters connected with legislation.'

On 16 December 1831 the Archbishop of Canterbury had a private interview with the King, who spoke very frankly about his own views on reform. Grey was much afraid that this knowledge of the King's critical opinions might have embarrassing consequences when the Bill came up for discussion in the Lords. Ten days later Sir Herbert Taylor told Grey that the King had authorized him to say to the Bishop of Worcester (who was allowed to repeat it) 'that his Majesty was of the opinion that the peers in general would be very ill-advised not to allow the Bill to go into Committee, and would place themselves in a very awkward position towards the country by rejecting the Bill without discussion'. [ASPINALL *The Cabinet Council 1783-1835* p. 241]

One bishop who argued to the end against the Bill was Phillpotts. Greville praised a speech he made just before the second reading, describing it as 'a grand speech, full of fire and venom, very able . . . he has a desperate and dreadful countenance, and looks like the man he is.' He likened him, not very flatteringly, to Bishop Stephen Gardiner, Lord Chancellor under Mary I, an instigator of the burning of Protestants in that reign. The Bishop had to endure some harsh verbal attacks in the Lords. One of Greville's diary entries, written in April, reads:

> Phillpotts got a terrific dressing down from Lord Grey, and was handled not very delicately by Goderich and Durham, though the latter was too coarse. He had laid himself very open and, able as he is, he has adopted a tone and style inconsistent with his lawn sleeves, and unusual on the Episcopal Bench. He is carried away by his ambition and his alarm and horrifies his Brethren who feel all the danger (in these times) of such a colleague. The episode, of

> which he was the object, was, of course, the most amusing part of the whole. [GREVILLE *op. cit.* p. 101]

Greville was not alone in that assessment of Phillpotts. The Tory ex-Cabinet Minister Lord Ellenborough frequently refers in his diary to the Bishop's debating skills. Here is part of his entry for 11 April 1832:

> We had in the debate a most extraordinary speech from the Bishop of Exeter, who has really wonderful powers – a degree of self-possession & readiness possessed by no man in either House, much eloquence, sarcasm and unction. Altogether he is a most vigorous debater. The conduct of the ministers towards him is quite ungentlemanlike. They lose all self-command. He only rises in consequence of it. I do not recollect to have heard any speech which has produced such a sensation. [ASPINALL ed. *op. cit.* p. 230]

Le Marchant, Brougham's PPS, wrote in his diary at the same time:

> Phillpotts was very successful. The Duke of Cumberland told Wetherell in my hearing that it was the most masterly speech ever delivered in the House. This of course was extravagant, but it must be admitted to have been very clever and admirably delivered. [*Ibid.* p. 222]

Lord Durham took a very different view, referring to Phillpotts's speech as full of 'coarse and virulent invective – malignant and false insinuations – the grossest perversion of historical facts – decked out with all the choicest flowers of his well-known pamphleteering slang.' [*Ibid.* p. 232] There seems to be little doubt that the Bishop of Exeter was a notable speaker, if not always expressing himself in the way one might expect a bishop to do!

Van Mildert, too, had no good thing to say of the Bill – quite the reverse. He believed that

> no great practical evil would be removed by it, nor any great practical good obtained; that it would go dangerously to abolish prescriptive rights and privileges, to weaken the executive Government, the Aristocracy, and eventually the Monarchy itself; that it would tend to deteriorate the character of the House of Commons, and, at the same time, to increase its power; and that it would have the effect of substituting for what were reproachfully called nomination boroughs, political-union boroughs, under an influence far more dangerous and degrading than any which aforetime had been exerted. [IVES *op. cit.* p. 124]

The bishops were divided and Murray of Rochester poured scorn on those of his episcopal colleagues who were now willing to vote for the Bill. On April 13, he referred with sarcasm to the 'light which appeared to dawn on some of his right reverend brethren' and stated that it 'had not cast its rays upon him.' He repented that he was still 'unilluminated but regretted it not, for he was convinced that the change in opinion of those individuals to whom he alluded was based upon expediency.' [W.G. SMITH *The Bishops and Reform* p. 369] Blomfield summarized the opinions of those bishops whom Murray had scorned in his statement that 'the time for neutrality has gone; and he was of the opinion that there must be extensive reform' and further that 'he would not support any amendment which would go to alter the Bill so as to mutilate or destroy its essential principles.'

Lord Holland noted in his diary about the debate in the Lords:

> The Bishop of London . . . took the plain, decided, and manly course of acknowledging that the bill, with all its imperfections or sins, of which he thought it had many, was not such an evil as its rejection would be, that he would attend to the Committee to improve it as much as he could, but that he was not prepared to vote against it even in its present form, nor would act the insidious or unmanly part of attempting indirectly to defeat by mutilating it in Committee. This, considering his character and abilities, was sufficient to cower such timid prelates as were at all disposed to reconcile themselves to the Court and the Ministry, and we had the support of twelve of that Reverend Bench. Though the Archbishops – the most timid, irresolute, and helpless of them all – gave a silent vote against the bill and a foolish unmeaning countenance to the opposition against it.
>
> [KRIEGEL *op. cit.* p. 169f]

When the Bill was eventually passed in the Lords on 4 June, the opposition had collapsed. Many peers simply absented themselves from the chamber. Several bishops had indicated that they would no longer resist it. The voting at the final reading was 106 in favour, 22 against. Those who had persisted in their opposition to the last were all lay peers.

Abuse continued, nonetheless, to be heaped on episcopal heads, and attacks were increasingly made by Dissenters as well as Radicals against the Church of England. Some bishops in their *Charges* used almost apocalyptic language to describe the plight of the Established Church but they remained confident, at least in their public statements, that the powers of hell would not prevail against them.

The social composition of the post-1832 parliament, however, was little changed: the landowning classes continued to send most members to Westminster. Professor Geoffrey Finlayson commented, 'When, therefore, the dust had settled and what had been achieved was clearly seen, it was evident that the Act had done little to shake the dominance of the established interests and classes. For the most part, it left the working classes outside the political nation altogether.' [FINLAYSON *Decade of Reform* p. 18] Grey's most recent biographer, E.A. Smith, believes it was never Grey's intention to bring about any radical changes.

> His object was to preserve, not to innovate; to ensure the continuance of aristocratic dominance and the traditional institutions of Monarchy, Church and Parliament, and not to subject them to the control of democracy. Reform was essentially a conservative solution to the problem of social and political change. Grey's principles and attitudes as well as his temperament were profoundly aristocratic, and it was as the servant of the English aristocracy and its tradition of paternalistic governance that he sought to guide the nation through the dangers of popular unrest and social upheaval.
> [SMITH *Lord Grey 1764-1845* p.3]

Viscount Morpeth, an MP for Yorkshire, wrote to Viscount Althorp on 26 December 1832 to share his impressions of the present state of public feeling in the north. His letter includes these lines:

> The general feeling is very keen in favour of a full measure of Church Reform, but I do not think there is any prevalent wish to destroy the Establishment. I feel sure that it is most essential to the welfare of the Church to take advantage of these dispositions by a large and decided measure of Conservative Reform. Church Rates, are the great rock of offence, I should say, more than tithes; but then I speak of a manufacturing district community. The power of the Bishops is not viewed with favour; cheap bread, more corn, a fixed duty of very moderate amount – but these are battles which we manufacturers must fight for ourselves.
> [E.A. SMITH *op. cit.* p. 153]

The Established Church had had little to fear, in reality, but that is not how bishops and parish clergy saw it at the time. Church reforms would soon follow with parliamentary backing but these were much needed reforms which would strengthen, not weaken, it. Some church leaders had the good sense to accept the changes the Reform Act would bring and to urge a conciliatory spirit among the clergy. Archdeacon Lyall, for example, in his *Charge* of 1833 delivered to the clergy of Colchester exhorted his brethren, however much they may have opposed the recent political changes, to devote themselves 'to the task of healing divisions, allaying animosities, and restoring harmony and good will.' They were to be ready for the ecclesiastical reform which was 'called for by the altered spirit of the age.'

In the aftermath of Catholic emancipation and the passing of the Reform Act, Jewish leaders hoped that they too might now benefit from the changed political scene. There were fewer than 27,000 Jews in Britain and Ireland at that time, of whom nearly 18,000 lived in or near London. Robert Grant, a Director of the East India Company and a keen Evangelical Christian but also a member of the Philo-Judean Society, agreed to introduce a bill into the Commons on their behalf, his brother Charles having been approached first and declined. When it failed in the Lords, he re-introduced it a year later. Both attempts to bring in Jewish emancipation were fiercely and successfully resisted. The Jewish Civil Disabilities Bill passed its third reading in the Commons on 22 July 1833 but the Lords threw it out. The Archbishop of Canterbury moved the rejection, and urged that the 'moral and intellectual capacity of the Jews was not such as to entitle them to any share in the Legislature.' Twenty bishops voted with Archbishop Howley in the majority of fifty against the bill at its second reading; three bishops supported it. When a similar bill was introduced the following year the Archbishop declared that Parliament would be 'degraded in the eyes of the country if there were among their members persons who were avowedly not Christians,' and fifteen bishops supported the rejection. Howley was anti-Semitic. He dismissed the Jews as 'a money-getting people' whose prosperity seemed proof that no concession was required to increase it, and alluded to the ultra-Orthodox arguments against emancipation of the type advanced by Rabbi Joseph Croolll as evidence that Jews were themselves divided on the wisdom of such a measure. [SALBSTEIN *Emancipation of the Jews in Britain* p. 73] Even the liberal-minded Thomas Arnold was opposed. In a letter to Archbishop Whately in May 1836, he wrote, 'The Irish being a Catholic people, they have a right to perfect independence, or to a perfectly equal union, if our conscience objects to the latter, it is bound to concede the former. But for the Jews I see no plea of justice, whatever; they are voluntary strangers here, and have no claim to become citizens, but by conforming to our moral law, which is the Gospel.'

One Act passed in the summer of 1833 which came into effect a year later has been described by Chadwick as 'the supreme moral act of those reforming years', was the emancipation of all slaves in the British Empire subject to an interim apprenticeship of not more than six years. Radicals, dissenters and a few Evangelical churchmen such as Fowell Buxton wanted immediate freedom for slaves without apprenticeship, and without compensation to slave-owners. But the Whig government was too conservative to accept that. The bishops' voices were not to be heard.

When it came to legislation affecting the working conditions of the masses, the bishops had singularly little to say. For example, in the debates leading up to the Factories Act of 1833, the only prelate to speak out strongly in its favour was Archbishop Howley. He did so on 1 March 1832 when he presented a petition to the House of Lords on behalf of the operatives in Rochdale. He deplored the system of 'cruelty and oppression' that kept children in factories for thirteen to sixteen hours a day.

> Up to the age of 14 or 15 the time was that of innocent pleasure and enjoyment, whereas under this system they were confined for an unreasonable number of hours each day at their labours without time for relaxation, or even for proper refreshment, and that too with very few holidays in the year. The effect of this was most pernicious to their health and it ought to be recollected that it was attended with most serious injury to their morals. It was a disgrace to a Christian and civilized country to allow such exploitation to continue merely for the sake of putting money in the pockets of the master manufacturers. [*Hansard* X (1832) p.985f]

That unusual outburst from the normally gentle Howley didn't stop the proposed legislation, which Sadler introduced in the Commons later that month, being watered down.

The northern bishops could hardly have been unaware of the 'Short Time' movement which organised a series of mass meetings in the north to awaken the public (middle class) conscience. Two Tories, Oastler and Sadler, were its leaders and Parson Bull of Byerley became one of its principal speakers. One of their largest rallies was a 'pilgrimage of mercy' which culminated in Castle Square at York on 24 April 1832. More than twelve thousand people took part and several MPs expressed their public support for it as did many clergy. Sadler's Bill, however, did not enjoy the support of the Government and he was pressed into agreeing that it should be remitted to a Select Committee. Evidence was taken from many workers who testified to their experience. 'They told of practised cruelties, of the brutality of overlookers – with millowners' connivance – and the effects upon the health of the children and therefore of the factory population. Indeed, no great powers of observation were necessary to see in the stunted and rickety adults the effects of child labour. Medical evidence supported the reformers.' [GILL *Parson Bull of Byerley* p. 69] Orders in Council prescribed for West Indian slaves a maximum working day of the same length that Sadler was asking for British young people between the ages of nine and eighteen years, yet the Government went on accepting as valid arguments advanced by mill owners identical with those they had eventually rejected when advanced by slave owners. The Bill fell when Grey's cabinet resigned and parliament was dissolved.

Sadler lost his seat in the following General Election, and Bull travelled to London to find a new MP to take it on. In the end he persuaded Lord Ashley to re-introduce the Bill in the Commons. It was this same Yorkshire clergyman who briefed Ashley and encouraged him in this momentous task which would last until 1847. Liberals in political reform were not necessarily liberal in social reform as the newly elected and reformed House of Commons proved. It contained many members who were sympathetic to the mill owners, and wanted to diminish the force of the Sadler Report which had roused much public support on humanitarian grounds. The Government was against legislation but they were now under pressure from public opinion which had swung in favour of reform on this matter too, so they resorted to a Royal Commission and yet more fact-finding. Bull appeared twice before it to give evidence and addressed a written 'Protest' to the Commission which included these hard-hitting lines of condemnation:

As a Minister of the Church of England, I conceive it my duty to maintain the cause of the oppressed and poor, and I regard this favourite system of *Commissions*, now so generally adopted, as so many parts of a Dexterous Conspiracy, which certain Political Philosophers are under plotting, the effect of which is, to establish the domination of wealth, and the degradation of industrious Poverty. I feel, too, that the interests of Christianity itself are betrayed, into the hands of unreasonable and wicked men, by the Judas-like conduct of many of its professors, whose capital is embarked in the Factory System, whose lips salute our altars with apparent devotion – who raise their hands in her sanctuary as if to adore, but who make them fall with tyrannous weight upon the children of the needy. Whether such bitter foes of the true Religion of Christ are shrouded in a Priestly Mantle, or dwell in those Mansions and are surrounded by those parks and lawns which the over laboured infant has enabled them to procure, my Ministerial duty to my Country is the same; and whether I regard its general prosperity its social happiness or its religious advantage, I am bound to rebuke and oppose them.

> I believe, the oppression of the Rich – of those especially who hypocritically assume a Christian profession, has done more to injure Christianity than all that Voltaire or Paine ever produced. [GILL *The Ten Hours Parson* p. 195]

No Bishop spoke so plainly and powerfully in the Lords on the matter. The result was a watered down version of the Ashley Bill which became the Althorp Act of 1833, in which some of its important features were omitted and others modified. Little improvement was achieved by that Act, which didn't come fully into force until three years later. The 'Ten Hours men' had, however, compelled an unwilling Government to legislate. Even a bad bill was better than no bill at all. It was a start.

Where were the bishops in all this? Ryder commended the Bill briefly in his *Charge* in 1832 and expressed his wish that 'the manufactory might prove, instead of a hotbed of moral mischief, a seminary of all that is useful and laudable.' Archbishop Vernon-Harcourt wrote in that same year to the Leeds Committee pledging his support and he gave Bull £20 in 1833 (worth more than £2,000 today) to assist the Ten Hours movement but he never spoke on that or any other question of social legislation. Oastler met Van Mildert on one occasion and he later related that the bishop had praised his campaign, 'It is a work which every Bishop and minister of Christ should take to heart: the Church of England is deeply interested in the success of your labours.' [WARD *The Factory Movement 1830-1855* p. 424] But such personal expressions of support were as far as it went. As recently as 1830, thirteen bishops had voted 'less from conviction, more from party obligation' [SOLOWAY] with the government against a proposal to establish a Select Committee to enquire into the condition of the working classes. Their sense of social responsibility was limited to acts of personal charity and to encouraging workers to simply accept their condition as God-given. None of them ever suggested that the physical condition of the poor was relevant to the Church's ministry to them. They believed that social and economic legislation was beyond their prescribed area of political activity and saw no reason to get involved in such debates in the Lords. Nor, with few exceptions, did they have any first-hand knowledge of the living and working conditions of the industrial poor which might have moved them to speak out on behalf of the poor.

Bowen warned that historians should judge the actions of churchmen by the standards of their day and not by those of today. He writes, 'You cannot abstract the Victorian churchman, or any other historical figure, from his age and its beliefs, to demand from him the insights of later generations.' [BOWEN *The Idea of the Victorian Church* p. 242] In other words, we should not be surprised or shocked that the bishops were not in the forefront of social reform at that time. That may be so, but the fact is that there were other churchmen such as Thomas Arnold who exposed the greed of the industrial *nouveaux riches* in his articles in the *Sheffield Courant* or Parson Bull and the many other parish clergy, especially in the West Riding of Yorkshire, who were seeking to reduce the working hours of children and the labouring masses. Such 'radical' views were being held and expounded by Christians at that time – but *not* by the bishops. And these men, after all, were supposed to be the guardians of the Christian Faith and who had the Gospels and the example of Jesus Himself with his special concern for those on the margins of society – 'a bias to the poor' as one modern bishop has called it. They just didn't seem to make the connection between that and their ministry as bishops. At least they did not in 1833. Fourteen years later when the Ten Hours Bill was successfully carried there was a strong episcopal attendance in the House of Lords and nearly every bishop voted in support. Three of them, Blomfield of London, Thirlwall of St David's and Wilberforce of Oxford spoke strongly in its favour. By then, they had been persuaded that they had a Christian duty to be involved. Lord Ashley recorded gratefully, 'This will do very much to win the hearts of the manufacturing people to Bishops and Lords, it has already converted the hard mind of a Chartist delegate.' [WARD *op. cit.* p. 344]

The 1833 Factories Act, in the end, only limited the working day for *children under thirteen* to a nine hours or a forty-eight hour week, except in silk mills, where ten hours was permitted. Children between the ages of thirteen and eighteen could not be worked for more than twelve hours a day or sixty-nine hours a week. An important innovation was that children under thirteen were supposed to have two hours' schooling each day. The establishment of travelling inspectors, absent in earlier legislation, gave this new measure some teeth but it was not effective everywhere.

Some bishops were so ignorant of the realities of industrial work conditions that they believed children working a twelve hour day thrived on it and were healthy because of it! A view put forward by some factory owners back in 1819 in a report they claimed was supported by 'medical opinion'. To his credit, that was a view which Bishop Law had challenged at the time, urging the Peers to 'assert the cause of defenceless and suffering youth'. He, at least, did have some first hand experience of visiting mills in Lancashire during his years as Bishop of Chester when he had been shocked by the conditions under which children laboured. But he and other episcopal sympathisers had no stomach for such radical ideas as the appointment of factory inspectors.

Law had moved to the more rural diocese of Bath & Wells in 1824 and there showed a particular concern for poor agricultural workers who subsisted on very low wages. When the agrarian troubles were sweeping across southern England in 1830 he had planned to address the Lords on the matter but 'the disturbed state of the country,' he wrote, 'induced him to return immediately to his diocese, feeling it to be his duty to be on the spot where . . . he might be enabled to do the most good.' Instead, he published his *Remarks on the Present Distresses of the Poor* in December of that year. He tried to analyse why the situation was as bad as it was. The main cause, he saw as arising 'from the scarcity or want of employment' – the contributing factors being the increase in population and the slump in trade and the land enclosures over the past half-century. The poor could no longer graze their domestic animals or find fuel for their fires. The consolidation of farms into larger units had seen men made redundant. Farmers had reduced wages, underpaying their employees, thereby requiring the parish to subsidize the poor. 'This practice tends to degrade and lower their good moral feelings. The labourer is, in all cases, worthy of his hire.' His initial recommendation was the assignment of land to each cottager and his family. He made some, what were for the time, radical proposals:

> In order, however, to secure, at present, the adequate sources of employment, the landlord must, where circumstances require it, lower his rent; the clergyman his tithes. Until this takes place, the farmer cannot offer to employ a sufficient number of labourers, or to give to those employed a due remuneration. The sum which I, myself, have given to those labourers whom I felt it my duty to employ, has been one shilling and six-pence per day; and with this sum (together with certain other advantages which they enjoyed) they expressed themselves, as being perfectly satisfied, and content.
> [LAW *Remarks on the Present Distresses of the Poor.* p. 18f]

Law had practised what he preached by setting up earlier that year a scheme in his diocese for providing poor families with tiny parcels of land where they could grow vegetables and perhaps have a pig or two. One of his clergy, John Skinner, visited the site in 1832 along with the bishop and recorded his opinion.

> Afterwards I accompanied the Bishop, who was on horseback, to the Park

and the potato grounds he has let to the poor people; nearly sixty acres in extent, and the plan seems to answer even beyond his expectations. The renters of these portions of good ground at twelve shillings a rood amount to upward of two hundred, and I was glad to hear that not only were they punctual in their payments, but so industrious in their habits that no one has received parochial help since he has become a renter.
[COOMBS. H. & P. ed. *Journal of a Somerset Rector* p. 448]

It was a commendable action by a genuinely caring man concerned for the welfare of unemployed and starving agricultural workers but he was fearful of those same workers being attracted to and influenced by the Chartists and by the new, socialist ideas. As were all his episcopal colleagues. Blomfield also provided land in Ealing in 1832 to be laid out as allotments for working men in the hope that gardening would prove to be more attractive to them than drinking. In time, he also developed a social conscience and through his membership of the Manufacturers' Relief Committee contributed to bringing some relief to the unemployed in industrial districts. Bishop Monk also followed Law's example in 1834 when he assigned a few acres of land near Gloucester 'to poor families to be cultivated by spade husbandry.' The condition of the poor was a real problem which was only recognized in part by a few of the bishops, and there was the real problem of Church reform which most of them did eventually acknowledge and seek to address. Sadly, no bishop seems to have seen a connection between the two. How could the Church thrive and minister effectively to the nation if it did not see that the two were interconnected?

In February 1832 Lord Grey invited two of the bishops, Blomfield and J.B. Sumner, who were known to be progressive thinkers favouring the new ideas of Political Economy, to be members of a Royal Commission given the task of investigating the administration of the existing Poor Law and of making recommendations for a new Act. Blomfield chaired the meetings and Edwin Chadwick was the Commission's secretary. Nassau Senior, a former Professor of Political Economy at Oxford, was another influential member. After some investigation, the Commission claimed that the Poor Law was being administered inefficiently. They failed, however, to take into account the causes of poverty such as chronic unemployment and sub-standard wages. All four men were influenced by the opinions of T.R. Malthus (a friend of Blomfield's) and Jeremy Bentham, especially the latter who had argued that a national poor law policy should be imposed by central government on clearly thought-out, rational principles such as encouraging self-help and discouraging reliance on the rates. The Commission recommended that persons in receipt of relief should have a 'less eligible' (i.e. less desirable) life than that of the 'independent labourer of the lowest class.' The principle the Act would apply was 'to let the labourer find that the parish is the hardest taskmaster and paymaster he can find and thus induce him to make application to the parish his last and not his first recourse.' [*Poor Law Commission Report* 1834 p. 229] Speaking in the Lords on 24 July 1834 in support of the Poor Law Amendment Bill, Blomfield said he hoped that 'the people would soon be induced to exercise a foresight which would render relief unnecessary; and that the time would come when it would be thought, as once it was, disgraceful to receive relief, except in case of extreme urgency.' This was a view which old-fashioned Tory and Whig paternalists alike found simply disgraceful.

Blomfield's most fierce critic in the Lords was the Bishop of Exeter who launched a powerful attack on the bastardy clauses in the Bill on 28 July, and returned to the attack on two further days of debate. It was proposed to discourage bastardy by transferring complete responsibility for the illegitimate child from both parents to the woman alone and making it a condition of financial relief that she and her child entered the workhouse. To Phillpotts this was a denial of the Christian principle of mutual accountability. When challenged by Phillpotts to defend legislation which denied a divine principle, Blomfield ducked the issue saying that it 'was a question upon which he was unwilling to enter, because to solve it would involve an abstract discussion on speculative points'. Political pragmatism was his *forte*, not speculative theology. The Bill was passed by a majority of just eleven but with the support of most of the bishops. Phillpotts had lost the argument in the Lords but not in the country. Michael Fealey writes:

> In sum, the father escaped from accountability and the burden of the child dropped squarely on the mother. The popular outcry over the radical change in the illegitimacy clauses remained a constant source of agitation inside and outside Parliament – particularly with Phillpotts' relentless attacks – until the Legislature essentially repealed the bastardy clauses in 1844. [FEALEY *Of Bishops and Bastards* p.17]

In the past, the Poor Law had been administered at parish level. That was to change. Responsibility and power were to be transferred from the local to a central agency. The Commission recommended the new law should be administered by unions governed by elected bodies of guardians under the national supervision of three commissioners who were to bring the unions into being, organize the building of workhouses, prescribe the rules on which relief was to be given and to control the servants employed in them. The Act was designed to reduce the rates and save money – always a welcome prospect for the wealthy who paid them. In the first year of the Act's implementation, 2,066 parishes were incorporated into 112 unions, and boards of guardians elected; in the second year 5,800 parishes were grouped into 239 unions. [FINLAYSON *op. cit.* p. 59].

The old practice of giving financial relief outside the workhouse to the able-bodied or their families, while they were in full or part-time employment, however pitifully remunerated, was to cease. Families which went into workhouses were to be split up, and any surviving goods they had were to be sold for the benefit of the parish. Family life was, in effect, under threat. It was as though poverty was a crime and should be punished by incarceration in a workhouse little different from a prison – the poor called them *'Bastilles'*. The Act was bitterly opposed even before it was passed in 1834. In the late 30s, which were years of deep depression and widespread misery, it was violently attacked in the manufacturing towns of the North. The truth is that whilst some union workhouses were humanely run far too many were the very opposite. As always, conditions were determined by the men actually employed in them.

Between 1837 and 1842 *The Times* printed scores of articles each year giving lurid details of the suffering inflicted on poor people in the workhouses. The annual reports of the Commissioners, on the other hand, provided a very different picture, claiming that the diet provided was as nutritious and the living quarters as comfortable as those of the average labourer. At the very least they provided a safety net of basic relief. David Roberts has examined the evidence in his article *How cruel was the Victorian Poor Law?* The diet may have been monotonous and the living conditions cramped but they were as good as, and in some places better than, that of those living in overcrowded urban slum dwellings and in cellars which flooded with effluent. Some of the smaller workhouses were little better than the crowded, dirty, cold prisons of that time – no wonder they were called *bastilles* – but that is not what the Commissioners wanted. They 'had always urged large workhouses with separate wards, warm and clean, with schools and infirmaries, playgrounds and chapels, and everywhere order and cleanliness . . . But they still imposed that dull institutional life, irritating regimentation, depressing incarceration, and humiliating submission to authority, which, however warm the bed and nourishing the food, bring a cruel edge to one's life.' [ROBERTS *How cruel was the Victorian Poor Law?* p. 104]

Many of the parish clergy had been happily associated with the administration of poor relief locally under the old dispensation. Fewer wanted to be associated with the new one which seemed to be so harsh and punitive. Denison of Salisbury discouraged his clergy from getting involved in the working of the Act, noting that the new Poor Law did not bear with it 'the gracefulness of charity, or have the character of almsgiving of Christian men.' Other bishops, however, did support it, among them Copleston and Grey:

> The Bishop of Hereford is a most conscientious, single-hearted man, affectionate & grateful to his brother – but as firm as a rock in every thing relating to the Church. He agrees also with me in supporting the principle of the Poor Laws Amendment Bill. Not that I approve it *in toto* – but having long been convinced that the authority of magistrates is most pernicious, & that it has been the great source of the frightful evil the county labours under – a transfer of it from their hands to some other body I think absolutely necessary - & I don't know how, under the complicated circumstances of the diocese, it can be better done than is proposed by this Bill. If it does not work well, Parliament may apply a remedy. But almost anything is better than the present system, which year after year is eating farther into our vitals.
>
> [BROWN. ed. *op. cit.* p. 171]

If the presence of two bishops on the Commission was ever intended by the Government to be seen as some kind of guarantee that its proposals would be humane and in the best interests of the poor, it failed. The Act was one of the most hated pieces of legislation of the 19th century. *The Times* called it 'the most disgraceful measure that ever emanated from a Christian legislature.' The involvement of bishops in its creation could only be seen by the poor as yet one more sign of the Established Church's indifference to their plight. A restriction of another kind was also upheld in 1834. The Lords rejected a special clause in the Poor Law Amendment Act which would have allowed nonconformist ministers to act as Chaplains in workhouses. The Bishop of London claimed the clause was unnecessary.

When the Palace of Westminster was largely destroyed by fire on 16/17 October 1834, watched by tens of thousands of Londoners, many of their cries and remarks were reported in the press. One such was 'Tis a pity the bishops are not in it.' Many more saw the fire as a judgement on the new Poor Law – 'There's a fire for the Poor Law Bill' one person was heard to exclaim. [SHENTON *The Day Parliament burned down* p. 130]

The Whigs tackled another longstanding grievance in 1833. This one was felt by the majority of the population in Ireland who were Roman Catholic. The Protestant Church of Ireland which since the Union in 1800 had been formally part of the Established Church of England was the minority Church yet Catholics were required to support it financially. It had twenty-two bishoprics, 2,436 parishes (18% of which had no church) but only 850,000 members. The cost was about £150,000 for the bishops and a further £600,000 for the rest of the Church, and the income was mainly derived from tithes paid by Catholic peasants. There were far too many dioceses and parishes, and some radical pruning was needed which the Whigs set about doing but not without encountering a good deal of opposition along the way. It was consistently argued and feared that if the Church of Ireland's internal organisation and finances could be interfered with by the Government, then the same treatment was likely to be meted out to the Established Church in England. During 1833 English as well as Irish clergy petitioned against the Irish Church Temporalities Bill which had been introduced into Parliament, on 12 February of that year. In July John Keble denounced the Bill in his assize sermon at St Mary the Virgin, Oxford – for him it was 'an act of national apostasy.' One consequence of the Bill and of Keble's sermon was what became known as the Oxford Movement which would lead to spiritual renewal in the Church.

A particular issue in the Bill which attracted much opposition, even from some Whigs, was clause 147 which would have allowed the Government to appropriate a large sum of the Church's revenues and apply the money to non-Church purposes such as education. Van Mildert of Durham said that if the object of the scheme was to suppress Protestantism and promote Popery, no better means could have been adopted. But such views were countered by Blomfield of London who argued that the measure was all that stood between the Irish Church and 'immediate ruin.' To get the Bill through the Lords required concessions to be made by the Government, and in the end a much revised Bill was passed. Fifteen bishops including the Archbishop of Canterbury voted against it, and eleven for it including Archbishop Whately of Dublin, Archbishop Harcourt of York, Copleston, Ryder and the two Sumner brothers. With the passing of the Bill, two Irish archbishoprics and eight bishoprics were eliminated, as vacancies occurred. And church rates which many Catholics had resisted paying for years were abolished, and a graduated tax on all clerical revenues introduced in its place.

The idea of such a tax had appeared in a plan for church reform in England produced by Edward Burton in 1832 and then incorporated by Lord Henley in his own reform proposals. The all-important battle as to the right of the State to appropriate ecclesiastical revenues for other than religious purposes in Ireland foreshadowed similar demands from Radicals in England about the Established Church. Likewise the establishment of an Ecclesiastical Commission with managerial as well as distributive powers in Ireland was a precedent for what would happen later in that decade in England.

The bishops returned to the defence of the Protestant Church in Ireland two years later when the Government, in the hope of pacifying the Roman Catholic majority in Ireland, introduced the Irish Church Bill. If passed, it would have resulted in the demise of some eight hundred benefices where less than fifty Protestants resided and the removal of the clergy from those places. Blomfield, who had supported the 1833 Bill, spoke powerfully in the Lords against it, arguing that 'in order to quiet the Roman Catholics, it will exterminate the Protestants . . .' [BLOMFIELD *Speech on the Irish Church Bill* p. 7] For him this was 'a measure, of which it is not too much to say, that it commences with spoliation and sacrilege and must end in ruin and confusion.' [*Ibid*. p. 30]

In March 1833 the Dissenting deputies in London resolved to form a United Committee 'to consider the grievances under which Dissenters now labour, with a view to their Redress.' A list of six was drawn up which they wanted the Government to deal with before any measures of Church reform. These were the compulsory use of the Anglican marriage ceremony, Church rates, the liability of Dissenting chapels to the poor rate, the absence of legal registration for births and deaths, the denial of burial rights in parochial churchyards, and their exclusion from the universities. Of these, the first three were declared to be the most pressing and important but it was the sixth which the Government tackled first.

A new attempt was made in 1834 to allow Dissenters to take degrees at Oxford and Cambridge. A flood of pamphlets appeared arguing the case for and against this proposed reform. The Bill passed the Commons but was rejected in the Lords by 187:85. Phillpotts argued in the Lords that to open the universities to dissenters was to 'persecute' the Church! Twenty-two bishops voted for the rejection, just two in its favour. A similar Bill was introduced the following year, which would have made subscription to the *39 Articles of Religion* no longer necessary at the Universities, and it met with the same fate; nineteen bishops voted against the

Bill, two were in favour, and it fell by 106:57 votes. Oxbridge would remain an Anglican academic preserve for a further thirty-six years.

Anti-Church feeling on the part of the Radicals and many Dissenters remained high. In May 1834, Edward Baines, the MP for Leeds, presided at a conference of 400 Dissenters which called for an end to the union of Church and State. That was exactly what many Churchmen feared might happen under a reformed House of Commons which included men like Baines. Earlier that year, Copleston had written to Bruce Knight:

> Let us be united, and resolute – and then if the storm should prove too much for us, we shall at least have the satisfaction of having done our utmost in the hour of peril. The peril is great & appalling – not from the opinions of the upper classes – but from the dreadful ascendancy which the Reform Bill has given to the mob. Three-fourths of the members returned on that interest dare not vote according to their own judgment.
> [BROWN ed. *op. cit.* p. 151]

Copleston claimed that he had never believed Lord Grey had any notion of altering the constitution of the Church or meddling in its Liturgy or Articles or polity – his reforming concerns were directed to such matters as tithes and pluralities and possibly cathedral endowments.

Peel came to power in November 1834 when the King dismissed Melbourne's government, partly because he did not approve of Sir John Russell becoming their new leader in the Commons. Peel was a sound Churchman who, like the Whigs, wished the Church to carry out its own reform rather than having unwelcome measures forced on them by the Government. He wrote to Church leaders seeking their co-operation. To Phillpotts of Exeter, for example, he wrote on 22 December, 'all mere political considerations . . . are as nothing in my mind, compared with the great objects of giving real stability to the Church in its spiritual character.' [quoted in MACHIN *Politics and the Churches* p. 48] He was indicating that the bishops had nothing to fear from him if they put their house in order and they could look to him for support if they did.

Whilst he was in power for only a few months, he did make one far-reaching decision following a meeting he had with the Archbishop of Canterbury and Bishop Blomfield on 4 January 1835. He wrote to the King next day and the result was that a new Royal Commission was appointed with the task of carrying out reforms in the Church of England.

> By the terms of its appointment, the Commissioners were 'to consider the state of the several dioceses in England and Wales, with reference to the

amount of their revenues and the more equal distribution of episcopal duties, and the prevention of the necessity of attaching by commendam to bishoprics benefices with cure of souls; also, the state of the several cathedral and collegiate churches in England and Wales, with a view to the suggestion of such measures as may render them conducive to the efficiency of the Established Church; and to devise the best mode of providing for the cure of souls, with special reference to the residence of the clergy on their respective benefices'. [BIBER *op. cit.* p. 157f]

It was axiomatic that the proposals for reform should come from a commission of responsible churchmen and not from the government. What happened subsequently is dealt with in the next chapter.

Peel also decided to tackle the controversial issue of the marriage of dissenters. On 7 January he wrote to Hobhouse at the Home Office setting out concisely what he required:

Retain the laws as to marriage, and the registration of marriage as they now stand without alteration for members of the Church of England.
For all who do object, not being members of the Church, require a civil ceremony, superadded to any religious rite which the Dissenting party may choose to adopt.
Encourage the religious rite, but do not make the performance of it essential to the validity of the marriage contract. Make the civil ceremony absolutely essential.
Let the civil ceremony be of the simplest kind – an acknowledgement before a magistrate by each party in the presence of witnesses, according to a form supplied by authority.
The difficulties in the way are difficulties of detail. [HURD *Robert Peel* p. 181]

Peel's administration was too short lived to allow this legislation, and it was left to Melbourne to deal with it finally and to face the opposition of some of the bishops.

With the return to power of the Whigs after just six months of Conservative rule, the Established Church suffered indirectly by the passing of the Municipal Reform Act in 1835. Hitherto many corporations had been self-perpetuating Tory (and Anglican) local oligarchies and usually with the Vicar/Rector of the town's civic church serving as the Chaplain. Now, the new town councils became directly elected by all householders of three years standing in the borough. Councils were to be elected for three years only with one third of the membership retiring annually. There was no property requirement made of those standing for election. This allowed for the active engagement of politically conscious upper working class men and lower middle class shopkeepers and artisans, many of whom were religious Dissenters. The result was that the political and denominational colours of many of these bodies changed radically. Here was the real political reform of the 1830s, yet the Whig Prime Minister at the time, Lord Melbourne, was not particularly concerned to see it passed. When the Bill was thrown out in the Lords at the first attempt, he commented, 'What does it matter? We have got on tolerably well with the councils for five hundred years. We may contrive to go on with them for another few years or so.' [CECIL *op. cit.* p. 130]

The Bishop of Hereford, the Hon. Edward Grey, tried to make his mark on a small piece of legislation in June 1835. He failed. On the third reading of the Newcastle-upon-Tyne Railway Bill, the Bishop moved an amendment which would have prohibited operation of the railway on Sundays. The House rejected it, 40:19. Lord Holland described it as 'a foolish attempt' but one which was supported by all the bishops present, of whom Maltby was not one, he noted. The fact is that bishops were divided on Sabbatarianism – Blomfield, for example, was hot on it, Copleston opposed it.

The Church of England's monopoly on officiating at baptisms, weddings and funerals, was finally broken in 1836 by the passing of the Bill which allowed marriages to be conducted in the offices of the newly established Registrars of Births, Marriages and Deaths. Parish clergy and the bishops were outspoken in their opposition to civil registrars effectively replacing them as the officiants and recorders of these three key life-events. A particular fear was that fewer babies would be brought to baptism. The 'Act for Registering Births, Deaths and Marriages in England' and its sister Act, the 1836 'Marriage Act', were the culmination of a long series of failed measures considered by parliament over the two previous decades. The first of these two Acts is particularly significant in that it marks the foundation of the modern era in vital statistics in England and Wales. By it the General Registry Office was created. [See CULLEN *The Making of the Civil Registration Act of 1836* in the *Journal of Ecclesiastical History* Vol. 25 pp. 39-59] It also remedied one of the major grievances of Dissenters by providing a civil, not ecclesiastical, registration of births, deaths and marriages. An Act of 1754 had required that, apart from those of Jews and Quakers, marriages could be recognized only if they took place under the auspices of the Church of England. By this Act one more bastion of the Establishment had been breached.

Whilst the Dissenting Marriages Act allowed nonconformist chapels to be used for the solemnization of marriages, it seems there was no great rush to take advantage of this, at least not in the country's largest rural diocese. Ambler records that 'only 33 chapels had been licensed in Lincolnshire by 1842. Civil marriage was possible from 1837, but only 3 per cent of marriages in the county were performed by this form of ceremony in 1850'. [AMBLER ed. *Lincolnshire Parish Correspondence of John Kaye* p. lix]

By now, feeling against the Church was subsiding and when Cuthbert Rippon moved a resolution in the Commons on 25 April 1836: 'That the attendance of bishops in Parliament is prejudicial to the cause of religion' Lord Russell coldly observed that he was sure that neither House nor the country would be prepared to entertain such a proposition, and it was rejected by 180 to 53. [TURBEVILLE *House of Lords in the Age of Reform* p. 317] A year later Charles Lushington, who thought bishops should spend their time and energies in their dioceses, brought forward a motion in favour of excluding the bishops from the House of Lords. It was defeated 197 to 92. Once again no support was given to the proposal by the Government. In Turbeville's judgement – 'To turn the bishops out of the House of Lords in 1836 might have proved a much more difficult task than to pass the Reform Bill in 1832.' [*Ibid*. p. 318]

The Government did, however, try in 1837 to secure one of the Dissenters' most desired objects: the abolition of Church rates. This was a form of national taxation in the interests of the Established Church which was spent largely, but not exclusively, on repairing the fabric of parish churches. Their proposal was to get the Ecclesiastical Commission to use £250,000 a year of money saved from the revenues of the bishops, deans and chapters on the repair of church fabric. The Commission had already considered this possibility and rejected it – the money was needed to augment poor livings. This attempt to conciliate Dissent provoked what the *Westminster Review* described as 'an outbreak of Episcopal fury unparalleled in the modern annals of Ecclesiastical turbulence.' Fifteen bishops meeting at Lambeth on 9 March, six days after the Government's plan was outlined in the Commons, declared unanimously against the Bill, and the same evening there was an angry clash between the Primate and Lord Melbourne on the issue in the Lords. 'What killed the measure, however, was the Anglican sympathies of the Whig gentry in the House of Commons.' [GASH *Reaction and Reconstruction in English Politics 1832-1852* p. 72] The Bill was dropped on the death of the King, and the premature end to the parliamentary session. It was a notable victory for the Church but a bitter disappointment to the Dissenters.

Lord Holland included in his diary some caustic reflections on how the Bill came to be defeated by the countrywide opposition of Churchmen:

> It had been from a punctilious feeling of propriety incautiously communicated to the Bishops composing the Commission for Church Reform, and those timid but artful Priests had expressed their doubts, apprehensions, and disapprobation, prevailed on most of their Colleagues on the Commission to postpone if not abandon it, and at the same time prepared the body of the High Church Clergy and party to take measures for resisting it with effect. The moment it was signified to the Archbishop that such a measure would be resorted to, cabals, consultations, and correspondences were instituted to counteract it, and little doubt can be entertained that the conservative party were apprized by their Clerical adherents or guides that the ensuing question of the Church rates would serve their turn almost as well as the appropriation Clause, and that they would lay the train and blow the flames in a way that would rouse the Country and perhaps the House of Commons itself against us. With this view innumerable petitions from the most remote rural parishes were procured by Archdeacons, Rural Deans, and other clerical vermin that infest the country, and it was evident from the language they contained and the comments with which they were delivered that the grossest arts of delusion had been practised to misrepresent the measure as one adopted and intended for the demolition of parish Churches and the elevation of dissenters at the expence (*sic*) of all Churchmen, lay and ecclesiastical. [KRIEGEL ed. *op. cit.* p. 358]

More Church-State confrontation took place in 1839 when the government introduced a measure which would have changed the way in which their annual subsidy of £20,000 [= £1,853,211] for education was allocated. Previously it had been divided between the National Society which supported schools attached to the Church of England and the British and Foreign Society which was largely a Dissenter-supported body and the subsidy was divided in proportion to the voluntary subscriptions each raised. This had favoured the former in a roughly 70:30 percent division. Under the new proposals the annual subsidy would be raised to £30,000 which could be allocated, according to need, to any body providing education. That could include Catholics and Atheists. And subsidies would only be granted subject to certain conditions which included allowing inspection by a new government inspectorate subject to a new committee of the Privy Council, in effect a Board of Education, on which no clerics could sit. It was also proposed to found a 'normal school', i.e. a college for training teachers. One of the functions of the proposed inspectorate would be to inform schoolmasters of educational innovations and improvements in the art of teaching, something which was unquestionably much needed.

Russell in his introductory speech in Parliament expressed the hope 'that the most simple rules of religion and habits of morality might be taught to children, without raising those great points of theoretical difference by which the country had been so long agitated.' Religion was to be combined 'with the whole matter of instruction and to regulate the entire system of discipline.' He was seeking to show that he was not a secularist and not an enemy of Christianity. Nonetheless, fierce resistance was expressed by Churchmen of different shades, from the Evangelical Lord Ashley (later 7th Earl of Shaftesbury) to the High Church Bishop Phillpotts. The veteran ultra-Tory Lord Winchilsea thought it was the most dangerous attack on Protestantism since the 1829 Relief Act. Blomfield described it in the Lords as 'the heaviest blow' yet struck against the Church of England. Both Howley and he recommended their clergy to refuse Government grants until the plan of inspectors unsanctioned by the bishops was given up.

The Government's plan came at a time when the Church had been doing much to improve its involvement in education thanks in part to a distinguished group of young Conservatives, including Lord Sandon, Sir Thomas Acland and Gladstone, who had pressed on Church leaders a scheme of diocesan education, the need for teacher training colleges and the creation of secondary schools for the sons of middle class parents, and all of it to be done in conjunction with the National Society. Their initiative produced results: in 1838-9 twenty-four diocesan or sub-diocesan boards of education were founded, more new schools were being opened and old ones improved, and the first Church college for training teachers was founded in Chester in 1839 – by 1845 there were twenty-four more. Acland and his friends stage-managed a great public meeting of the National Society in May 1839 presided over by the Archbishop of Canterbury with many of the bishops in attendance. The meeting passed a resolution, moved by the Earl of Chichester and seconded by Bishop Blomfield, that 'it is an object of the highest national importance to provide that instruction in the truths and precepts of Christianity should form an essential part of every system of education intended for the people at large, and that such instruction should be under the superintendence of the clergy and in conformity with the doctrines of the Church of this realm as the recognised teacher of religion.' [quoted in the printed edition of Blomfield's Speech] In his speech, Blomfield set out the claims of the Established Church to be the educational agency of the nation. 'Though we do not assert an empire over the consciences of those who are not within the pale of her communion, nor pressure to interfere with them in the education of their own children,' he declared, 'we say that the Church is the authorized and recognized organ and instrument of National Education in the largest sense in this country.' [BLOMFIELD *Speech on National Education* p. 10]

It was an issue that figured in episcopal *Charges*, among them that of Edward Stanley, the Whig Bishop of Norwich, who had been very active educationally as a parish priest. He advanced the claims of the Church on the grounds of social utility – 'Christian education alone deserves the name of education; it is through Christian knowledge only that we can hope to see the social and political condition of our countrymen purified and perfected.' [STANLEY *Charge* 1838 p. 19]

The parliamentary battle commenced that summer. In the House of Lords an address to the Crown, containing a series of resolutions against the scheme, was carried on the motion of the Archbishop of Canterbury by a massive majority. The controversy raged all year and ended with the Government capitulating and agreeing to many of the Church's demands.

> On 15 July 1840 it was agreed that inspectors of National Society schools were to send reports to the bishop of the diocese and the archbishop of the province as well as to the Education Committee of the Council; and that the archbishop would have power to veto the appointment of these inspectors, and to remove them from office. The old method was revived of allocating grants in proportion to private contributions, a system which favoured the Church. Roman Catholic schools made no applications for grants, so their admission to the scheme was purely academic. [MACHIN *op. cit.* p 68]

Harmony between the Whig Government and the Church was restored on that front but it had all left bitter feelings among the Church's conservative supporters. Wellington advised his local bishop, C.R. Sumner of Winchester, to refuse to allow his schools to be inspected or to accept any further government financial aid which might thereby justify state interference. He wrote to Sumner, 'As an individual I must decline to take part in any meeting which might have for its objective to raise subscriptions for establishing schools; unless on the condition that such Diocesan Associations shall engage that they will not receive aid from the fund at the disposal of the Privy Council.' [G.H. SUMNER *op. cit.* p. 267] When the National Society did accept further government funding, one of its founding fathers, Joshua Watson resigned as Treasurer. Gash comments on this confrontation between Church and State: 'What is striking about the

1839 episode is the strength and self-confidence of the Anglican Church in contrast to its weakness and self-consciousness in 1832. Between the Reform Act and the accession of Victoria the position and morale of the Church had in fact been revolutionized.' [GASH *op. cit.* p. 80]

1840 saw the passing of the Ecclesiastical Duties and Revenues Act (also commonly called the Cathedrals Act) which effected the most radical shake up in centuries of cathedral revenues and staffing, but consideration of that belongs to the next chapter.

Church Reform

Major reforms took place in the 1830s but the need for them had been publicised half a century earlier by Richard Watson, Bishop of Llandaff. He had sought the support of the Archbishop of Canterbury and the Prime Minister but without success. In a *Letter to the Archbishop of Canterbury* (1782) he called for such reforms as the equalization of episcopal incomes and the appropriation of cathedral chapter monies for the relief of impoverished clergy. In his *Memoirs*, Watson tells how he sent a copy of the letter to all of the bishops 'and of them all the Bishop of Chester alone (Porteus) had the good manners so much as to acknowledge the receipt of it. I had foreseen this timidity of the bench, and I had foreseen also that he must be a great-minded minister indeed, who would bring forward a measure depriving him of his parliamentary influence over the spiritual lords: but I believed that what was right would take place at last, and I thought that by publishing the plan it would stand a chance of being thoroughly discussed.' [WATSON *Anecdotes of the Life of Richard Watson* p. 107] Lord Shelburne discouraged him from publishing the letter on the grounds 'it was not the time.'

As Arthur Burns notes, that letter 'could almost be called the founding document of the modern church-reform tradition . . . Watson insisted that his letter was not prompted by 'a silly vanity of being considered a Reformer; a character which in all ages has met with as much detraction as praise', and at its conclusion he resigned himself to bear any censure resulting from becoming, 'as some will scoffingly phrase it, a Reformer.' [BURNS & INNES ed. *Rethinking the Age of Reform* p.145]

In the decades following the publication of Watson's *Letter* there were a number of church-reform initiatives aimed at making the Church more effective in pastoral terms and less vulnerable to hostile criticism. Pitt's abortive 'Ecclesiastical Plan' of 1800 was one such. It envisaged augmenting clerical incomes to a minimum of £70 for curates and overhauling the system of monitoring and disciplining the residence of clergy but it was not supported by the bishops. Watson wrote to Pitt about his plan and put forward his own suggestions:

> As, however, there are many benefices utterly inadequate to affording even a bare maintenance to an *unmarried* clergyman, a law abolishing *in futuro* all pluralities ought to be accompanied with another making a decent provision for every resident minister. An hundred pounds a-year ought to be the very least stipend annexed to any benefice, and, such sum being annexed service

twice every Sunday should be required in all. Benefices above an hundred a-year should remain, I think, as they are; unless it should be judged expedient, on a vacancy, to take the first fruits on real valuation, constituting thereby a fund towards augmenting benefices under an hundred to that sum.

Houses of residence for the clergy should be bought or built at the public expense, or by the Governors of Queen Anne's Bounty, for livings under an hundred pounds a year.

The number of livings under an hundred a-year, their respective values, and the state of their parsonage-houses, should be accurately ascertained, and laid before parliament, in order that the additional public burden attending the giving a decent maintenance to the clergy might be known: it would, I am persuaded, whatever the magnitude might be, meet with no opposition from the judicious part of the community. The bishops would be able to make, if required, this return to parliament by means of their officers.

[WATSON *op. cit.* p. 351f]

Nothing came of Pitt's plan or Watson's proposals but they show this was a live issue long before the 'age of reform' and Watson's thinking presaged what would happen. By 1830, the Church was under such scrutiny and criticism that the bishops knew they had to put their house in order, though some chose to disregard the fact.

Archbishop Howley had been in conversation about church reforms with Wellington in 1830 before the latter resigned. Blomfield was even more keen than the Archbishop on reform. Lord Holland noted in his diary on 29 July 1831, 'I missed the House of Lords, where Bishop Blomfield spoke so earnestly in favour of thorough enquiry and fearless reform in ecclesiastical matters, that the Archbishop, after writhing some time, exclaimed loud enough for his brother of London to hear, "These things should not be said without consultation." [KRIEGEL ed. *op. cit.* p.19f] Howley tried to get three modest measures through Parliament in 1831 to tackle the problems of pluralism and non-residence but only one on augmentation of poor livings succeeded. Then the crisis of parliamentary reform intervened.

John Wade's *Extraordinary Black Book* which was published in 1831 exposed much that was rotten in the Establishment. The first 137 pages dealt with the Church of England. The book had originally appeared as a series of articles and was then published as *The Black Book* in 1820. It proved to be a best-seller despite the very many inaccuracies in the early editions about the wealth of the Church, which, to be fair to Wade, he sought to correct in the following years but not always with success.

Wade's was the most comprehensive and detailed attack on the abuses and evils prevalent in Church and State, and it can reasonably be reckoned to have been one of the direct causes for the reforms which followed. There was also a flood of shorter pamphlets written between 1831 and 1833. R.M. Beverley's *Letter to the Archbishop of York on the Present Corrupt State of the Church of England* which appeared in 1831 sold 30,000 copies and went through fourteen editions. Beverley was a former Anglican who had become a Congregationalist. The thrust of his attack was the Established nature of the Church – any Christian body which had the backing of the State and was dependent on the State and receiving State funding (as in the case of the two Parliamentary grants for building churches) would be corrupted. This one sentence from the 4th edition gives the tone of his pamphlet, 'England is thoroughly sick of the Church Establishment, and your Grace's diocese perhaps reckons more persons who feel this nausea, than any other in England.'

He was particularly incensed by the patronage system which had produced such a poor bench of bishops. He claimed that, with one or two exceptions, they had obtained preferment only by flattering the great and making themselves useful to the Government – the latter charge was hardly the case when they voted on the Reform Bill later that year! He attacked too their abuse of the patronage they acquired once they had set foot on the episcopal ladder – it was reserved, he wrote, for the benefit of family and personal friends. It is a virulent attack on the current bench of bishops – 'the majority of the Bishops of the Church of England *always* are persons whose main object is to amass wealth, and to aggrandize their families.' He caricatures the worst of the bishops and regards all as being as bad as them:

> But what are the labours, watchings, fastings, perils and difficulties of our Baron-Bishops? These holy men, perhaps, pass many a sleepless night in the first stage of their exaltation, to discover by whatever possible means they may escape the persecution of Llandaff or Bristol, or some other poor see with which they find themselves disagreeably saddled . . . By dint of voting and jobbing in the House of Lords, the successor of the Apostles finds his prospects brighter a little, for, after infinite exertions of soul and body, he is translated to Exeter, peradventure whereby his apostolical pocket is replenished with a greater number of orthodox guineas. But not in Exeter is the godly man at ease . . . In the course of time, Winchester or Durham is vacant – then do all the eagles gather at the carcase; loud are the screams of the apostolical vultures, and sad the dismay of the First Lord of the Treasury, to know how to satisfy so much pious voracity . . . [BEVERLEY *A Letter* p. 11]

It is a caricature but one with a touch of reality about it which may explain why his pamphlets sold so well.

The most glaring example of episcopal greed was Dr Sparke of Ely, one of the few prelates who had voted neither for nor against the Reform Bill. He had liberally endowed his two sons and a son-in-law with the good things in his gift. Wade estimated their joint annual income at £39,942 [= £4,074,890 in 2014]. Wade listed in great detail the many appointments he had made to just these three close family members between 1815 and 1831, excluding others made to more distant relatives and friends:

1815   The Rev. John Henry Sparke, the eldest son, took his BA degree; he was then about 21; he was immediately appointed by his father to a bishop's fellowship in Jesus College Cambridge.
1816   He was appointed steward of all his father's manorial courts.
1818   He took his degree of MA, and was presented to a prebendal stall in Ely Cathedral, on the resignation of the Rev. Archdeacon Brown, who had been holding it one year: he was also appointed to the sinecure rectory of Littlebury, and in the following month he was presented to the living of Streatham-cum-Thetford, by an exchange with the Rev.Mr Law for the living of Downham, which last living had been held for three years by the Rev. Mr Daubenny, the bishop's nephew, who now resigned it in favour of Mr Law, and retired to the living of Bexwell.
1819   The Rev. J.H. Sparke had a dispensation granted him from the Archbishop of Canterbury, permitting him to hold the living of Cottenham with his other preferments.
1818   The Rev. Henry Fardell, the bishop's son-in-law, was ordained deacon.
1819   He was presented to a prebendal stall in Ely, the degree of MA having been conferred on him by the Archbishop of Canterbury.
1821   He was presented to the living of Tyd St Giles.
1822   He was presented to the living of Waterbeach, on the resignation of the Rev. Mr Mitchell.
1823   He resigned Tyd St Giles, and was presented to Bexwell, on the resignation of the Rev. Mr Daubenny, the bishop's nephew, who was presented to Feltwell; but in a few weeks when the value of Feltwell was better understood, Mr Daubenny was required to resign Feltwell and return to Bexwell. This, it is said, he did with great reluctance; he was, however, presented to Tyd as well as Bexwell, and the Rev. Mr Fardell was then presented to Feltwell.
1824   The Rev. J. Henry Sparke was appointed Chancellor of the diocese, and this year he resigned the prebendal stall he held, and was presented to the one which became vacant by the death of the Rev. Sir H Bate Dudley; the

house and the gardens belonging to the latter stall being considered the best in the College.

1826 The Rev. Edward Sparke, the bishop's youngest son, took his degree of BA, and was immediately presented by his father to a bishop's fellowship in St John's College Cambridge, on the resignation of Charles Jenyns, Esq. a friend of the family, who had been holding it for three years. He was also appointed register (*sic*) of the diocese.

1827 The Rev. J. Henry Sparke resigned the livings of Cottenham and Streatham, and was presented to the rich living of Leverington.

1828 The Rev. J. Henry Sparke was presented to the living of Bexwell.

1829 The Rev. Edward Sparke took his degree of MA and was presented to a prebendal stall on the resignation of Rev. Ben Park (another friend of the family) who had been holding it three years. He was also this year presented to the living of Hogeworthingham, and to the living of Barley.

1830 He resigned Hogeworthingham and was presented to Connington. This year he resigned Barley also, and was presented to Littleport.

1831 He resigned Connington and was presented to Feltwell, at the same time he resigned his prebendal stall, and was presented to the one become vacant by the death of the Rev. George King – the rich living of Sutton being in the gift of the possessor of the latter stall.

1831 The Rev. Henry Fardell resigned Feltwell, and was presented to the rich living of Wisbech.

The Rev. J. Henry Sparke now holds the living of Leverington, the sinecure rectory of Littlebury, the living of Bexwell, a prebendal stall in Ely Cathedral, is steward of all his father's manorial courts, and Chancellor of the diocese. The estimated value of the whole, £4,500. [= £407,353]

The Rev. Henry Fardell now holds the living of Waterbeach, the vicarage of Wisbech, and a prebendal stall in Ely Cathedral. The estimated annual value of his preferments, £3,700. [= £334,935]

The Rev. Edward Sparke holds the consolidated livings of St Mary and St Nicholas Feltwell, the vicarage of Littleport, a prebendal stall in Ely, is Register of the diocese, and Examining Chaplain to his father. The estimated annual value of his appointments not less than £4,000. [= £362,092]

The bishop's see of Ely and dependencies £27,742. [= £2,511,287]

Total income of the Sparke family, £39,942. [= £3,615,667]

[WADE p. 25f]

Wade seems to have seriously overestimated the revenue of the see itself but not of what the Bishop's family members earned from his patronage. He rightly claimed, however, that 'Bishop Sparke is not the only prelate who has shown regard to the temporal welfare of his family' and duly provided ample evidence of its truth. And it was all being done with the connivance of the Archbishop of Canterbury who behaved no better himself. Le Marchant recorded in his diary in February 1833 a conversation he had had with Bishop Maltby on this very issue,

> Maltby, the Bishop of Chichester, told me that Bishop Murray [of Rochester] had boldly avowed to him that there were no abuses in the Church. "What do you say," says Maltby, "to the Bishop of Ely [Sparke] giving five large pieces of preferment to one of his sons?" – "That is no abuse, it is not contrary to the law."' Le Marchant had a high regard for Maltby but he regarded Murray as a 'High Church bigot . . . opposed to all reform.'
> [ASPINALL ed. *op. cit.* p. 303]

An irregular practice which several bishops were party to because of the inadequate endowment of the diocese was that of holding additional posts *in commendam*. The Commission of Enquiry set up in 1832, which reported two years later, provided details of this undesirable practice. The disparity in the value of stipends also meant that men appointed to the poorest sees were quickly looking for translation to richer ones, thereby depriving the poorer dioceses of any continuity in episcopal oversight and care. Christopher Bethel, for example, was Bishop of Gloucester worth £2,282 [= £194,282] at the beginning of 1830 and Bishop of Bangor worth £4,464 [= £379,972] by the end of the year but had also been Bishop of Exeter worth £2,713 [= £230,929] for a few months in between the two! There were some noble exceptions to this such as the pious, hardworking Evangelical John Bird Sumner who stayed at Chester, one of the largest and most onerous dioceses in the country, for twenty years. His 'reward' came when he was translated to Canterbury in 1848.

In addition to the evils of pluralist and non-resident incumbents and the poverty of most curates who did the work in their absence and the inequitable distribution of funds even at the highest level, Dissenters too made justifiable complaints against the Established Church. They were required to pay rates for the upkeep of the parish churches and chapels of an institution to which they did not belong. And they were still being required to submit to using the religious rites of baptism, marriage and burial of that institution when they wished to avail themselves of the ministry of their own denominations and use their own buildings. And they were excluded from taking degrees at Oxford and Cambridge though not from the universities in Scotland, and after 1828 they were able to study at the newly founded University College of London. Both the College and the University, as a separate institution, were eventually granted charters, and students could be awarded degrees irrespective of their religious allegiance but this right was won despite opposition from the bishops in the House of Lords.

Lord John Russell tried to make a start on alleviating another of the complaints of Dissenters by introducing the Dissenters' Marriage Bill on 25 February 1834 but his particular set of proposals did not find support among those it was intended to help, and the Bill was abandoned. There were also plans for a Church Rates Bill and a Bill for the commutation of tithes, but both were withdrawn for the time being. The issue of reforming the Poor Law took precedence. Peel too in his short-lived time as Prime Minister in 1835 introduced a Dissenters' Marriage Bill but again without success.

The Whigs had some ideas for Church reform from an early stage which included creating new sees to take account of population changes, redistributing the wealth of the Church by reducing the income of the richest bishoprics to the benefit of the poorest parishes but the Archbishop of Canterbury indicated that the Church would immediately begin to put its own house in order. So, with the support of Lord Grey, he introduced three Bills in to the Lords on 24 June 1831, the Augmentation Bill, the Pluralities Bill and the Tithe Composition Bill but they proved to be too little too late. Only the first of the three, which made augmentation of livings by ecclesiastical bodies easier, was passed in both Houses. Lord Holland records in his diary on several occasions the opposition that the Archbishop encountered in debates in the Lords on the Pluralities Bill – this entry is dated Friday 23 March 1832:

> In the house there was a long debate on the Archbishop's plurality bill. It is liable to all the objections which half measures of reform are sure to meet with. It does too much or too little. It admits the existence of abuse and it does not remedy it. It must be allowed the Bishops are placed in this particular in rather a hard situation. They have been badgered for years for not doing something, and when they bring forward their plan they are attacked by one party for abandoning the interests of the Church and by the other for deluding the public by the semblance of reform while they in fact perpetuate and even aggravate the abuses of it. They do not deserve much compassion just now, for their political conduct is at once irresolute and factious.
>
> [KRIEGEL ed. *op. cit.* p. 159]

It was, indeed, exceedingly modest in scope, and would have limited pluralities by vesting discretionary power in the Archbishop of Canterbury to revoke dispensations to hold them. It never reached a second reading in the Commons. Another entry dated 2 April shows Grey trying to be supportive of the Archbishop's modest efforts at reform:

> In the Lords Lord Suffield made a tiresome and Lord King somewhat unfair attack upon the Archbishop's bill against pluralities. It is a weak and unsatisfactory measure but, as Lord Grey observed, a bill which endeavours to correct an obnoxious abuse with which the Church has been often reproached, originating with the Bishops, deserves to be treated with some little indulgence and may, even by those who are not satisfied with it, be hailed as the harbinger of further and effectual reforms. The Bishops seemed pleased with Lord Grey's temperate and gallant defence of them, but will one of them give him a vote for the reform bill more readily? [*Ibid*. p. 166]

Towards the end of 1832 Grey asked the Archbishop to call a meeting of the bishops in order to obtain their opinion on certain questions of ecclesiastical reform which were then before the cabinet. Blomfield set out his views in a letter he sent to the Primate on 11 December:

> I have long been convinced of, and have for some time been urging, the necessity of a mixed Commission of clergymen and laymen to consider what measures should be adopted in the way of Church reform, whether as to the establishment of a consistent scheme of discipline or the arrangement of ecclesiastical property. Whether this Commission should be permanent and be invested with the power of initiating all legislative measures affecting the Church in its spiritual character or in its secular provisions, or in both, I am not quite prepared to say. [quoted in MATHIESON *op. cit.* p. 171]

Blomfield was, in effect, predicting Peel's Commission of Enquiry of 1835 and its conversion a year later by Parliament into the Ecclesiastical Commission. The meeting of bishops convened by Howley met in December and according to Phillpotts, who was present, the chief topic of discussion was the future of cathedral bodies. He said that Blomfield and two other bishops were 'disposed to go far in breaking in upon them,' but that the great majority were in favour of upholding 'all the institutions of the Church in their full integrity.' That majority was to be disappointed and Blomfield's view would prevail.

Le Marchant's diary entry for February 1833 throws some light on the politico-episcopal negotiations going on at this time:

> I was employed about this time by the Chancellor [Brougham] in preparing the English Church Reform, a topic that frequently engaged the attention of the Cabinet. The Chancellor had several meetings on the subject with the

Archbishop of Canterbury and he found him by no means obstinate in his opposition, though they could not agree in their plans of amendment. The fact is that the Archbishop is a very timid man, and preferred a partial, vague, qualified assent to the Chancellor's measures to a candid expression of his disapprobation of them. At home he was less reserved and Bishop Maltby told me that in the conferences at Lambeth he would hear of no reform, and upon Bishop Blomfield urging its necessity, he withdrew his confidence from him. This week Maltby tells me he has announced an entire change of opinion. Maltby ascribes it to the death of his son.

[ASPINALL ed. *op. cit.* p. 302]

Peter Virgin in his magisterial study *The Church in an Age of Negligence* has identified fifty-one contributions to the church reform debate, excluding episcopal *Charges* and sermons, published in 1832-3, and a further eleven between 1834 and 1836. Of these many pamphlets Lord Henley's *A Plan of Church Reform*, published in the early summer 1832, was the one which attracted most attention and was frequently reprinted. Henley was Peel's brother-in-law and a Master in Chancery. He regarded plurality as 'the most prominent evil in the Church' and proposed prohibiting it with few exceptions. He wanted all sinecure posts in the Church to be abolished and the problem of poorly endowed parochial cures to be addressed. He also suggested redrawing the boundaries of dioceses and a levelling of episcopal incomes at £5,000 with the exceptions of the two Archbishops, and the Bishops of London, Durham and Winchester, and the creation of two new sees at Windsor and Southwell. Bishops should be excluded from Parliament ('be relieved of their duties in the House of Lords' as he put it euphemistically) but by way of compensation the Church Convocations should be revived. He wanted much of the Church's revenues to be transferred to 'Commissioners for the management of Ecclesiastical Property.' He also highlighted another widespread problem: 4,809 livings did not have habitable houses for the incumbent, and some livings were worth as little as £12 a year. Henley's thinking was clearly noted by the Ecclesiastical Commission when it came to making its proposals later. In a second publication in which he welcomed some of Dr Edward Burton's suggestions, Henley argued that if cathedral staffs were reduced to just a dean and two assistants, the savings made could fund the endowment of eight new bishoprics.

> If the vast livings, with a cure of 20,000, 30,000 or 50,000 souls, are consigned to one Rector with a sufficient assistance of curates, surely the superintendence of the services of a cathedral, which include no such pastoral

duties, may without scruple be entrusted to one superior minister with the assistance of two chaplains.

[HENLEY *Union of Dr Burton's & Lord Henley's Plans* p. 14]

In some places, he considered it possible that the bishop himself could be the principal officiating minister in his own cathedral.

Henley returned to the matter of bishops in his 1834 pamphlet *A Plan for a new arrangement and increase in number of the dioceses in England and Wales.* He proposed that the annual value of episcopal revenues, as stated by Lord Althorp in the House of Commons, of £158,527 could be redistributed in such a way as to allow 'six additional Bishops not being Peers of the Realm' to be funded at a stipend of just £3,000 a year. Canterbury would be reduced to £14,000, York to £10,000, London to £8,000, Durham and Winchester £6,000 each, and the other twenty-one bishops would get £4,500. His preferred six new sees would be Bodmin, Halifax, Hexham, Huntingdon, Ipswich and Lancaster. He also recommended re-drawing the boundaries of most dioceses. Chester, Lincoln, York, Lichfield & Coventry, Exeter, Norwich, London, Durham and Winchester were to be reduced in size, and six would be increased: Worcester, Hereford, Oxford, Ely, Peterborough and Rochester.

An anonymous clergyman, who welcomed Henley's plans in part, felt bishops could manage on much lower stipends. He wanted them all to have just £3,000 a year and the archbishops alone £4,000 – 'an income still, it is to be feared, more than is required *by duty*, and, therefore, leaving room for *pomp*.' And as sees fell vacant, he recommended that surplus residences be sold off, leaving just the most convenient palace for the use of the new bishop. 'Thus the palace at Fulham will be sold, and London House remain as the episcopal residence; and Auckland Castle and Farnham Castle will, in like manner, augment the clerical fund.' [A CLERGYMAN *Safe and Easy Steps towards an efficient Reform* p. 42]

Another pamphleteer expressed concern not just about non-resident parsons but also about bishops.

Instead of hurrying down from their town residences, to discharge what they appear to consider the irksome task of visitation, it is respectfully suggested that every bishop should reside within his diocese more than one half of the year; and that he should annually, instead of triennially, make his visitations, and perform his episcopal functions. . . . The bishop, by living so much and so long among his clergy, would gradually become acquainted with the character, and the habits of every individual; would be able to afford his advice and assistance, whenever difficulties might arise, and would

naturally feel anxious to acquire the esteem, and attachment of a people, amongst whom he would then regard himself as settled for life, instead of considering his see as a mere resting-place, on which he is only to remain, until he shall be enabled to wing his flight to some more lucrative eminence.
[A LAYMAN *Thoughts on the Church Establishment* pp. 20-22]

Dr Thomas Arnold, Headmaster of Rugby, also published his ideas on *Church Reform*. His aim was to make the Established Church truly and effectually the Church of England by incorporating Dissenters into an enlarged Church. The future of the Church, he believed, lay in its becoming comprehensive. Episcopacy was to be preserved but bishops in future would act only on the advice of a council comprising laymen as well as clerics 'and partly elected by the officers of the respective parishes' who in turn should have been elected directly by the inhabitants. The bishops would be further restricted by a diocesan assembly but have smaller dioceses to administer. Parishes too should have elected bodies with a greater say in the appointment of ministers. What he had in mind was akin to the system of synodical government and bishop's councils which exists today. Arnold's pamphlet went through four editions in six months but his proposals for a more inclusive and comprehensive church body enjoying a form of democratic government and where traditional liturgical forms such as the *Book of Common Prayer* would be used alongside freer forms of worship did not find many supporters. Though there was some desire for liturgical reform at this time, more particularly for the removal of the Athanasian Creed from the Liturgy. His proposals met with little support as they were deemed to be impracticable. *The Times*, not usually critical of him, thought nothing would be gained but a kind of ecclesiastical Noah's ark.

George Wilkins, the Archdeacon of Nottingham, published a *Letter to Earl Grey on the Subject of Ecclesiastical Reform* in 1832. He was an advocate of reform, not least in respect of how bishops exercised their ministry. They could do better! He recommended reducing their number in the Lords to the two archbishops and the three most senior English bishops, London, Winchester and Durham and two of the Irish archbishops 'and thus throw the valuable services of the rest upon the business of their dioceses, and upon that of such a Synod or Convocation as it may be deemed necessary to establish in future connection with Parliament.' [WILKINS *A Letter...* p. 11f] And he goes on to argue

> It must be evident, that by enjoining twenty-one Prelates to reside for a period of, at least, two-thirds of the year within their diocese; to mix and

live more with their Clergy; to hold Confirmations more frequently, and in a much greater number of their Churches than is at present the custom, instead of permitting the demoralizing practice of bringing numerous bodies of young persons from various and great distances into the contaminating focus of a large town; incalculable benefits would arise; their stations and services would be more highly appreciated; the character of the inferior Clergy would be improved; their ministrations would be more perfect and effective; and the solemn rites of the Church would be freed from that reproach to which they have been too often exposed. [Ibid. p. 13]

He has one final dig at the current practice of the bishops. He notes that they have often been so long detained in London and exhausted by their duties there that 'an additional period has been required for their restoration; so that their actual residence in their diocese has been much curtailed.' [Ibid. p. 14]

Pusey also wrote a pamphlet in late 1832 attacking Lord Henley's proposals regarding using the assets of the cathedrals to fund the Church's ministry in the parishes. Newman advised him to wait and publish it as a defence of the ministry of cathedrals. Pusey did this and his *Remarks on the Prospective and Past Benefits of Cathedral Institutions* appeared a year later. He showed how cathedrals had in the past been centres of theological learning and could be again. More specifically, he envisaged a dozen cathedrals having a collective intake of about 450 students a year for a two year course taught by members of the cathedral's staff. Pusey was critical of the two universities for failing to provide full theological and professional instruction for the clergy. His pamphlet was a substantial piece of work but it bore little fruit, and much of the cathedrals' assets were in due course re-distributed as Henley had proposed. He did, however, exercise some influence in two ways – the founding of Chichester theological college was in accord with his thinking, and his proposal that there should be two further theological professorships, one of Ecclesiastical History and the other one of 'Practical Theology' at Oxford attached to cathedral canonries. Eventually the chair of Pastoral Theology was founded in 1842 and would prove to be of immense value to future generations of ordination candidates.

Dr Bloomfield, the Vicar of Bisbrooke in Rutland, who published his analysis of five of the reform pamphlets, probably represented the views of many country clergy. For him the 'evils and abuses' being written about were only 'alleged', and so he urged great caution: 'do nothing rashly, nothing for mere political consideration . . . and in those instances wherein it [i.e. the Church] may seem defective, it may, with the least change, be made to do so better.' [BLOOMFIELD *Analytical View of the Principal Plans of Church Reform* p. 51] The plan he disliked most was Henley's. He wrote, 'The scheme looks well on paper; but the question is how it would work?' and, after examination, concluded it was 'wholly inadmissible both on the score of *injustice* and of *inefficiency*.' [*Ibid.* p.15]

A Royal Commission was appointed on 23 June 1832, just three weeks after the passing of the Reform Act, with the support of the Archbishop of Canterbury as well as the Prime Minister who announced the names of the Commissioners. Its task was to inquire into the financial position of the Church. This was a task even the most hardened anti-reformist could support because there was so much ignorance about its true wealth and consequently critics and enemies of the Church were free to exaggerate and distort things with impunity. Some hard, factual statistics were urgently needed. A brief report was published on 16 June 1834 showing the annual yield of episcopal, capitular and parochial endowments, a classification of benefices according to their value, and the number of incumbents and curates. The full report was signed and published exactly one year later. Amongst its many findings it revealed that there were eighteen livings worth over £2,000 a year [= £232,184 in 2014], and that the *average* stipend received by the 4,224 curates who did the work for non-resident incumbents was £81 a year [= £9,403].

Peel appointed a second Commission early in 1835 and it submitted its first report just six weeks after its first meeting. It was based on the statistical information provided by Grey's Commission of Inquiry which revealed that half the sees were insolvent. The income was not sufficient to balance the outlay, and the expenses incident to appointment consumed a whole year's revenue in most cases and in others much more. Had the public known this earlier, there would have been far less criticism of the poorer bishops holding additional posts *in commendam*. Mathieson has drawn attention to the gross disparity in duties, revealed in the report, which was as important an issue in need of reform as the disparity in remuneration. 'The Bishop of Rochester had the oversight of 94 incumbents, whilst his brethren of Norwich and Lincoln were responsible respectively for 1026 and 1251. Ely, one of the richest sees, had a population of 126,000 and 149 livings. Chester, a poor see, had a population of almost two millions and 554 livings.' [MATHIESON *op. cit.* p.113]

This was an issue that John Henry Newman had addressed in his pamphlet on *The Restoration of Suffragan Bishops* in 1835. His recommended solution to the unequal distribution of episcopal duties was not to rely on changing diocesan boundaries but to appoint episcopal asssistants where they were most needed: 'Suffragans may be appointed *at once* for certain twenty-six towns, under an existing Act of Parliament, viz, 26 Henry VIII.c.14., nothing being needed for their restoration, but the approbation of the Ecclesiastical Commission to the revival, on the part of the Bishops, to a statute which having slept, may need some such sanction.' [NEWMAN *The Restoration of Suffragan Bishops* p. 20] His suggestion did not win the support of the Commission, though it was an idea Peel was interested in as he had written to Phillpotts on 21 January 1835 in a letter marked 'Most Private' asking for his views on appointing Suffragans.

Thomas Gisborne, a prebendary of Durham supported Church reform from the provision of 'a decent abode and a competent income' for all the parish clergy to reducing the number of bishops in the House of Lords so that they could spend more time in their dioceses. He supported the redrawing of diocesan boundaries and made some specific proposals; he also wanted bishops to have more power to correct 'immoral or unbecoming conduct on the part of beneficed clergymen.'

> For such cases his hands must be strengthened. He must also be relieved from the odium of appearing as the prosecutor and from personal expenses in the course of the business. Provision at the same time should be made for securing to the person accused means of defence together with a fair trial, in some way sufficiently analogous to the principle of a jury.
> [GISBORNE *Considerations on Objections current against Ecclesiastical Establishments* p. 57f]

He was also one of those advocating the eradication of pluralism and non-residence among the parish clergy. Whilst it was now clear that the commonest cause of pluralism was the poverty of benefices, a far too common cause was the abuse of the patronage system. To quote Mathieson's summary of the Report again:

> Lord John Russell declared that there were many instances of clergymen holding two or three livings to the value of about £3,000; and a writer who had analysed the Report said that he had before him a list of 485 pluralist incumbents, each with a benefice of at least £500 a year, whose total net income, derived from both cathedral and parochial endowments, was £654,579, an average of nearly £1350. One finds that the Marquis of Bath, having three livings (£1236) in his gift, had bestowed them all on his son, and that the Duke of Beaufort had disposed similarly of four livings – two being sinecures – to the value of £2422. Peel was horrified to find that a large country parish 'overrun with Dissent', could have only one church service on Sunday, because Trinity College, Cambridge, absorbed the whole

tithes to the amount of £2000 a year and allowed the Vicar only £24. We learn also from Peel that the Vicar of St Mary's Nottingham, was wholly dependent on pew rents and Easter offerings; but the Report shows that he raised in this way £700 a year and derived £780 from three other livings. [MATHIESON *op. cit.* p. 113f]

The Report's Tory authors made recommendations in line with the earlier Whig ones, for example, creating the two new sees of Ripon and Manchester, and the redistribution of Church income. It fell to the Whigs to implement these reforms. Melbourne replaced most of Peel's lay nominees on the commission with Whigs who were less committed to the work and left it to the bishops to make the running. A second report was issued in March 1836 which proposed a radical shake-up of cathedral establishments and revenues in order to provide churches and clergy for the new industrial urban communities. A third report in May 1836 recommended making the Commission a permanent body. The fourth was published a month later which outlined proposed changes to benefices. When the Commission's proposals became law, there were teething problems and consequently complaints and opposition from bishops who felt they were being badly treated. Joseph Allen, for example, on his translation to Ely in 1835 had Bedfordshire added to his new diocese and he was asked to pay, as of 1836, £4,000 a year towards supplementing the incomes of poorer dioceses. He published his correspondence with the Commissioners arguing that their figures were wrong, and declining to pay. A few months later the Commissioners conceded a reduced annual contribution of £2,500 but on 3 December 1836 he informed them that he had received no payment so far as Bishop of Ely and was living on money borrowed from his banker! So, he still couldn't pay them.

An anonymous critic of bishops for amassing wealth argued that they didn't deserve the income they received:

> There is nothing in the *duties* of bishops to call for extravagant stipends. They are neither difficult of execution nor multifarious, and are mostly performed by *deputy*. They employ archdeacons to visit for them; rural deans and others to preach for them [i.e. at visitations]; they have a vicar-general to issue licences, hold courts, and do other drudgery; and if otherwise engaged, they employ a brother bishop to ordain for them: in short, their work is *light*. It is not half so burdensome and difficult as that of many curates, equally learned and pious, who do not receive a five-hundredth part of their remuneration. [ANON *Statistics of the Church of England* 1836 p. 65]

He was also highly critical of the proposal to increase the patronage of bishops – 'It is the abuse of church patronage by Sparke, Pretyman, Sutton, and other prelates that has brought so much disgrace on the establishment.' [*Ibid.*]

Another anonymous critic writing under the pseudonym of *Clericus Anglicanus* published three Letters to the Archbishop of Canterbury in 1836 attacking the proposals contained in the first three reports of the commission, notably those relating to diocesan boundary changes which would affect Llandaff, Bristol, Bath & Wells and Gloucester. Almost inevitably he was also opposed to alienating cathedral funds which, he believed, would ruin those institutions, and in his third Letter he deals with what he calls 'the vital interests of the Clergy'.

The first piece of legislation based on these reports was the Established Church Bill (Ecclesiastical Commissioners Act) of 1836 which abolished the practice of bishops holding livings *in commendam* and made the income of most of them more equal with the exception of the two archbishops and the three most senior diocesans. Two other pieces of legislation were framed which Melbourne introduced but they did not come into immediate effect: the Pluralities and Residence Bill which was passed in 1838 and the Ecclesiastical Duties and Revenues Bill (usually known as the Cathedrals Act) in 1840. The latter was bitterly resisted by most cathedral clergy. The Dean and chapter of Canterbury convened a meeting at St Paul's in July 1836 of representative canons from all cathedrals, and opposition was planned. Philip Barrett in his book *Barchester. English Cathedral Life in the Nineteenth Century* includes many extracts from the submissions (p. 17-19). Some of them are quite laughable – the Revd Canon Dr Smith of Durham, for example, pointed out that if canonical houses were alienated 'this would be productive of great inconvenience to the members of the chapter, and might lead to the introduction of very objectionable inhabitants'! [BARRETT p. 18] The only three cathedrals in the end not to submit objections to parliament were Chichester, Gloucester and Peterborough.

Archbishop Howley successfully moved an amendment to the Established Church Bill to omit the requirement that the bishops of Welsh dioceses should have a knowledge of Welsh. He regarded it as an unnecessary restriction on the choice of bishops as all the Welsh clergy understood English. That was not true, however, of very many parishioners and consequently an opportunity was lost of making the Church more attractive to the Welsh-speaking inhabitants of the principality. A.J. Johnes, a Welsh Anglican layman, published a *Letter to Lord John Russell on the Operation of the Established Church Bill with reference to the Interests of the Principality of Wales.* In it he protested at the Archbishop's amendment and behaviour to the Welsh Church, spelling out in detail how the assets of Welsh dioceses had been plundered in the recent past by English bishops and bestowed on their sons and other relatives. He argued fairly that it made no sense to require incumbents to be fluent in Welsh but not bishops. He opposed too the proposal to take some of the assets of the sees of Bangor and St Asaph to fund the proposed new see of Manchester when the money could be so much better spent on the augmentation of the many poor livings in Wales and in the provision of a university college. Lampeter, he described as 'a valuable institution' but 'is suited exclusively for the education of the Clergy.' What Wales needed was an institution in which 'every branch of learning and science' would be taught.

The Commissioners, however, did not always get their way. One of the provisions of the Established Church Act of 1836, for example, was the suppression of the Diocese of Sodor and Man, which had only 45,000 inhabitants. It was proposed to amalgamate it with Carlisle at the first vacancy but it was successfully annulled despite both Howley and Blomfield having spoken in the Lords in support of the original decision. Bishop William Ward, although in ill health, rallied Manxmen and lobbied peers to secure a reprieve for his diocese. After much lobbying by Manx clergymen and by others on the mainland, a Bill was introduced in the Lords in February 1838 and it passed its third reading in June by a majority of sixty-four with just five voting against.

Ward listed six arguments for retaining the see: its antiquity – there had been an almost uninterrupted succession of bishops for over 1,400 years; its geographical position; the Manx laws, civil and ecclesiastical were different to those of England, and their legislature was independent; the bishop was head of the council, the principal branch of the legislature with duties that could not be exercised by an archdeacon as deputy; the bishop was one of the principal resident gentlemen who knew the wants and needs of the people; and, lastly, the presence of the bishop had great moral influence upon society of all ranks. His absence would affect the interests of religion. He listed the munificent acts of previous bishops who had built churches and chapels and funded schools on the island. He ended with a personal plea 'as a dying man' that his words would not pass unheeded and the Manx Church be spared 'as a memorial of happier days that are passed, and as an earnest of brighter days to come.' Despite being the least influential bishop in the country Ward took on the episcopal heavyweights of the Commission and won.

Another of its proposals, although passed, never came to fruition namely the merging of the two Welsh dioceses of Bangor and St Asaph because the Earl of Powys successfully led opposition to the merger.

In addition to reorganising bishoprics, the Act more importantly set up a permanent body, the Ecclesiastical Commission, which was to administer these changes and bring forward recommendations for further reforms. It was this latter body which was to provoke most episcopal opposition. Bishop Phillpotts of Exeter and Bishop Grey of Hereford were particularly opposed to the permanent nature of the Commission as 'a perpetual corporation.' Phillpotts in his visitation *Charge* that year described the Commission as 'a machinery of the most formidable and portentous nature . . . threatening us with a series of changes in our ecclesiastical constitution so often as the convenience of any government, which may be dependent on the will or caprices of a faction hostile to the Church, shall dictate such changes.' The Act was amended in 1840 which provided for a much larger membership and one that was dominated by Churchmen: all the bishops, the Deans of Canterbury, St Paul's and Westminster, and – provided they were Churchmen – six leading judges, four laymen appointed by the Crown and two appointed by the Archbishop of Canterbury were to have seats on the Ecclesiastical Commission; and every Commissioner was to be irremovable so long as he 'well demean himself.' What it did was to allow the Church to reform itself from within rather than having Parliament force reform upon it. It proceeded by way of Church Measures for Parliament to put into effect, once passed. Machin has described this Act as 'the most important parliamentary victory for gradual Church reform' whereby the Whigs saved the Church from the Radicals who would have preferred to have seen it disestablished and disendowed. By the end of the decade many of the abuses which had attracted so much public criticism had been put right and that was in part thanks to the work of the Commission and in particular to Charles James Blomfield who deserves some lines in gratitude for his titanic efforts.

Sydney Smith commented caustically about his bishop that he had 'an ungovernable passion for business.' It is true that Blomfield did not do things by halves. That had ever been the case from childhood and then as a student when he worked inordinately long hours at his books. He had won the highest classical and mathematical honours at Cambridge and gone on to be one of the foremost representatives of the new school of Greek criticism which included his future episcopal colleagues Maltby, Kaye and Monk. He had proved his worth as an effective parish priest in

London and then as a driving, reforming bishop in the vast diocese of Chester. The man was born to lead and whilst not the Chairman of the Commission, he dominated its business. In the oft repeated words of Archbishop Harcourt, 'Till Blomfield comes we all sit and mend our pens and talk about the weather.' As its leading member, he inevitably became the target for much of the criticism thrown at its doings. But he rightly claimed, 'They now blame me for these measures, but they will hereafter confess that those very measures have been the saving of the Church.'

The Commission had many other critics besides Sydney Smith. One of them, Christopher Benson, addressed an open letter in 1837 to Bishop Kaye in which he deprecated the delegation of such powers 'to a few selected Commissioners to whom it gives a perpetual existence, and over whose acts it [i.e. parliament] gives up almost all control.' [BENSON *On the Proceedings of the Ecclesiastical Commission* p. 4] He expresses his fears that the independence of bishops will be affected – even to making them move house and transferring some of their real estate.

> They have, in fact, destroyed one of the best securities for the permanency of ecclesiastical property, the undisturbed antiquity of title, and the long proscription it has enjoyed. They have placed it, at least the episcopal possessions upon a purely Parliamentary foundation. Henceforth every Bishop must plead his right to what he retains or receives . . . [*Ibid.* p. 8]

Benson also argued against extending the patronage of bishops by looking at how they had exercised their patronage in the past. 'The list of incumbents shews, that a very great number of livings have been conferred by Bishops upon their own children, relations and friends, when they had any . . .' [*Ibid.* p. 25] It would not be a beneficial reform, in his judgement, if the patronage of deans and chapters was transferred to the bishops.

There was other legislation too besides establishing the Ecclesiastical Commission as a permanent body. Peel introduced a measure, on which the Whig statute of 1836 was based, for the commutation of tithes, i.e. the payment as an addition to rent of a fixed sum of money instead of the annual contribution of a certain fraction of crops and livestock. It was clearly welcomed as within a year of its passing most payees and recipients had arrived at mutually acceptable agreements. What many people had not previously realized was that these tithe payments, although originally intended as a means of providing financial support for the Church and its clergy, had since the Reformation been paid to lay impropriators in many places and had not benefited the Church at all.

W.R. Ward has argued that the catastrophic decline in the influence of the Church in the countryside in the early nineteenth century was due in part to the tithe question. [WARD *The Tithe Question in England in the Early Nineteenth Century* in the *Journal of Ecclesiastical History* Vol. 16 1965 pp.67-81] The payment of tithes in kind was particularly burdensome at a time of poor harvests and depressed agricultural incomes, as in the years following the end of the Napoleonic Wars. Agrarian discontent came to a head in the autumn of 1830 when labourers in Kent revolted and trouble spread across the southern counties as far as Dorset. Demands for higher wages were backed by rick-burning and machine breaking. The farmers convinced the labourers that wages could not go up till tithe came down, in effect putting the blame for the labourers' sufferings on the clergy and lay impropriators. The government put down the revolt ruthlessly but the bitter feeling remained. The resolution of the issue in the Tithe Commutation Act 1836 by which the value of the tithe was fixed by a money payment, which in turn was based on an average of seven years, was a blessing but the Church got a much worse bargain than in the days of the enclosure bills earlier in the century when the tithe element had been commuted, usually half for money and half for land. Glebe acres had increased significantly in many parishes at that time as a result of that commutation. Not so this time.

The problems of plurality and non-residence were also being addressed directly by some of the bishops in their dioceses. They are twin themes that figure frequently in episcopal *Charges* of the period along with pressure on incumbents to provide two services a Sunday (which was a statutory requirement) instead of just one which many of them were making do with. Phillpotts, for example, declared in 1836 that in his diocese 60 parishes were now being served by residents which three years earlier had had non-resident clergy. Bishop Marsh of Peterborough said in 1831 that there were 60 churches in his diocese which a few years earlier had had one service and now had two.

Melbourne's government, as noted earlier, also produced in 1836 a more comprehensive measure which established a civil register of births, marriages and deaths for the whole of England, and enabled marriages to be celebrated in places of worship other than the Anglican Church, provided that a registrar was present, and in exceptional cases could be performed by the registrar, in effect permitting civil marriages. The complaints and criticisms of Dissenters were thereby to some extent disarmed, and by now the Church of England was beginning to regain its confidence and could move forward. New societies were being established, such as the Church Pastoral Aid Society in 1836 and the Additional Curates Society a year later, which provided more ministers for service in the most populous parishes where help was most needed. And the Oxford Movement which had its origins in events of 1833 would eventually bring spiritual renewal to many parishes.

In 1837 a Church Rates Bill was introduced which would have resulted in the Church itself being financially responsible for the upkeep of the fabric of its buildings, but it ran into trouble even among the Whigs, and consequently came to nothing. The ministry wanted rates abolished and the money needed for church repairs to be raised possibly by increased pew rents and by the transfer of the management of some of the Church's estates to a government committee. At a meeting held in Lambeth Palace on 9 March, fifteen bishops declared against the plan, and that same evening there was an angry interchange in the Lords between Archbishop Howley and Blomfield with Melbourne. They refused to cooperate in any further reforms – in effect the Ecclesiastical Commission went on strike! When the Government failed to get sufficient support even in the Commons, the scheme was abandoned – church rates would have to wait until 1866 before the matter was resolved. It was a notable, albeit temporary, victory for supporters of the Church.

A Pluralities Bill framed by the Commissioners of Inquiry had passed the Lords in 1836 but too late to permit its passing in the Commons. It was brought again in 1837 but abandoned and only finally became law in 1838. It bore the title 'An Act to abridge the holding of benefices in plurality and to make better provision for the residence of the clergy.' What had started life as a measure for the partial abolition of plurality had turned into one which partially prevented it. The old system of exemption and licence was retained; but two benefices could not be held by the same person unless they were under ten statute miles apart, and not even then if the population of one was over 3000 or the joint value over £1000. No clergyman was to hold preferment in more than one cathedral, and no pluralist in any cathedral, archdeacons in both cases exempted. Provision was made for uniting and disuniting parishes, for building parsonages, and for the appointment and remuneration of curates. Where there was no parsonage, the bishop could authorise a house within three miles of the church in the country and within two miles in town. Further restrictions would come later when the Act was amended in 1850. How effective this measure was may be judged from this comment by R.W. Ambler about the diocese of Lincoln where Kaye had told his clergy that he intended 'to carry into effect the declared intention of the legislature in every possible case':

> The effectiveness of the 1838 Plurality Act and the powers that it gave to the bishop can be seen from the fact that by 1853 only 3 per cent of the Lincolnshire incumbents who had been instituted to their livings after 1838 were non-resident under the exemptions permitted by the Act, compared with some 25 per cent who had been in their livings before the Act became law, and therefore not covered by its provisions. [AMBLER ed. *op. cit.* p. xix]

Sydney Smith wrote to Lord John Russell criticizing particular clauses in various Bills and repeating his constant refrain that if the number of pecuniary 'prizes' were reduced in the Church, then a flow of capital from wealthy parents will be cut off as they will dissuade their sons from offering themselves for Ordination. He did it with his customary touch of humour. 'Your Bill, abolishing Pluralities, and taking away, at the same time, so many dignities leaves the Church of England so destitute of great prizes, that, as far as mere emolument has any influence, it will be better to dispense cheese and butter in small quantities to the public, than to enter the Church.' [SMITH *A Letter to Lord John Russell on the Church Bills* p. 16]

The one which took longest to be passed into law was the 'Cathedrals Act' because hundreds of men had a vested financial interest in retaining the old system. Dean Blakesley of Lincoln in a letter to Gladstone called the Commissioners 'ecclesiastical butchers'. Christopher Wordsworth, the Master of Trinity College Cambridge and Incumbent of Buxted in Sussex wrote a lengthy and reasoned defence of the value in allowing Heads of Colleges and university professors to continue to hold office as a cathedral dignity or be an incumbent in addition to their university post. He cited his own case to show how well the current, unreformed arrangements worked – he spent four to five months a year in his living and employed three resident curates. There was one church and two chapels, each of the latter with its own district and resident minister. He had built a new chapel, a school and a house for a curate, all at his own expense. Had he simply been an incumbent, he would have employed just one curate and there would have been no new buildings. The parish had, in fact, benefited greatly from the present arrangements which allowed a Head of House to hold a living too. Were Heads of colleges and professors no longer to be allowed to be Deans or Prebendaries or incumbents, or even clergymen, under the Commissioners' proposals? he asked.

One of the most frequently pressed arguments in defence of cathedral chapters was their role as theological educators. The fact is that the only cathedral dean and chapter to have done anything about this was that in Durham who, with further financial support from the Bishop, had funded the foundation of Durham University in 1831. When this argument was raised in the Lords in 1840, Melbourne dismissed it with the words, 'The study of theology may be a very good thing in its way, but it is not a thing that we want in these days.' What was needed much more was the better provision of churches and of properly remunerated clergy to serve in them. Archbishop Howley cited in the same debate a district in Yorkshire which had a population of 400,000 and church-room for just 29,000. The second reading of the Bill was carried in the Lords on 27 July 1840 by 99:48, eleven bishops voting against it and nine for it (including the five who were Commissioners).

Bagot of Oxford had predicted in his 1838 *Charge* that the cathedrals would 'eventually fall into ruin and decay, through the inadequacy of the funds now left to defray the necessary expenditure on repairs. The Established Church generally would receive no benefit from the alienation of cathedral property.' [BAGOT *Charge* 1838 p. 9] Charles Sumner of Winchester in his 1837 *Charge* and Edward Denison of Salisbury in his *Charge* in 1839 were two more bishops who sought to defend cathedral property and interests. Howley, Kaye and Monk had all once held similar views and had expressed their support for cathedrals in earlier *Charges*, but faced with the harsh reality of having to fund parochial ministry in deprived areas and in the new industrial centres they now recognized sacrifices had to be made where they could be best afforded. Monk in his 1838 *Charge* said that he 'yielded to none in his respect and attachment to cathedral establishments', but he pointed out that 'such a deficiency of spiritual instruction' confronted the Commissioners, that it seemed only right to ask the chapters to make a material sacrifice. A graduated tax on benefices would have been inadequate, because by far the greater number of livings over £500 in annual value were in the patronage of laymen, who would have called any such scheme confiscation. [MONK *Charge* 1838 pp 13-17 *passim*] He concluded:

> When I regarded the frightful deficiency of spiritual instruction under which such numbers of my countrymen were suffering, when it was clear that no earthly resource was available, except what might be spared from cathedral appointments, it became a question, not of predilection or of taste, but of duty to the sacred cause of Christ's Church. [*Ibid*. p. 19]

Kaye went further by publishing a *Letter to the Archbishop of Canterbury on the Recommendations of the Ecclesiastical Commission* which set out cogently and fully the reasons for his conversion to the principle of redistribution of capitular income. Prior to the investigations of the Commission and the publication of their findings in the Second Report of the Commission, he had had no idea of the enormous spiritual needs of large urban parishes. They had looked at all possible alternative means of providing the necessary funds – none sufficed. He stated to those opposing the Commission's proposals: 'No man can be competent to deliver a fair judgment upon our recommendations who has not carefully perused and weighed that portion of the Report which particularly related to the deficiency of Church and Ministers in populous places.' [KAYE *Letter to the Archbishop* p. 21]

After all the debate which had roused such strong passions the actual legislation had an easy passage through parliament. The House of Lords gave it a second reading on 29 July 1840, voting 99:48, and passed the Bill one week later, twelve bishops voting against it. It received the royal assent five days later. Welch in his study of it concluded 'There was in fact no alternative. Very few Anglicans outside cathedrals opposed it; those who did not actively support it acquiesced in it, because of "the utter absurdity and inefficiency" [*Times* 28 July 1840] of any other plan.' [WELCH *Contemporary Views on the Proposals for the Alienation of Capitular Property in England (1832-1840)* in the *Journal of Ecclesiastical History* Vol. 5 1954 p. 195]

Most cathedrals and collegiate churches would in future have only four canons in addition to the dean. Canterbury, Westminster, Durham and Ely would have six, and Winchester and Exeter five. Christchurch Oxford, being a college chapel as well as a cathedral was to retain its present staff but three of its canonries – in addition to the two already so applied – were to be annexed to professorships; and any canonry at Ely which might be attached to a professorship at Cambridge was to be retained. All the non-residentiary prebends were retained as titles of distinction but devoid of their previous income; and in cathedrals where such preferments did not exist there were to be honorary canons. It was now provided that the Dean of Durham should pay to the Ecclesiastical Commissioners such fixed annual sum as should leave him with an average income of £3,000, that the Deans of St Paul's, Westminster and Manchester should each retain £2,000, and the canons of all these four churches £1,000. Elsewhere, in England, deans, whether by deduction or addition, were to have £1,000 and canons £500. The annual savings thus made by the new arrangements would eventually provide about £130,000 a year to be used by the Commissioners for augmenting poor livings. One additional provision welcomed by the bishops was that capitular patronage would be passed to the bishop in whose diocese the parish was located. Monk welcomed it on the grounds that a diocesan bishop was far more likely than a far-away chapter to know the merits of an obscure and friendless clergyman. W.L. Bowles, a canon residentiary of Sarum published a series of articles and letters attacking the Commission's proposals to transfer almost all patronage of deans and chapters to the bishops.

One of Sydney Smith's arguments advanced against the Bill sounds bizarre in a clergyman's ears ministering in the 21st century but was presumably a fact of life in the 1830s. He argued that hefty differentials were a way of attracting men of wealth and property into the ranks of the clergy, and that attempts to equalize stipends would deter gentlemen of means from offering themselves for ordination:

> The most important and cogent arguments against the Dean and Chapter confiscations are passed over in silence in the Bishop's [i.e. Blomfield] Charge. This, in reasoning, is always the wisest and most convenient plan, and which all young Bishops should imitate after the manner of this wary polemic. I object to the confiscation *because it will throw a great deal more of capital out of the parochial Church than it will bring into it*. I am very sorry to come forward with so homely an argument, which shocks so many Clergy men, and particularly those with the largest incomes, and the best Bishoprics; but the truth is, the greater number of Clergymen go into the Church in order that they may derive a comfortable income *from* the Church. Such men intend to do their duty, and they do it; but the duty is, however, not the motive, but the adjunct . . .
>
> I have no manner of doubt, that the immediate effect of passing the Dean and Chapter Bill will be, that a great number of fathers and uncles, judging, and properly judging, that the Church is a very altered and deteriorated profession, will turn the industry and capital of their *élèves* into another channel. [S. SMITH *Third Letter to Archdeacon Singleton* p. 264f]

Whilst his verbal attacks in his three *Letters* were mostly aimed at Blomfield and, to a lesser degree, the Archbishop of Canterbury, he regarded Bishops Monk and Kaye, whom he mentions, as nonentities – to him the Ecclesiastical Commission was Blomfield, Howley and Sir John Russell. He ends a letter, provoked by Blomfield's speech in the Lords on the Dean and Chapter Act, with a highly personal attack on his bishop. The letter appeared in *The Times* on 5 September 1840:

You are fast hastening on, with the acclamations and gratitude of the Whigs, to Lambeth, and I am hastening, after a life of 70 years, with gout and asthma, to the grave. I am most sincere, therefore, when I say, that in the management of this business you have (in my opinion) made a very serious and fatal mistake: you have shaken the laws of property, and prepared the ruin of the church by lowering the character of its members, and encouraging the aggression of its enemies. That your error has been the error of an upright, zealous, and honest man, I have not the most remote doubt. I have fought you lustily for four years, but I admire your talents, and respect your character as sincerely as I lament the mistakes into which you have been hurried by the honest and headlong impetuosity of your nature.

I remain, my Lord, your obedient humble servant, SYDNEY SMITH

Another area of church life which had long needed attention and reform was the ecclesiastical courts and clergy discipline in general. Attempts had been made repeatedly throughout the decade to tighten up clergy discipline but without much success, beginning with the establishment of the Ecclesiastical Courts Commission in 1830. It reported in 1832 and recommended that future disciplinary cases should be heard personally by the bishop assisted by an expert legal assessor, that oral evidence be admitted, and that delinquents should be suspended pending appeals. It would be another eight years, however, before any successful general legislation on clergy discipline resulted. Arthur Burns comments, 'In the interim, a succession of failed initiatives had been wrecked on the parliamentary shore'. [BURNS *Clergy-Discipline Legislation in Parliament c1830-1870* p. 84 in *Parliament and the Church 1529-1960* ed. J.P. Parry & S. Taylor]

Previously if a bishop wished to take disciplinary action against one of his clergy, it could involve him in considerable legal expenditure – at times prohibitively costly – and justice was not done. Phillpotts, for example, who had not been averse to threatening legal action or taking it against libellous journalists before he became a bishop soon discovered how expensive it could be when he was having to pay all the legal costs in a case against one of his clergy. Following the publication of the Commission's Report in 1832, the old Court of Delegates was abolished and its jurisdiction transferred to the Privy Council. In 1833 appellate jurisdiction passed to the Judicial Committee of the Privy Council. 1840 saw the passing of the Clergy Discipline Bill. Where a clergyman was accused of any offence or had given occasion for scandal, the bishop was empowered to issue a commission of inquiry to five persons, one of whom must be his vicar-general or one of his archdeacons or rural deans. If these persons reported that there was sufficient ground for suspicion, he might summon the accused and pronounce sentence on his confession; but, if the accused did not appear or did not confess, he might try the question with the advice of three assessors, one of whom must be an experienced lawyer, or he might remit the case to a provincial court of appeal either before taking action or on the report of a *prima facie* case. It was a small step in the right direction. The revival of the system of rural deans who could be used as investigative officers under the command of the bishop and his archdeacons had been a constructive reform, or more correctly the restoration of an earlier church office, in the life of the church at diocesan level. They had been introduced gradually in all dioceses during the previous twenty or so years, and at no cost as the post did not bring the holder any extra remuneration.

The outcome of this Act, however, was not always what the bishops had hoped for, as beneficed clergymen with the freehold of their living remained very hard to dislodge. Frances Knight provides examples of this in the diocese of Lincoln. [KNIGHT *The Nineteenth Century Church and English Society* pp. 163-166] She comments:

> The Church Discipline Act represented a victory for the continuation of the parson's freehold; that is to say it permitted no permanent deprivation of livings, even those of notoriously dissolute clergy. The Church in 1840 was not ready for a measure that would have struck at the heart of its belief in the supremacy of the freehold, even though it might have reduced the level of public opprobrium over clerical scandals, which, though relatively few, attracted wide publicity. [*Ibid*. p. 166]

One of the provisions of the Clergy Discipline Act had unforeseen consequences. Appeals against episcopal judgements in clerical cases were to be allowed to be dealt with by the Judicial Committee. Norman observes about that, 'In these arrangements the State was actually practising a very thorough erastian control of the Church. And the body involved, the Judicial Committee, was not even one that provided that its membership was restricted to members of the Church.' [NORMAN *op. cit.* p. 121] Its judgement in the Gorham case a decade later caused immense controversy.

In April 1840 Blomfield took an important initiative of a different kind, without any prodding by hostile critics of the Church, when he wrote a letter to Archbishop Howley proposing the setting up of a Colonial Bishoprics Fund. As Bishop of London he had an historic role in providing episcopal oversight in any British colony where there was no bishop.

SPCK (the Society for Providing Christian Knowledge) was the oldest missionary society and had been providing Christian literature for the Church at home and overseas since 1698, and enjoyed the patronage of the Archbishop of Canterbury. SPG (the Society for Propagating the Gospel), a High Church initiative, had come into existence in 1701 to provide pastoral and spiritual support to expatriate Brits initially in the West Indies. These two societies benefited from a measure of financial support from the Government. CMS (the Church Missionary Society) was an Evangelical foundation started in 1799, and initially active in West Africa and India. The latter society did not have any episcopal support to begin with and experienced difficulties in getting its missionaries ordained in England. That changed in 1819 when, by an Act of Parliament, the Archbishops of Canterbury and York and the Bishop of London were empowered to ordain men for ministry in the colonies. When the policy of the British East India Company changed in 1813 the way was opened up for the employment of Chaplains. The bishopric of Calcutta had been founded with Thomas Fanshaw Middleton as its first bishop (1814-22), with archdeacons in Madras, Bombay and Ceylon. The bishop also had oversight of Australia until 1836 when William Broughton was appointed – he had been archdeacon there since 1829. There had been some increase in the number of Anglican bishops overseas with the creation of sees in Madras in 1835 and Bombay in 1837, and Newfoundland and Toronto in 1839. There had been bishoprics, supported by SPG, in Barbados and Jamaica since 1824.

Blomfield's proposal was radically different in that he wanted bishops to be pioneers in Church extension, i.e. to be there from the start rather than being sent later in response to needs. He recognized that there was little chance of Government aid in establishing new dioceses and that the Church of England had to take matters into its own hands. He proposed, consequently, that a fund should be formed by voluntary contributions for the endowment of bishoprics in the colonies and distant dependencies of the British Crown, and that the fund should be held in trust and administered by the archbishops and bishops of the Church. His letter to Howley included this passage about what was novel in his proposal:

> The difference . . . between our past labours in the work of erecting colonial churches, and those which are now called for, must be this: that whereas we formerly began by sending out a few individual missionaries, to occupy detached and independent fields of labour, - unconnected with one another by their relations to a common oversight in the execution of their task, although deriving their spiritual authority from a common origin – and then,

after an interval of many years, placing them under the guidance and control of Bishops; we should now, after having supplied the wants of those older colonies which are still destitute of the benefits of episcopal government, take care to let every new colony enjoy that blessing from the very first. Let every band of settlers which goes forth from Christian England, with authority to occupy a distinct territory, and to form a separate community, take with it not only its civil rulers and functionaries, but its Bishop and clergy. [quoted in CNATTINGIUS *Bishops and Societies* p. 199]

The idea of pioneering missionary bishops had been first suggested in 1835 at the General Convention of the Episcopal Church in the USA, and news of the appointment of their first 'missionary bishop' had reached England. Blomfield undoubtedly knew of this when he wrote his letter to Howley but it is thanks to his initiative that the Fund was established a year later and in June 1841 all the bishops and archbishops of the United Church of England and Ireland issued a manifesto specifying the six dioceses which they considered should be established first, beginning with New Zealand in 1841. Blomfield's initiative resulted in fourteen new colonial sees being erected between 1841-50. [*Ibid*. p. 204] Here, surely, is a sign of a resurgent and renewed Church emerging from the troubles of the 1830s.

Another area of work where the Established Church had improved its performance was in the provision of week-day schools as well as Sunday schools, and this was in large measure thanks to the funds raised and distributed by the National Society founded in 1811. It had enjoyed from its conception the support of Archbishop Manners-Sutton who chaired the first two meetings held in October 1811 which brought it into being. The patronage of the Prince Regent was also immediately secured. All the bishops were *ex officio* vice-presidents and members of the committee, so it was firmly placed in the Establishment. In the very first *Report* of the National Society (1812) the principle was set out that 'the national religion should be made the groundwork of national education.' At the first annual meeting, held in June 1812, there were 52 schools with 8,000 children in union with it; a year later that had grown to 240 schools with 40,000 children, and in 1824 there were 3,054 schools and 400,000 children instructed in them. This amazing growth had been achieved by voluntary subscriptions as it was not until 1833 that the Government made its first grant. But trouble came, as related earlier (see p. 136f) when the Government decided in 1839 to set up an Inspectorate of Schools and that its grants would be made only to schools accepting its inspection. A compromise was reached but the Society and individual bishops, such as

Sumner in Chester and Otter at Chichester, also decided the time was ripe to found proper training colleges to provide a supply of professional teachers.

There remained one immensely important need for reform: the provision of appropriate theological education for ordinands and for innovation in the area of professional ministerial training. Whilst this was an issue of national importance as it affected every diocese in the land, the bishops as a collective body were unable to do anything about it. Consequently it was left to a few local initiatives to meet the need which we will look at in a later chapter. Let it suffice to say here that institutions founded to meet the needs of a particular diocese, such as St Bees College in West Cumberland to serve the Diocese of Chester, quickly became a resource for the whole Church.

In 1838 the young, up-and-coming politician William Ewart Gladstone published his reflections on *The State in its Relations with the Church*. Keble welcomed it for here was a new champion of the Church, 'a statesman of the highest talent for business, an orator who commands the ear of the House of Commons.' Newman too thought that the book would do good. Gladstone began it on an ominous note, 'Probably there never was a time in the history of our country, when the connection between the State and the Church was threatened from quarters so manifold and various as at present.' [GLADSTONE *The State . . .* p. 1] He ended it, however, on a confident, hopeful one, redolent of the best of the bishops preaching at that time.

> It is true that we have nothing to fear for her, who bears a charmed life that no weapon reaches. She pursues her tranquil way of confession, adoration, thanksgiving, intercession, and Divine communion, concentrated alike for the present and the future, upon one object of regard, her Lord in heaven. This of the church of Christ. And in the Church of England we find all the essential features unimpaired, which declare her to be a fruit-bearing tree in the vineyard of God. The Scriptures faithfully guarded, liberally dispensed, universally possessed and read; the ancient bulwarks of the faith, the creeds, and the sound doctrine of catholic consent, maintained; the apostolical succession transmitting, with demonstration of the Spirit, those vital gifts which effectuate and assure the covenant; the pure worship; the known and acknowledged fertility in that sacred learning which, when faithfully used, is to the truth what the Israelitish arms were to the ark; and every thing reviving and extending zeal, courage, love: these are the signs which may well quiet apprehensions for the ultimate fate of the Church of England in the breast of the most timid of her sons. [*Ibid.* p. 320]

Alec Vidler in *The Church in an Age of Revolution* named his chapter on the period 1830-1845, *The Anglican Revival* which, given the fears and threats to its very existence in the 1830s as the Established Church, was an optimistic retrospective view. Reading the *Charges* delivered by the bishops to their clergy in that decade does not give the impression of a Church experiencing revival. Yet, the reality was that long-needed reforms were effected, some of which needed further attention in the following decades, but the long-term effect was a positive, hopeful one. The Thirties marked an important turning point in the Church's history. By 1840, the Church was in a far better position to meet the demands made upon it by a greatly increased population than it had been just ten years earlier. All those episcopal exhortations to the parish clergy to stand firm and serve their people faithfully and to be conciliatory to Dissenters and other critics may have contributed to the more confident mood in the Church. For it was at that level, in the villages and towns and cities, that the struggle for the spiritual health of the nation was being waged. The parish clergy were in the front line but they needed the practical support and care and encouragement of the bishops who were supposed to be their 'fathers in God', the *pastor pastorum*. How effective they were in this respect, we shall see in the next chapter.

The Bishops in their Dioceses

The much maligned Bishop Watson of Llandaff who administered his diocese from Westmorland, there being no adequate residence in Llandaff, wrote in his private notes in 1780:

> Give every Bishop income enough, not for display of worldly pomp and fashionable luxury, but to enable him to maintain works of charity, and to make a decent provision for his family: but having done these things for him, take from him all hopes of a translation by equalizing the bishopricks. Oblige him to a longer residence in his diocese than is usually practised, that he may do the proper work of a Bishop; that he may direct and inspect the flock of Christ; that by his exhortations he may confirm the unstable, by his admonitions reclaim the reprobate, and by the purity of his life render religion amiable and interesting to all. [WATSON *op. cit.* p. 72]

It is to his credit that when he was sounded out in 1787 by the Duke of Norfolk with regard to his being translated to Carlisle, he made it clear that he had no wish to seek such an appointment as he wished to retain his independence of action in parliament. He closed his letter with the admonition, 'I sincerely hope, for the credit of the Church and of religion, that neither the bishoprick of Carlisle, nor any other bishoprick, will be prostituted in promoting the purposes of parliamentary policy.' [*Ibid.* p. 188] The fulfilment of that hope lay far in the future. Watson has often been criticized for being an absentee bishop preferring to live in Westmorland where he grew up as a boy when his father was headmaster of Heversham Grammar School. But he was an able theologian, one who thought about the social issues of his day, an independent minded prelate politically and one who had some real understanding of what a bishop should be.

We get a rare glimpse into the thinking of a recently appointed bishop, who had a high and solemn view of his work, in Edward Stanley's journal. He recorded his reflections a few months after his arrival in Norwich and at a time when he was being assailed by insinuations of ambition:

> Little do they guess how engrossed I altogether am in one sole object – the spiritual and temporal welfare of the diocese. By night, in my many waking hours, the working of my mind is how and what can be done by me to promote the end for which I accepted a situation for which in every other point I feel myself so unqualified and so unfit. I accepted it with a determination not to make it a source of profit to myself or patronage for others, it being

> my unshaken determination to expend not only the whole proceeds of the emoluments on the diocese, but the greater part of my private fortune also, saving little or nothing, more than it was my wish to do at Alderley; that, with regard to patronage, no motives of private interest, or mere connection, or personal friendship, should sway me in giving preferments; and that the names hitherto on my list consist of individuals known to me only by respectability and fitness for the situations to which I could appoint them. Such are the feelings with which I accepted the office of a Bishop – on such I have acted hitherto; and God grant that nothing may induce me to depart from principles which will alone justify me in entering on a line of life and arduous responsibility, drawing me aside from pursuits and tastes with which my habits were far more congenial. [A.P. STANLEY op. cit. p. 30]

Stanley now laid aside his earlier love of scientific pursuits and concentrated on studies which were more related to his new post – church history, systematic divinity, biographical literature which bore upon the duties of a clergyman, and even NT Greek which he had long neglected.

We have seen how men achieved episcopal preferment but having reached that goal in their career, there was no help or advice available to a bishop-designate (apart from the Ordinal in the *Book of Common Prayer*), and no spiritual or practical preparation for the responsibilities which lay ahead. What there was, as M.L. Clarke in his *Greek Studies in England, 1700-1830* has noted, was 'a wealth of Classical talent on the episcopal bench, with Blomfield at London, Monk at Gloucester, Burgess at Salisbury and Maltby at Durham.' Some of whom even still managed to devote time amidst their diocesan responsibilities to their first academic love, and Blomfield found refuge in it when laid low by sickness. But far more than classical or mathematical talent was needed if a diocese was to run smoothly. The gifts of administration and public speaking, not least, were needed, and, above all, a heart for the clergy and the people committed to their care.

Maybe it was this perceived lack of any official guidance for new members of the bench which prompted a lay friend of a newly appointed bishop to write fifteen letters to him in 1841, which were subsequently published anonymously as *The Bishop: a series of letters to a newly created prelate* by William Cooke Taylor. The writer was clearly a well-educated churchman with a better than average knowledge of the ordained ministry as practised at that time, and of the ministry of oversight a bishop ought to exercise, and a writer wishing to see much needed reforms brought about. Taylor may have been the actual writer, for he was a graduate of Trinity College Dublin, a prolific writer on religion, history and social affairs and a notable biographer whose religious views were influenced by Richard Whately. The letters tackle most aspects of a bishop's ministry from such high profile things as 'The conduct of a bishop in parliament' [letter VII], 'Visitations – Intercourse between a bishop and his clergy – Confirmations – Education' [letter XIII], 'Candidates for holy orders – Examinations – Charges' [letter XI] through to more personal aspects such as 'The manners of a bishop – Intercourse with superiors, equals and inferiors' [letter VIII] and 'Mildness of demeanour – Influence of literary habits and reputation' [letter IX]. The final one is headed 'The opposition which must be expected by those who propose wise schemes of practical reform' [letter XV]. The writer provides many refreshingly common-sensical and practical observations.

Nigel Scotland claims in his biography of J.B. Sumner that the bishop 'saw one of his major roles as that of *pastor pastorum*. This was not something that he had to do with conscious deliberation; he had a pastor's heart and took naturally to the task.' [SCOTLAND *The Life and Work of John Bird Sumner* p. 50] His wife died just a year after his arrival in the diocese but he resolved to put that great loss behind him and focus on his ministry.

> It soon became clear that his diocese and particularly his clergy had become his family. For almost twenty years Sumner gave himself unstintingly to the task of encouraging and supporting them. He travelled great distances to preach to their congregations, he entertained many of them with gracious simplicity in his home and he arranged meetings where he could hear and learn about their needs and concerns. [*Ibid*. p. 50f]

Sumner was not alone in this, Van Mildert showed similar concern and kept a room at Auckland Castle, supplied with refreshments, available for clergy calling to see him.

Jenkinson and Kaye in their primary visitation *Charges* explicitly appealed to the younger clergy, in particular, to turn to them for help and advice. Copleston's letters to his Chancellor, Bruce Knight, reveal how well informed he was of the poverty and problems which some of the curates and incumbents were facing, and how he tried to support them. A letter dated 30 September 1828 can serve to illustrate this and also how limited a bishop sometimes was in the help he could provide.

> The next day was employed in visiting the Church [at Merthyr Tidvill] & Dowlais Chapel & in conversing with Mr. John Jones and Mr. Jenkins on the circumstances & conditions of the parish.

They appear to me to be both excellent men – but both sadly underpaid. Mr. Maber [the absentee Rector of Merthyr Tydvil] allows £75 & £15 for a house – but if the living is worth £600 or £700 a year, which I am told is the value, surely an addition might be made. He also allows £30 to Mr. Jenkins – but here there is some difference of opinion as to the terms of the grant. Mr. Jones understands that Mr. Jenkins is to take part of the surplice duty, in consideration of it, but this not done, nor understood by Mr. Jenkins to be the subject of the grant. I think of settling it by requiring Mr. Maber to give all the fees to his curate, & by letting them (i.e. Messrs. Jones & Jenkins) make an arrangement between themselves as to this portion of duty. Upon this subject I shall be glad of your advice when we meet.

[BROWN ed. *op. cit.* p. 61f]

Phillpotts made real efforts to get to know his extensive diocese and to meet many of his clergy in his first year. He was consecrated at Lambeth Palace on 2 January 1831, did homage to the King in Brighton on the 4th and arrived at Exeter's East Gate at 1 p.m. on Saturday 8th where he was met by the Mayor and Chamber of the city, in full regalia, who welcomed him warmly. On Friday the 14th he was enthroned and two days later preached his first sermon in the cathedral. He stayed for three weeks before returning to London and the business of parliament. In May he was back, having taken passage in a coaster to Plymouth calling at Exmouth on the way. 'The spending a few weeks at a good central spot in Cornwall will enable me, I hope, to make myself well acquainted with a considerable portion of that member of my diocese,' he wrote to his secretary. [DAVIES *Henry Phillpotts* p. 104] He spent three weeks in Penryn with Archdeacon Sheepshanks. In July he stayed at Ilfracombe, then several days at Tawstock, going on via South Molton to Lord Fortescue's residence at Castle Hill. His very hospitable host invited 'all the neighbouring clergy, in divisions' to meet him. At the end of August Phillpotts made a tour of the most westerly part of his diocese, arriving in the Scilly Isles on board HMS Hermes, accompanied by his chaplain and the Archdeacons of Cornwall and Totnes. He was accommodated at the house of the Duke of Leeds's agent, and from there visited the islands of St Martin's, Tresco and Bryher, inspecting churches and schools and the various parishes. [*Ibid.* p. 105]

Wolffe comments 'One fruit of his early foray into the diocese was his discovery of how inadequate the endowments of certain livings were - the Dean and Chapter of Windsor were the impropriators of fourteen livings in the diocese and levels of stipends were generally unsatisfactory and he put it "strenuously, though courteously" that there was a case for improvement and by March 1832 was able to report that he had persuaded them to augment the value of the livings.' [WOLFFE *Bishop Henry Phillpotts and the Administration of the Diocese of Exeter 1830-1865* in the *Devonshire Association Report & Transactions* Vol. 114 p. 101]

He also laid down some principles he intended to be guided by in his dealings with junior clergy. There were many assistant curates, some of whom were only in Deacon's orders and unable to celebrate Holy Communion, but who were in sole charge of parishes for absentee incumbents. This inevitably caused requests to be submitted to the bishop for reducing the usual length of the diaconate. He wrote to his secretary on 30 March 1831:

> I object *generally* to deacons being ordained priest till they have been deacons a year. Cases of particular urgency may admit of remission of this general rule, but the delay of their ordination as deacons does not affect the reason, or the principle, of the rule. If any of these deacons have particular reasons to urge, let them urge them, and they shall be attended to.
> [DAVIES *op. cit* p. 118]

He made clear to incumbents that no assistant curate should be paid less than £70 a year – though even that was below the recommended national minimum. Pluralist incumbents were required to reside on their larger benefice, and employ a curate in the other parish. Phillpotts believed this arrangement would provide useful probationary experience for newly ordained men who, he insisted, must remain in their first curacy for at least two years to gain experience. He also required that a new licence should be issued in every case where a curate's conditions of employment were changed. In this way he was able to exercise some kind of control over them and where necessary press for improvements. A memorandum dated 7 May 1831 gives a list of eight curacies with new licences for increased salaries – some were modest additions of £10 but one recorded an increase from £40 a year to £75. By 1835 the average stipend of a curate had risen to £89 a year, the fourth highest in the country. Incumbents who were being pressed to pay the increases were not happy about it and some protested in writing to the bishop.

Sadly many of the bishops, though pious, well-meaning and generous in their support of Church-based charities and of indigent clergy families, had no idea of the conditions in which ordinary people lived and worked in their dioceses, simply because they had never done any visiting among poor agricultural labourers and had never spent even a single day observing the working conditions in a mill or industrial factory or seen at first hand the overcrowded, disease ridden slum dwellings the workers went home to. And, at the other end of the social divide, prior to their appointment to the bench of bishops, they had no experience of how the upper house functioned. Archbishop Howley hosted an annual meeting of the bishops in London in the week after Easter and they met frequently at Lambeth during times of crisis. What is clear, however, is that the bishops were not of one mind when they deliberated in private about the Bills which came to the Lords. Norman gives this example of the division of opinion which existed between the new 'progressive' thinkers and the old.

> Thus in 1833 Blomfield had opposed the Duke of Richmond's Bill to provide public relief for distressed agricultural workers – a model of the old view of social responsibilities – on the grounds that the measure would 'affect the free circulation of labour', and would 'relieve one class of the Community at the expense of another.' This was the voice of Political Economy. Bishop Law of Bath and Wells, on the other hand, supported the Bill because it 'would have the effect of preventing much misery,' regardless of the economic principles involved. He spoke for the paternalists. [NORMAN *op. cit.* p. 137]

It didn't help that a bishop was expected to be in London for several months of the year for the parliamentary session, and, if he had an additional office, such as Copleston had as Dean of St Paul's where he was expected to serve half his time, there were few weeks left over to be spent in his diocese. In Charles Sumner's case, however, when in London he preached every Sunday in one of his churches south of the Thames as they were in his vast diocese. Such lengthy absences from his diocese simply meant the bishop was not available when a curate or incumbent needed his advice and help. In many cases it was left to the archdeacon or chancellor to deal with.

The clergy's only regular and direct contact with their diocesan was when he came on a visitation. The frequency of episcopal visitations varied from diocese to diocese but the norm was every third year in accordance with Canon 60 of the Canons of 1604. In most cases a questionnaire about parish life was sent out and had to be returned in advance of the Bishop's coming so that he had some factual knowledge about what was actually happening in the parishes. Some of the bishops, notably C.R. Sumner, took great care over reading them and analysing the results, and then commenting on his findings in the *Charge* he delivered. A visitation *Charge* was an occasion when their chief pastor could inform and inspire them. Some did but clearly not all. It is hard to hold a listener's attention when the bishop spoke for two or more hours, and that was after listening to a sermon which could be more than an hour long.

In Arthur Burns' judgement 'by the 1830s and 1840s it [the visitation] was the most important diocesan occasion and was crucial to the relationship of bishop and clergy and the development of diocesan consciousness.' [BURNS *The Diocesan Revival* p. 39] Whilst the norm was once every three years, the Norwich clergy had to make do with seeing their bishop just once every seventh, and Winchester, previous to C.R. Sumner's appointment, just once in an episcopate. Sumner established a quadrennial pattern and in 1833 increased the number of centres to thirteen where he delivered his *Charge* and then entertained the clergy to a dinner. Bathurst carried out his last visitation in 1820 and the diocese of Norwich then had to wait eighteen years before Stanley carried out his first following Bathurst's death at the age of 93. The Bishop of Lincoln divided his diocese in two, visiting half one year and the other the next, and then had a year without any. In preparation for a visitation, articles of enquiry were issued to church wardens and incumbents. The bishop usually wanted to know the state of ecclesiastical affairs in every parish – how many services were held a Sunday, how many parishioners attended, what schools were there in the parish, what was done about catechizing the children, was the priest resident, the value of the living and what the curate was paid (if there was one), the state of the church building and of the parsonage (again, if there was one), how strong were the Dissenters locally, and much else. [See JACOB *op. cit.* p. 274f]

Not all bishops were keen on creating additional labour for themselves by having to read and note the answers to the questions in their Articles of Enquiry. Copleston, for one, took this line in a letter, written whilst on holiday in Sidmouth on 1 August 1836, to his chancellor.

> You will, I fear, not agree with me – but I really am not disposed to send circular Visitation Queries. They are almost entirely useless – they are very troublesome & if I am to frank them all, I don't know how & when it is to be done. But the chief objection is that I believe it is by no means usual to send them *every* Visitation. In this Diocese, they do not - & I am sure they are much more needed here than in mine. At a primary visitation their propriety is obvious. They are in fact indispensable – but having received two sets, I think myself sufficiently informed as to all such details, without having recourse again to such heavy machinery. [BROWN ed. *op. cit.* p. 221]

That is not a view shared by C.R. Sumner who attached great value to the information about the parishes in his diocese that these returns provided him with every four years.

In addition, archdeacons visited the parishes in their designated area, in theory, twice a year – once to admit church wardens, and the other to inspect churches and make recommendations about repairs and improvements. In practice, these duties were occasionally delegated to rural deans where they existed for not all dioceses had them. Or the chancellor of the diocese might carry out the visitation in lieu of the archdeacon, some of whom were inactive. They received only scant financial reward for their labours – in 1831 the mean net annual archidiaconal income was just £87 [= £8,061] Like its episcopal counterpart, an archidiaconal visitation brought clergy and churchwardens together in one of the main churches in the archdeaconry for a service, at which a sermon would be preached, usually by a local clergyman who had been invited to give it, and to hear a *Charge*. Churchwardens were admitted to office, and made their returns. The proceedings ended with a clerical dinner. Samuel Butler was assiduous in this respect and published his annual archidiaconal *Charge* but he managed to deliver only one as a bishop before death took him off the ecclesiastical stage. Not all archdeacons, of course, were as assiduous as Butler. Copleston complained about this when he arrived in his diocese in 1828.

> The more I reflect on the state of discipline in this diocese, the more convinced am I that there is something wrong in the system. That an Archdeacon should be a cypher & without duties & without authority is certainly an abuse. It cannot have been so originally. The Chancellor indeed takes a great part of his duties – but he does not personally visit the Churches & the Glebe-houses – neither do the Rural Deans report to him. They would report to the Archdeacon, if there were one - & to him, who also personally inspects, the reports would be of use. But to the Bishop, who cannot personally inspect, such reports are of little use. [BROWN ed. *op. cit.* p. 64]

The office of rural dean was gradually being restored in most dioceses but what these office holders were permitted to do varied considerably. They were, however, all involved in providing the bishop with local knowledge and information about clergy as well as the state of buildings. [See BURNS *op. cit.* chapter 4 on the revival of the rural dean and the ruridecanal chapter.]

By 1828 with the knowledge of impending reforms of various kinds in the public domain, bishops found their visitation *Charge* to be a useful vehicle for expressing their own views, and, if so desired, advertising and implementing reforms in their dioceses. As we shall see when we look at some of their *Charges*, there was a handful of issues the bishops repeatedly spoke about: the better provision of churches and of more free seating in them for poor people; more resident clergy providing two services a Sunday; better remuneration of curates and the augmentation of poorly endowed livings; and the better provision of parochial elementary schools. Much improvement was achieved on those fronts but the rural and industrial working classes continued to drift away from the Established Church. Many of those who retained an active interest in the Christian Faith now expressed it in the fellowship of a dissenting chapel, with the Methodists as their first choice, as the 1851 census would later reveal, though Horace Mann's report on that census shows that no denomination was having any real success with the poorest layers of society. The Church of England did, however, continue to draw many of the middle and upper classes to its Sunday services and attract their support for parish activities, and financial support for diocesan initiatives such as building new churches and providing clergy to minister in them.

After the parliamentary session had ended, many bishops took some weeks for recreation, and then spent the late summer and early autumn in their dioceses carrying out visitations and confirmation tours. Ordinations were often held in late December. Van Mildert in a letter dated 31 August 1831 from Auckland Castle gives some indication of his ministry and public duties,

> The bustle of public days here, of the Assizes, and of company staying with us, have left me but little time at my command. The day after tomorrow I set out for Newcastle, where I am to preach for the Sons of the Clergy on Thursday, and to hold a Confirmation on Friday. On my return, I am also to preach at Durham Cathedral on Sunday, and to confirm on Monday. An Ordination is fixed for the Sunday after Michaelmas. Afterwards, I expect to have two or three Consecrations [i.e. of new churches], which will probably close my *public* labours for this session. [IVES *op. cit.* p. 109]

The only occasion on which an ordinary layman might see and hear a bishop was when he came to a neighbouring town to minister the rite of Confirmation. In the recent past, that was only likely to happen once in every three years and these occasions could be singularly impersonal. In the 18th century, confirmations and visitations had been carried out in tandem – the visitation charge being delivered in the morning and the bishop confirmed candidates in the afternoon and into the evening, as long as daylight permitted. Norman Sykes in his *Church and State in England in the 18th Century* has given a comprehensive account of the problems and difficulties which beset bishops as they set off on horseback or by coach over poor roads and tracks to carry out this tri-ennial task. Bishop Hurd of Worcester, for example, who had a more compact diocese than many of his fellow bishops carried out his primary visitation and confirmations between 20 July and 4 August 1782 halting at nine places where he laid hands on a total of 6,490 persons. The greatest number was 2,000 at Shipston and 1,200 at Alcester. He repeated the process three years later but by 1788 he had separated his visitations from his confirmation tours. [SYKES p. 124f] Other bishops too changed their practice and were beginning to confirm in places never visited before. He cites the case of Bishop Watson of Llandaff who, though over seventy years of age, 'went over the mountains from Neath to a place where no bishop had ever had a confirmation before, Merthyr Tydvil. In his time this place had become, from a small village, a great town containing 10,000 or 12,000 inhabitants occupied in the fabrication of iron; and he thought it his duty not only to go to confirm the young people there, but to preach to those who were grown up.' [*Ibid*. p.137] Bishop C.R. Sumner, in his Llandaff days, confirmed at fourteen places. Copleston increased that to sixteen in 1834 but retained the old practice of just doing it triennially. He did not approve of his neighbour, Bishop Grey of Hereford, holding confirmations every year – 'not, in my opinion, very judicious', he wrote in November 1834.

Because of the infrequency of episcopal visits, the problems of huge numbers attending the few centres remained well into the 19th century. Blomfield of Chester, for example, confirmed 7,991 candidates in six different places in six days – there was no opportunity for the candidates to 'meet' him in any meaningful sense. By the 1830s, some bishops were doing an annual trek to different parts of their diocese for this purpose, and ministering confirmation in more and in smaller centres of population with fewer candidates at each service. They were also giving directions to the clergy about appropriate preparation of the candidates and the right age at which to present them – preferably no younger than sixteen. When C.R. Sumner came to Winchester, confirmation was ministered in only 22 centres in Hampshire, he raised it to forty-five in 1832 and by 1867 the list had swollen to sixty-seven. In 1830 the number of centres in Surrey was twenty-four, and by 1863 had increased to fifty-six. [G.H. SUMNER *op. cit.* p. 216] In his early years he set aside a month for each confirmation tour, often ministering twice a day. And then in the evening was usually required to meet a party of guests over a meal who had been invited by his host for the night who was often a clerical or lay friend.

S.R. Hole recalled his confirmation under the old regime of Vernon Harcourt in the early 1830s when the Archbishop was well into his 70s:

> My first recollection of dignitaries is of Archbishop Vernon-Harcourt, who confirmed me at Newark – a tall, aristocratic man in a wig, which became him well. There was in those days a scant administration and a large abuse of this Apostolic ordinance. Seldom offered, and only in cities and towns, the ceremony was attended by crowds from the surrounding districts, who came with little or no preparation, behaved with much irreverence and levity within the church, and outside as though at a fair. From a parish adjoining my own the candidates went in a wagon, and gave a fiddler half a crown to play them merry tunes on their journey.
> [HOLE *The Memories of Dean Hole* p. 142f]

Edward Boys Ellman tells a similar story from his boyhood in Chichester diocese:

> When I was confirmed, in 1829, the Confirmation service was held in St Anne's Church, Lewes. And on that occasion, some of the confirmees were brought all the way from Seaford in wagons – a distance of eleven or twelve miles, great boys and girls riding together, and all feasted before they returned home. The day was looked upon by most of the young people as a regular outing, the greater part of the day being spent on the road, going backwards and forwards. It is easy to imagine how little they came prepared for the solemn rite.
> At that period a bishop would frequently only repeat the prayer "Defend, O Lord, this, Thy child," once for a whole railful, (*sic*) and then pass along the rail laying his hand on the head of each... At that time, and for many years after, in the Chichester Diocese, as well as in other dioceses, confirmations were held only once in every three years, and then only in the towns, so that all the villages around had to send their candidates to the nearest town. I was only thirteen when I was confirmed, which was rather an early age at that date; but I was anxious to be confirmed, and my parents also wished my confirmation to take place before I left home.
> [ELLMAN *Recollections of a Sussex Parson* p. 96f]

Harford gives a lengthy description of how Bishop Burgess in old age at Salisbury ministered this rite to batches of candidates in turn, presumably to make it a more intimate and personal occasion for them.

Admission into the church was allowed only to the catechumens, their ministers, and their parents or guardians. All of these were, if possible, admitted some half hour previously to the commencement of the service . . . (the males on one side of the church, the females on the other), and had time to collect their thoughts, and offer up without distraction a prayer for the blessing of God . . . before the entrance of the Bishop, who, on proceeding to the chancel, found there a moderate number of young people, seldom exceeding seventy or eighty, in readiness for him. The ceremony which consisted only of the Confirmation Service, commenced by the officiating minister reading the introductory preface. The Bishop then delivered to the division of catechumens about to be confirmed, who were kneeling before him, a few words of exhortation . . . He then confirmed them, repeating the Prayer of Confirmation after imposition of hands on four or six only, never more, at a time, pronounced over them; and dismissed them with a short charge, referring principally to the 17th chapter of St John's Gospel, and very touching from its simplicity . . . This division was then allowed to retire altogether from the church, and another division was brought up from their seats, and confirmed and dismissed in like manner . . . [HARFORD *op. cit.* pp.402-404]

Harford comments on how fatiguing this was as he would confirm 700 or 800 persons in the course of a morning but he insisted that personal inconvenience mattered little to him – he wanted the service to be a memorable one for the candidates. It was whilst ministering confirmation in Warminster in 1835 that he suffered a slight stroke which affected his speech and bodily strength from which he never fully recovered. [*Ibid.* p. 405]

Another bishop who took particular care over confirmation was Ryder. In his Gloucester days he used to send out a printed letter to the parents and godparents of every candidate before he came to confirm, and after his translation to Lichfield his chaplain gave a second letter to each of the candidates as they rose after the laying on of hands.

Charles Linnell describes the situation as experienced by Bathurst, the sixty-five year old Bishop of Norwich:

In the summer of 1809, he undertook an exhausting Confirmation tour. Between sixteen and seventeen thousand people were confirmed at Bury St Edmunds alone, and in the pouring rain of the July of that year the roads of North Norfolk were almost impassable. The episcopal coach trundled along often getting stuck in the mud. Sir George Chad of Thursford Hall rescued him from such a predicament after a Confirmation at Holt, and after lurching along the roads of North-west Norfolk he was glad to break his journey after a Confirmation at Snettisham and stay a few days with Mr Styleman, 'very genteel and a gentleman with £7,000 a year.' 'It is' he wrote, 'a consolation to me to meet and become acquainted with such characters, and it is a full reward for my trouble.' [LINNELL *op. cit.* p. 141f]

Bathurst normally only carried out a confirmation tour every seven years, and as he visited only a small number of centres, some children had to travel far. Stanley changed that to it being an annual event and he tried to ensure that no child had to travel more than four miles to get to the church where the rite would be performed. He also evinced the kind of personal care and individual attention for children which had marked his ministry as a parish priest. One of his chaplains describes this:

> He made accurate observation of the candidates; and the pains taken with them by their respective ministers – the open Prayer-book – the devout and serious demeanour – seldom failed to receive his commendation; whilst anything like carelessness or levity of conduct met with his prompt and sharp rebuke. When adults presented themselves to him, they almost invariably went away with some kind word of encouragement, spoken with an earnestness that could never be forgotten. But the objects that would especially engage his attention were the friendless children that came from the different union-houses. His eye was always quick to discover their homely appearance, and before they were allowed to leave the rails of the communion table he would address them individually: he used then to request that the chaplain to the workhouse might be summoned, to whom he would express his satisfaction that these children had been brought to him, and would desire that he might be furnished with the list of their names. And it was his habit on his return home to forward to each a Bible and a Prayer-book, in which the name of the child, the date of the Confirmation, with the words 'Remember the day,' and the donor of the book, were written with his own hand. [A.P. STANLEY *op. cit.* p. 42]

F.E. Witts, the active and conscientious squarson of Upper Slaughter in the Cotswolds has given us a vignette of the fifty-two year old Bishop Monk of Gloucester hurrying about his diocese ministering this rite in August 1838:

> The Bishop arrived at the Unicorn Inn at Stow from Campden, where he had confirmed and visited yesterday, complaining of fatigue and over-exertion and suffering from the increased infirmity of his eye-sight. He received me with his wonted friendship. When his Lordship had robed, he went to the church where confirmation was administered to, I suppose, nearly 400 young persons of both sexes. All was done with much order and decorum. The Bishop delivered a suitable, plain but rather feeble and commonplace discourse on confirmation. The Bishop and clergy retired for an hour to the

Rectory. Several ladies were present; Mrs Leigh of Stoneleigh Abbey with a daughter who has been confirmed. My son and daughter who were greeted by Bishop Monk with the utmost cordiality and kindness. At 2 o'clock we returned to the church for evening service. The Bishop's charge was very long and laboured; his imperfect vision led to much hesitation. . . his unwillingness to exhaust the attention of his hearers led him to curtail his charge by omitting considerable portions, and consequently the line of argument was interrupted.

Bishop Monk is a man of very kindly disposition very well meaning; but lacks judgement, and is of a very susceptible, irritable, and sensitive temperament. The evening exceedingly damp and cold; but the labours of the day not yet over as we sallied forth in our chariot to meet the Bishop at Mr Ford's (at Little Rissington) where he was to sleep preparatory to two Confirmations fixed for to-morrow at Bourton-on-the-Water and Northleach. The Bishop adverted to a subject of some local importance as regards his now greatly extended diocese, in which there are no less than three charitable associations for affording pecuniary relief to distressed clergymen, their widows and orphans; that long established in the old diocese of Gloucester, a like association for the City of Bristol, and a third in North Wiltshire. The Bishop thinks it desirable that these should be concentrated into one; but it is obvious that such an arrangement will be fraught with many difficulties.

[WITTS *The Diary of a Cotswold Parson* p. 150f]

As the above quotation shows, that particular bishop had chosen by the late thirties to stick with the old practice of combining his confirmation and visitation tours into one.

As some of the earlier quotations have already shown, diocesan geography and poor road communications made it very difficult for a bishop to have direct personal contact with his clergy. Given the number of parishes and clergy and the distances and difficulties involved in travelling, even the most hard-working bishop had little hope of seeing and really knowing his clergy. John Kaye, as diligent as any of the bishops, had over 1,250 clergymen in his care scattered over a very large area. Moving through the countryside over rough roads was a slow and laborious process, so no bishop ventured out into the sticks unless the journey was essential. The much less diligent and very aged Bathurst of Norwich had nearly 1,100 clergy spread across an equally large diocese, and York (no youngster either) had about 825. And there were no suffragan bishops to assist them. At the other end of the scale, Rochester covered less than a hundred parishes and Carlisle just 130, but neither bishop made visiting the clergy a priority. Both Murray and Percy came from aristocratic families, so there was the additional problem of the wide social gap between them and their inferiors: the poor curates and incumbents. If an incumbent had some pressing reason to meet with his bishop, he was just as likely to have to travel to London to see him there during the many months he spent in London as to visit him at his diocesan residence.

Even conscientious archdeacons would have found it hard to get to know the clergy when they carried out their annual visitations. It is unlikely that the Bishop even knew all their names – not least because some incumbents had not bothered to get their curates formally licensed by him. A frequent plea to incumbents made in episcopal *Charges* was to do so. Or, as in the case of Bathurst with almost as many clergy in his diocese as Kaye had, he was too infirm and with no prospect of taking retirement as pensions, in the sense we know them, did not exist. So he soldiered on (if playing whist in Malvern can be so described) and only visited his diocese for brief periods, leaving diocesan business to his aged secretary and to his son. In a letter to his daughter he complained about the strain of getting back to Norwich from London to ordain over 50 men – hardly surprising as he was eighty-seven years old by then. It is unlikely that any of the clergy in that diocese ever thought of their bishop as a 'father in God', even if they had written a begging letter to him asking for financial aid which had produced by return ten or more pounds, equivalent to a thousand pounds today. Bathurst held his last ordination in 1833, when he was 89, prior to leaving the diocese. He wrote to his good friend Thomas William Coke Esq. of Holkham Hall on 22 September,

> My ordination is fixed for Sunday the 6th of October. Soon after that I shall pay a visit to my daughter in Hampshire; and about the end of that month it is my intention to be settled in London, where my hours will glide on smoothly, with the assistance of an elbow-chair, a good fire, and a book in the morning, and a rubber of whist in the evening, with three or four ancient ladies, who win just enough of my money to keep them in good humour, without making me bankrupt. [THISTLETHWAYTE *op. cit.* p. 411]

One can hardly blame this old man for wanting to enjoy his closing years relaxing in such harmless ease but the sad fact is that he still remained in office as Bishop of Norwich and none of those whom he had ordained that Sunday in October would ever experience any episcopal care and oversight from him. His successor, Edward Stanley, took far more care. He instituted a mandatory three day examination, inquired more closely into a candidate's previous career, requiring private letters as well as official testimonials for each, and entertained them at the palace. Stories were told of his exceptional care for individuals – one runs as follows:

'Hearing that one of the candidates was very nervous and in low spirits concerning his fate, he took the trouble to walk up, after dinner, from the Palace to the hotel where the man was staying, to assure him that his work was well done, and that he need be under no alarm about not succeeding.' [A.P. STANLEY op. cit. p. 43]

In theory, all bishops should have known many of their clergy personally because they had ordained them but that was not the case in practice. It was possible in a diocese such as St Asaph where Christopher Bethel ordained just forty-one Deacons between 1830 and 1840, most of whom he saw a year later when he ordained them Priest. But other bishops had that many and more every year. Another problem was that many bishops were lax in their ordination discipline because if a candidate possessed a degree, had provided appropriate character references and a Title for Orders, and was willing to subscribe to the Thirty-nine Articles, there were no grounds for refusing him.

A few bishops, however, did examine candidates for holy orders very thoroughly but it was done with the prime purpose of weeding out those who did not share his Lordship's view on such theological issues as baptismal regeneration. Marsh who was a leading figure among the "Orthodox" or High Churchmen became infamous for this. Pollard describes him as 'an attractively unpleasant because incurably quarrelsome character.' [POLLARD A Trap to catch Calvinists in CQR 1961 p. 447]

Overton rated him more highly: 'Bishop Marsh, of Peterborough, was one of the ablest prelates of his day, and not the sort of man to fight with shadows. Yet he was so alarmed at the progress of Calvinism, that in 1822, he framed 87 questions for his ordination candidates, on purpose to exclude those who held Calvinistic views.' [OVERTON The English Church in the 19th Century 1800-33 p. 187] The questions fell under nine heads or chapters, dealing respectively with redemption by Jesus Christ, original sin, free will, justification, everlasting salvation, predestination, regeneration, resurrection, and the Holy Spirit. Overton explains the controversy in this way, 'Calvinists held that no man was in a justified state until he had a conscious sense of pardon and peace with God. The "Orthodox", on the other hand, held that all baptized Christians were in a justified state, and that there was no such thing as a second birth after that which took place in the Sacrament of Holy Baptism; they made, of course, a marked distinction between regeneration and conversion, and laid stress upon the daily renewal by God's Holy Spirit which most Christians in their present imperfect state required.' [Ibid. p 190]

When the matter came up in the House of Lords in June 1831 Marsh declared that his intention was not simply to exclude Calvinists. It may not have been his object but it was certainly the result. He stated that the questions were 'adapted to the present wants of his diocese; they operate as a check to some particularly prevailing irregularities.'

Sydney Smith launched a scathing attack on Marsh in the *Edinburgh Review* under the title *Persecuting Bishops*:

> The Bishop has at least done a very unusual thing in his Eighty-seven Questions. The two Archbishops, and we believe every other Bishop, and all the Irish hierarchy, admit curates into their dioceses without any such precautions. The necessity of such severe and scrupulous inquisition, in short, has been apparent to nobody but the Bishop of Peterborough; and the authorities by which he seeks to justify it are anything but satisfactory. . .
> The Bishop who rejects a curate upon the Eighty-seven Questions is necessarily and inevitably opposed to the Bishop who ordained him. The Bishop of Gloucester ordains a young man of twenty-three years of age, not thinking it necessary to put to him these interrogatories, or putting them, perhaps, and approving of answers diametrically opposed to those that are required by the Bishop of Peterborough. The young clergyman then comes to the last-mentioned Bishop; and the Bishop, after *putting him to the Question*, says, "You are unfit for a clergyman," – though, ten days before, the Bishop of Gloucester had made him one!

Having illustrated in some detail the method and injustice of Marsh's interrogatory practice, Smith concludes his article, 'Now we have done with the Bishop. We give him all he asks as his legal right; and only contend, that he is acting a very indiscreet and injudicious part – fatal to his quiet – fatal to his reputation as a man of sense – blamed by Ministers – blamed by all the Bench of Bishops – vexatious to the Clergy; and highly injurious to the Church.'[*Ibid*. p.133] Marsh reduced the number of questions to thirty-six but refused to change his practice.

Burgess too examined candidates personally and thoroughly but not with a view to excluding any who held Calvinist views. His purpose was more to ascertain that they had a real sense of vocation and were serious about entering upon the sacred ministry. One of those he ordained described many years later the lasting impression the bishop had made on him at his examination.

> He did not entrust to others the examination of candidates for Holy Orders. He took upon himself that important task, and no man was better qualified; for, having once satisfied himself of the competency of the person examined, he blended his queries with such admonitions as were likely to pro-

duce the most beneficial effects. For my part, I trust, the benignity of his countenance, and the kind, the solemn, the emphatic manner in which he spoke to me, once in particular, during my examination, concerning my duties as a Christian Minister, will never 'while memory holds her seat', be erased from my mind. During the ordination week he frequently exhorted us to be constant and regular in the practice of family devotion, of which he every morning gave us a beautiful example. [HARFORD *op. cit.* p. 227f]

Frances Knight describes how equally thorough Kaye was in examining candidates himself. She cites the case of John Rashdall who was ordained Deacon in 1833 and Priest a year later. On both occasions he first had to undergo a theological grilling by the Bishop.

On the Thursday he began the examination, and 'answered at some length all the papers' which were chiefly doctrinal, Burnett on the Articles and Paley's *Evidences*. Then followed an hour long *viva voce* examination with the bishop, during which they discussed the examination papers and 'divers theol. subjects' including the 6th chapter of St John's Gospel and Moore's controversial *Travels of an Irish Gentleman*. The examination continued the next day, with more papers on Paley, and one on Pretyman-Tomline, presumably his *Elements of Christian Theology*, which was widely recommended to ordinands but which Rashdall admitted to not having read. The examination ended with a second, shorter, conversation with the bishop . . . On Saturday Rashdall signed the Thirty-nine Articles, paid three shillings and seven pence and dined with the bishop at a 'sumptuous dinner – venison – all kinds of wine etc.' The next day, in a service that lasted three hours, Rashdall was ordained. The sermon, preached by J.A. Jeremie, moved him and other men to tears. His ordination to the priesthood followed a similar pattern twelve months later.   [KNIGHT *op. cit.* p. 113]

In contrast to that, Howley left examining candidates to his Chaplain. Blomfield had that task when Howley was Bishop of London and he set a high standard which was kept up by his successor in the post, W.R. Lyall. 'He took up references, conducted interviews, set written question papers. He did everything he could to stop the incompetent and the immoral slipping through the net; and judging by his subsequent promotion, he succeeded.' [DEWEY *The Passing of Barchester* p. 16] Lyall succeeded Blomfield as Archdeacon of Colchester, and later became Dean of Canterbury.

Copleston also used to leave interviews and examination of candidates to his examining chaplain, Bruce Knight, who was also the chancellor of the diocese. The bishop then met with the candidates on the Saturday when he delivered a *Charge* to them before ordaining them the next day. To a conscientious clergyman like Knight, examining candidates took its toll. Copleston commented on this to J.M. Traherne:

> There will be twelve candidates for Ordination – the best set upon the whole we have had for many years. Bruce Knight was particularly pleased with the Saxon portion of them as compared with the Celtic: I am afraid this examination has been too burdensome & harassing. Now it is over he tells me how ill he has been, and how great the fatigue & anxiety of the two long days were. [BROWN ed. *op. cit.* p. 246]

Right from the start of his episcopal ministry, Copleston had felt the need for some reform in the matter of ordaining deacons, though, in reality, the only avenue open to him was by enforcing an even more selective process prior to ordination.

> That Deacons should only be ordained as Assistants, except in certain strong cases - & that these Orders shd. not be indelible. How absurd it is, to confide the whole care of a parish to a man not authorised to administer the Sacrament? And again, if a deacon is a probationer, what is to become of him after his probation if he is not worthy of Priest's orders. He is deprived of subsistence altogether – if precluded from entering into any other profession. I have in my diocese two cases of this kind. In fact, it is no *probation* if the first step is decisive & irrevocable. [*Ibid.* p. 74]

Today, men and women who feel they have a calling from God to the ordained ministry usually have to undergo a lengthy period of probation and discernment at the diocesan level before attending a national advisory/selection conference after which their bishop makes his/her decision about letting them begin professional training at a residential theological college or at one of the regional, non-residential theological institutes. Whilst not a perfect system, it does allow for unsuitable candidates to be identified at an early stage. In the period under review none of this pertained.

Bishop Bathurst called the Ember seasons 'the burden and vexation of my life.' In a letter to his wife dated 24 December 1810, he wrote:

> The responsibility is painful to me, and the best of my candidates are more versed in Greek and mathematics than in "Pearson on the Creed" or in "The Pastoral Care." Of those who are not versed in anything I hold my tongue. If I could perceive more frequently, even in the latter, a deep sense of the

serious obligations they enter into I could dispense with their want of literary attainments. [quoted in LINNELL *op. cit.* p. 142]

He was at that stage in his ministry still personally interviewing candidates for ordination but that stopped as old age and fatigue took hold. He also became less careful about whom he laid his episcopal hands on and about those to whom he gave *letters dimissory*. Blomfield in his Chester days complained formally to the Archbishop of Canterbury when Bathurst ordained a man he had rejected. Howley duly wrote a gentle letter of admonition to Bathurst who explained in his reply that he did not know that the Bishop of Chester had rejected the man, and added that Mr Burdon 'is a very well-informed and exemplary young man, and nearly related to one whose memory I shall never cease to love and revere.' [THISTLETHWAYTE *op. cit.* p. 323]

He had been criticised by others of his episcopal peers for being too ready to ordain men who were not Oxbridge graduates but Bathurst was always of the opinion that 'a pious turn of mind was of much more consequence in that state, than a certain quantum of learning.' He stated his view in a letter to the Bishop of Winchester in 1817 who had criticised him for being willing to ordain a graduate of the University of Aberdeen – Bathurst regarded a Scottish degree 'as fair a criterion of literary talents as one at Oxford or Cambridge.'

> I have since my first appointment to this laborious diocese, uniformly felt anxious in the discharge of the most important duty of my episcopal office, to ordain those only of whose religious, moral, and literary character, I had good reason to think well. At the same time, being firmly persuaded, that a serious turn of mind and genuine piety, accompanied with a moderate degree of human learning, are far more useful qualifications in a clergyman than a large share of the latter without a sufficient portion of the former. I have never scrupled, and never shall scruple, under the guidance of a sound discretion, to receive occasionally as candidates for holy orders, young men, some of whom have not the advantage of an academical education, and others who have never taken a degree. Nor do I recollect any instance in which I have had the least reason to repent of having done so.
> [THISTLETHWAYTE *op. cit.* p. 250]

Copleston, too, was unhappy about Bathurst in this respect. In a letter to Bruce Knight in February 1836, he wrote 'Since my arrival in town I have mentioned to several Bishops the gross attempt made to get me to lay hands upon one of the Norwich factory. Everyone has reprobated it – and if the Bishop of that diocese were not a superannuated person I would certainly bring it before the Archbishop.' [BROWN ed. *op. cit.* p. 198] But other normally strict bishops also turned a blind eye to the rules when it suited them to do so. Again Copleston's correspondence from the same month and year provides an example.

> The Bp. of Exeter, it is said from Devonshire, will be attacked in the H. of C. He has made a slip, in ordaining his own son privately, upon an uncanonical day, viz. Saturday the 19th of last Dec[r]. Having been a rigid disciplinarian in his dealings with Dr. Carwithin, he cannot wonder if they retaliate upon him when they have an opportunity. [*Ibid*. p. 199]

Whilst many men did surely have a personal sense of vocation, that was not the norm. In Virgin's words, 'Ordination was for many prospective clergy a conditioned reflex rather than a conscious decision of active intelligence and will. Tradition decreed that a son, often a younger son, should take Orders; and tradition was adhered to, even in the midst of a changing society.' [VIRGIN *op. cit.* p.137] He goes on to cite a prime example of how the process worked at that time.

> In 1822 the Hon George Spencer, the youngest son of George John, the second Earl, and a brother of Lord Althorp, the future Whig Chancellor of the Exchequer, was seeking Orders in the Diocese of Peterborough. He therefore wrote to the diocesan examiner, the Revd. T.S. Hughes, asking what books to read in preparation for his ordination examinations. The reply was inimitable. It was, Hughes assured him, 'impossible that I could ever entertain any idea of subjecting a gentleman with whose talents and good qualities I am so well acquainted as I am with yours, to any examination except one as a matter of form, for which a verse in the Greek Testament, and an Article of the Church of England returned into Latin will be amply sufficient.' The diocesan examiner was as good as his word. Spencer was duly ordained in December of the same year. [*Ibid*. p. 137f]

Things were done differently during Sumner's episcopate at Winchester:

> The examinations began on the Thursday morning preceding the day of the ordination. The candidates were lodged either in the Castle or in lodgings selected for them in the town (which were under a sort of collegiate surveillance); and the candidates spent the whole of each day at the Castle. The examinations began at ten – two examining chaplains taking respectively the paper work of the deacons and priests, and another the *vivâ voce* examinations. Each candidate went in turn to the Bishop, who commented on special points in his examination, on his work during the year of his diaconate, or on the sermons sent up for inspection by the candidates for the priest-

hood. To each was said some words appropriate to his special case. With the exception of a short interval for luncheon, the examination was continued each day till four or five. Dinner was at seven. A general invitation was sent to some of the neighbouring clergy, whom the Bishop thought likely to influence the candidates for good, who, if they wished to dine, simply left their names at the porter's lodge. A service was held in the chapel at ten o'clock, at which the Bishop always expounded some appropriate passage of Scripture. On Saturday afternoon, when the examination was concluded, he delivered a more formal charge, generally touching on some of the topics of interest in discussion at the time.

There was one point, the importance of which he never seemed weary of impressing upon the candidates – the necessity of "preaching Christ."

[G.H. SUMNER *op. cit.* p. 142f]

We have another contemporary account from Dean Hole who was ordained Deacon and Priest by Bishop Kaye of Lincoln. Like Rashdall whose examination was described earlier, he had a searching but memorable experience and consequently retained a high regard for the bishop.

Ever to be remembered by those who had the privilege of knowing him, with admiration of his learning and veneration of his character. Spiritual and intellectual beauty made sunshine on his countenance . . He had, as I afterwards discovered from converse with others, an invariable system of dealing with those whom he examined personally for Holy Orders. He took an exact measurement of each before he let him go. He led us by the hand into shallow waters, and onward until we were out of our depth; and then, giving us one plunge overhead, he brought us gently and lovingly ashore. The process commenced, on my first interview, with easy passages from the Greek gospels, and I was congratulating myself on the serenity and security around, when I found the waters rising rapidly, as I made mistakes in my translation of the shipwreck in the Acts, and finally lost my foothold and my Greek in the epistles, as huge billows, lingual and doctrinal, surged and roared overhead. Then I grasped the outstretched hand of his sympathy, and heard, as I reached the land, that he was fully satisfied.

[HOLE *op. cit.* p. 143f]

Owen Chadwick in his book *Victorian Miniature* provides a fascinating account of the extraordinary clash of wills between a Norfolk squire and his Evangelical vicar. It, coincidentally, offers some glimpses of Bathurst. On first interviewing the devout young Evangelical William Wayte Andrew in October 1831, the bishop dismissed him angrily for declining to answer some questions he had put to the candidate about the life of his prospective rector. Later, when Andrew had found an alternative incumbent, he tried his luck again with Bishop Bathurst who, not wishing to ordain him and looking for a reason to reject him, passed the matter to his chaplain, Mr Drake, who held two livings in Norwich and two curacies elsewhere, to see if Andrew knew any Latin, any Divinity, and his Bible.

> The examination was no matter of form; questions all one morning, next day two themes to write, one in Latin and one in English; a bald and routine affair, during which the candidate was tense, and said his prayers over every word that he wrote down on paper, and knelt down in prayer before he presented the result, and tried to compose his mind with the thought that if he failed he would see that this was the Lord's way of hindering him from following a wrong path, and that he might be contented to spend his days as a layman.
> Andrew passed the test, and the chaplain said 'You will do very well, sir. You will present yourself for ordination tomorrow.'
>
> [CHADWICK *Victorian Miniature* p. 21]

Edward Boys Ellman (1815-1906) who was Rector of Berwick, East Sussex for 60 years tells in his *Recollections of a Sussex Parson* how he came to be ordained. His father made the decision and bought the advowson for the living of Berwick without consulting or telling his son until the deed was done. The young man was happy to be ordained and wished to become a Naval Chaplain but there were no vacancies. The arrangement his father had was that his son would succeed the Revd Harry West, the existing non-resident incumbent when he died. West had had a string of unsatisfactory curates and in the Spring of 1838 he wrote to young Ellman who had graduated at Wadham College Oxford with a First. He offered the curacy to him at a stipend of £40 a year plus the right to live in the Rectory free of all rates and taxes. Ellman took his time over the decision:

> In the end I consented. Mr West himself had only lived in Berwick for a very few months, and never went near the place. Time passed on, and Mr West was anxious that I should become a Curate as soon as possible, and wished me to be ordained in the September ordinations, which would take place a few days after I was twenty-three. But there was no September ordination in the Chichester diocese or in any of the adjoining dioceses. Mr West wrote to the Bishop, saying how anxious he was for me to be ordained as soon as possible. So the Bishop sent for me on the 18th of June, and offered to give me "Letters Dismissory" (*sic*) for the September ordination.
> On Sunday, September 23rd, I was ordained Deacon at the parish church of Buckden. On the Monday I left, reaching Glynde [his home] on the Tuesday,

thankful for a few days' quiet before entering upon my sacred charge. On Sunday, September 30th, I rode over to Berwick and took the prayers, and the former Curate preached his farewell sermon. In the afternoon I took the whole of the service. . . It is not good for a young man to have to begin as I did. Curate in sole charge. From the first Sunday I had two sermons to prepare and preach each week. [ELLMAN *op. cit.* p. 147]

It seems from this account that there was minimal examination or involvement or support by Carr, his diocesan bishop. With no professional training or preparation for ministry, he was dropped in the deep end – fortunately he showed he could swim!

A story is told about the Archbishop of York not taking any particular care. Baring Gould tells it in his book *Church Revival*:

The Revd John Sharp whose curate I was, used to tell the story of his ordination in 1833. 'Well Mr. Sharp', said the archbishop in the only interview with the candidate, 'so you are going to be curate to your father, Mr Sharp of Wakefield. Make my compliments to him when you go home. My Secretary has your testimonials: he will give you full instructions. Be sure to be at the Minster in good time. Good Morning'. [TINDALL HART *Ebor* p. 157]

Henry Alford, later to become Dean of Canterbury, recorded in his journal his experience of being ordained Deacon in 1833. On 2 October he went to Norwich to be examined as a candidate by the bishop's chaplain, Mr Drake, who, he said, was 'very civil' to him. But the ordination was fixed for 5 October, two days before his 23rd birthday (the minimum canonical age), so he returned home and received *letters dimissory* from the Bishop of Norwich to the Bishop of Exeter. His journal states on Saturday, 26 October:

At 10 a.m. I went to the Cathedral; a very fine interior and venerable exterior . . . Very beautiful chant in the morning at twelve. Went to the Bishop's Palace and heard his Charge. Altogether it was the most solemn thing I ever heard. He talked to us most seriously for nearly two hours on the inward call, the ministerial duties, &c. Oh! May I never forget it, and may this be to me a lesson among many others I have had of late, not to judge of men harshly, or before the time, as I certainly had of the Bishop of Exeter.

Next day to the Cathedral at ten, and I was ordained. What a service it is! And the Bishop's manner was most solemn, and altogether all was most suitable and proper. I am very thankful to God for having brought me to such a place and such a man.

[F. ALFORD ed. *Life, Journal and Letters of Henry Alford* p. 91]

Alford wrote to his friend Charles Merivale that he had a most wonderful time at Exeter, was delighted with Bishop Phillpotts in every way, had dined with him on the Saturday evening, had sat near him and talked on many subjects. A year later, and just a month after being elected a Fellow of Trinity College Cambridge, he was ordained Priest in St Margaret's Westminster. 'It is close to Westminster Abbey and the burning Houses of Parliament', he noted, 'May God's blessing rest on me in that solemn and responsible office.' [*Ibid*. p. 99] He had gone to London on Friday 4 November and was ordained two days later. He makes no mention of being examined prior to it.

Phillpotts let it be known shortly after his arrival in the diocese that he would actively discourage 'the increasing practice of strangers coming hither. So many of the clergy of this diocese, and others, breed sons to the Church, that I do not like that their prospects be unnecessarily interfered with by strangers.' [DAVIES *op. cit.* p. 123] This has direct relevance to curacies but also to ordination candidates – he preferred home-grown ones.

Sometimes a man was ordained because he could conveniently fill a local need rather than that he had a definite vocation to ordained ministry. Copleston in a brief PS to a letter written to Bruce Knight in 1831 shows he was open to doing this – 'Old Mr Thomas of Pentyrch has applied to me to know if I will ordain Richards upon the title of assistant curate to him. I shd. be glad of a line from you before I answer his letter. He is 85 & quite incapable himself. I am therefore inclined to say *yes*.' [BROWN ed. *op. cit.* p. 87]

Phillpotts took the opposite view in such cases. He wrote to his secretary on 31 December 1831, 'I have received an application from Mr W. Churchward, late usher at Exeter schools, desiring to be ordained deacon and priest for the sake of enabling him to hold the living vacated by his father. I am sincerely sorry for him; but I must not establish so very dangerous a precedent.' [DAVIES *op. cit.* p. 118]

The Suffolk squarson, John Longe, who was the Vicar of Coddenham-cum-Crowfield from 1797-1834 illustrates in his diary how compliant a bishop could be in the matter of procuring ordination. He wrote to Bishop Bathurst on 27 April 1826 'to request him to dispense with the requisite of a title in my son Henry's case, who applys [*sic*]for deacon's orders next ordination.' He was, in effect, asking his bishop to trust him to take interim responsibility as young Henry had no curacy to be ordained to. A diary entry three days later reads, 'Answer from the bishop: he very kindly will admit my son Henry without a title.' The next mention is dated 17

May, 'I sent my son Henry's testimonials, &c, for ordination to Mr Kitson, for tomorrow morning's mail'. He gave his son some preparation on 31 May, 'I began reading the ordination service for deacons with my son Henry, with Bishop Mant's *Notes*, &c,'. It seems the young man wasn't very responsive for the next day entry reads, 'I wrote to Robert saying that I find Henry very deficient in his preparation for the ordination examination, I could not satisfactorily leave him next week, in hopes of rendering him some assistance.' On 11 June he wrote to Bathurst thanking him for dispensing with the requirement for a title in Henry's case. On the 18th, he records that Henry was ordained in Norwich Cathedral that day. There is no mention of Henry being examined beforehand. There is just one more related entry – John Longe notes on 3 July that Henry had left them for London, 'on a tour in Scotland'. The young man could disappear on three weeks' holiday so soon after ordination because he had no job to go to. [STONE ed. *The Diary of John Longe* pp 63-70]

The Cotswold parson, F.E. Witts, tells in his diary how he fixed for his son to be ordained by Bishop Monk of Gloucester:

> August 4. 1837. Reached Gloucester about 1 o'clock. On calling at the Palace found the Bishop engaged with other clergymen and sat for some time with Mrs Monk. My object in seeking a conference with his Lordship was to obtain his promise to receive my son as a candidate for ordination at the Christmas ordination. The Bishop very kindly and cordially acceded to my request. [WITTS *op. cit.* p. 140]

Witts was a wealthy country incumbent, an active magistrate and civil administrator who took his clerical duties seriously, and like most of his kind a Tory but he was no great fan of his diocesan. Another diary entry gives his view of the bishop at the time of the Reform Bill:

> April 18 1832 The Reform Bill has passed the second reading in the House of Lords. The votes were for the second reading 184, against it 175; majority 9. The Bishop of Gloucester maintained his opinions against the measure with more firmness and boldness than I had anticipated. It required some nerve in Dr Monk to detach himself from his Cambridge friends (Kaye, Bishop of Lincoln, and Blomfield, Bishop of London). A strong temptation was to be resisted by a junior bishop, the holder of a poor see; but it seems that Dr Monk is not devoid of firmness and vindicated his views with judgement, and answered with much spirit a very intemperate attack which the violent Popish Earl of Shrewsbury had made on the episcopal order, whom he denounced as the enemies of liberty. From what I had seen of him (the Bishop) I was led to regard him as a learned Greek, but incautious, injudicious and

precipitate. What I have seen and heard of him in his diocese does not prepossess me in his favour. [*Ibid*. p. 89]

Another entry, dated 3 January 1838 describes the second general meeting of subscribers to the Gloucester and Bristol Diocesan Church Building Association, as relating to the archdeaconry of Gloucester. The Bishop chaired the meeting. 'It appears that about £13,000 have been subscribed in the whole Diocese, of which the clergy have subscribed £4,000. . . The Bishop urged the claims of the association earnestly and at considerable length; but he is a hesitating public speaker, not very effective.' [*Ibid*. p. 143f] An entry from January 1839 tells of the Bishop's hospitality to clergy; Witts was in Gloucester in his role as a magistrate on that day: 'From the Tolsey I returned into Court, and attended on Trials for felony, etc. till it was time to dress for dinner at the Palace, whither I repaired after 6 o'clock. We had a large party, chiefly of clergy with some ladies, and much civility from the Bishop and Mrs Monk; but the tone of the party was not particularly social or cheerful.' [*Ibid*. p. 153]

One way in which bishops showed their religious preferences and prejudices to their clergy and the laity was by the financial support they gave to particular voluntary societies and by their public disapproval of certain others. As we have already seen, Marsh in his pre-episcopal days led the opposition to the British and Foreign Bible Society because they printed the Scriptures apart from the *Book of Common Prayer*. The Church Missionary Society founded by Evangelicals in 1799 was without any episcopal support at all to begin with, though that changed as the years passed and some bishops came to appreciate what effective work it was doing as an agency for missionary work abroad. The Church Pastoral Aid Society, another Evangelical foundation, was disapproved of by some bishops because it financed not just curates in populous parishes but also *lay* workers. Such opponents gave their support to the aptly named Additional Curates Society. There were exceptions - Shute Barrington of Durham made himself generally agreeable to Evangelicals by joining both CMS and the Bible Society. He also took a deep interest in week-day and Sunday schools and was a liberal supporter of both. Although not an Evangelical himself, he invited Hannah More to come to Durham to assist him in his plan to establish schools in his diocese. Such breadth of sympathy in a bishop was unusual. Ryder was the most supportive of CMS and was the first bishop who ordained missionaries direct to the country in which they were to serve, accepting as a title the Committee's agreement to employ them. All the other bishops required a man to serve a title first in an English diocese.

To be *seen* to be a generous benefactor and a donor to respectable charities mattered to bishops. Lists were published and it was important that they were seen to be high on the list in support of causes in their own diocese (such as in the provision of new churches and schools) as well as of national organisations (notably the National Society, SPCK and the Sons of the Clergy), and that they gave unpublicised financial aid to poor clergy and to clergy widows and orphans in need. Van Mildert, after his translation to the wealthier see of Durham, continued to send £100 a year for that last mentioned purpose, equal to about ten thousand now, to Bruce Knight, his former registrar in the diocese of Llandaff, for distribution to the needy there. Bishops could hardly exhort their clergy to be generous and charitable if they did not set an example. Ryder was active in his support for many more societies than CMS, among them the London Jews Society, the Sons of the Clergy, the Bible Society, SPG and SPCK.

Providing parochial elementary schools came high on a bishop's wish list for improving things in his diocese. But education could be a contentious subject. 'Schools were a remedy for sin and social disorder, not to provide worldly learning,' wrote Edward Royle in his essay on *Evangelicals and Education*. [WOLFFE ed. *Evangelical Faith and Public Zeal* p. 117] 'Despite the limited objectives of Evangelical educators of the poor, they offered more than those conservatives who thought it dangerous to provide them with any knowledge at all. Indeed, because Evangelicals expected the poor to be able to read not only their bibles, but also the tracts they issued to persuade them of the truths of the gospel and the errors of their ways, the teaching of reading to the poor was central to evangelical mission.' [*Ibid*. p.119] Hannah More's tracts were used widely by all shades of churchmen, her *Shepherd of Salisbury Plain*, for example, sold two million copies in four years.

One of the most famous and effective parish priests of the period was W.F. Hook who became Vicar of Leeds in 1837. It was a vast parish with 88,000 parishioners but with church accommodation for just 13,000. He realized the parish boundaries had to be reformed and new parishes carved out of the old one which he succeeded in getting Parliament to approve with the support of Longley, the first Bishop of Ripon. He summed up his aims in a sentence towards the end of the long letter in which he laid his plan for the Vicarage Act before the people of Leeds. 'We must never rest until we have provided for every poor man a pastor, and for every poor child a school.' [STRANKS *op. cit.* p. 66] It was a goal shared by the best of the reforming bishops.

Bishop Stanley went further than simply helping to provide schools, he frequently visited the children in them when he was at home or out visiting in the diocese. In Norwich when he discovered that the children of the workhouse school were not being properly provided for educationally, he asked one of his city incumbents to see if he could find any teachers among his congregation who would willingly devote their evenings to the work of teaching hitherto neglected children. This was done and the Bishop duly went to the opening of this evening school and even instructed a class of boys. Perhaps more surprisingly, when the clergyman offered up a prayer of blessing on the undertaking, Stanley knelt down on the stone floor of the hall together with the poor children, many of whom had probably never knelt in prayer before and certainly never seen a bishop do it.

Sunday schools had been a major contributor to elementary education ever since Robert Raikes had started one in Gloucester in 1780. It is reckoned that by 1800 there were 200,000 children attending them and by 1851 ten times that number. Some taught writing as well as reading but most did not. What was important was that a child should be enabled to read the Bible. The Chaplain of Trinity College Cambridge in a sermon he preached in Bridlington on education in 1838 warned against over-educating a man, by which he meant giving him 'knowledge uncalled for by that station in life in which the providence of God has placed him.' That was a view shared by most bishops – society was unequal because God had ordained it to be so! And education, it was believed, should focus on eternity, not just on meeting present needs. Kitson Clark comments:

> It was certainly realized that attendance at a day school, and possibly at a Sunday school, would provide secular advantages for a child; for it was clearly to his advantage in this life to learn to read, to write, and to have some smattering of arithmetic. But it was natural for a clergyman to think that a child's most urgent need was to be fitted not so much for this life as for eternity. For this end it was more important than anything else that he should be taught the doctrines of the Church, and those rules of conduct which should bring a man peace at the last. [KITSON CLARK *op. cit.* p. 101]

In 1832 the National Society produced a report on the state of education in the country based on a nationwide survey they had carried out with the help of the parish clergy. Of the returns received, 6,730 had some form of church school and 6,020 had both daily and Sunday schools, but of these only 3,058 were in union with the National Society. Staffing day schools founded by the Society and by the non-denominational British Society was a problem as elementary school teachers came from a lower social class than clergymen and lacked any higher education. In 1838, as noted earlier, Gladstone and some friends brought new life to the workings of the Society and in an attempt to provide some professional training, the National Society founded a Teacher Training College at St Mark's Chelsea in 1841. Diocesan education societies began founding local ones; the decision to build the first one was taken by the Board for Education in Chester in 1839. Nigel Scotland comments on this:

> The jewel in the crown of Sumner's educational strategy was to be his major role in the founding of Chester College. The prime mover was Sumner's Chancellor, Henry Raikes, but without his bishop's gracious and good relations with other sections of the wider Church, it is doubtful whether the project would have been as successful. Sumner backed the institution because he saw clearly that good teachers would result in larger schools, for 'when parents realised there were good teachers in National Schools they would be prepared to pay a little for their children's education.'
> [SCOTLAND *op. cit.* p.59]

Then came the Bishop Otter College in Chichester in 1841. By 1845 there were twenty-two church training colleges in England and Wales. Given that schools would be subject to inspection by government inspectors after 1839, such training became all the more important. Archdeacon Samuel Wilberforce in his *Charge*, delivered in 1840, describes an inter-diocesan initiative between the boards of education in Winchester and Salisbury.

> In Winchester a training school has been founded. Ten scholarships of £10 a year each for three years have been established for this diocese (the whole expense of each pupil being £23, board, lodging, education, &c) four of which scholarships have been filled up . . . Further, we have for one purpose formed an union with the diocese of Salisbury – we admitting their boys into our training school for masters, and they, in a similar establishment for mistresses, (which is about to open) giving us the like advantage. They have founded two scholarships in our institution, and we have founded three in theirs. Thus far a good beginning has been made; and we hope further to assist parochial schools by allowing young men who are engaged already, or are about to be engaged, as masters, to join the classes of the training-

school without living in the house; by instituting and paying sufficient inspectors; and by making grants towards erecting schoolrooms.

[WILBERFORCE *Primary Charge* as Archdeacon of Surrey p. 27f]

He also said that they wished to institute commercial schools where such were wanted but funds were needed for all this work.

The four Welsh dioceses had a particular problem which affected episcopal as well as parochial ministry: the language barrier. Overton states that whilst the Welsh dioceses were part of the Province of Canterbury, from an ecclesiastical point of view there was no more reason to appoint a Welshman to a diocese in Wales than a Yorkshireman for one in Yorkshire. But practically it was a different matter – 'the Welsh people were of a different race, different language, different habits and temperaments.' [OVERTON *op. cit.* p. 18] It was a source of weakness that these differences were so long ignored but at that time a man's special fitness for a special post was not the first consideration in the minds of those with the responsibility and power to make appointments.

It is to Copleston's credit that when he was appointed to Llandaff in 1828, he required a knowledge of the Welsh tongue from the clergy whom he instituted to livings. It was a small step in the right direction if the Established Church was to regain the ground that it had lost to Dissenting chapels. Thirlwall was even better – one of the first things he did on his appointment to St David's in 1840 was to learn the language in order to be able to converse and preach in Welsh. That was something A.J. Johnes had argued the need of a few years earlier. Sadly, Thirlwall's pronunciation was such that few understood what he was saying!

The Association of the Welsh Clergy in West Riding of Yorkshire sent a petition in 1835 to Sir Robert Peel welcoming the proposed 'measures for the removal of all proved abuses connected with the Temporalities and Discipline of the Established Church' and begging

> A provision be graciously made to secure in future the appointment of pious and approved Welsh Scholars to each of the Welsh Bishoprics, as long as the Welsh tongue shall remain the vernacular language of that Country: to the intent that every Bishop shall be able to decide for himself, and not by proxy, on the competency of Candidates for Orders and Applicants for Preferments, 'to preach the Word and administer the Sacraments' in the Welsh language; and that at 'the laying on of hands', in the solemn and Apostolic Rite of Confirmation, he may be able to bless the Welsh Children in the only language they understand.
>
> [quoted in BROWN *In Pursuit of a Welsh Episcopate* p. 11]

The inability of English bishops to communicate with very many of their parishioners in a Welsh diocese was a cause of constant and justified complaint. The most frequently used argument to justify their appointment was that a bishop was there for the *clergy* and not for the people, and the clergy all understood English. Archbishop Howley used this argument in the Lords when he moved the deletion of the clause in the Established Church Act 1836 which would have required those appointed to Welsh sees to be fluent in the language. Bethell, Carey and Copleston all used this argument to justify their own appointments. Copleston even felt the need to address the larger language issue in his *Charge* of 1836, that is eight years after his arrival in the diocese, and more particularly the 'grievance' that bishops who are unacquainted with the Welsh language should not be appointed to preside over Welsh dioceses. A view he robustly rejected in his own defence.

> But is a knowledge of the Welsh language essential to the discharge of the Episcopal office in this part of the kingdom? I confidently maintain that it is not. The inspection and regulation of the Clergy, the appointment of fit men to the several churches respectively, as far as his patronage and influence extend – the settlement of disputes and differences, the correction of what is wrong or deficient in their lives and in their ecclesiastical duties – this is unquestionably the main province of a Bishop. With the Clergy, the English language is the sole medium of conversation, not only with their Bishop, but among themselves. In all towns the English language universally prevails. To require a knowledge of Welsh then, as a necessary qualification for the Bishoprick, argues either an excess of that local partiality to which I before adverted, or a morbid spirit of discontent, which seems in the present age to regard every institution with a jealous eye, bent upon discovering some flaw, or some circumstance which may excite a popular prejudice among them.
> To this cause we must attribute the querulous objection, that Bishops reside during a part of the year in the metropolis, whereas, say these objectors, they ought to be constantly in their Diocese.
> [COPLESTON *Charge* 1836 p. 25f]

He tried, unconvincingly it seems to me, to justify his long absences in London on the grounds that that is where 'all institutions connected with the National Church transact their business' and that he could transact the greater part of his official diocesan duty by correspondence wherever he was. He also claimed that such complaints came very largely from those who 'have little or no regard for the Establishment.' [*Ibid*. p. 26] In his *Charge* he also clearly indicated that the use of the Welsh language should be discouraged – the natives should learn 'the more modern and useful tongue', English! What is striking, even shocking, about the description he gives of his role as a bishop is not just that the care of the laity does not figure in it at all but also that he does not seem to think that encouraging and supporting his clergy had any part in what he calls 'the main province of a bishop.' Disciplining them, yes; caring for them as a father-in-God, not a mention! Yet, other letters written to his chancellor reveal him as having a good knowledge of the needs and situation of particular men, and a desire to do the best he could for them.

Copleston was not alone in this paltry self-defence of his inability and unwillingness to learn to speak the language. Bethell claimed that as the candidates who came to him for confirmation had been instructed by a clergyman in the meaning of the ordinance and the words of the prayer used, and that his chaplain repeated the prayer in Welsh after he had said the words in English, it was not necessary for him as bishop to be bilingual.

Brown quotes two contemporary accounts of episcopal ministrations performed in English and the negative effects they had on the native Welsh present at them; the first relates to Bishop Carey of St Asaph and the second to Bishop Jenkinson of St David's. In 1837 Carey went to Rhosymedre to consecrate a new church:

> His lordship arrived at the hour fixed, accompanied by his officials. There were present several of the dignitaries of the church: the service was read in English, the sermon was English, and the consecration of the church and churchyard, English. The Welsh people gazed, they heard a sound, and wondered; doubting whether it was the voice of the shepherd of a Welsh Christian flock . . . The language was unintelligible, but their persons and performances were seen, and became the subject of much conversation and astonishment. That the people of the village and neighbourhood might not spend the whole day in empty gazing, the good curate of the parish had a Welsh service in the afternoon. The new church was full, the service was read, and the native preacher delivered his discourse with a clear enunciation, and considerable power: it was no dry moral disquisition, but one containing the pure truths of the Gospel, plainly and yet forcibly set forth. The attention of the assembly was arrested, and their minds seemed solemnly impressed. But where was the bishop? Gone! His officials? Gone! The dignitaries of the church? Were they also gone? Gone! They had turned their back on the Welsh service; and the peasantry of Wales, the poor of the neighbourhood, had not a share in their sympathies; but what was perhaps better, they had, in their absence, the Gospel preached unto them.
> [BROWN *op. cit.* p.21]

One could, of course, make out a reasonable case for why the bishop and his entourage did not stay or were not able to stay for the afternoon service, but there is no mistaking the hurt and incomprehension felt by the locals. The second story comes from a Welsh cleric who wrote:

> I was confirmed when I was about the age of thirteen by the late Bishop Jenkinson, previous to which I was examined with several others in the church catechism, by the curate of the parish in which I then resided. The curate was an English settler, a sportsman and a fox-hunter, who had acquired a reading acquaintance with the Welsh tongue, peculiar to himself, in which it was most difficult to understand him. For I can truly say that, though I attended the church in which he officiated for many years, yet I never was able to make out two consecutive sentences of his Welsh sermons. I went to be confirmed in the parish church of a country town. The whole of the service usual on the occasion was performed in the English language, of which I was then, with the majority of those confirmed at the same time, entirely ignorant, except indeed that I had been taught to read in it fluently and correctly, without, however, comprehending the meaning of what I read. And when I reflected that a solemn rite of apostolic origin, and sanctioned in the New Testament Scriptures, had been performed in an unknown tongue, and thereby converted into a meaningless ceremony, I felt truly disgusted that such a mockery of divine things should be perpetrated in the church which I most dearly loved. [*Ibid.* p. 22]

That sounds more like an adult's reflections on an episode in his youth rather than the puzzlement he presumably felt at the time as a thirteen year old. But, nonetheless, an important point is being made about the ministry of Bishop Jenkinson and his fellow bishops in Wales.

Back in England, one of the topics most frequently referred to in their *Charges* was the requirement to hold two services (and possibly two sermons) every Sunday. Croker asked Phillpotts about this in October 1840 as he did not understand something the Archbishop had said in his recent *Charge*. Phillpotts set out his own views on the matter:

> Respecting the demand of a second sermon from every minister on every Sunday, though the recent statute empowers the Bishop to make it, my own judgment is very far from being that it ought to be generally made. In *rural* parishes especially, I should much prefer the public catechizing of the children, with an effective explanation of part of the Catechism, or a familiar, but grave, and avowedly or manifestly premeditated, though not written comment on one of the Lessons of the day – to a second sermon. In truth, the more we elevate the Liturgy, the *intelligent* reading of Scripture, or the different offices of the Church (the Baptismal and Burial Service especially),

and render them by explanation familiar to our people, even if this be done at the expense of what is called *preaching*, the better in my opinion it will be. By the bye, *Hooker* calls all these things *preaching*.
[CROKER *The Croker Papers* Vol 2 p. 372]

Sumner in Chester took a quite different view, encouraging more informal services in the evening which would appeal to working class people. He was aware of the failings of the Church in attracting unchurched people to its services but was unaware of just how hard their working lives were. How could the bishop of one of the most industrialized dioceses in the land truly have his people's welfare at heart when he was so ignorant of their lives? That John Bird Sumner had a deeply held concern to provide more church buildings for the expanding population of his diocese was praiseworthy but he failed to recognize that people would not come to an institution which, in their eyes, showed no real understanding or sympathy for them. Indeed, one whose chief pastor genuinely believed it was God's plan that some should live in poverty and that it was confirmed by natural law! Sumner had, however, distinguished between poverty as a natural class distinction and as an economic condition in his early work, written in the comfort and security of Eton:

> These conditions, it must ever be remembered, are essentially distinct and separate. Poverty is often both honourable and comfortable; but indigence can only be pitiable, and is usually contemptible. Poverty is not only the natural law of many, in a well-constituted society, but is necessary that a society may be well constituted. Indigence, on the contrary, is seldom the natural lot of any, but is commonly the state into which intemperance and want of prudent foresight push poverty: the punishment which the moral government of God inflicts in this world upon thoughtlessness and guilty extravagance. [J.B. SUMNER *A Treatise* Vol. 2 p. 92]

Soloway comments, 'The future bishop of the most industrialized diocese in the country had not yet been disabused by experience and the later reports of the great enquiry commissions investigating the working and living conditions of the labouring classes.' [SOLOWAY *op. cit.* p. 115]

The need for new churches to be built and for old ones to be restored was a problem for most bishops, especially those in the emerging industrial towns and cities of the North and the Midlands but also in the rapidly expanding capital. In 1818 largely through the influence of Lord Liverpool, who was a committed Churchman, a parliamentary grant of one million pounds was voted for the erection of new churches. No opposition to the measure was voiced in either House – a sign that legislators at that time still acknowledged the confessional obligations of the State. When in 1824 a further grant of half a million plus Exchequer loans to about the same amount was made, there was some opposition in the Commons – radicals and Dissenters were becoming more confident and vociferous.

Those two grants were a big help but by 1835 the stream of churches wholly built from these grants had almost ceased to flow, with 212 of the "Commissioners' Churches" complete and 208 other churches assisted by grants in aid. [See WEBSTER *Joshua Watson* pp. 68-71] Most money by then had come from voluntary donations given either to the newly established Diocesan Church Building Societies or for particular local churches. Wealthy Churchmen, including some bishops, paid the entire cost of erecting a particular church. Pusey, for example, built and endowed St Saviour's in Leeds in 1845, Joshua Watson paid for the building of a church in Homerton, a church was built in memory of Bishop Ryder in Birmingham, and Blomfield built St Stephen's in Hammersmith. That was just one of the latter's many gifts to his diocese. Biber claims that it had been calculated that 'the total amount of outlay incurred by Bishop Blomfield for promoting the erection and endowment of new churches in his diocese cannot be much under £30,000' [BIBER *op. cit.* p. 186] That equates to about three million pounds today.

The marks of a reforming bishop intent upon bringing new life to the parishes of his diocese were to be seen not only in the leadership and support he gave to building new churches and where possible creating new parishes, helping fund the repair of habitable parsonages for the poorer clergy,but also in providing schools and teachers for the children. Sumner in his Chester days was just such a tireless promoter of church extension. In 1834 he organized and founded the Chester Diocesan Church Building Society whose main purpose was to encourage the building of new churches in the most heavily populated centres. A second society, the Cheshire Building Society, was formed to promote the building of chapels in rural areas. By 1841, 170 new churches had been built and clergy provided, especially in Liverpool and Manchester. The building of new schools had been another priority in Sumner's diocesan strategy which had met with equal success.

Burns lists nineteen diocesan church-building societies as having been founded between 1825 and 1839, and concern for schools lagged not far behind – he lists eleven being in place by 1841. [BURNS *op. cit.* p. 116]

Otter, likewise, in the four years he was at Chichester showed what a reforming bishop could achieve in such a short time. In 1838 he established a Diocesan Association, in 1839 he founded a training college for women teachers at Brighton, and the first theological college for graduates was opened in Chichester with his support in that same year, and in 1840, encouraged by his cathedral dean, George Chandler, and by his two archdeacons, he revived rural decanal chapters. Not bad for a man who was aged 68 at the time of his appointment in 1836. Only Salisbury had chapter meetings for the parish clergy. The hope was that younger clergy might learn from their older and more experienced brethren, and professional standards be generally improved. They could also serve as a two-way process of communication between the bishop and his clergy.

The office of rural dean had been revived in a few dioceses by the early nineteenth century – Salisbury had them in 1811 and Chichester the following year. Marsh introduced them in Llandaff and then Peterborough in 1820. Burns describes the growth –

The revival gathered pace, and episcopal translation remained a potent factor in its diffusion. The office was revived in Bath and Wells; John Kaye restored rural deans first at Bristol (1824) and then at Lincoln, beginning with the archdeaconry of Lincoln with the encouragement of Archdeacon Goddard (1829). Charles Sumner, translated from Llandaff, soon restored the office at Winchester. Bagot appointed deans at Oxford (1831); Blomfield and Howley restored them at London and Canterbury in 1833; in 1834, Carr of Worcester followed suit while at Gloucester Monk reinvigorated the office where he found it and revived where he did not. [BURNS *op. cit.* p. 78f]

Stanley instituted seventy rural deans in his large diocese, and had them visit him at the palace once a year, where in addition, to giving them a good dinner, examined their reports in their presence. In a memorial presented to Stanley's family after his death, they wrote: 'We feel that if we have been in any degree useful in carrying out the wishes of our chief pastor, much of our success is due to the opportunities which his generous hospitality so often afforded of associating with one who was ever vigilant and active himself, and anxious only to spend and to be spent in the service of his fellow-creatures.' [A.P. STANLEY *op. cit.* p. 45]

Rural deans served as a ready supplier of local information to the bishop and could be used by him as a means of securing effective remedial action. In some places they replaced inactive archdeacons. A sensitive area was that of clerical misconduct. Some bishops directed trusted rural deans to inquire informally into alleged misconduct, but others, such as Marsh at Peterborough, explicitly disavowed it. They assisted in disseminating information and requests sent to them by the Bishop and were a conduit for, and representative of, grass-roots clerical opinion back to him. The revival of ruridecanal chapters [i.e. the clergy licensed in the deanery] meeting on a regular basis, as we have seen, came later. But rural deans, valuable as they were to the bishop, were clearly subordinate to the archdeacons who were the 'eyes of the Bishop' and played a central role in the effective administration of the diocese. Burns says of them –

> Archdeacons were crucial to the diocesan societies, organizing schemes for Church improvement and extension, and as discreet investigators of lapses of diocesan discipline. Where an individual exhibited the requisite qualities – authority without remoteness, local knowledge backed up by episcopal charisma – the limited legal powers of the office did not prevent an archdeacon having a considerable impact on the effective functioning of his diocese.
> [BURNS op. cit. p. 74]

A common problem in every diocese was the provision of parsonages. Legally it was the responsibility of the incumbent, not the patron or the bishop though either or both might assist (as Monk of Gloucester did late in life), but few of them could afford to build a new house despite the availability of loans from Queen Anne's Bounty and later from the Parliamentary Grants Fund. The income of the living was simply too small to allow them to take up and repay a mortgage. This was a widespread problem – in 1833 there was no parsonage at all in 2,878 parishes, and a further 1,700 incumbents reported that the residence, in their judgement, was 'unfit.' Virgin elucidates that word:

> The state of parsonages officially described as 'unfit' was very variable. At one extreme were residences whose unfitness was blatantly apparent - decay, neglect, or a combination of both, had rendered them uninhabitable; next came parsonages which, although structurally sound, were unsuitable for married clergy with families; then there were houses which some well-to-do incumbents, anxious to imitate the gracious living of the gentry, considered insufficiently commodious, and lastly came a number built upon such a palatial scale that upkeep had become prohibitively expensive.
> [VIRGIN op. cit. p. 147]

Some bishops recognizing that the provision of a new parsonage or refurbishing an old one, would facilitate greater residence did what they could to help. Stanley, for example, saw a hundred additional parsonage houses erected in the first seven years of his episcopate.

Blomfield had an impressive record of building new churches and finding the money to provide clergy to minister in them. Soloway has dubbed him 'the dean of church-building bishops'. One of his clergy, the Revd Baptist Noel, addressed an eighty-eight page *Letter* to him in 1835 about the spiritual needs of the metropolis. He began with a statistical review of church attendance in the city arriving at the conclusion that half a million people were totally unchurched. He then highlighted the moral and spiritual destitution of these people.

> 500,000 Sabbath-breakers, at the very least, in total neglect of the restraints of religion, communicate the plague of ungodliness to all around them. 10,000 of these are devoted to play; above 20,000 are addicted to beggary; 30,000 are living by theft and fraud; 23,000 are annually picked up drunk in the streets; above 100,000 are habitual gin-drinkers; and, probably, 100,000 more have yielded themselves to systematic and abandoned profligacy. [NOEL *The State of the Metropolis Considered in a Letter to the Lord Bishop of London* p. 29]

They were living in a missionary situation and the Established Church had a responsibility to the whole populace, and he challenged Blomfield to be the first Bishop of London since the Reformation to pour 'the light of the Gospel upon the darkness of the lowest and the vilest haunts of the metropolis.' Some of his suggestions, such as building more church schools and making it easier legally to sub-divide parishes and build new churches and chapels were already favoured by Blomfield but there were other things the bishop would not countenance – 'if we cannot attract them to our churches, we must seek for them [the unchurched masses] wherever they are congregated: if we have not buildings within which to gather them, we must preach to them in the open air.' For which he cites the good precedent set by Jesus! [*Ibid*. p. 42f] Street-preaching and co-operating with evangelical dissenting ministers (another of Noel's suggestions) were simply not acceptable.

A year later, Blomfield established a voluntary Metropolis Churches Fund to solicit funds for building new churches to which Noel gave £60. Pusey made an anonymous donation of £5,000 to it, and Blomfield gave £2,000, including the building and endowment of St Stephen's, Hammersmith at a cost of some £8,000. The King was its patron and contributed £1,000 as did Queen Victoria on her accession to the throne. The scheme met with much success initially – it raised £106,000 in the first six months

- and within ten years forty-four new churches had been built, ten more were being built and a further nine about to be. The seating capacity of the churches and chapels in his diocese grew by 65,000. But in the same period the population of the city had grown by 300,000. He would live to see that his success in building was not matched in congregational growth in them – he raised funds for ten churches in Bethnal Green in as many years but only 6,024 persons out of a population of 90,193 there attended any service on Church Census Sunday in 1851. [SOLOWAY *op. cit.* p. 444]

That census provided figures which correlate the growth in population and the provision of 'sittings', the term used for church accommodation. These figures represent all churches and not just the Established Church.

	Population	Estimated no of sittings	No of sittings for each 100 persons
1831	13,896,797	7,007,091	50.4
1841	15,914,148	8,554,636	53.8
1851	17,927,609	10,212,563	57.0

[WEBSTER *op. cit.* p.76f]

Buildings and raising money were practical problems which could be tackled with some assured degree of success. Finding able, conscientious clergymen was another matter. All bishops were the patrons of some livings in their diocese, and occasionally of livings situated elsewhere in the country and consequently they had to find suitable clergy. In fact they had the right of appointment to 12% of all livings in England and Wales. They usually gave the best endowed livings to their own sons, or to other close male relatives, then to the sons of friends or of men who had some claim on the bishop's patronage. Even that hardworking, re-forming bishop, Blomfield, was not innocent when it came to nepotism. William Cobbett ironically dedicated his *Legacy to Parsons* to Blomfield who had conferred a prebendal stall and two rectories upon his son. Kitson Clark describes him as 'a man of both the old and the new dispensations.' His nepotism was a deplorable hangover from the old way of doing things.

Bathurst was still at it almost to the end of his very long life. He wrote to his nephew, the Revd John Prowett, on 15 August 1833

> I am happy to inform you that it is in my power to offer you a piece of preferment, which will enable you to pass the remainder of your days in comfort, as far as pecuniary matters are concerned. The rectory of Catfield is

vacant; the value of it, nearly, if not quite, £600 a-year; Lord Bathurst having kindly consented to rest satisfied with Heigham for his friend, the resignation of which is no great sacrifice on your part. The sooner you repair to Norwich for institution the better. I have neither strength nor leisure to say more. [THISTLETHWAYTE *op. cit.* p. 410]

Seven days later he was collated by his uncle, and on Sunday the 25th read himself in at Catfield Church. The speed of that appointment from the date of the offer to actually officiating at a Service must have been one of the fastest in the history of the diocese!

All was not always sweetness and light between a bishop and his clergy. One of the most trying situations a bishop faced was when a cleric in his diocese decided to abandon the Church of England either to become a Roman Catholic or to become a dissenting minister. Grayson Carter in his study of Evangelicals who seceded writes:

Though Anglican bishops deplored these secessions, whether to Protestant Dissent or to Rome, and complained about them in private (and sometimes in public), they assumed that they had little choice but to accept them as *faits accomplis.* Those who departed from the communion of the Church of England were assumed to be misguided, but not in breach of the law.
[CARTER *Anglican Evangelicals - Protestant Secessions from the Via Media* p. 356f]

Some bishops, however, did take action. Burgess of Salisbury, for example, threatened the Evangelical William Tiptaft upon his secession from the parish of Sutton Courtney, Berkshire to become a Baptist, but nothing came of it. Tiptaft published a pamphlet setting out his fourteen objections to Anglican belief and practice (among them the right of bishops to sit in the Lords) which sold 3,000 copies almost immediately and went through eight further editions. Burgess argued that whilst Tiptaft had resigned his living, the man still remained in holy orders, and as such was culpable for his itinerant ministry and for preaching doctrines 'inconsistent with the principles of the Established Church'. When Tiptaft published his correspondence with the bishop, Burgess backed off [*Ibid.* pp. 283-290 for the whole story].

Henry Phillpotts of Exeter was made of sterner stuff and in 1844 chose to prosecute James Shore who ministered in an Anglican chapel built by the Duke of Somerset in his diocese. Shore intended to continue ministering in the same chapel with the Duke's consent but as a dissenting minister. The prosecution was based on a long forgotten canon which had never been invoked since the Reformation. It became a *cause célèbre* at the time. Phillpotts won and Shore was imprisoned until a committee in London set up to support him paid all the fines and re-imbursed Phillpotts' legal expenses. This foolish action simply portrayed the bishop as a tyrant and Shore as a martyr.

Among those who followed Newman to Rome was a son of Bishop Henry Ryder - George Dudley Ryder who was Rector of Easton in the diocese of Winchester. Fortunately his father had died before it happened.

Inevitably, there were other difficulties with individual clergymen about whom the bishop had received complaints from church wardens or other leading laity, but trying to discipline an incumbent was not easy. Legal proceedings were expensive and the press was all too ready to give publicity to a story about conflicts between the clergy and their bishop. Not all clergy, including the bishops, were of a conciliatory nature. Murray of Rochester was reputed to be arrogant and distant in his relations with his clergy. Phillpotts of Exeter, as we have seen repeatedly, was pugnacious by nature and determined to get his way whatever the legal costs. Bowen says of him, 'He was continually quarrelling with someone, and during his episcopate he engaged in more than fifty law suits which cost him in all between £20,000 and £30,000.' [BOWEN *op. cit.* p. 96] – that is millions in today's terms! He was not a model of harmony and reasonableness bent on finding non-confrontational solutions.

Some bishops tried to be pastoral rather than disciplinary even when there was some fault in the clergyman's behaviour. Copleston, for example, describes one such case in a letter to his chancellor.

> Can you devise any sort of provision for the poor ex-curate of Lantillo. He has a wife & six young children. He has not a shilling of his own - & I believe he is involved in debt. They represent to me the hardship of being turned out in the middle of winter without a home or even shelter. I have authorised Mr. Lewis to give him some money for immediate use – but it is impossible for me, who have withdrawn his licence, to *recommend* him to another curacy. I may yield to the solicitations of others founded upon humanity - & if a *small* Welsh curacy could be found I would not refuse to license him – altho' I fear his habit of drinking is inveterate & almost incurable. [BROWN ed. *op. cit.* p. 79]

And then there were the cases of greedy rectors treating curates unfairly such as this one that Copleston brought to his chancellor's attention.

Wm. Williams has allowed £15 to his Rector R. Knight out of his salary of £80

for having administered the Sacrament four times in Newton Church when he was Deacon. R. Knight contended for a proportionate deduction out of the second year – to which Williams demurred & applied to me. My answer was a sharp reprimand for having made such an allowance the first year & I referred him to the Marginal note in his Licence, & telling him the consequences would be serious, if I was compelled to notice the thing at all. I expressed a hope that to prevent this disclosure Mr. K. & he would speedily settle the dispute.
Williams now tells me that he has sent my letter to Mr. K. but he has heard nothing further from him. I feel no scruple about exposing Knight, but if the matter is noticed at all Williams also must smart, & that more severely perhaps than the other. Have you any means of bringing this man to his senses. I told Williams that he must reclaim the £15 as well as insist upon no such deduction being made from his second year's salary. In this I think you will agree with me. [*Ibid*. p. 134]

But sometimes even a pastorally minded bishop such as Copleston had to put an end to a minister's career:

I had a lamentable letter from the ex-curate of Cadoxton, who says he is a ruined man, with four helpless children. He asks for part of the Barrington money. Something of course must be sent him, either from my own pocket, or from some charitable fund – but I should like to know whether you think he has any resource for subsistence. Employment in the Church is out of the question. [*Ibid*. p. 161]

A frequent problem faced by bishops was that of securing a sufficient stipend for newly appointed curates. Incumbents needing help did not necessarily have the means to pay them, and sometimes patrons who could have afforded it simply refused to help or were niggardly in their response. Copleston complained bitterly about one such wealthy patron whom he had solicited help from to provide the stipend of a much needed curate in Merthyr. There was a suitable candidate available who had attended St David's College and who would also act as a teacher in the parish's school but where was the money to pay him to come from. Copleston himself was willing to contribute £20. As usual, he shared the problem with his chancellor.

The Merthyr affair as to an assistant curate will soon take effect. I think Lord Bute might, under the circumstances, which I fully explained to him, have offered a salary of £50 himself. What he does offer, is to give as much as I give. Now that is a strange way of meeting a Bishop, who is a common Guardian of all the parishes in his Diocese – whereas he is Patron of this, & a great proprietor. It reminds me of a similar speech from Lord Grosvenor to the then Bishop of Chester (Blomfield) about subscribing to a new Church in his neighbourhood, 'Whatever you do, I'll do.' [*Ibid*. p. 169]

Lloyd rapidly showed his unfitness to be a bishop by his inept handling of a number of problematic pastoral situations of which this is one. An anonymous letter arrived from the parish of Swalcliffe revealing a remarkable case of pluralism, non-residence and general neglect. The vicar was a man he had already had difficulties with when he refused to ordain a candidate nominated by the vicar to a curacy. The letter reads:

> The parishes of Swalcliffe, Sibford, Burdrop, Sibford Gower, Epwell, and Shutford, containing three churches and a very large population are all served by one clergyman wherefrom the services at each are obliged to be shamefully hurried over, and the duty at Shutford is always at one o 'clock, an hour inconvenient to all the Parish who also never have the opportunity of hearing the morning service at all. Besides this the Rectory house at Swalcliffe is let to poor people and the prayers that there always used to be twice a week are now never performed though several of us much wish to go to Church on those days and to have a proper resident clergyman which always used to be, nor was the church at Shutford ever added to these till the present incumbent. From this neglect there are four or five Methodist places in the Parishes all within a few years and the interests of the Church are gradually falling into decay.
> There can be no fault found with the clergyman [a temporary curate] who now does the duty with great solemnity and has drawn many people back to the Church but *it is said* that the Curacy is about to be sold for a title and this is the *third time within four years* that it is *believed* so to have been disposed (for the Rector (*sic*) though a rich man would sell himself if he could).
> It is earnestly hoped that the Bishop will restore the accustomed duties to Swalcliffe, and cause the Clergyman [i.e. the Vicar] to reside in the parish and also take it into his kind consideration whether a Church and Parish so large ought not to have two services on the Sunday and separate churches that ought never to have been united. [quoted in BAKER *op. cit.* p. 158f]

It was a depressing and difficult situation commonly found in rural dioceses which bishops had to use their admittedly limited authority to try and sort out. Lloyd proved not to be up to it. He recognized that, in the absence of the vicar, two curates were needed, but failed to get more than one appointed whilst the elderly incumbent remained far away. Baker rightly comments 'it is obvious that Lloyd's forte was not in episcopal administration' though he then goes on to make allowances for a man who 'was not given to assertive intrusion against the established pattern of authority even in the lower echelons of the ecclesiastical order.' [*Ibid*. p. 167]

There were other problems too which a reforming bishop such as Blomfield felt he had to tackle head on. On his appointment to Chester, he attempted to raise clerical standards in the diocese and encourage them to be more 'useful' in their ministry.

> I do contend, that the members of our sacred profession are bound, in the first place, to exercise great caution in the choice of their pursuits and amusements; secondly, to practise great moderation in the use of them; and lastly, in whatever occupation they may be engaged, into whatever society that they may be cast, never to forget the dignity and importance of their calling; nor wholly to lay aside that serious and quiet demeanour which bespeaks a mind habitually occupied in the duties of sacred trust.
> [BLOMFIELD *Primary Charge to Clergy of Chester* 1825 p. 17]

Inevitably he met with some opposition and unpopularity. He wanted to see changes in his clergy's lifestyle, so such favourite pastimes as hunting and fishing were banned as was dancing at public balls. This provoked Sydney Smith to parody his *Charge*:

> Hunt not, fish not, shoot not;
> Dance not, fiddle not, flute not;
> But before all things it's my particular desire
> That once at least in every week
> You take your dinner with the squire.

Blomfield told each newly ordained man that his licence would be withdrawn if he transgressed any of the new commandments.

He was also unusually strict about Sabbath observance – an issue that came to the fore during his years as Bishop of London when he did his best to prevent ordinary working people enjoying themselves on Sundays. In May 1830 he published a letter to the laity of his diocese entitled *On the Present Neglect of the Lord's Day* which covered a lot of practices he condemned, firstly Sunday trading especially market trading (which was illegal but met a social need when most people were working long hours the other six days of the week). Then came 'the resort of the lower orders to the almost numberless wine-vaults and gin-shops, in which the work of ruin goes on throughout the week, without intermission'. [BLOMFIELD *A Letter on the Present Neglect* p. 12] He notes that there were 'more than eighty liquor shops in the single line of street between the two churches of Bishopsgate and Shoreditch.' But his criticism is not directed solely against poor people, he tackles the sins of the rich too: Sunday dinner parties which could lead to intemperance and gambling and certainly made more work for servants, and card parties. And then there were 'the troops of boys' playing ball games in Green Park when their families should have been in church, and the thousands who each Sunday enjoyed a boat trip on the Thames, passing his palace bound for Richmond 'crowded with gaily dressed Sabbath-breakers.' Blomfield writes, 'A waterman who lives near my own house, has told me, that he has known more than five hundred boats pass under Putney Bridge on a fine Sunday, carrying parties of pleasure.' [*Ibid.* p. 15] In his eyes, this was sin on a mega-scale but not all bishops agreed with him – Whately, for example, argued that this Jewish practice did not apply to Christians.

On the other days of the week, Blomfield set an example to his clergy by his stewardship of time. Mornings were devoted to correspondence. His copy books, now kept at Lambeth Palace Library, show him giving practical instructions to incumbents as well as many letters of a more pastoral nature. His average was thirty letters a day. Friday mornings were set aside for clergy interviews when he saw twenty to thirty men. Johnson comments,

> Their needs were dealt with briskly and efficiently, even to the point of abruptness. The Bishop sat at one end of a table, with a notebook beside him in which he noted rapidly the subjects of discussion. Incumbents of the very large parishes were told that they could come at any time even if he had to travel to town specifically to see them. One of his diocesan clergy noted in his diary, 'When you go to a man of business keep to your business, finish your business and then go about your business.' [JOHNSON *op. cit.* p. 153f]

Clearly some of his men learned from his example. Blomfield is an interesting example of the metamorphis taking place in the episcopate. He had progressed from being the pluralist editor of Greek plays to becoming the most committed of Church-reforming bishops. The things he had done himself as a country clergyman, such as being a JP and a commissioner of turnpikes, he told his clergy not to do once he became a bishop in Chester. Secular duties, such as those of a magistrate, were not to interfere with carrying out their spiritual duties as a clergyman. How times were changing! Despite having once been a pluralist himself and had a curate to minister in his place, Blomfield as a bishop pressed non-resident incumbents to mend their ways and was very successful at it in

London. 'According to the official return for 1827, there were 255 resident incumbents among 577 benefices in the diocese of London. Within four years the number of residents had risen to 287, within another four it was up to 325, and within three more it had reached 409.' [VIRGIN *op. cit.* p. 208] Phillpotts too enjoyed a similar success, he who had been a flagrant pluralist and non-resident clergyman, and who had even tried to hold on to the immensely wealthy living of Stanhope after his appointment to Exeter. Yet he cracked the whip over similar sinners in his diocese and between 1831 and 1838 he persuaded 154 non-resident incumbents to return to their parishes. Virgin rightly comments, 'Their efforts show how large a measure of change a really strong-minded diocesan could bring about.'

Of course, not all bishops regarded pluralism as such a great offence; Archbishop Howley in his *Charge* to the clergy of Canterbury diocese in 1832 said, 'The holding of more Benefices than one by the same individual has been always allowed under certain restrictions in our Church, with a view to the more liberal maintenance of its ministers, the encouragement of sacred learning, and the remuneration of professional merit.' It is hardly surprising, then, to learn that when he brought an abortive measure to the Lords in 1831, and again a year later, whose ostensible purpose was to limit pluralism and non-residence there was a let-out clause in the small print which allowed all clergy with the degree of MA to be exempt from the proposed prohibition against holding a second living if an incumbent's first was worth over £400. Howley was not a keen reformer!

In contrast to hyper-active bishops such as Blomfield and litigious ones such as Phillpotts, there were gentle – even shy – souls among the bishops who cared deeply about the men and the families who looked to him as their father in God. Thomas Burgess at Salisbury was one such whose close friend and biographer J.S. Harford describes how on a drive back to Bath from Clifton, the bishop opened up about his own spiritual life and the importance of habitually cultivating and maintaining a devotional frame of mind. It reveals the 'spiritual knapsack' he carried daily and which sustained him in his episcopal ministry.

> After touching on the mental serenity and the firmness of purpose which are its characteristic accompaniments, he proceeded (casting aside the reserve which he generally maintained in reference to his own religious feelings) to repeat to me, with equal simplicity and fervour, a fasciculus of prayers, collects, and select passages from psalms and hymns, with which, variously modified, he told me he was in the habit of commencing the day. All that he

said proved how truly his religion was an indwelling principle of holy living; a salient spring of pure and heart-felt joy, and that the Bishop of Salisbury, in the midst of continual engagements, and the engrossing circumstances of station and influence, retained the humble and devout feelings of the retired Rector of Winston. [HARFORD *op. cit.* p. 358]

And there were those who went out of their way to befriend and support the 'little men' who never expected any attention from their bishop. Stanley exemplifies this kind of pastoral care. One rural parson described the impact a visit from him made:

I was Rector of Waldringfield – one of the smallest and most obscure parishes in the remotest corner of the Diocese, containing a population of less than 170 persons. Nevertheless, to this remote, obscure, and diminutive parish, the Bishop found his way. He came, and spoke kindly and encouragingly to the rustic priest, accompanied him to his church and school, and walked with him through his straggling parish. He took a lively interest in all my parochial arrangements, as if my parish had been one of the most important in the Diocese . . . To a country parson who is old-fashioned enough to believe in the Apostolical Succession, and to regard a Bishop as (in reality what he is professedly) a 'Father in God', all this was delightful in the extreme. I felt as if a sunbeam had passed through my parish, and had left me to rejoice in its genial and cheerful warmth. From that day I would have died to serve him; and I believe that not a few of my humble flock were animated in a greater or less degree by the same kind of feeling.

[A.P. STANLEY *op. cit.* p. 47]

Hostile critics often argued that all the bishops were concerned about was to build up their personal wealth at the expense of the Church, rather than being godly pastors and leaders in their dioceses. This was apparently true of some but by no means of all. A few, who had ample private means, spent all the emoluments of their see on the ministry and infrastructure of their diocese. Shute Barrington of Durham and Archbishop Vernon Harcourt were two such but they were exceptional as a primary concern for most bishops was to provide for their children financially, as we shall see in a later chapter when we look at family life in the episcopal palace.

Howley who was Primate during the whole period under review represents the old regime which was passing. Bowen calls him 'the last Prince-Archbishop.'

Howley had driven to Westminster from Lambeth in a coach flanked by outriders; when he crossed the courtyard of Lambeth Palace, from chapel to Mrs. Howley's lodgings he was preceded by men bearing flambeaux. Once a week during the season he kept open house. Anyone was welcome to these dinners if he wore court dress. The food and wine were served by thirty flunkeys in livery, and fifteen without livery. [BOWEN *op. cit.* p. 39]

By contrast, his successor the pious Evangelical John Bird Sumner, led at Lambeth 'the simple life of a country clergyman, lighting his own fires and walking to the House of Lords with an umbrella beneath his arm.' [*Ibid.*] Change was coming even in an archbishop's lifestyle.

Visitation Charges 1828-1840

Not all bishops issued *Charges* – in the twenty-three years that Manners-Sutton was Archbishop, the clergy of Canterbury heard not one. And not all bishops had their *Charges* published but enough have survived from the period for us to gain a pretty clear picture of the topics they dealt with most frequently and the concerns that exercised them in their episcopal ministry. Henry Ryder is exceptional in having actually explained to his clergy at his first visitation in 1816 what he believed such an address should contain. 'The grand object originally designed and properly to be pursued in these occasional addresses, appears to consist in *general* exhortation, and in *appropriate* instructions and admonitions, as suggested by the peculiar exigencies of the time; by public acts and occurrences, which affect the interests of the Church, chiefly as a spiritual body; and by the ever-varying state of opinions and manners amongst our flocks.'

Publication after delivery at the visitation highlighted the efforts of reforming bishops and served as a counter to anticlerical criticism. Some were more widely read than just by the diocesan clergy - C.R. Sumner's primary *Charge* at Winchester, for example, went quickly through three editions. Burns notes that 'topicality and local colour encouraged more frequent printing of charges for wider dissemination; appendices and partial delivery necessitated it.' [BURNS *op. cit.* p. 31] This chapter is based on a reading of sixty-two *charges* delivered by tweny-five bishops and on twenty-five given by other dignitaries.

For ease of treatment I have divided the period into three sections: 1828-1830, 1831-1833, and 1834-1840.

Charges 1828-30

As Bishop Marsh of Peterborough did not carry out a visitation in this period but did deliver an important one in 1827 on 'the influence of the Roman Catholic question on the Established Church' I have included it too as that was a burning issue at the time.

Marsh was vehemently opposed to any amendment in the Church-State relationship and defended the right of his clergy to make representations to Parliament in the form of petitions. The clergy had been accused of 'bigotry and intolerance'. Not so, he argued, the issue under discussion was 'not about *religious liberty*, but *political power*; and surely we may oppose an extension of political power, without incurring the charge of bigotry and intolerance.' He noted that if Catholic emancipation was passed, then Dissenters too must be granted the same, and that the Corporation and Test Acts would need to be repealed. He then delivered a passage which borders on scare-mongering and carried an appeal to their clerical self-interest.

> When all religious parties in this country are placed on the same footing in regard to civil power, when the ascendancy of the Church of England has thus merged into equality with other religious parties, and is virtually become a sect among sects, the question will soon arise, whether the emoluments, which are set apart for the service of religion should be *exclusively* enjoyed by the ministers of *one* sect . . . . . And when all religious parties have the same political power, exclusive possession of Church emoluments cannot be urged by one party on the ground that they belong to the present Establishment; for the very question at issue will be, whether the present Establishment should remain. [MARSH *Charge* 1827 p. 12f]

He argues disingenuously that it is not about self-interest and not wanting their families to be reduced to beggary but about truth because as ministers of the Established Church they believed they were ministers of the true Church, and 'therefore bound to support it for its own sake' as well as for their own. He then moves on to a fear that would be rehearsed frequently in the next decade by the opponents of Church reform, namely the loss to the ranks of the clergy of well-educated men. It would not be a profession worth entering. Marsh shows no sense here of a man having a vocation to ordination from God. 'Men so educated and so qualified would never be content to owe their subsistence to voluntary contributions dependent on the favour or the caprice of the donors' (i.e. as dissenting ministers did) nor could it be expected any longer to see 'a Clergy numerously allied to noble, and other distinguished families in the State, whence they confer on their profession additional lustre, while they personally adorn it by their individual conduct. If a Clergy so educated, and so formed, should be destined to fall, the calamity would not be confined to themselves, but would extend to the nation at large.' [*Ibid*. p.19]

It is to their credit that seven other bishops who delivered their visitation *Charges* the following summer did not echo Marsh's views. C.R. Sumner in Llandaff, Jenkinson in St David's, Blomfield in Chester, Bethell in Gloucester, Ryder in Lichfield, Kaye in Lincoln and even the ultra-conservative Van Mildert in Durham were more concerned about the exercise of the sacred ministry in their dioceses. Van Mildert did tackle the issue of the Church under attack but exhorted his clergy to put your adversaries to rebuke, by such well-regulated zeal, and such irreprehensible conduct, as shall render ineffectual any efforts to deprive you of that strong hold on public opinion, which will be a shield against a host of foes. An assiduous discharge of all your pastoral duties is indispensably requisite; not only such as relate to the public ritual of the Church, and your discourses from the pulpit; but also the visiting of the sick, the instruction of the ignorant, the consolation of the afflicted, the relief of the necessities, and the education of the children of the poor in the principles of our Established Church. [VAN MILDERT *Charge* 1827 p. 17f]

Christopher Bethell told his clergy that he had voted for the repeal of those parts of the Corporation and Test Acts which had imposed a sacramental test on those entering on public office. He noted that some clergy were apprehensive about a door having been opened which might allow Catholics into corporate and civic offices but he (mistakenly) did not expect that to happen. He ended his *Charge* with some reflections on the role of a bishop and made an appeal to the young clergy among his hearers, intimating that he wanted to be their friend and counsellor.

The Constitution of the Church presumes that the Bishop is the centre of Clerical unity, who is to moderate between you, if need be, and to conciliate your differences, and to guide and superintend you in the discharge of your duties; to whose advice and instructions you owe a reasonable and respectful deference; and whose legitimate authority you have engaged yourselves to obey. In me you will find, I trust, a friend, a counsellor, and a fellow servant, who is desirous both to possess and deserve your confidence. To my younger brethren, especially, I would willingly offer such aid and instructions as are the result of years and experience; and shall be glad when they open up their minds to me on their studies, their success, their difficulties, the whole circle of their Pastoral labours. [BETHELL *Charge* 1828 p. 38f]

Ryder chose to comment in 1828 on the need for new churches and on the progress made since his previous visitation four years earlier. That visitation had shown there was extreme need in 27 parishes where there was church accommodation for less than one-fifth of the population. 'Of the twenty-seven I have already consecrated six churches which will hold about 8,000 persons. Grants have been made by the Commissioners, which in union with Subscriptions, will erect sixteen more – capable of containing about 24,000, and the buildings are most of them commenced or commencing, and several nearly ready for consecration.' [RYDER *Charge* 1828 p. 38]

As an Evangelical bishop, he naturally wanted a copy of the Bible to be in every home, so he urged his clergy, 'Provide to the utmost of your power, for every one of your Parishioners, who will accept or will purchase them at the lowest rate, a Bible and a Prayer Book – they will be, as it were, the Christian *Penates* of each Cottage Household – and far more than the Amulet or the Patron Saint of each individual.' [*Ibid*. p. 49] And, above all, they were to 'Preach Christ more freely – more fully – more practically.'

John Skinner who heard Law deliver his *Charge* at Frome on Monday 14 July 1828 recorded his very positive impressions. The Bishop had already confirmed 'multitudes' in the morning during a two hour long service before turning his attention to the clergy.

> The Bishop afterwards read a very impressive charge to the clergy, confining himself more particularly to the enforcing the parochial duties of the resident minister, in performing which with propriety, he said, much of the evil we had to complain of might be obviated, as the resident minister would thereby conciliate the affections of his flock and prevent their straying after new pastors. He lamented that the sacraments of Baptism and the Supper of the Lord were so much neglected; that the former was by some considered as a mere ceremony which must be complied with in order to admit a new member into the Church, of which Confirmation was the seal. That the Sacrament was indeed still more neglected – that few but females now were communicants, and not so many of them as ought to attend. He also alluded to the ceremony of Marriage, which had of late been considered rather as a civil rite than connected with the offices of the Church . . . He also spoke in decided and very appropriate terms of reprobation against the increase of licensed Ale Houses which, although they might increase the revenues of the State, must also increase the immorality of the people. It was a very good Charge; the delivery was excellent, and had double effect, as the sentiments thus conveyed evidently came from the heart.
> [COOMBS. H. & P. ed. *op. cit.* p. 350f]

Law, who had always been ambivalent about educating the poor beyond enabling them to read the Bible, expressed his opposition in this *Charge* to what would soon become an accepted practice, namely amending the curriculum in Church schools towards slightly 'higher scholastic attainments.' He feared it would cause the poor to 'puffeth up' suddenly and seek employment for which they were unqualified. The result would be a 'dangerous and pitiable' frustration among educated youths. [LAW *Charge* 1828 p. 24] Promoting and enabling such education was not part of a Christian minister's spiritual duties.

Kaye's *Primary Visitation Charge* to the clergy of the diocese of Lincoln delivered in the summer of 1828 majored on the work of ministry, the importance of residence and the provision of two services each Sunday. His insistence that the legal requirement of two services a Sunday should be observed figures in many other episcopal *Charges* in the following decade but was it really such a good idea in sparsely populated rural parishes, of which there were very many in Lincoln diocese? Frances Knight argues that there is evidence to show this requirement had a negative effect.

> In the period after 1830 double duty became the norm throughout England, and diligent clergy watched what had once been good congregations ebbing away. Double duty could have the effect of splitting - and demoralising – scattered congregations. This occurred at Cowbit, Lincolnshire, where the perpetual curate, John Steel, decided to introduce an evening service after seeing it recommended in the bishop's Charge of 1828. Soon he lamented that on some Sundays the aggregate of the two congregations scarcely exceeded the single one. Steel's puzzlement at this, and his claim that Dissent was weak, suggest that for the parishioners of Cowbit, one visit to church on Sunday was perceived as quite sufficient, a consideration that does not seem to have occurred to senior Anglicans in their wholesale advocacy of the importance of going to church twice on Sundays.
>
> [KNIGHT *op. cit.* p. 78f]

Cowbit was not the only rural parish in that diocese to experience this negative consequence of double duty whereby one good congregation became two scanty ones.

Kaye added as an appendix to his *Charge* the text of the speech he had given in the House of Lords at the second reading of the Bill to repeal the Corporation and Test Acts. He ended with these words,

> I should feel it my bounden duty to resist the repeal of the Corporation and Test Act if I thought that the safety of the Church of England would be compromised by the repeal. I entertain no such apprehension; the best security of the Church of England is the hold it possesses on the esteem and affections of the people. The legislature may, undoubtedly, contribute essentially to its stability and well-being; not, however, by throwing around it the external fences of restrictive laws, but by defining more accurately the privileges which belong to it as an Established Church, by improving its internal polity, and by providing it with less expensive and less circuitous in order of administering its discipline. [KAYE *Primary Charge* 1828 p. 44]

Jenkinson in his *Primary Charge* to the clergy of south-west Wales responded to the information provided by the clergy in response to his Articles of Inquiry. He was clearly determined to make his diocese a much better regulated one than it had become during Burgess's last years there. He insisted curates must be licensed by him (i.e. no more local, private agreements!), the rules concerning exemption from residence had to be complied with, and curates had to give him three months notice of their intention to quit a post. 'Another very gross abuse which calls for animadversion is, the too frequent practice of clergymen, Incumbents as well as Curates, undertaking to serve *three* Churches on a Sunday.'

He then dealt at length with the related issues of incumbents appointing curates and/or requesting ordination for potential curates. They must 'never suffer the suggestions of friendship, the solicitations of interest, or any view to your own private advantage, to prevail over a sense of duty, and the regard which you owe to the spiritual welfare of your flocks.' [JENKINSON *Charge* 1828 p.17] He went on

> I trust that no attempt will ever be made to impose on me by fraudulent and fictitious titles, where there is no intention, on the part of the Incumbent, of employing *bona fide* as his Curate, the person to whom he gives the title; and that there never will be any agreement, expressed or implied, direct or indirect, between the parties, that no stipend shall be paid, or a less stipend than I may think it right to assign, nor any contrivance for repayment, by the Curate or his friends. [*Ibid*. p. 18]

The fact that he felt it necessary to spell out in such detailed, quasi-legal, language, suggests this particular bad practice had been a frequent occurrence in the diocese which he was determined to put an end to. In future he would refuse to ordain candidates unless the rules had been followed. And that included curates must be paid a minimum stipend of £80 a year. It was essential that testimonials were honest and deserved.

> In their veracity, candour, and firmness, the Bishop must confide. . . If you abuse the confidence reposed in you, and, by signing testimonials at random, suffer yourselves to be made the instruments of misleading the Bishop, he is most unjustly and cruelly treated; for the world will be too apt to ascribe the consequences to a want of vigilance on his part . . . By the introduction of an unfit or disreputable member, the credit of your order is deeply affected, the Church of God is injured, religion receives a wound and the best interests of your fellow Christians are sacrificed. [*Ibid*. p. 25f]

Jenkinson wanted well-educated clergy so he intended to look exclusively to the recently opened St David's College at Lampeter and to the universities for a supply of candidates, so no more 'literates' as in the past. But he promised to note and reward diligent and successful students. The *Charge* marked a promising start to his episcopate but he seems to have quickly lost the confidence of his clergy. Copleston in a letter to Bruce Knight dated 19 February 1834, reports that the Archdeacon of St David's had told him Jenkinson 'does not satisfy his clergy – and, I fear, is very inactive to the details of his Diocese.'

Both of the Sumner brothers delivered *Primary Visitation Charges* in 1829. J.B. in Chester dealt very largely with the ministry of his clergy, (a theme he returned to in almost every *Charge* he delivered) their preaching, public discourses and catechetical instruction.

> I begin, then, by observing, that the object of the Parochial Ministry is, to carry into effect the merciful purpose of God in the dispensation of the Gospel: that wherever an assemblage of men is collected and located together, provision should be made for their souls; that is, provision that they be "brought to God" through Jesus Christ, that they be instructed and maintained in his faith, and thus enabled to render this present life an habitual preparation for eternity. [J.B. SUMNER *Primary Charge* 1829 p. 2]

Unlike many of his episcopal brethren who did not share his evangelical faith, he was keen to see the laity much more involved in a shared ministry with the clergy, especially in populous parishes. He was, in effect, launching a major diocesan initiative by urging upon them the benefits of district visitors.

> Let the minister of a populous district, using careful discrimination of character, such as 'are worthy' and 'of good report', and assign them their several employments under his direction: they may lessen his own labour by visiting and examining the schools, by reading and praying with the infirm and aged, by consoling the fatherless and widows in their affliction.
> [*Ibid*. p. 23]

A lengthy appendix deals in some detail with this suggestion, and he cited the example of Brighton which had been divided into six districts for some years and had a 'District Visiting Association' with clearly stated aims. He was among the first of the bishops to acknowledge that the urban masses were not flocking to the new churches as had been expected. Young and old alike were unreached by their local clergy, so all the Church's resources, lay as well as clerical, were needed if the people were to be won into a lively faith and active membership of their parish churches.

His younger brother Charles, who had been translated to Winchester, shared 'the very full and detail returns' made by the clergy to the questions he had sent out. He seems to have loved statistics for he regarded them as the 'register of our moral power.' They enabled him to pinpoint both the strengths of certain parishes and the areas of particular deficiency which needed attention. He wanted, he said, authentic sources of information as there had been no such episcopal enquiry in the diocese since 1788! It revealed that the diocese had 460 churches and chapels (141 in Surrey and 319 in Hampshire) with church sittings of 81,701 in the former and 15,106 in the latter – enough for about one quarter of the population in Surrey and about half in Hampshire. The recently appointed rural deans in Surrey and the chancellor in Hampshire had examined and reported on the state of church fabric. A few churches had three services on a Sunday, over half had two, but only one in a sizeable minority (132 in Hampshire and 29 in Surrey). In Hampshire there were 216 glebe houses for residence, of which 18 were unfit for residence; in Surrey the figures were 95 of which four were just cottages. In Hampshire 236 parishes had resident incumbents or curates, leaving 83 without a resident minister. In Surrey there were 118 parishes with resident clergy, and 24 without one. Some were in hamlets with chapels attached to a parish where there was a resident cleric. Sumner made it clear that he did not approve of non-residence: 'Without personal residence there can be no daily oversight and inspection, no influence of example; no seasonable counsel, reproof or comfort; no encouragement of good, no restraint of evil practices.' [C.R. SUMNER *Charge* 1829 p. 14]

He told them that curates had to be properly licensed 'strictly conformable to law' with a minimum stipend of £80 a year or the whole value of the benefice; £100 if the population was 300, £120 or the whole value up to 500 souls, £150 up to 1,000 souls. He wanted names and details of candidates for orders and details of the curacy to which they were nominated. Like Jenkinson he was clearly determined to put an end to the private agreements some non-resident clergy had been making in order to acquire a cheap curate. He was similarly concerned about candidates for confirmation who should be at least fourteen years old; he planned to visit every part of the diocese for this purpose every three years. There was a need for more day schools – 69 churches and chapels in Hampshire had no school; in Surrey 19. All parishes should have a Sunday school as paid teachers were not needed, and he told of a visit he had recently made to St Peter Port, Guernsey. It was a town of 12,000 souls and on the day he visited 348 boys and 327 girls were present with 69 teachers and 20 members of the committee. Sharing this information was clearly intended to be an encouragement to his hearers: Go and do likewise!

He also commented on the intolerable living conditions for labourers and their families crowded into inadequate cottages and tenements. He told of one parish where 210 people were crowded into 29 dilapidated cottages. Several people were forced to sleep in the same bed, and in many cases children had to sleep under the bed of their parents. [*Ibid*. p. 48] Such conditions needed to be improved – not least because it interfered with the effective ministry of the clergy!

There was another unhappy topic in his *Charge* – 'the profanation of the Sabbath'. It was a particular local evil he had spotted on his travels in the diocese, e.g. keeping shops open, the payment of wages that day, the habits of cricketing, village festivals and other desecrations of a similar nature which in too many instances robbed the Lord of his own day. [*Ibid*. p. 28]

The aged Thomas Burgess of Bath and Wells remained a staunch opponent of Roman Catholic emancipation even after it had been passed. The thrust of his *Charge* in 1829 was to prove that 'the Church of Rome, which arrogates to herself the exclusive title of *the Church*, and holds all others to be excommunicate and heretical, which are outside her communion, is not the true Church.' [BURGESS *Charge* 1829 p. 46] He also attacked Unitarianism as being 'next to Popery, the greatest enemy of the Gospel.' [*Ibid*. p. 20f]

Archdeacon Samuel Butler's 1829 *Charge* touched on the danger that the hierarchical structure of society was facing by the expansion of educational opportunities for the children of the labouring classes. 'For the possession of knowledge without the power of exercising it, must not only be unprofitable, but a source of restlessness and uneasiness to its possessor. It must tend to make him dissatisfied with his condition . . . ' [BUTLER *Charge* 1829 p. 10] After reminding his clergy of what followed from eating fruit from the tree of knowledge, he indicated his hostility to the 'sentimentality' that encouraged further education for the poor along with 'other acts of charity and benevolence'. Was it not possible that more education would, in fact, so alienate the poor from their established role that they would 'withdraw . . . from useful and honest industry, to idle and unprofitable speculation; from cheerful and active employment in the duties of their calling, to a reluctant and dissatisfied discharge of so much labour as the wants of nature required, or to lazy and degrading dependence on the bounty and services of others?' [*Ibid*.]

Butler shared the fears of other ultra-conservative churchmen such as Bishop Law that the divinely appointed social order was under threat. His opposition to any improvements in the education of the poor never wavered and this, despite being a notable educationalist himself. When in 1836, as Bishop of Lichfield, he was asked to support a society for the promotion of 'normal schools' to train teachers to educate the poor, he condemned the plan as a European innovation which would lead to a compulsory levelling system of education.' [SOLOWAY *op. cit.* p.388]

Blomfield delivered his *Primary Visitation Charge* to the clergy of London in July 1830. He had already shown himself in Chester to be a disciplinarian who expected high standards of his clergy. London got the same treatment. Whilst pressing for the duty of residence and wanting pluralities restricted, he accepted that there was sometimes a case for permitting it. Two services a Sunday had to be the norm, 'Every parish is entitled by law to morning and evening services; and nothing can justify the omission of either, but the poverty of the benefice, which renders it necessary for the Bishop to allow the minister to serve a second Church.' [BLOMFIELD *Charge* 1830 p. 21] He cautiously recommended the use of lay visitors but warned his clergy that they were responsible for seeing that lay visitors never assumed the ministerial role of interpreting Scripture. Laymen were to be confined to visiting and encouraging the poor to attend church where the clergy would provide the necessary teaching. He wanted to see Holy Communion celebrated more frequently than the traditional three times a year though he did not go so far as to require it weekly, and ruled that a surplice should be worn at it by the priest.

He also urged upon them the importance of education: 'It is hardly going too far, to assert, that a Clergyman's attention to his parochial schools is the most hopeful part of his ministerial exertions.' The presence of a church school did not excuse a clergyman from 'catechizing in church; and by catechizing I mean not merely examining, but instructing young persons in their catechism; trying their understandings as well as their memories; inquiring into their notions and the grounds of their knowledge; correcting their mistakes, explaining difficulties, opening to them by degrees the great truths of religion.' [*Ibid*. p. 29] Candidates for confirmation were not to be brought to him before they were sixteen years old. He then expressed his desire for a better educated clergy and set out his expectations of candidates which inevitably included their classical linguistic competence – that was an essential qualification even for a man who would be ministering in the slums of the capital!

There was nothing very controversial in Copleston's *Primary Charge* at Llandaff in 1830. He paid tribute to his immediate predecessor (C.R. Sumner) who had passed on 'a mass of information admirably digested and arranged, the fruit of his own diligent enquiries, seconded as they were and assisted by yourselves.' He mentions one striking statistic relating to confirmation – 'the number actually confirmed in 1830 was 3439, or just double the number confirmed three years ago.' He spoke at length about the preparation given by the clergy to candidates for confirmation and the need for them to have a thorough grounding in Scriptural knowledge. 'Among the most effective instruments for advancing this work, are parochial schools, frequently visited and superintended by the minister.' One issue on which he did not accept the opinion of reformers was that of non-residence of the clergy.

> I must be allowed to protest against the unjust clamour which has been lately raised on the subject; and to profess my belief, that not only has the extent of the evil been greatly exaggerated, but that both the causes and the consequences of the thing complained of are very ill understood. Residence is, in many instances, either physically or morally impossible.
>
> [COPLESTON *Charge* 1830 p. 27]

Charges 1831-33

The Reform Bill and the perceived threats to the Establishment inevitably figure in just about every *Charge* delivered in this period but it was not the only issue addressed.

Bishop Law issued a Pastoral Letter to the clergy of Bath and Wells on 9 November 1831 in which he described himself as 'a decided friend to Reform. But . . . a Reform, just, considerate and constitutional.' The letter is an exercise in danger limitation. He favoured a measure of electoral reform such as closing down rotten boroughs (Old Sarum and its like) in favour of Manchester, Birmingham and other unrepresented places. He had wanted the Bill to go into Committee to allow for modifications and amendments, but this was not allowed. So, because he could not approve of the whole Bill, he felt he had to vote against.

He uses the letter to express concern for the poor and to raise wages when possible, and then turns to the contentious issue of episcopal stipends, more particularly his own. Figures quoted in the press and in pamphlets, he said, had been greatly exaggerated. The value of his own see was reputed to be one of the most valuable and was alleged to be worth £20,000 a year whereas in reality 'its average amount does not exceed a fourth part of that sum.' And adds 'with respect also to the disposal of Episcopal Incomes . . . they are nearly all expended in the discharge of public duties, and circulated throughout the neighbourhood in which they are received.' [LAW *Letter* 1831 p. 16] When the Ecclesiastical Commission produced its findings, his diocese was in fact the ninth wealthiest with an average of £5,946 over the previous three years.

In his *Charge* of that same year, Law returned to the topic of education. God had given to his creatures different faculties and endowments, both of mind and body, in order that 'the great machine of the world' could work properly. Education gave power to all who received it, even the poor, but by going beyond the dictates of natural law and social harmony, 'we render them dissatisfied with their station, we lay the foundation of civil insubordination and discord.' Consequently, a basic religious education was sufficient for them 'to discharge the duties of that station in life, in which it hath pleased Almighty God to place them'. [LAW *Charge* 1831 p. 16f] Poverty was another concern he addressed as it was seriously affecting the stability of society. In agrarian districts it was clear 'that the strong tie which had for ages bound together the Clergyman and Parishioners, the Landlord and his tenants by a sense of benefits mutually conferred and received, appears now to be inauspiciously weakened, if not entirely rent and torn asunder'. [*Ibid.* p. 18f] Poverty was a topic he had addressed at length the previous year when his *Remarks on the Present Distresses of the Poor* was published. In it, he had pressed for poor labourers to be paid a living wage. Landowners, industrialists and even the Government were attacked by him for their lack of concern. It was inevitable that social turbulence would be a consequence, as indeed it proved to be, unless fairly remunerated employment was provided.

> We are called upon therefore, by every principle of humanity and justice, to reverse, in this respect, the present order of things: to pay the labourer that which he fairly earns, and to pay it to him as his right, and as his due. Thus shall we secure the willing and effectual services of the labouring classes of the community, and remove from their minds, every ground of discontent and murmuring. [LAW *Remarks* p. 11]

The 1831 *Charges* were all delivered in the late summer and before the political storm broke over the heads of the bishops in October.

Kaye made a passing reference to Roman Catholic emancipation and its importance in his *Charge*, 'the principle that the legislature of this country should be exclusively Protestant was abandoned. Last year, a further change was attempted, though unsuccessfully; it was proposed to remove the civil disabilities affecting the Jewish subjects of the realm. Had that attempt succeeded, the legislature would have ceased to be exclusively Christian.' [KAYE *Charge* 1831 p. 51] That would have been a step too far even for a reforming bishop such as Kaye. This *Charge* is particularly valuable for the exposition it provides of his ideas about ordination and appropriate reading he recommended to candidates.

Marsh produced another defence of the clergy in July and August. He believed that with the exception of the period which preceded the overthrow of the Established Church in the time of Charles I, there never was a time when the clergy were assailed with so much calumny and so much violence as at present. Not all but most are 'loving and diligent in their parochial duties' he stated. More than sixty churches in his diocese which previously had had only one service a Sunday now had two. Pluralism, likewise, was not a major problem and he claimed that the clergy with two livings

> do not deserve the reproach, which their adversaries cast on them. And there is *no* accusation so grossly unjust, as that, in which pluralists are represented as a set of idlers in the vineyard, who enjoy in indolence the riches of the Church, while the *working* clergy (as Curates are now called, in order to throw odium on the beneficed clergy) perform the duties of the Church for a pittance. Of the thirty-two clergymen who have more than one living in this diocese, there is not an individual who does not strictly and literally belong to the class of the *working* clergy. [MARSH *Charge* 1831 p. 15f]

Nor were curates working for a pittance, he said, 'They not infrequently receive the greater share in the income of a living.' He readily admits that the primary object of this *Charge* has been

> to defend the parochial clergy against the unjust complaints which are now industrially made against them; to show that their moral conduct is not such as their adversaries pretend; that so far from being negligent in the performance of their duties, they perform those duties more efficiently than ever; and that, instead of being overloaded with wealth, the average amount of their remuneration is hardly so much as the expense of their education, and the extent of their services require. [*Ibid*. p. 26]

Van Mildert referred to the need for more places of worship in the *mining* districts 'where for the most part, there is no provision of the kind, sufficient to insure to the multitude belonging to them those spiritual ministrations, without which there is danger of almost all sense of Religion being either lost or perverted.' [VAN MILDERT *Charge* 1831 p. 9] Yet, after giving thought to a proposal made by some colliery owners to provide land and endowments for erecting and maintaining auxiliary chapels in Durham's new mining areas, he dropped it. Soloway comments, 'To the rigid bishop, however, such a proposal was too reminiscent of Methodist sectarianism to permit his consent.' [SOLOWAY *op. cit.* p. 334]

Robert Gray in Bristol also urged his clergy to reach out to the labouring classes who had disappeared from Church worship, in part because of the lack of free seating. That situation, he claimed, was being reversed with more free seats. The clergy had an important role in educating the masses in 'just and patriotic principles . . . right doctrine and moral conduct of the general classes of society, at this time exposed to much misguidance and many seductions.' [GRAY *Charge* 1831 p. 29]

He addressed some of the issues which had been before parliament – the Archbishop's Bill 'for encouraging and facilitating composition for tithes. . . Such is the projected arrangement by which it is proposed that the maintenance of the Clergy may be secured without that disagreement which has sometimes arisen, and proved prejudicial to the cause of religion. . . A Bill has been brought in by the Archbishop to restrain and regulate the holding of plurality of dignities and benefices by spiritual persons – the tendency of which is to prevent the recurrence of that accumulation of preferment on individuals which justly excites complaints.' [*Ibid.* p. 17]

The temperate tone of his *Charge* contrasts with the vitriolic attacks made by some of the Church's critics. 'The great object which seems now to be in the contemplation of the legislature, and of all who are well affected towards the interests of religion as promoted by the Establishment, is to extend by different regulations greater competency to the Parochial Clergy, and to secure the effectual discharge of their important duties.' [*Ibid.* p. 18] But he goes on to defend aspects of the *status quo* in allowing 'large emoluments of a few elevated stations' which 'afford encouragement to distinguished talent' though they are too often the objects of envy.

The Archdeacon of Colchester's 1831 *Charge* entitled *The Nature and True Value of Church Property Examined* went through three editions as it was a robust defence of the parochial system which, he claimed, needed the finance brought in by tithes and glebe and church rates in order to serve everyone in the land. He argued that the Church was doing its job well.

> I do not believe that since the Reformation, there was ever a period . . . when the Church of England . . . possessed stronger claims upon the regard and affection of its members. Never was there a period when there was more learning and talent, more activity and propriety of conduct among her ministers; nor when the great truths of the Gospel were laid more fully before the people, or more zealously enforced. [LYALL *Charge* 1831 p. 10]

The Archbishop of Canterbury delivered and published his *Primary Visitation Charge* in 1832, four years after he had taken office. It is thoroughly conservative and traditional in its tone and content when dealing with the parochial ministry. It is almost as though he is advising his clergy to ignore the political turmoil they are living through and simply get on with their job. Here are three short passages:

> In respect to the duties of the pulpit, let your discourses be Scriptural, illustrating the doctrines of the Gospel, and enforcing its precepts from the sacred text, explaining the grounds of justification through the Cross of Christ, of sanctification through the aid of the Holy Ghost, the true nature of Christian holiness, and its absolute necessity to salvation. Take care to be audible, and not less care to be intelligible. A discourse not understood by the hearer is like food hard of digestion to a weak stomach, and, misunderstood may have the effect of poison. . . [HOWLEY *Charge* 1832 p. 28]

> But your zeal for the salvation of others will be of little avail, if it is not accredited by your own example: when the life of the teacher exhibits a contrast to his doctrine, his instructions lose all their weight. Irreproachable purity of morals, habitual piety, a gravity suitable to his calling, and the strictest propriety in all his demeanour, are required, and not without reason, of the professional teacher of godliness, the steward of the mysteries of Christ. What may seem in a layman excusable levity, is criminal indiscretion in a Clergyman. Addiction to worldly pursuits, or frivolous pleasure, occupations and habits inconsistent in any respect with the clerical character, will diminish the reverence due to his office, and expose him to the suspicion of hypocrisy. [*Ibid*. p. 31]
>
> In most instances, the state of the Schools, the numbers prepared for Confirmation, attending the Services of the Church, and partaking of the Lord's Supper, may be taken as a tolerable criterion of the ability and diligence of the Pastor. [*Ibid*. p. 35]

Towards the end of his *Charge* Howley addresses the need for reforms but says, 'I am unwilling to hazard its [i.e. the Church's] safety by rash innovation, nor could I venture to act without full consideration of the probable consequences of any given change. These feelings have rendered me cautious, but, I trust, not inactive.' His desire was 'the pursuit of the greatest attainable good, by the least violent methods.'

Monk of Gloucester also carried out his first visitation that year. He too chose to major on the work of the ordained ministry and touches on issues that have already been heard in the *Charges* of other bishops: residence is essential to the effectual and edifying performance of its various pastoral duties, the need for two services a Sunday in all single benefices, curates must be licensed properly, etc. He reports that there are above a hundred benefices in the diocese entirely destitute of a residence, or anything that can be converted into a residence for a pastor. He then deals at some length with his expectations of candidates for Holy Orders. 'To raise the standard of intellectual qualification among the Clergy is not only expedient, but necessary, with a view to the present condition of the country.' And he adds that in future he will expect all candidates who mean to offer themselves at his half-yearly ordinations to communicate to him their intention at least two months before Christmas Day or Trinity Sunday. His expectations and recommendations are reported more fully in the next chapter.

Monk then deals with the way the clergy should answer the attacks and calumnies of the Church's enemies – by fulfilling their ministry with love and diligence:

> The real and effectual safeguard of the Church of England is founded on the attachment of the people; which attachment will continue so long as they are convinced by experience of its usefulness and efficiency in promoting the true ends of its establishment. It is my sincere conviction that there never was a period at which the ministers of our Church were more generally attentive to their duties, correct in their lives, ardent in their piety, and zealous in their spiritual labours than at the present moment.
> [MONK *Charge* 1832 p. 32]

Co-incidentally, J.B. Sumner, who carried out his triennial visitation that same summer, added a very long Appendix devoted to his practice regarding ordination. One of his requirements was that candidates should give three months' notice; he was planning to contact their referees before giving them an appointment for a personal interview. He also used his *Charge* to report on the positive results some clergy had achieved who had acted on his advice given in 1829 with regard to lay assistants. In the town of Lancaster, for example, during the first year of using lay workers, more than a hundred children had been added to schools which were short of pupils and seventy-nine persons had begun attending worship regularly. In the following year 'eighty-one more persons were reclaimed by like means, and an hundred and eighteen fresh scholars united to the schools.' [J.B. SUMNER *Charge* 1832 p. 9]

By 1832 Sumner had come to see that merely building new churches was not the solution to engaging with the unchurched masses. And it was no longer possible to take some negative comfort in the likelihood 'that if the people are not in the established churches, they are in dissenting chapels, and are therefore not destitute of religious instruction. The truth is not so. The mass of the ADULT manufacturing population is . . . without religious instruction of any kind.' [*Ibid*. p. 12] A grave change had occurred in English society in his life time, he noted. Apathy and unbelief had become a lower-class, uneducated way of life in contrast to the eighteenth century, where it had flourished among the upper classes. 'The careless apathy, or the dissolute sensuality of former times, though it had as much ungodliness in it as may be found now, was far less dangerous. Our lot has been cast upon a period, when there is nothing neutral. Every man who is not a friend, is the enemy of religion.' [*Ibid*. p. 11] The labouring poor would be irretrievably lost to the Church unless maximum effort was applied immediately – 'one thing is evident: the ordinary means of grace are unavailable. The church is open, but neglected: the voice of truth is raised, but never heard. . .'

> If the minister waits . . . for times of penitence or messages of invitation, he will wait for ever. We might as justly expect that a Lazarus should rise unsummoned from the tomb, as that the man who lies in the darkness of spiritual death, should by any natural process begin to feel his ignorance, and his sin, and shake off his grave clothes, and come forth to seek religious knowledge . . . What he needs is, not precepts, but motives: not merely a condemnation of present habits, but an effective reason why they should be changed. [*Ibid*. p. 17f]

It was an urgent call from their bishop that clergy and laity alike should get out in the streets and alleys of those blighted, heathen districts visiting lost souls and showing them the way to the empty churches waiting to receive them. He was also calling for a more dedicated kind of ordination candidate with leadership abilities:

> It is no longer sufficient that a man have shewn a decency and respectability of conduct, against which nothing blameable can be alleged: he must also have the talents and disposition from which much that is laudable can be expected. He must have received such education, and be possessed of such

strength of character as may raise him above the level of those over whom he is to rule. He must have such natural and acquired powers, as shall enable him to take the lead among his fellow creatures; to guide the flock, not follow it.

I trust therefore that those who may require the assistance of Curates, will not be induced by friendship, or relationship, or neighbourhood, or amiable feelings, to recommend any persons to me for ordination, who do not give promise of essential usefulness. [*Ibid*. p. 29f]

Henry Ryder in his large and industrialized diocese of Lichfield-Coventry faced a similar situation. Since his arrival in 1824 he had seen non-residency reduced, new churches and chapels built, and more churches providing double services on Sundays but he was not confident about the future. Existing churches were filled to no more than one-third of their capacity. Less than one quarter of those attending received communion, while no more than one in twelve parishioners attended. He told his clergy he was saddened by this 'grievous disproportion' and saw it as 'an unfavourable sign, demanding on our part a searching examination into the cause.' [RYDER *Charge* 1832 p. 35f]

Archdeacon Thorp of Durham, who was Chaplain to Earl Grey and who would become the first Principal of Durham University, delivered a more upbeat message to his clergy. He expressed his hopes about that new foundation in his annual *Charge* in 1832.

> The establishment of the Durham University, made at great personal sacrifices on the part of the Bishop and the Dean and Chapter, will have a happy effect in furnishing sound instruction for our children, in securing the residence and the service of men eminent in all the walks of literature, and capable of directing human learning to the highest purposes; in strengthening the ties between ourselves and the laity; and providing the means of a liberal clerical education, combining general learning with professional pursuits. The class of divinity students will have advantages equal to those enjoyed at either of our famous Universities; and will, we trust furnish to the northern dioceses a perpetual supply of men duly qualified to serve in the ministry of the Church. May God look upon this also for good!
> [A footnote on p.27 adds: An Act was passed in the last Session, settling an estate belonging to the Dean and Chapter upon the University, which now produces to the University chest £3,000 a year. The Bishop of Durham gives £1,000 a year, and the Bishop and Dean and Chapter have provided houses for present use at a considerable cost.] [THORP *Charge* 1832 p. 27f]

The first part of his *Charge*, however, had been a defensive rant against critics of the Church and an attempt to justify its practices. He referred to 'the popular objections which are urged against the Church, and which, to suit the spirit of the day, are drawn from its *Revenues*. They are said to be *excessive*; - *ill-spent*; - *unfairly distributed*.' [*Ibid*. p. 11] He then sought to defend current practices, and, on the third point, argued

> The Church to be efficient in an advanced state of society such as ours, must secure the service of the able and informed persons of every rank and station, drawn from all classes, intimately united with them in the intercourse of life; - and it must embrace men of literature and study, securing to them leisure and independence; - and this forbids *Equality*. Nay more, it bespeaks great *Inequalities*. [*Ibid*. p. 16]

He then attacked Lord Henley's proposals for Church Reform as being 'destructive of the constitution and character of the Church.' [*Ibid*. p. 19] Here speaks a die-hard conservative!

At the other end of the country, George Chandler, the Dean of Chichester, who would later play an important role in bringing the first postgraduate theological college into being, was taking a rather different line. He was happy to accept the recommendation that such peculiar jurisdictions as his should be brought under the control of the bishop and the archdeacon. He supported the Plurality Bill before Parliament – 'I should say the measure steers a happy medium between rash innovation and a morose retention of ancient usage.' And he welcomed measures which would allow delinquent clergy to be prosecuted 'both by remodelling the appellate jurisdiction, and also by giving to the Diocesan (a due regard to the fair liberties of the accused being still retained) a much more summary cause of proceeding to correction and punishment. When these things are effected, I think we are likely to see the removal of some scandals, which now are seriously injurious to our Church.'   [CHANDLER *Charge* p. 15] It would, in fact, be some years before these changes came into being as the Archbishop's mildly reforming Bills were not passed.

Bishop Blomfield in his *Charge* of 1832 gave his clergy a new version of Laud's 'beauty of holiness' – any 'ornamental parts' of the Church should be discarded if they 'stand in the way of improvements calculated to enhance and give lustre to the true beauty of the Church – the beauty of its holy usefulness.' Olive Brose comments, 'Stretching ahead of this delightful utilitarian sentiment lay the strategy of the Bishop of London: to use efficiency and usefulness as necessary means for survival, to the end that the Church might function in the terms of the society in which it found itself. But it could do so only through the spheres available at the time –

the education of the people and the whole enterprise of Church extension – and in both these spheres it did grapple, however unsuccessfully, with the problems of the connexion between the Church and its people.' [BROSE *The Irish Precedent for English Church Reform* p. 225]

Thomas Burgess in his *Charge* of 1832 included 'the education of young men intended for the Ministry of the Church' as 'another subject of Reform'. He was critical of the lack of adequate theological preparation at the universities,

> . . . their previous studies being too general, too inappropriate to their future prospects, too neglectful, not only of the evidences of Christianity, but of the first principles of our Faith; too neglectful of the writings of the Primitive Church, in which may be found admirable rules of faith and life for the formation of the Christian character, and beautiful specimens of fine writing for the cultivation and exercise of taste and judgement, and models of eloquence in pastoral instruction. [BURGESS *Charge* 1832 p. 24]

He adds an appendix detailing the directions for candidates for Orders in his diocese.

We come now to Henry Phillpotts's *Primary Visitation Charge* delivered at various locations in the diocese of Exeter in August, September and October 1833. His friend, Bishop Copleston, commended it in a letter to Bruce Knight, dated 22 November 1833, 'It is written with much ability and legal knowledge – but it is too little like a *charge*. It is rather a pamphlet on behalf of the Established Church.'

Phillpotts started on a doleful note, speaking of the gloom and darkness which hung over every worthy institution at that time, and in particular over 'the Ark of the Lord, the Church'. He then turned to one of the current burning issues – that of the Church's endowments. 'The endowments of the Church,' he argues, 'are mainly to be valued as a means to an end, the greatest of all ends, the full instruction of the *people* in the knowledge of those truths which can "make them wise unto salvation."' [PHILLPOTTS *Primary Charge* p. 7]   The Church's endowments allowed it to bring the blessings of the Christian Faith to the poor – to those who could not pay for the maintenance of a pastor. He deals more particularly with the question of tithes and their commutation into cash payments. He rehearses a history of the tithe and then declares that the clergy, as a body, are ready and anxious to concur in any measure of fair and secure commutation. The cash tithe was, in fact, already in operation in almost every parish in his diocese where the clergy had the right to tithes. He then turns to what one noble lord had called 'the necessity of a *more equitable distribution* of the revenues of the Church.' He defends one aspect of this which had enabled 'one of the main bulwarks of the English Church – I mean a learned Ministry.' The holders of cathedral stalls and dignities, he claims, have done 'so much for the common cause of Christian truth. . . The opportunities of learned leisure, afforded in these retreats, have produced a very large portion of the immortal works, which have placed this Church on an eminence.' [*Ibid*. p. 28] And then, with Durham in mind, adds

> In some instances, it might be practicable, and expedient, to append to the Chapter (I am confident it might be most usefully done at Exeter) an institution in the nature of *a School of Theology*, at which candidates for orders might be required to reside during one or two years after they have left the University, and immediately before their Ordination; thus acquiring the knowledge necessary for their holy vocation, and giving testimony of their fitness for it, by their previous conduct, under the immediate eye of the Bishop, or of those who are best able to judge, and report to him.
>
> [*Ibid*. p. 29f]

His wish for a training college attached to the cathedral was eventually met, thanks in part to his generous financial support, but not until 1861.

Recognizing that the Church could no longer expect help from a reformed legislature which now included Dissenters and even Catholics, he called upon those who profited from the labours of the poor to provide for their spiritual welfare before it was too late. He then addressed a number of other current issues: pluralities and ill-endowed benefices, non-residence and the stipends of curates, the frequency of translations of bishops and to *commendams* necessary to some by reason of the poverty of their sees (including Exeter).

> In respect of translations, I cannot forebear adding, that in my own opinion, as they ought not to be necessary, so, if not necessary, they ought never to be made, on pecuniary grounds. If the income of every Bishopric were made adequate to its fair demands, translations from one to another ought no longer to be allowed, except for the manifest good of the Church, - more especially, in order to place the fittest persons in sees requiring peculiar qualifications. [*Ibid*. p. 53]

He did not, however, support the idea of the bishops' property being centralized and redistributed – rather let individual wealthy bishops voluntarily alienate part of their property. He, then, defends some richer emoluments on grounds we have already heard expressed by others.

'The eminent station, and ample means, assigned to a few, exalt the order generally, - thus rendering it attractive to those who would disdain to consign their sons to a profession, in which nothing was seen but that humble mediocrity, which must be the result of anything like an equalization of the emoluments of the Clergy.' [*Ibid*. p. 54] He recognized that some non-resident clergy were in fact ministering in their parish but were living just outside its boundaries. That he would accept but notorious non-resident clergy he intended to call to account, and the number of parishes with a resident incumbent duly rose.

Copleston and C.R. Sumner also carried out visitations that autumn in their dioceses, the latter after having spent some time in Norwich carrying out confirmations and consecrations on behalf of the aged and infirm Bathurst. Sumner valued the statistical information he gathered from his careful reading of the articles of enquiry the clergy returned. In this *Charge* he chose to report on the demands being put on ministers in heavily populated areas: 'The Southwark parishes, which cover six hundred acres have a population of about 91,500, and only nine parochial ministers. In Lambeth, there are 90,000 inhabitants, and eleven clergy with cure of souls. In Portsea, there are more than 42,000 with four parochial clergy.' And whilst the theory of a national church, he said, supposed there were seats for everyone, that was manifestly not the case. 'In one of the Surrey parishes, not one in twenty, and in another, not one in forty, can obtain a sitting. In another parish, of 14,000 souls, there are only 150 free and unappropriated sittings for the poor! The shepherd, in too many instances, is so far from being able to know his sheep, that he can scarcely count them. . . . He is disabled by the magnitude of his Charge.' Moreover, a traditional and fundamental bond of social cohesion was at breaking point: 'there is no sympathy or bond of holy union between pastor and people; [it is] despised and disowned, motives are suspect, confidence is withdrawn, respect is violated,' and the classes of society are full of enmity. [C.R. SUMNER *Charge* 1833 p.16-18]

Sumner suggested some things his clergy could do, 'Have we tried any of those expedients of District Visiting Societies, and Bible Classes, and Adult Teachings, and Cottage Readings, which are often found effective in breaking up the fallow ground, where the harvest might be plenteous were not the labourers so few?' [*Ibid*. p. 29] He also offered advice to young ministers to earn people's respect and not to assume it by their status, and to preach in a temperate way and not inflict degradation and peril on the people.

Copleston began his *Charge* on a hopeful note, referring to the storm which the Church had safely passed through.

> Formidable as the threatenings of this moral storm were, yet the evils we naturally apprehended have not yet burst upon us; and I am willing to believe that much of that angry passion has now subsided which disturbed the general tranquillity, and alienated the affections of men from things they were once accustomed to esteem and love; while it is beyond doubt ascertained that the ravings of infidelity and blasphemy, which accompanied these convulsions, are no longer popular. [COPLESTON *Charge* 1833 p. 6f]

He touches on the 'reproaches' of the Church's enemies and even of some of its friends relating to the Church's wealth and argues that these endowments are needed for its nationwide ministry.

> The property of the Church is emphatically the inheritance of the poor. It is given, that the Gospel may be preached *to them*. It is their portion in the land in which they live; their bread of life springs from it; and whoever alienates, or lessens this portion, does, in the same degree, take from the common stock destined to their comfort and instruction. [*Ibid.* p. 13]

Another issue which troubled him greatly was the immoral conduct of some clergy and the inability of bishops to punish the culprits.

> The part, however, of our ecclesiastical constitution which appears to me most defective, is one which has least provoked animadversion among the advocates of reform. I mean, the difficulty of removing unworthy ministers, or even of suspending them from the exercise of their sacred office. If it be hazardous to entrust a superior with absolute authority in such cases, let it be remembered, that the hazard is infinitely greater, and affecting the interests of far greater magnitude, when a minister of the Gospel brings a scandal upon his profession, grieves and disgusts the better part of his flock, corrupts the weak, and confirms the wicked in their sins; all of which may be done artfully, as to baffle for a long time the formal interposition of the law, and in many cases defeat it altogether. [*Ibid.* p. 22]

He hastens to add, however, that he is not thinking about the clergy in his own diocese in particular when he says this. Six years experience of Llandaff has shown him 'an improvement manifestly, not only in the exterior decencies of life, but in the assiduous and exemplary discharge of all parochial duties. It is this general improvement which has made any deviation from it more conspicuous, and more to be lamented.' [Ibid. p. 23] By mid-December Copleston was back in residence at St Paul's in

London and had had his *Charge* printed and made it available via Bruce Knight in Llandaff for all his clergy as he wished them to have a copy.

The Archdeacon of Colchester, W.R. Lyall, had also had his *Charge* printed under the title *Sentiments of the Clergy on the Question of Church Reform briefly stated*. He noted that most clergy did not favour parliamentary reform but it had been passed so the clergy's duty now was to promote obedience to the law, and to strive for peace 'by private persuasion and example. In this way let it be our endeavour, then, laying aside all party feeling and distinctions, to do as much good, and prevent as much evil, as shall be in our power; by devoting ourselves to the task of healing divisions, allaying animosities, and restoring harmony and good will, wherever either the weight of our authority, or the influence of our example, may be supposed likely to extend.' [LYALL *Charge* p. 9]

He saw calls for reform of the Church as being more threatening as they came largely from those opposed to the Established Church such as Dissenters whose attacks on the Church's finances appealed to anyone who had paid church rates or tithes. He believed the clergy would support reforms where they were *genuinely* needed and he argues that the clergy are a fair and reasonable body. But he imputed bad motives to the Church's critics:

> One person seeks to benefit his estate – and he proposes to do away with tithes; another seeks to strengthen his party – and he proposes to turn the Bishops out of the House of Lords; a third looks to the advantages of his sect – and his plan is to abolish Church rates, and to obtain a share in marriage and burial fees. But what has all this to do with the interests of Christ's Kingdom? How is the glory of God, and the salvation of mankind, concerned in schemes of this kind?
> We have at least a right to protest against such propositions being dignified with the name of Church reform. To proposals such as these, the Clergy are not, and, I hope, never will be parties. [*Ibid*. p. 18f]

Lyall's *Charge* ends on the depressing note that the poor can accept 'subordination of ranks, and the inequalities of condition in society' if they consider them as 'founded upon God's will' and not 'merely upon the will of his fellow man.' The implication is that they will get their reward in heaven.

His fellow archdeacon, Samuel Butler of Derby, had published a pamphlet entitled *Thoughts on Church Dignities* that same year which he mentions in his annual *Charge*. He quotes in the *Charge* the recently published returns of Church property which was worth about three and a half million, including all bishoprics, cathedral dignities and livings.

> Of these, the whole revenue of the bishoprics of England and Wales, including that of Sodor and Man, amount to £158,527. The whole of that belonging to Deans and Chapters amounts to £236,358; and the whole belonging to the 11,400 livings in England to very little more than 3,000,000, giving an average of £285 a year to each Parochial Clergyman, or, if the whole income arising from Deans and Chapters were added thereto, an average of £300 p.a., and no more . . . Thus ends the fable of the enormous wealth of the Church. [BUTLER *Charge* 1833 p. 5]

His pamphlet was an attempt to defend what he calls 'the higher clergy' from the charges that they were underworked and overpaid, and that a bishopric was a sinecure. 'The present bench of Bishops, must surely be redeemed from the charge of idleness by the labours of Van Mildert, Blomfield, Marsh, Kaye, Sumner, Maltby, Copleston – I speak here, be it observed, of Theological Works alone.' [BUTLER *Church Dignities* p. 16] He defended many of the cathedral dignitaries by name for their contribution to the life of the Church, and suggested that residentiary canons could form a school of theology for the training and examining of young divines in the interval between taking their academical degree and their entering holy orders. He claimed that anyone who had the 'ordinary measure of coming to the truth' would know how busy bishops actually were.

> When the general care of the interests of the Church which his high station demands of him, and the discharge of his episcopal functions in ordinations, confirmations, and visitations; in the superintendence and regulation of his clergy; in answering the numberless appeals to his benevolence; in preaching for public charities, and public occasions, as well as in the course of his diocesan duties, are all considered, it is impossible to say that a bishop's office is a sinecure; and in more than half the sees, it is not only not underpaid but in many cases a sum is received notoriously inadequate to its support; hence, indeed, arises a principal ground of odium. To help out a bishopric of £800 or £1,200 a year, stalls or other sinecures are given, or rich livings are allowed to be held *in commendam* with the bishopric, giving a colourable ground for exclaiming against the accumulation of church preferments in the person of one individual, where a grant of £5,000 a year would not appear disproportionate to the duties and dignity of the situation. Improvement therefore might be made . . . especially as it would lead to the abolition of that greatest real evil in the constitution of the Episcopal Bench, the frequency of translations. [*Ibid*. p. 5]

He also argued at length for some of the clergy, at least, to be well paid using the argument often repeated later in the decade that if this wasn't the case only men of a lower class would offer themselves for the ministry – 'Were these offices either wholly abolished or very materially reduced, I conceive one inevitable evil would be the introduction of a grade of persons lower in point of birth, habits and education into the Church. For what man of high attainments and cultivated mind will enter into a profession which holds out no honourable distinctions as a reward for merit and a stimulus to exertion?' [*Ibid.*] We saw earlier how Butler himself had pressed for his own promotion on the grounds of his own high attainments as a clerical headmaster. Three years after the pamphlet appeared, Butler, at the age of sixty-two, was elevated to the see of Lichfield, the one he had particularly requested.

Charges 1834-40

These years were dominated on the one hand by the investigations, initial findings and then the controversial recommendations of the Ecclesiastical Commission, but also, on the other hand, by the continuing fear of Church reforms imposed by a hostile parliament which would try to address the grievances of Dissenters who were now better represented in the House of Commons. These years also saw many diocesan initiatives in church building and the provision of parochial schools, and the reduction in pluralism and non-residence.

The opening words of the Archdeacon of Nottingham's *Charge* delivered in May 1834 express graphically the fear felt by many:

> Reverend Brethren, - A most awful period has elapsed since we last assembled here – a period of "trouble, rebuke, and blasphemy," in which the combined enemies of Zion have let slip the Dogs of War to pursue us to our extinction. This war of extermination has been opened with very extraordinary feelings of hostility; for under the pretend colours of religious liberty, political advantage and the spoliation of our property have alone been sought. But the same holy arm which has shielded us in past time of peril, has hitherto been extended for our protection. In that arm is our only trust, we pray that "under the shadow of thy wings, O God, we may find refuge until this tyranny be overpast." (*sic*) [WILKINS *Charge* 1834 p. 3]

In his *Charge* Wilkins resisted all claims by Dissenters to marry and bury their members. That was an attitude shared by some bishops but not by all.

Bishop Blomfield opened his *Charge* that year on a similar note, accusing Dissenters of having recourse to 'the grossest calumnies, and the most unfounded accusations' in their attacks on the Established Church over the past three years. 'Our endowments have been exaggerated, our labours depreciated, and our services disparaged, in the face of recorded evidence, and in defiance of the testimony of all experience.' [BLOMFIELD *Charge* 1834 p. 4] He then adopted a more critically positive line by setting out the needs of the Church. 'We want more churches, and more clergymen', he declared and stated the statistical facts relating to the eastern and north-eastern districts of his diocese to justify that view: ten parishes with a total population of 353,460, served by eighteen churches or chapels and twenty-four incumbents and curates, an average of one building per 19,000 people and one clergyman for every 14,000. His ideal was a church and two clergymen for every 3,000 people. He then argues for reform of the system:

> If any changes can be made in the actual distribution of its resources, which would have a clear and unquestionable tendency to increase its usefulness; and which are not inconsistent with the fundamental principles of its polity, we ought surely to carry them into effect, even if it be at the expense of some of those ornamental parts of the system, which have their uses, and those by no means unimportant, as that they should be suffered to stand in the way of improvements, calculated to enhance and give lustre to the true beauty of the Church – the beauty of its holy usefulness. [*Ibid.* p. 16]

He was setting his gun sights on prebendal stalls and sinecures, and on the wealth of cathedrals such as St Paul's. Two things needed immediate attention, he declared, non-residence and pluralities. And, again, he provided the relevant statistics: 'That part of the City of London which is under my jurisdiction, contains 88 parishes, and 57 benefices; 20 of which have no residence house, and 16 are returned as having unfit houses.' The clergy needed to make use of the facilities afforded by the Gilbert Act to improve the houses – a request he had made in his previous *Charge*. On a quite different matter, one that figures in a number of other episcopal *Charges*, namely liturgical reform, Blomfield said now was not the time for that. He acknowledged that the *BCP* needed improving but it risked the peace of the Church. There were more pressing issues which needed attention. Among them was the question of who would be responsible for educating the nation's children – the State or the Church? He concluded that ' the extension and improvement of the National system will probably decide the question, whether the education of the poorer classes shall be suffered to remain, in the hands of the parochial clergy; or whether an attempt will be made, to place it under the control and direction of the government, with a compulsory provision for its maintenance.' [*Ibid*. p. 37] More specifically, Blomfield felt it was time to widen the curriculum and include such subjects as history, geography and elements of useful practical science. He felt there was no longer any reason why the education of the poor should differ from that of their superiors. As we have already seen, that was not a view shared by all his episcopal colleagues.

Maltby delivered his *Primary Visitation Charge* at Chichester in May and also chose to comment on the grievances of Dissenters and their demands for reform, including the separation of Church and State. They wished, he claimed, 'to destroy the Church Establishment altogether.' On the question of their admission to the universities, he felt the decision should be left to the universities and not to the legislature. He personally favoured making arrangements which would allow Dissenters to take degrees. He also wanted to see the introduction of a new examination for students in Theology which would prepare them 'much more suitably, than they are in general now prepared, for admission into holy orders.'

> My notion is shortly this . . . Instead of admission to the degree of A.B. in the January Term, it might take place in the June preceding. Then, such young men, as are looking forward to lay professions and employments, might betake themselves without loss of time to their destined occupations; while such, as were intended for the ministry, should have a course of study laid down, to which they might apply themselves diligently till the ensuing spring or summer. They should then repair to their respective universities, and there undergo an examination. Unless they acquit themselves to the satisfaction of the examiners, no college testimonials for orders should be granted, nor should they be permitted to appear as candidates before any Bishop. [MALTBY *Charge* 1834 p. 15f]

He also favoured Poor Law reform despite knowing that the poor would react with anger. 'Divine Providence when it laid man under the original curse of earning his bread by the sweat of his brow, mercifully sweetened the morsel by annexing to the exercise of industry the pride of independence, and the comfort of rest, which is rendered so grateful by exertion.' [*Ibid*. p. 23f] The workhouses would guarantee the return of that exertion, and derivative oral and material advantages would soon follow, he believed.

Bishop Kaye of Lincoln started his *Charge* by referring back to his earlier predictions that the union between Church and State might be dissolved. Not at present, he asserted, 'But the attack, though suspended, is not abandoned.' He expressed his willingness to co-operate cordially in the removal of any real grievances that Dissenters were subject to, and he listed these as their liability to the payment of Church rates; the want of a legal registration of Births, Marriages and Deaths, without having to submit to religious rites to which they conscientiously objected; compulsory conformity to the rites and ceremonies of the Established Church in the celebration of marriage; their exclusion from the privileges of the universities of Oxford and Cambridge; and the denial to them of the right to burial by their own ministers, according to their own forms, in parochial cemeteries. Kaye's analysis of their grievances was spot on but he showed, in reality, little sympathy with them.

He then turned his attention on those who wished to reform the Church rather than destroy it: 'those who propose changes in the Articles and Liturgy of the Church; others in its constitution and discipline; others, and they compose the most numerous class, cry aloud for a new distribution of the ecclesiastical revenues.' He was able to show the real (as opposed to the exaggerated) facts about the wealth of the 1248 benefices in his diocese, as provided by the Ecclesiastical Commission's report. The average of three years ending 31 December 1831 showed that the income of 206 was below £100 a year, 837 between £100 - £500, and 205 had above £500; the income of 21 of those was over £1,000 a year. At this stage (his opinion would change later) he preferred to see archdeacons properly remunerated from Cathedral income than that it should go to the augmentation of small livings. Whilst deploring non-residence and pluralities, he acknowledged the realities on the ground made it so – too many livings were simply too poor to support a resident incumbent and in too many places there was no suitable parsonage house.

His closing reflections were on the hard times they were living in.

> Our lot, my revered brethren, has not been cast in those happier days when the clergy of the Established Church, secure of not being called to tread the thorny paths of controversy, could devote their time and thoughts exclusively to the guidance of an affectionate flock in the way which leads to salvation. The doctrine, the services, the polity of the Church, are now the daily objects of attack; and ill are we qualified for our office, if we are not prepared at all times to enter on their defence. Let us only beware lest, in our zeal to defend them, we allow ourselves to be carried beyond the bounds of Christian charity. Far be it from us to assume the tone of defiance; or to resort to the language of angry recrimination.
>
> [KAYE *Charge* 1834 p. 152 in Vol 7 of his published *Charges & Speeches*]

Bethell of Bangor chose similar topics and referred to the Commissioners' report showing the real state of the Church's finances, and blamed the scanty revenues of poorer benefices on Reformation history when lay Impropriators had been given the right to the tithes belonging to the Church, and who after three centuries were unwilling to return them. He did not favour taking cathedral endowments from them: 'The long list of distinguished men who have filled from time to time these eminent stations, is a sufficient test of their usefulness.' He reflected on the various Bills affecting clergy before parliament and referred to the call for the revision of the liturgy and public formularies. Alterations to forms of worship 'so familiar to the minds and feelings of so many', he declared, should 'be undertaken with much caution and reserve.'

He did, however, support moves to reform the registration of marriages: 'The Marriage Laws were not intended to be a boon to the Clergy of the Established Church, but to guard against clandestine marriages, and to give publicity and security to the marriage contract.' But he was opposed to allowing Dissenting Ministers to officiate in 'Parochial Cemeteries' or for people 'to be admitted without any test or subscription to the privileges and emoluments of our Universities.' He argued that the universities were *not* 'National Institutions. They are aggregates of several corporate bodies founded and endowed by individuals for the express purpose of upholding the Established Church, and providing for the education of its Ministers.' [BETHELL *Charge* 1834 p. 20] He also referred to complaints which had been voiced about appointing Englishmen to Welsh (speaking) Dioceses and Parishes; he refused to comment on his own appointment but assured them that there were Welsh-speaking English incumbents in his diocese.

Richard Bagot of Oxford also delivered a visitation *Charge* that summer and chose issues we have already heard about repeatedly – the lack of church seating for all the people though the situation was not as serious as in manufacturing districts in other parts of the kingdom. The population of the 177 places which had returned his articles of enquiry was about 115,000 with church accommodation for about 60,000. Worse still, however, was that only about 40,000 people attended worship, and of those just 7,000 were communicants. 'It is impossible but that the knowledge of such a state of things must fill us with anxiety,' he commented. Like other bishops, he accepted that pluralism and non-residence would continue to exist as long as so many parishes were so poorly endowed. He, too, made use of the Commissioners' findings about parish revenues – 'The gross annual value of Livings in the Diocese of Oxford amounts to about £50,000 averaging an income to each Incumbent of £250, if the whole sum were thrown into a mass, and equally divided.' [BAGOT *Charge* 1834 p. 19] One encouraging statistic he gave related to the provision of education – 'In the 177 parishes alluded to, there are no less than 229 day, and 154 Sunday Schools affording instruction to more than 13,000 children.' [*Ibid.* p. 20] And he commented appreciatively on the rural deans who had been appointed since his first visitation.

He ended his *Charge* on a gloomy note but also with some words which were intended to inspire his hearers.

> The present condition of the Church of England is a crisis in her eventful history . . . that her position is one of extreme difficulty and peril, we are all painfully aware . . . yet, whatever may be our difficulties, our case is far from desperate. The Church of England has seen more trying times than these . . . It is, however, on the character of the Clergy that the stability of the Church of England mainly depends. [*Ibid.* p. 21f]

One bishop who should have carried out a visitation in 1834 and delivered a *Charge* but declined to do so, was Henry Bathurst who was by then ninety years old. He wrote to his son Henry on 11 March 1834 about the visitation.

> With respect to a Charge of my own composition, the wishes of my brethren have, as they ought to have, great weight with me, and the subjects you allude to are certainly both interesting and important; but in these feverish days, the attacks upon the clergy and the established church, from all quarters, are so *numerous* and so *violent*, that a *cursory, superficial* discussion would answer no purpose; and an *angry* one "would tend to *aggravate*, and not to *heal*". To these considerations, I am sorry to add, that my abilities are not equal to the task of composing a *learned, comprehensive, moderate,* and *judicious* defence of an establishment, the welfare of which I have sincerely at heart; silence therefore appears to be, upon the whole, the most prudent step I can take; and I trust that my very kind friend the Bishop of Rochester will be of this opinion. In truth, my strength of mind as well as body begins to fail me exceedingly. [BATHURST *Memoir* vol. 2]

He was to continue in office for a further three years.

In 1835 Monk of Gloucester dealt in his *Charge* with 'the assaults upon our Establishment' also known as 'Church abuses', and gave an account of what had happened in the previous three years as regards Church reforms. He had been appointed to a new Commission set up by Peel in 1834 and later confirmed in office by Melbourne when Peel's government fell. Copleston seems to have been a bit peeved that he hadn't been appointed for he wrote in a letter to Knight dated 7 February 1835, 'The name of the Bishop of Gloucester in the Ecclesiastical Commission caused in me some surprize – not that I expected to be named myself – for I knew fulwell (*sic*) from the profound silence both of the Archbishop & of the Bishop of London towards me on this subject, that I was not to be included – but I am still at a loss to account for the choice made of my neighbouring Diocesan.' [BROWN ed. *op. cit.* p. 190]

Monk told his clergy about the new Commission and what he expected from it: 'Each of the three last sessions [i.e. of parliament] has commenced with a promise from the Government that legislative measures should be proposed for a temporal reformation of the Church; and each year the hopes that excited have been disappointed.' [MONK *Charge* 1835 p. 10] The first effectual stage, he said, had just been taken in setting up a Royal Commission, which included the two archbishops and three bishops to inquire into and recommend improvements as might increase the efficiency of the Established Church and improve the conditions of the poorer clergy. He then discussed the findings of their first report, and added

> Before we quit the subject of Church Reform, I will observe, that I have no reason to apprehend that the present Church Commissioners contemplate, as has been rumoured, the abolition of Cathedral Dignities, any more than the equalisation of the incomes of parochial incumbents. The former will, I trust, continue to minister to the same good object which they have hitherto served, in becoming the reward and encouragement of literary and professional merit, and the maintenance of learned theologians; to which purpose it is devoutly to be wished that the appointments were confirmed.
> [*Ibid*. p. 17]

He feared the defection of the sons of the aristocracy from the future ranks of the clergy if financial differentials were removed. He acknowledged, as critics charged, that it might appear that 'the low-minded and worldly motive of pecuniary benefit' was a consideration of the well-born in entering the clerical profession. But he believed it was the parents, and not their sons, who expected adequate recognition and advancement for their sons. [*Ibid*. p. 18]

Later in the *Charge*, in paying tribute to his diocesan assistants, Monk expressed his hope that they might have a role to play in future disciplinary procedures. 'To the Archdeacons and to the Rural Deans of the diocese my best acknowledgements are due for the prompt, zealous, and intelligent assistance and advice which I constantly experience at their hands, and I will not omit this opportunity of expressing my hope, that whatever new arrangements are made in respect of the discipline of the Church will extend their sphere of usefulness, and increase their power of aiding the perfect organisation of our ecclesiastical system.' [*Ibid.* p. 40] That hope was realized in the provisions of the Clergy Discipline Act of 1840.

In his *Charge* of 1835 J.B. Sumner said that the Sunday School was the only formal education that many people ever had because the young were made to go to work at so early an age that they were removed from the day school before they had received much permanent benefit. He commended his clergy warmly for their labours in this vital component of the education of the poor: 'there is nothing on which the eye can rest with greater satisfaction than on the Sunday-schools, as conducted under our establishment in most of our populous towns; and containing I rejoice to say, in Lancashire and Cheshire, not fewer than 120,000 persons.' [J.B. SUMNER *Charge* 1835 p. 22]

Joseph Allen carried out his primary visitation in the diocese of Bristol in October 1835. His *Charge* was short and plain speaking which addressed just one major topic and one minor one. He concentrated on the Church's need for well educated clergy who would continue to read and study after their ordination and so become better equipped for ministry.

> It is impossible for the most inobservant amongst us not to perceive, that the times we are living in are those of great difficulty; and that, as far as concerns our own profession, the utmost prudence and caution are necessary to prevent even the good we do from being evil spoken of. . . we must be blind not to see the dangers before us, and utterly inexcusable not to exert our best endeavours to ward them off.
> [ALLEN *Primary Charge to Bristol* 1835 p. 5]

His solution is to do everything possible to ensure that only men of the right character and education should be admitted to Holy Orders.

> At no time has it ever been proper to admit indolent, careless, and ill-educated young men into our sacred profession; and that *such* should be admitted *at present upon any account* whatsoever, and for *any reasons, however plausible,* is utterly inexcusable; because both the credit of the Bishop is at stake, and the Church itself will be endangered by the inefficiency of such ill-qualified ministers . . .
> My advice, therefore, to all here present is this; whatever your future prospects be, stick close to your studies . . .

Highly, however, as I estimate the studious habits of the Christian minister, I would not be misunderstood upon this subject, as if application to study alone was all that is required to exalt his character. For the cure of souls requires a great deal more. It requires a constant communication with those committed to our care, an easy access to us of all persons in every rank of life to consult and speak with us, and a searching out of many who without that searching out, would never avail themselves of our assistance.

[*Ibid.* p. 8 – 18 *passim*]

The only other topic he deals with is 'the *enthusiasm* so apparent in the present times, and that evident tendency to puritanism which is but too visible amongst us.' He doesn't use the word 'evangelical' but it seems it was this party he was attacking. He warned his clergy they needed to be 'thoroughly understanding the principles of their religion, and conscientiously practising, and inculcating its precepts' if the country was not to be overrun with enthusiasm. [*Ibid.* p. 22]

1836 provided a goodly crop of published *Charges*. Jenkinson's in St David's is valuable for its extensive appendix which is a long list of theological books he recommended to his clergy plus shorter lists of required reading for candidates for Deacon's orders and Priest's. Much of the *Charge* is taken up with his suggestions for their general conduct as ministers of the Gospel. He begins it with this admonition, 'We may complain as long as we please of a want of that esteem and reverence which are due to the pastoral office; but the most effectual means to prevent or remove an evil, is for the Clergy to apply themselves diligently to the most necessary duties of their respective stations, and to be particularly careful that there be nothing in their general deportment repugnant to the sacred nature of the office they bear.' [JENKINSON *Charge* 1836 p. 8]

Phillpotts dealt extensively with a whole series of Bills and Acts: the Tithe Commutation Act; Irish Church Bill; the Registration and Marriage Acts; the Established Church Act; the reports of the Church Commissioners; the Pluralities and Non-Residence Bill; and the Church Discipline Bill. Inevitably, he had some acerbic comments to make. The Irish Bill, for example, was 'in plain English, for seizing on the revenues of the Protestant Church in Ireland, and applying them to some undefined purpose of teaching morality without religion, and religion without a creed.' [PHILLPOTTS *Charge* 1836 p. 12] On marriage – 'Englishmen, in short, were never, before this year, invited to enter into matrimony with as little solemnity, as if they were engaging in some partnership in trade, or bargain of convenience.' His expectation, however was that people would 'spurn the boon thus thrust upon them. All honest persons, certainly all honest women, will avail themselves of the option which is yet left to them, and will adhere to the religious rite.' [*Ibid.* p. 16]

He was particularly critical of the Ecclesiastical Commission's policy of one model suits all, e.g. that every cathedral should have just four residentiary canons, when the size and needs of cathedrals differed. That was an issue later addressed by the Commission and their proposals amended. He also questioned the right of the Commission to devote some of the Durham capitular assets to the University of Durham. 'If the Commissioners of 1836 are allowed to apply the revenues of the Chapter of Durham [Phillpotts had a personal interest as one of its Canons] to the maintenance of the University of Durham, why may not the Commissioners of 1837 apply the revenues of the Chapter of London to the maintenance of the University of London?' [*Ibid.* p. 24] This precedent, he saw, as more mischievous than the measure itself. He was severely critical of proposals relating to the remuneration of archdeacons and that one cathedral stall should be assigned to an archdeacon, in order to bring his stipend up to £200. This showed no regard to the vastly different expenses of such office holders and he compared the Archdeacon of London, who received £1,200 or £1,300 a year, serving a compact area 'with comparatively few duties . . . almost at his door' with the Archdeacon of Cornwall whose district was 100 miles long but only getting £200, half of which he had to use to pay for a curate as he was away so much on archidiaconal business.

> Now, that to a Bishop of London should be assigned an income more than twice as ample, as to a Bishop of Exeter, I readily admit to be very reasonable: for the former fills a station of higher dignity, demanding higher qualifications, and bringing with it the necessity of a more costly establishment. But why an archdeacon of London should receive twelve times the stipend, with less than a twelfth part of the labour, care, or responsibility of an archdeacon of Cornwall, and with no higher demands of qualification or expenditure, is not quite so intelligible; and when I witness such an inequality, an inequality not arising out of the casualties of time or the incidents of property, but voluntarily created by the Commissioners themselves, in new-modelling our Establishment, it requires more than all my confidence in their wisdom, and deference to their authority, to make me acquiesce in the propriety of this part of their plan. [*Ibid.* p. 27f]

One great error influenced the proceedings of the Commission, he said, and impaired almost every part of its usefulness – 'There is not enough (indeed there is hardly anything) of adaptation to the special wants and circumstances of the several dioceses. . . All is marked by what most of the wisest men around us consider to be the vice of modern legislation – all is "centralisation". . . London, in short, is to be all in all. ' [*Ibid*. p.32f]

Three years earlier, Edward Copleston had wondered if the Establishment could survive but now he was much more upbeat in his assessment of the threats made to the Church.

> We are still, it is true, involved in difficulties and perils – still surrounded by fierce and irreconcilable enemies, exposed to false accusations, envied, hated, reviled and threatened. All the arts of seditious and intriguing men are still practised to inflame the popular mind among us. But the adversary is daily becoming more and more impotent, in proportion as his falsehoods are detected and his hypocritical pretences unmasked. We have not shrunk from inquiry: we have nothing to conceal – nothing to gloss over: we desire that what is amiss may be corrected: and our chief regret is, that the measures prepared in Parliament for this object have not proceeded with that expedition which the governors of the Church themselves desired.
> [COPLESTON *Charge* 1836 p. 6f]

He went on to give his views on recent legislation. He was happy to see the civil registration of births and deaths in place, and 'did not apprehend much actual evil' from registrars officiating at civil marriages. He welcomed the Commutation of Tithes and hoped every facility would be given by the clergy to a voluntary and amicable adjustment. He greatly regretted the failure of the Clergy Discipline Bill to pass in the Commons but was less concerned about the failure of the Pluralities Bill. A reform which he would like to have seen but there was no prospect of it was the abolition of private patronage of livings.

> If the Rulers of the Church had the power of appointment to all benefices, it would be their duty to adapt the pastor to his flock – to select men specially qualified for the province in which they are to be employed – to allot the work and to distribute the labourers, according to their respective fitness for the several operations of the vineyard. But it is an evil incidental to the right of private patronage, that this duty cannot be exacted from the Patron, and that it is seldom recognized as a duty. The Bishop can exercise but a very slight control over a careless nomination. If the Clerk presented to him be not absolutely disqualified to act as a Clergyman *anywhere*, the Bishop cannot refuse institution, whatever the circumstances of the parish may be.
> [*Ibid*. p. 13]

This was an issue he felt deeply about as his private correspondence with Bruce Knight in Llandaff about appointments in the diocese shows. Another issue about which he had strong feelings was that of the use of the Welsh language in Wales. 'It is sometimes insinuated, sometimes broadly asserted, that the native population of Wales have not the benefit of our ministration and instruction in their own language: and this fact is alleged as accounting in great measure for the prevalence of dissent and schism among us', he said and proceeded to show how untrue this was in his diocese. His arguments did not sound convincing. He trotted out the standard argument that bishops did not need to speak Welsh as all their clergy were English-speaking, and dealings with them formed the 'main province of a Bishop'. He claimed that there was no parish in which all the residents were Welsh-speaking – possibly true but there were parishes with a large majority of Welsh-speakers. He argued that native Welsh residents usually understood English but English settlers didn't understand Welsh, so the cleric needed to know only English in order to minister effectively. The sad truth is that he would have much preferred to see the use of the language die out and he spoke and wrote witheringly in private about the poverty of Welsh poetry and literature. [*Ibid.* pp 18-26 *passim*]

Wilkins, the Archdeacon of Nottingham, headed his annual *Charge: The National Church re-adjusted.* Unlike Copleston and Phillpotts, he was a fan of the Ecclesiastical Commission. He comments on the Commission's report, part one of which deals with the hierarchy, the territorial extent of dioceses, and with the jurisdiction and duties of bishops. He gives some account of the pressures on bishops.

> They are subject to expenses which, with very few exceptions, their professional incomes, very inadequately maintain. With respect to their labours, their correspondence alone engages them for some hours in every day, - their intervention in matters concerning the clergy individually and their dioceses generally – the discharge of their public duties – their long and expensive residence in the metropolis to watch over and to direct the affairs of the Church in Parliament, where, also, their days are consumed in the constant routine of business, and in discharge of duties connected with the management of the endless charitable and religious societies of the Country at large; - all these press so continually upon them for time, for attention, and for pecuniary support, that they are left without leisure or repose, and in general, without much such superfluity. Yet so, it must be while means are wanting to multiply their number. [WILKINS *Charge* 1836 p. 9]

He also had things to say about the work of archdeacons, predicting that they were to become not only the 'eye' of the Bishop but also his 'hand'. They discharged an important duty in making a periodical personal visitation of the churches in their jurisdiction, 'a service which, though requiring both time and expense for which there is no remuneration.' He himself had experienced the frustration of inspecting and making recommendations for repairs to a church only to have it blocked because a church rate was refused and consequently there was no money to pay for the work. [*Ibid*. p. 18]

Copleston, co-incidentally, had expressed a wish to the Commission that the stalls in his cathedral should be retained for archdeacons and rural deans who did their work with no financial reward.

Thorp, who was now Warden of Durham University, remained an archdeacon and in his *Charge* of July 1836 began with warm words of appreciation for Van Mildert's ministry: 'And now, surrounded as we are with difficulties; hardly discerning, in a day of change and confusion, how we ought to walk; we feel severely the want of such a guide, of one so entirely endeared to us, and so fully possessed of our trust.' [THORP *Charge* 1836 p. 4] Those were hardly welcoming words to the new bishop. He then attacked the Established Church Bill. He said it would grant extraordinary powers to the Ecclesiastical Commissioners and it would have negative effects on the parishes in Durham diocese which Van Mildert had assisted financially. The new bishop would be on a reduced income, in effect, a stipendiary minister and no longer an independent proprietor. 'I have ever thought there was a beauty in these inequalities of property, and a great convenience in translations.' [*Ibid*. p. 11] 'We find our most important concerns delivered over to a new, confined, and secret tribunal, neither appointed nor controlled by us, with the full authority of Parliament, but freed from the important checks of publicity and discussion'. [*Ibid*. p. 13f] And as for the coming Bill on Deans and Chapters, that would be one of 'a more disastrous bearing.'

Edward Maltby had been translated from Chichester to Durham in 1836, and carried out his primary visitation the following year. He began by welcoming the removal of all civil, secular powers and responsibilities from the see, and that the revenues of the bishop had been reduced. £13,000 [= £1,326,263] had been withdrawn in order to meet the deficiencies of poorer dioceses and to avoid *commendam* arrangements and too frequent translations from those dioceses. But he wished much more of it could have been applied to supply much needed churches in the new mining townships and to pay for the provision of clergy to serve in them. That was something his predecessor, Van Mildert, had done munificently from his episcopal revenues. He commented on the 'rapid social movement' which was a way of life for large numbers of people in his diocese who moved to work in the new coal mines. Railways would encourage even greater migration. It meant that 'cottages are quickly built, people flock in, but as they diligently seek their daily bread, they seek in vain for that bread, which sustains the vital principle even to everlasting ages.' [MALTBY *Charge* 1837 p. 7]

He welcomed the founding of a new Church Society which Van Mildert had supported financially: the 'Society for Promoting the Employment of Additional Curates in Populous Places'. Joshua Watson, Sir Robert Inglis MP, and Archdeacon Benjamin Harrison had founded ACS in 1833 which was pledged to work through the bishops. [See WEBSTER *op. cit.* p. 75 for an account of Watson's central role in the society.] But Maltby was less favourably inclined to the Church Pastoral Aid Society as it admitted 'the agency of laymen In the offices of expounding Scripture and of administering spiritual consolation.' He regarded this as 'an anomaly in the administration of sacred duties.' [*Ibid.* p. 12] He was sanguine about the Church's future, 'I am satisfied that the Established Church has nothing to fear from its opponents, so long as its ministers continue true to themselves, and true to the holy cause, to which they are in so especial a manner devoted.' [*Ibid.* p. 21] Their best security, under Providence, he said, would be found in their learning, their piety and their moderation. He closed with much praise for the founding of Durham University and for the way in which it was being managed and 'the talents, attainments, and diligence of all the instructors.' He appended a list of required reading for candidates for Ordination – it is the same one he had published earlier in Chichester. Candidates, he said, should not need reminding that, by the 34th Canon, they were expected to 'be able to yield an account of their faith *in Latin.*' Hardly a practical requirement for ministering to the mining and agricultural labourers who constituted the majority of the working population in his diocese!

Unlike Maltby, Charles Sumner of Winchester welcomed the assistance of *both* ACS and CPAS, and said he did not agree with the critics of the latter for allowing the employment of laymen. Lay catechists were welcome in the large towns of his diocese. There was a need for many more new churches but also for clergy to staff them, and some relief could be expected from having additional approved lay assistants. With his usual interest in statistics, he was glad to report an increased church attendance in several parishes, and an increase of about one seventh in the number of communicants since 1833. On the negative side, the number of children in church schools seemed to have decreased even though the number of schools had increased. This then led him to share his fear that church schools would soon suffer in another way.

> A bill has actually been brought into one of the houses of Parliament for the appointment of a minister and council of public instruction. As clergy of the Church of England, we should certainly esteem it a grievous evil to witness the children of our poorer parishioners taken out of our hands, and a series of new school-rooms erected in all our villages, within sight of the church and parsonage, but unconnected – specially and intentionally unconnected – with either. We should augur ill for our country if we were to see the education of our youth dissociated from religion; and the families of the working classes left to collect their creed, as best they might, without direction or authorized teaching. [C.R. SUMNER *Charge* 1837 p. 26]

He also had some critical things to say about the Ecclesiastical Commission, to which body he objected, and its proposals. He opposed the proposed new arrangements for cathedrals which would in future have a reduced staff of just a dean and four canons. He argued for cathedral chapters being 'nurseries of theological learning.' Nor could he concur in the forcible transfer of property, originally granted for particular use, to general ecclesiastical purposes. [*Ibid*. p.16] The removal of eighteen parishes from his diocese did not have his approval either.

Kaye of Lincoln was not happy about measures passed by parliament during the previous three years affecting not just the temporal interests of the clergy 'but also the relation in which they have hitherto stood to the community at large.' The Marriage and Registration legislation was flawed, in his view, as it was now possible to celebrate a marriage in the office of a superintendent registrar which would now be degraded into a mere civil contract.

> In England the inviolability of the marriage union has been secured by the deeply-rooted persuasion in the minds of the people that it is a Divine institution, and by the religious ceremonies with which it is contracted; by the pledge of mutual fidelity which God is called to witness, and the blessing pronounced in his name by the minister. Remove the religious sanction, and there is too much reason to fear that the engagement will soon cease to be regarded with the same feeling of reverence; and that we will learn to treat its violation as a comparatively venial offence. [KAYE *Charge* 1837 p. 16f]

The Act had also allowed the couple to have the banns read over at three meetings of the guardians of the poor rather than by a clergyman in church. In effect, the clergy were being cut out of relationships in which they had traditionally played a major role. Kaye also expressed concern that the Act in its relation to registering births and deaths would affect not only surplice fees but more importantly the clergy would lose 'the occasions of friendly intercourse with the laity.'

He then expressed his surprise that men favourably disposed to the Establishment should be entertaining the possibility of abolishing Church rates – though its supporters claimed that they were seeking 'to promote religious peace, by putting an end to the heart-burnings and animosities arising out of the present system.' Kaye felt the existence of the Established Church was threatened by the removal of this general levy. And he was critical of proposals emanating from the Commission, of which he was a member, regarding the management of all the episcopal and chapter estates into the hands of a board of commissioners. 'The Bishops will, therefore, cease to be independent proprietors and be converted into annuitants; and an opportunity will be afforded for raising every year invidious discussions respecting the amounts of their incomes.'

Joseph Allen had been translated to Ely and carried out his primary visitation to 'the Isle of Ely and the County of Cambridge' in September 1837. He focuses attention on what he perceived as dangers to the Church at large and not simply in his own diocese: various erroneous opinions currently held, such as 'an absolute licentiousness and extravagance in regard to the indulgence of private religious opinions'. Against which he regarded the *BCP* and the *Thirty-nine Articles* as being safeguards. Those who are 'enthusiastic' about religion and show a liking for Puritanism also figure on his hit-list. He closes with some remarks about his new diocese in which, he claimed, Dissent was very prevalent in parts and one principal cause of this was the non-residence of beneficed clergymen. 'Dissenters also are made by the Church service being fixed at inconvenient hours; by there being only one sermon on the Lord's Day; and sometimes, also, by the inconvenient situation of the Church.' The first two, he says, are easily remedied where a proper sense of pastoral duty is entertained. Bedfordshire had been added to his diocese and he regretted it was such a distance from his two residences that it would be difficult for clergy to meet him personally but he promised to be regular and prompt in his correspondence with them.

1838 was another good year for *Charges* from some of the more impressive members of the bench of bishops. Blomfield devoted his to commenting on parliamentary legislation and the recommendations of the Ecclesiastical Commission, whose most prominent member he had by now become. He welcomed the Act restricting pluralities and promoting residence although many had objected to it. One of the things the Act did was to give bishops the authority to require incumbents to employ a curate in any benefice, the income of which exceeded £500 and the population exceeded 3,000, or where there were less than 3,000 but there was a second church or chapel two miles away from the parish church with a population of four hundred.

He told them that the Commission had fought shy of appointing suffragan bishops or changing diocesan borders [i.e. creating new dioceses] as it did not wish to have two classes of bishops, those with a seat in the House of Lords, and those without. A possible 'remote consequence' was that eventually *no* bishop would be part of the legislature. Cathedral reform he described as 'a more delicate subject.' He reminded them of the paramount object of the Commission: *'to devise the most effectual mode of making an increased provision for the pastoral superintendence and religious instruction of the people at large.'* [BLOMFIELD *Charge* 1838 p. 31] Critics had seen the Commission's work as a 'suppression of Cathedral establishments'. The Commissioners on the contrary, acted upon the principle of preserving to those bodies all that was indispensably necessary to their dignity and usefulness; and of appropriating to the unspeakably more important object of supplying, with the means of grace, millions who are now destitute of them, only that which could well be spared.' [*Ibid.* p. 33]

The needs of populous parishes were immense – in the four dioceses alone of York, London, Lichfield and Chester there were 108 parishes each having a population exceeding 10,000, the aggregate being nearly 2,600,000 with church room for only 276,000, leaving a deficiency which ought to be supplied by the addition of *at least* 800,000 sittings, or about 600 new churches, the endowment of which at the rate of £200 p.a. each would require an annual sum of £120,000. [*Ibid.* p. 38] And that was just *four* dioceses! The Commissioners expected, in time, to obtain £120,000 - £130,000 a year from the cathedral and collegiate churches.

Monk of Gloucester, who was another Commissioner, had had the diocese of Bristol annexed to Gloucester. The increased work load, he complained, had not been helped by an 'affection of my eyes, which has impaired my vision, and the progress of which threatens to consign me to darkness.' The merger of the two dioceses was 'finally embraced rather from necessity than choice.' He would have preferred to see an increase in the number of dioceses but 'there was no prospect of obtaining for additional prelates either the station or the maintenance befitting the character, and necessity for the due performance of their functions.'

He told them that the Commission's investigations had revealed in the populous towns and districts 'an appalling picture of destitution' and the growth and movement of the population had resulted in the Church plainly incapable of fulfilling the object of its institution. As a former dean himself, he valued highly the role of cathedrals as seats of learning but 'when millions were destitute of the bread of life, those could not be faithful disciples of our blessed master, who would refuse to feed the hungry. The ornamental parts of our system, however beautiful they may be . . . are yet not to be put in competition with the souls of multitudes now abandoned to error, or ignorance, and to heathenism. Convinced that a material sacrifice was demanded, I would not shrink from partaking of the responsibility.' [MONK *Charge* p. 17f]

Having, in effect, made out the case for more churches and more clergy, he congratulated them on the successful establishment of a Diocesan Church Building Association. He then turned to the contentious plans for state schools, and taking a positive line described how the National Society was planning a three pronged approach to improving its contribution to church schools: 1. To provide a better class of teachers, by improving the education, conditions and prospects of schoolmasters; 2. To ascertain and bring into notice, improvements in the management of schools; 3. To offer to the middle classes, on moderate terms, a useful general education [i.e. at secondary level] based on the religious principles of the Church. [*Ibid.* p.39] And he then set out plans for a Diocesan Board of Management under his presidency, lower boards at deanery level, and connected to the cathedral a central school for the joint purposes of training schoolmasters and parish clerks for the diocese, and choristers for the cathedral! It was hoped to have a 'Commercial School' in each deanery. The intention was clearly to demonstrate the usefulness and improved effectiveness of Church schools.

William Otter, formerly Principal of King's College London, had been a lifelong supporter of the National Society, so it is hardly surprising that education also figured prominently in his *Primary Visitation Charge* to the clergy of Chichester diocese. He began on an encouraging note by referring to positive signs of 'Divine favour' such as the recently founded Association for 'church building and clerical aid', and 'the extension and improvement of our parish schools, and the increase of clerical influence and superintendence in the conduct of them.' He then addressed the fears, which he shared, of a coming change in the system of general education away from the Church. 'They tell us that the National Society . . . is no longer adequate to the important task it has undertaken; that the matter of its instruction is too confined, the training of its masters imperfect, its operations languid and dilatory, and the whole effect of its system disproportionate to the wants and expectations of the age.' [OTTER *Charge* 1838 p. 13] He defended the Society's record but he must have taken seriously some of those criticisms as one of the first teacher training colleges in the country was founded in Chichester two years later and aptly named Bishop Otter College. He also endorsed the idea of an expanded curriculum in Church schools – 'Hitherto the poor have been treated as children – they must now be considered as men.' But if they were to become independent and mature, they must be properly trained and educated – one day most of the poor currently in National schools would have the right to vote, something he welcomed. [*Ibid*. p. 50f]

He also had things to say about higher education.

Another pleasing feature which the present state of society presents to us is the increasing estimation and importance attached to Christian instruction in the highest seminaries of education, public as well as private, and this not only in reference to those who are destined for the ministry, but also to the great body of our youth, whatever be their prospects or destination . . . It cannot be concealed that this general advancement in Christian knowledge, diffusing itself through our lay brethren in the Church, constitutes an additional call upon the clergy for a more diligent application of their own minds to those studies which serve either directly or indirectly to increase their usefulness, and to shed grace upon their profession. [*Ibid*. p. 33 and 35]

He urged the younger clergy, in particular, to give themselves to being perpetual students. Every day, he stressed, must have some time in it for study and contemplation and for advancement in scriptural knowledge. What he did not apprise his hearers of was that he was even then in the process of setting up a clerical training institution in the diocese.

Bagot of Oxford also attacked the government's plans for schools 'independent of all spiritual instruction, and from all interference' of the clergy' and, echoing Phillpotts, called it a 'plan for teaching morality without religion, and religion without a creed.' He was equally harsh in his words about the Ecclesiastical Commission, which he denounced in words reminiscent of Phillpotts's attacks.

> In the appointment of the Board of Ecclesiastical Commissioners we have witnessed the creation of a power as irresponsible as it is gigantic – an *"imperium in imperio"*, which, before long, must supersede all other authority in the Church. . . . I disapprove the Commission, as utterly unconstitutional in its *permanence,* in the *extent* of its *powers,* and in the obstacles which it throws in the way of fair and open discussion, - in the limited selection of its clerical members, taken from one rank of the Ministry only, - in the exclusion of four-fifths of the Bishops from all participation in the consultation on Church measures . . . and lastly as being under the controlling influence of the Government for the time being. [BAGOT *Charge* 1838 p. 7f]

He refused to enter into the controversy surrounding the *Tracts for the Times* emanating from Oxford, but had, nonetheless, some things to say about their writers.

> Where these publications have directed men's minds to such important subjects as the union, the discipline, and the authority of the Church, I think they have done good service; but there may be some points in which, perhaps, from ambiguity of expression, or similar causes, it is not impossible but that evil rather than the intended good, may be produced on minds of a peculiar temperament. I have more fear of the Disciples than of the Teachers. In speaking therefore of the Authors of the Tracts in question, I would say, that I think their desire to restore the ancient discipline of the Church most praiseworthy; I rejoice in their attempt to secure a stricter attention to the Rubrical directions in the Book of Common Prayer, and I heartily approve the spirit which would restore a due observance of the Fasts and Festivals of the Church; *but* I would implore them, by the purity of their intentions, to be cautious, both in their writings and actions, to take heed lest their good be evil spoken of; lest in their exertions to re-establish Unity, they unhappily create fresh schism; lest in their admiration of antiquity, they revert to practices which heretofore have ended in superstition. [*Ibid.* p. 20f]

An appended note reads, 'As I have been led to suppose that the above passage has been misunderstood, I take this opportunity of stating that it never was my intention therein to pass any *general censure* on the *Tracts for the Times*. There must always be allowable points of difference in the opinions of good men, and it is only where such opinions are carried into extremes, or are mooted in a spirit which tends to schism, that the interference of those in authority in the Church is called for.'

J.B. Sumner alluded to the Oxford Movement in his *Charge* but without naming it; he denounced those who were bringing about 'a revival of the worst evils of the Romish System.' He continued,

> Under the specious pretence of deference to antiquity, and respect for primitive models, the foundations of our Protestant Church are undermined by men who dwell within her walls, and those who sit in the Reformers' seat are traducing the Reformation. It is again becoming a matter of question whether the Bible is sufficient to make a man wise unto Salvation.
>
> [J.B. SUMNER *Charge* 1838 p. 2]

He then touched on what he felt was really important – 'I direct myself, as I have formerly done, to the one object of transcendent and universal importance, - the spiritual state of our diocese and its component districts; the local advancement of religion in the particular field which is assigned to each of us for cultivation.' [*Ibid.* p. 3] He referred to the deficiencies in children's education, caused by child labour which was all too common in the diocese. He acknowledged realistically the poor needed the income that their children could earn in order to survive, and the Church in its provision of education had to accept that. He reckoned that 112,000 children had never seen the inside of a classroom. 'We must provide for things as they are, and not as we think they ought to be; and must make the best use we can of partial and imperfect education.'

He reported that in the past three years, thanks to help from the Government and the National Society, 59 new schools, containing 21,690 scholars, had been brought into operation between Macclesfield and Preston. Church building too had continued apace – 'During the last three years, in that important district which lies between the Ribble and the Mersey, the erection of more than 50 churches has been undertaken of which 32 have already received their ministers and congregations, and the rest are fast advancing towards completion.' [*Ibid.* p. 21f] Help too, for which he was appreciative, had been received from the Pastoral Aid Society and the Additional Curates Society – at least 150 labourers have been thus supplied to the field, and consequently 'in the most needy districts of Lancashire the effective force of the Church is more than doubled.' [*Ibid.* p. 25] Sumner became a Vice-President and active supporter of CPAS.

He claimed that the clergy were determined to recover 'our population to the Church' but he realistically acknowledged the demoralizing effect of poverty on church attendance, and wondered if it was not unrealistic to expect the depressed poor to mingle readily with those better off even once a week.

> Those who are in this state are naturally reluctant to mingle themselves with the richer: they are unwilling to exhibit poverty and rags in contrast with

wealth and splendour. The very act of attending the house of God requires in them something of an effort; and they are moreover continually and importunately tempted to withdraw themselves . . . [*Ibid*. p. 62]

He suggested the use of schoolrooms and lecture halls as alternative places of worship for labouring people. Soloway comments, 'In effect, what the bishop was suggesting was the abandonment of social mixing in many of the churches. Economic and social realities were apparently too strong to permit even spiritual integration any longer.' [SOLOWAY *op. cit.* p. 271] A compromise arrangement that many a wealthy pew-holder would have welcomed.

The new diocese of Ripon had been created with Charles Longley as its first bishop in 1836 but he waited two years before carrying out his primary visitation as the legality of such an action on the part of the new bishop had been questioned. But as Longley rightly commented, important as visitations are, they are not the only means available to a new bishop becoming acquainted with his clergy personally and with his diocese. His archdeacons and other diocesan officers had helped greatly in this. His *Charge* is of especial interest as he set out clear standards and expectations about such important episcopal functions as ordinations and confirmations. A new broom was going to sweep clean in the parishes of the newly formed diocese.

He commented briefly on the legislative business dealt with in the present session of Parliament – the 'Clergy Resident Act' and the 'Benefices Plurality Bill'. With regard to the latter he would have preferred even stricter limitations so that where two parishes were served by the same incumbent, they should be contiguous. He did not share the fears of those who had opposed the bill on the grounds that it would reduce the number of parishes in which young curates could be trained. The 'Clergy Discipline Bill' had been postponed to another session. He then thanked them for all the information they had provided as to the existing state of each parish. One immediate conclusion was that the spiritual needs of this densely populated diocese were not being adequately provided for – the now all-too-common observation of too few churches and too few clergy. But thanks to CPAS and ACS help in the form of 30-40 grants had been received and it was proposed to found a Diocesan Association for building, enlarging and endowing churches.

He told them that he was reluctant to grant *letters dimissory*. In future incumbents would have to make their arrangements for the appointment of curates to coincide with his own regular periods of ordination, which he proposed to hold in the months of January and July. He contrasted the disadvantages of ordinations and examinations far away with the advantage of it being done in the home diocese.

> When all who are admitted into holy orders are assembled together for many successive days under the roof of the Bishop, at the periods fixed for the diocesan ordination, an intimate acquaintance with their habits of thought, their religious views, and the light in which they regard those sacred obligations which they propose to undertake, may be arrived at; a mutual understanding between themselves and their Diocesan may be originated, which will lay the foundation of personal confidence in all future stages of communication; the bond of union formed by their relative positions will thus be more firmly cemented, while the Bishop will feel an increased interest in watching over the progress of his younger Clergy, and imparting to them, as occasion may arise, that Godly counsel and admonition, which as their spiritual father and friend, he first bestowed upon them at the solemn period when they undertook the vows of their holy calling.
> [LONGLEY *Charge* 1838 p. 15f]

He urged all incumbents to comply with his wishes in this respect.

His articles of enquiry had revealed that the important duty of catechizing the young was observed 'in very different degrees' by the clergy. He told them it needed to be done and suggested they transfer the Sunday School to the church for one hour previous to the afternoon service during the greater portion of the year. This would allow older parishioners as well as the young to profit from simple explanations of the faith and duty of a Christian. It would also make preparation for confirmation easier which he described as 'the turning point for many a heedless wanderer, the decisive moment from which many a humble follower of his Saviour may date his first *abiding* impressions of Divine truth.' [*Ibid*. p. 19] He praised what he had seen on his first confirmation tour the previous autumn – 'the decent solemnity which almost everywhere prevailed; the sober and serious demeanour of the candidates betokening the pastoral care which had generally been bestowed in training for this public act of self-devotion to the service of their God and Saviour, and the feeling of responsibility with which they appeared to be impressed.' [*Ibid*. p. 20] He made clear that he expected far more from candidates and clergy in the preparation than a simple knowledge and ability to repeat the Catechism, Creed, Lord's Prayer and Ten Commandments. He planned to hold confirmation services in more localities and thereby obviate long journeys for candidates, and in the hope that parents too would attend.

Like his fellow bishops, he was opposed to the idea of state schools for all but he acknowledged the need to raise standards and the scale of education throughout schools in connexion with the National Society, which would provide proper training for all future teachers. He hoped Ripon might be among the first dioceses to make trial of the proposed scheme.

Edward Stanley also carried out his primary visitation of the diocese of Norwich that year. His *Charge* met with a mixed reception as he pressed upon the minds of his clergy the realities of a new political and social age. The 'circumstances of the age' had placed the relationships of society into new forms, and whatever opinion one might have about expanded political rights and extended knowledge, they were here to stay.

Much of the opening part is predictable from a new bishop – his desire to work with them and support them: 'If we would achieve the good which is our object, we must join hand in hand, and heart to heart, fervent in the Spirit of the Lord, with unanimity and perseverance.' He reminds them that in the battle against sin and error, they have to rely on spiritual resources: 'Study the Scriptures then earnestly, fearlessly, reverently; not exaggerating nor neglecting any part of them, but endeavouring to learn from them the whole counsel of God.' Thus armed, what is the sole object of your ministry, he asks. And answers his own question

> It is, beyond the shadow of a doubt, to grapple fearlessly and perseveringly with evil wheresoever found, - to turn men to God by preaching to them our Divine Redeemer, as the sole sacrifice for sin, the defence against sin, and the judge of sin, - to awaken all, in whatever rank or station, to a sense of the duties and privileges to which they are heirs by being born in a Christian country and baptized into a Christian Church. [STANLEY *Charge* 1838 p. 11]

He then challenges them to look critically at their style of preaching – if there is no fruit to be seen in the reformation of lives, the blame may be the preacher's! He begins to get more controversial when he tackles the question of educating the children of the poorer classes. He asserts explicitly that 'Christian education alone deserves the name of education', and that any extension of the educational system must 'be founded upon the knowledge of God in Jesus Christ.' So far, so good, but he had long supported providing a much wider curriculum, including secular subjects, for all children than simply offering a religious education, important as that was. All the signs of the times, Stanley continued, point out that in education as in so many other areas, the salvation of Church authority did not depend upon resistance to innovation, but upon advocacy and guidance of new proposals. To his critics, there was worse to come - relationships with Dissenters had to be improved.

> I am aware that the subject is delicate, and ought to be guardedly worded, to avoid the possibility of erroneous motives or opinions being imputed to him who advocates conciliation; but feeling as I do how much depends upon it, and how imperative we are called upon to take it into our most serious consideration, viewing it all in its bearings, I feel that I ought not to allow this opportunity to pass without candidly giving the result of my own experience. [*ibid* p. 23f]

He then bravely argues the case that Churchmen hold far more in common doctrinally with Dissenters than is generally acknowledged, and that more extreme views are held by opposing parties in the Church of England. 'And if they can live at peace with one another within the same forms, why should not conscientious Dissenters and conscientious Churchmen live, I do not say within the same forms, but within the same feelings of Christian love and harmony?' There is much more of the same – Stanley is being at his most Arnoldian. Many of his hearers did not like his appeasing talk. He then challenges them, 'Let us then abide by the faith of our Protestant ancestors, whose object was to proclaim that there was a deeper and more scriptural unity than the unity of ecclesiastical organisation or of ecclesiastical details, - I mean the unity of Christian principle, the unity of the Spirit.' [*Ibid.* p. 27] He argues that he is not depreciating the Establishment. He sees an Established Church, 'when purified, as it ought to be, from those blots or abuses which time never fails to introduce into the most perfect of human institutions' as being the keystone of one mighty arch which holds society together.

In the closing pages of his *Charge* he shares some of the statistical information gleaned from their replies to his articles of visitation. There was manifestly a great deal of clerical poverty in the diocese and in the 863 benefices, parsonages were lacking in 326 and a further 162 had houses but described as 'unfit for residence'. He set his face firmly against two common clerical abuses: 'I look upon every case of nonresidence or pluralism as a blot upon the spiritual character of our national Establishment, and a matter of regret that such should ever have been sanctioned by law, or allowed by prescriptive right.'

William Dealtry, the Chancellor of Winchester Diocese, also carried out a visitation that year, and included in his *Charge*, to which he gave the title *The Obligations of the National Church,* topics already addressed elsewhere – the need for more churches and schools and clergy. He opened with a clear statement of what they were about as a national church.

> It is included in the very design and notion of an Established Church, that it should afford the means of religious instruction and of public worship to the entire population: not, however, interfering with any man's conscience, but taking care that everyone who wishes these benefits shall have the opportunity to possess them. The obligations of the Church are co-extensive with the spiritual wants of the people; its doors should be open to all, and all should be invited to enter them. [DEALTRY *Charge* 1838 p. 3]

To that end, the diocese had benefited from grants given by CPAS and ACS; the former had voted grants to 146 incumbents, which had provided for an additional 137 clergymen and 24 lay assistants. ACS had contributed over £6,000 to 83 parishes in all. He also gave some statistics relating to the Church's ministry in British dominions overseas – presumably in the hope of encouraging support for the work. SPG according to its 1837 report was employing 235 clergymen and 15 catechists. CMS had 68 English clergy, 11 Lutheran, 81 laymen, 3 women, 5 native clergy, 355 native lay workers and 15 women – in all 541.

Copleston also addressed the hot issue of education in his 1839 *Charge*. 'On the subject of National Education happily no law has been proposed . . . Much praise, therefore, and warm thanks are due to those distinguished men, chiefly of our own order, who boldly withstood an innovation which threatened to undermine the very principles upon which the Constitution of this country is based.' [COPLESTON *Charge* 1839 p. 24] He admitted that there were too few schools in some populous districts but believed that generally the National Society had kept up with the demand. If anything, he argued, the poor were not taking advantage of existing facilities. Poor parents saw no secular advantage in letting their children go to school and it was more profitable to send them to work. Nor did he think any benefit would come from the State either extending financial aid to all denominations or of it centralizing and regulating all education. This would be a step in the direction of compulsory education, which he saw, as 'that offspring of despotic governments'. He reluctantly accepted government funds for Church schools, but only so long as it was clearly recognized that 'we are almoners of the State for religious purposes'. [*Ibid.* p. 30f] He preferred to see local needs being met by those who benefited from the labours of the poor and he called on the rich industrialists of south Wales to provide for the religious instruction of the poor. Those who create 'congregations of people' by their mercantile efforts, 'ought surely to contribute, not only to their own immediate neighbourhood, but still more in remote parishes which have not their due proportion of wealthy inhabitants, and of whose swarming population the conflux of rich families to the metropolis is the cause'. By moving away from the industrial communities they had brought into being, the rich 'see them not, and therefore think they are not specially connected with them.' This, the Bishop insisted, makes it especially necessary 'that the truth should be plainly told, and their own duty forcibly pressed upon their attention.' [*Ibid*. p. 28] His closing remarks are directed against using the term 'catholic' of the 'Romish Church'. And he is equally critical of those who refer to them as the 'old faith' and of Protestant confessions as a new form of Christianity. 'The truth as you well know is, that *ours* is the old faith.' [*Ibid*. p. 39]

His friend, Henry Phillpotts of Exeter shared his opposition to any extension of government interference in education but he did not share Copleston's support for Political Economy. It was utilitarian confidence in the power of practical, secular instruction that was causing the country's abandonment of the stabilizing and saving virtues of religious education. Phillpotts thought it was complete lunacy that 'the *sole* means' of correcting the moral evils of the nation would be the instruction of 'the working people in the true causes' of the way matters are. 'In plain English, Political Economy is henceforth to be the Poor Man's Gospel; and the true way of making him contented under all his privations in this life, is to open to him no prospect of an inheritance of happiness and glory beyond the grave!' [PHILLPOTTS *Charge* 1839 p. 28f]

Phillpotts commented at some length (pp. 58-76) on the Oxford Tracts dealing with the Divine Commission of the Christian Ministry, the Sacraments and Tradition. He declares that he is no advocate of these writers – not even their partisan – 'for I am far from subscribing to all they say, and still further from always approving the mode in which they say it.' [*Ibid*. p. 77] He then spells out where he differs from them, yet concludes 'Neither shall I forbear to avow my own opinion, that the Church is, on the whole, deeply indebted to them.'[*Ibid*. p.84]

Edward Denison delivered his first *Charge* to the clergy of the diocese of Salisbury in 1839. Commenting on the effects of the Marriage Act, he quotes one striking statistic: in 1838 107,201 marriages had been celebrated in the Church, and just 4,280 in all the other ways possible including at a Registry Office. He comments, 'It is gratifying evidence of the hold which the Church retains on the affections of the people, while the removal of the restraint, which obliged those who do not belong to her communion to conform to her rites on so solemn an occasion, appears to me an act of justice alike to Dissent and to the Ministers of the Church.' [DENISON *Primary Charge* 1840 p. 10] He also has some interesting things to say about priorities in and the nature of education.

> I will only say, that the only improvement I look to does not so much consist in teaching the poor more things, as in teaching them better the same things which they now learn. The goodness of education is not to be estimated by the amount of knowledge acquired, but by the degree in which the faculties of the mind are developed, and the religious and moral character improved; and especially in the case of very young children, the cultivation of an obedient and teachable disposition which may bring them to seek and profit by further instruction, when they are more capable of comprehending it, will be far more valuable than that knowledge of facts which is apt by too many to be more highly appreciated. [*Ibid*. p. 23]

Lord George Murray, Bishop of Rochester, published a *Charge* in 1840 in which he lamented that it would only be a matter of time before there would be no more ecclesiastical dignitaries like him offering themselves for ordination. The episcopal reforms of 1836 and the cathedral reforms of 1840 indicated that the Church was abandoning all the social advantages it had won, and that it would 'drag on a mutilated and degraded existence . . . It will soon sink into the state . . . where the clergy are one degree removed from the labourer and the mechanic'. [MURRAY *Charge* 1840 p. 31]

Archbishop Howley, now aged 76, was also experiencing negative feelings and fears. In his 1840 *Charge*, he recalled the French Revolution 'which like a dormant volcano, bursting forth on a sudden, spread terror and desolation over Europe'. Since that time 'the antagonist powers of good and of evil have been in constant activity, and the period seems to be approaching which will decide the issue of the conflict.' He feared that the forces of evil, long preparing 'in darkness and secrecy', were again coming into the open with their 'hostile designs against our Established Church'. Above all, he was alarmed at their influence over the vast working populace who still lay beyond the reach of the Church's ministry. Chartists and socialists, whom he regarded as the new agents of evil, were leading them into a coalition with the traditional enemies: Dissenters, schismatics, and lately, 'professors of liberal sentiments'. [HOWLEY *Charge* 1840 pp. 14-17]

He was despairing too of the Church's failures in urban ministry. 'We can hardly conceive the want of religious ministrations which is felt in the districts where hundreds of thousands of poor and ignorant workmen, collected from all parts of the country, are employed in mines or manufactories, without places of worship for public devotion, and beyond the reach of pastoral care . . . ' [*Ibid*. p. 20] Sadly he resigned himself to the realisation that irrespective of the Church's best intentions and efforts, 'multitudes must necessarily be left in a state of heathen darkness.' And this was spoken at the end of a decade of unprecedented expansion in church building and the provision of more clergy and lay workers. But he did have some positive things to say about the reforms achieved since his last visitation:

> The changes effected in respect to Bishoprics have, as far as I can learn, been generally approved. The points which required correction were the unequal allotment of territory into the jurisdiction of the several Bishops, the unequal distribution of revenues, and the necessity arriving from hence, of assigning Cathedral preferments, or benefices with cure of souls, to make up the deficiencies of income in the poorer sees. These anomalies have now been removed. The labours of the Bishops have been more fairly apportioned by the union of sees, the division of dioceses, or the transfer of districts from one diocese to another, with regard to the exigency in each particular case. A competent maintenance is provided for every Bishop by taxation of the richer sees. The necessity of commendams being thus done away with, all subordinate preferments will be left to the Clergy; and the Bishop, having no other charge to distract his attention, will be able to devote the whole of his time to the care of his diocese, his Parliamentary duties, and the general concerns of the Church. The approach to equality in the revenues of Bishoprics will have the further advantage of diminishing the frequency of translations . . . generally speaking, it is better that a Bishop should remain in the station in which he was originally placed, where he has the advantage of local experience, and of that personal influence which is the slow growth of years. [*Ibid*. p. 9f]

The last one we shall look at briefly was delivered by Kaye, who was at the mid-point in his episcopate at Lincoln in 1840. Inevitably, the question of who was to be responsible for primary education in the country and the content of the curriculum figured in his *Charge*. Fearful that the controversy over education would pry Church and State even further apart, he joined with Blomfield and Denison and others in praising the spirit of mutual compromise. Whilst it was obvious that churchmen could not give their blessing to strictly secular education, there was no reason why it could not be blended with religious instruction, with the State regulating the temporal sphere. Realism demanded that they accept as a fact of life the existence of the Educational Committee of the Privy Council which controlled the funds available to support Church schools. It was also a fact, as Kaye noted, that 'of the present generation many have been estranged from us; some, it is to be feared, by our own remissness; more by our inability to supply the wants of the rapidly increasing population.' [KAYE *Charge* 1840 p. 32] he then outlines the plans for diocesan boards of education and diocesan training schools to provide better qualified teachers, and the introduction of a system of regular inspection.

Earlier in his *Charge*, speaking about the provisions of the Plurality Act, he picked on the requirement that there be *two* services a Sunday but acknowledged that compulsory enactment was at best a poor substitute for a sense of duty. A piece of practical advice was then offered as a means of their retaining the loyalty of their parishioners.

> But I am satisfied that no single cause has contributed more to the prevalence of dissent in this diocese than the too frequent practice of omitting a second service. When the parishioners see that a resident clergyman, having the care of a single church, opens that church once only on the Lord's Day, the impression naturally made in their minds is, that he is more desirous of consulting his own ease than of promoting their spiritual welfare; and if they are seriously disposed, they turn to any teacher who professes to supply them with the spiritual food for which they hunger.
> With respect to the delivery of a sermon or lecture at each service, our experience tells us that, when the Prayers of the Church only are read, and no sermon delivered, the parishioners are very remiss in their attendance. [*Ibid.* p. 14f]

He ends his *Charge* on a contrite note:

> I have spoken of the present state of the Established Church, as a state of difficulty and trial – a representation of which even our adversaries will not dispute the correctness. The fact is to them a source of rejoicing. Let it operate on us, my Reverend Brethren, as a motive to self-examination, and anxious enquiry, whether this state of things may not be traced in some degree to our own neglect: as a motive to increased circumspection in our life and conversation, increased activity, and zeal in the discharge of all our ministerial duties; above all, as a motive to increased earnestness in our prayers to Almighty God. [*Ibid.* p. 43]

PLACES OF ANGLICAN THEOLOGICAL LEARNING 1800-1850

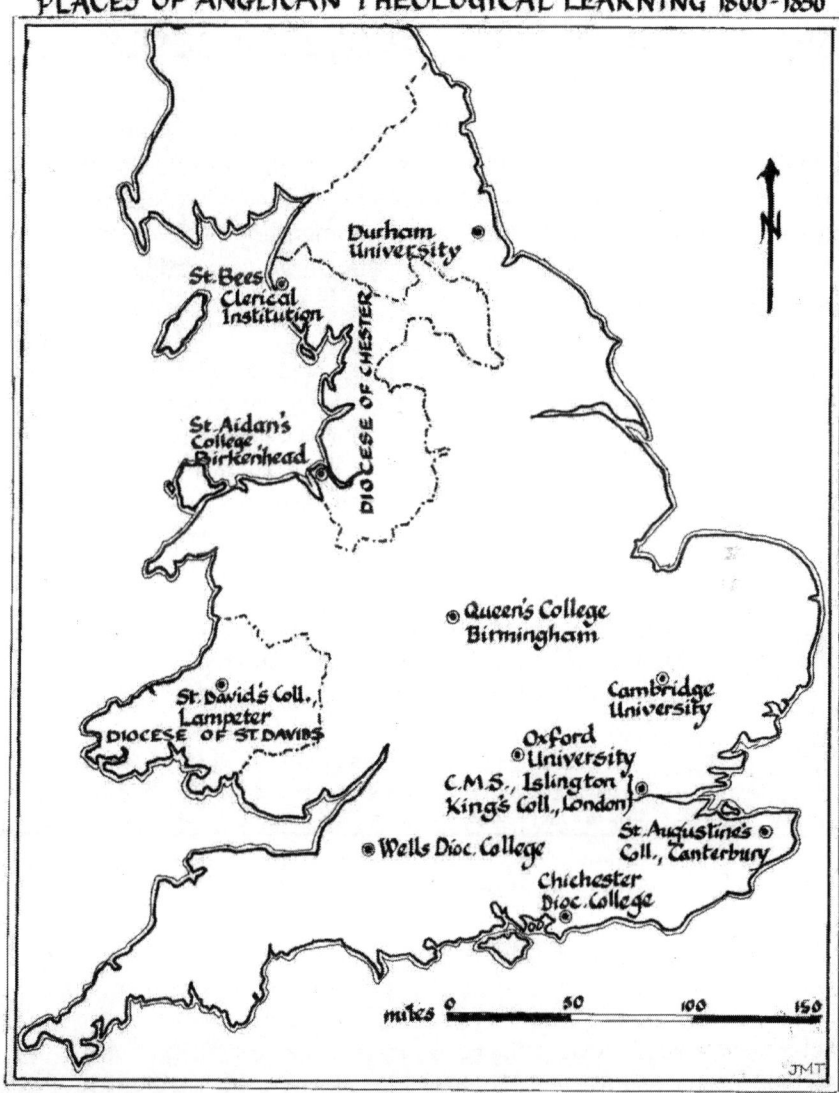

New foundations

1816 St Bees Clerical Institution
1817 CMS Training College, Islington
1825 St David's College, Lampeter
1828 King's College, London
1833 University of Durham
1839 Chichester Theological College
1840 Wells Theological College
1846 St Aidan's Theological College, Birkenhead
1846 St Augustine's College, Canterbury
1850 Theological Department at the Queen's College, Birmingham

Ministerial Training in the Dioceses

Strange as it may sound, not everyone regarded academic or professional training as a necessary prerequisite to becoming and ministering as a parish priest. In 1830 at a time of agrarian hardship and strife in southern England when farmers were pressing for a diminution in tithes, (and consequently a reduction in the income of the clergy) a meeting at Penenden Heath in Kent resolved that,

> however essential the aid of wealth and honours may have hitherto been to the Church of England, to enable her to hire to her service men of learning and talent . . . the necessity for such aid happily no longer exists. . . . The well-paid labours of those eminent men, who attracted by the splendid revenues of the church, have enlisted in her cause, have so simplified the clerical duties as to make them practicable by persons of ordinary capacities and acquirements . . . for its comprehensive liturgy, by supplying all the formularies of devotion, whether for prayer or praise, imprecation or benediction, disavowal or belief, and also strictly enjoining the various occasions on which they are to be respectively used, affords no opportunity for the exercise of judgement, the exhibition of talent, or the display of learning. . . . Nor do the duties of the preacher any more than the minister require an education superior to that which is usually bestowed upon the middle class of society; for the inexhaustible stores of invaluable sermons which have eminated from the labours of those highly gifted divines who have, at different periods, shed a lustre upon the English Church, afford a fund of instruction admirably adapted for every purpose, and to select from which requires but a moderate portion of literary attainments. The qualifications for the proper performance of these functions being few, and the acquisition of them not requiring expense, as they consist principally of propriety of demeanour, and the possession of the natural advantage of suitable voice and delivery, but moderate stipends would be necessary to ensure a sufficient number of candidates, and the payment of those stipends might be safely left to the generosity of their respective congregations. [quoted in WARD *op. cit.* p. 79]

It was, in effect, a plea for cheaper clergy to be paid on the voluntary support principle of Dissenting congregations. So, there was no need for tithes! It was also a politely worded but hostile put down of the Established Church's ordained ministers.

It was not, of course, a view shared by any of the bishops who still required candidates for holy orders to be graduates and competent classicists. But it did inadvertently highlight a problem which some bishops had had to struggle with, namely how to provide ministers for parishes which could not afford to pay a living wage. This inevitably meant ordaining and appointing men who had not been able to afford a university education. In the case of St David's diocese where so many curacies and livings were worth as little as £20 a year, about 90% of all those ordained were non-graduates. 'Of those admitted to Deacon's Orders 1750 - 1799, 45 were graduates and 680 were literates. Another 37 had been at Oxford or Cambridge but had not taken a degree'. [O.W.JONES *The Mountain Clergyman; His Education & Training* p. 167] Burgess had faced this problem soon after his appointment to St David's in 1803. A letter he wrote to a friend a few weeks after his first ordination sets the scene for his coming great work in raising clerical standards in the diocese.

> You will be glad to hear that I found the circumstances of my Diocese, in some respects, much better than I expected. At the Ordination in September most of the candidates who were admitted to Orders were very well prepared. There were twenty candidates; fifteen were ordained; four were refused, and one *arena sponte decessit*. There are no active Archdeacons: (there are four Archdeacons, but they have long since ceased to visit) but there are in the whole of the four Archdeaconries twenty Rural Deans, who make very minute reports of the state of the churches in their respective districts. Their assistance to the Bishop is, I think, capable of being turned to a very good account. The whole Diocese is full of Dissenters of different denominations and mostly Methodists. The evil of schism has been so long prevalent in South Wales from a variety of causes that I do not expect to be able to lessen it. But I shall use my best endeavours. I shall hold my primary Visitation next year; and I shall avail myself of every opportunity of information that it will afford me. [BODLEIAN MS. Eng. lett. C.139, fols 100-1]

On 10 October 1804 twelve of the rural deans met with him at Abergwili Palace and at the conclusion of their meeting they formed a Society for Promoting Christian Knowledge and Church Union in the diocese. It was to have five educational objects, the third of which was 'to facilitate the means of education to young men intended for the Ministry of the Church of England in this Diocese, who are educated in this Diocese'. He did this initially by authorising seven grammar schools to have a 'divinity class' lasting four years where young men could be prepared. These were at Brecon, Cardigan, Carmarthen, Haverfordwest, Pembroke, St David's and Ystradmeurig. The bishop had convened the meeting but the result of it, the formation of a reforming Society, came about thanks to the rural deans too who knew the clergy and the needs of their areas far better than he did. There was a grassroots element as well as an upfront episcopal leadership element in this important diocesan initiative.

When he wrote to his clergy following that meeting, he shared his wish that a residential clerical training college should be established in the diocese. He asked all incumbents to consider giving one tenth of one year's income towards a building fund – he himself immediately gave £120 which he believed was a tenth of his own stipend. The project attracted wide support and by 1820 the fund stood at £11,000 [= £949,573] Various locations for the College were considered by Burgess, among them Landdewi Brefi (where there had been a college of priests from 1287 until the Reformation) and Carmarthen which Archdeacon Thomas Beynon favoured. Burgess produced draft regulations and submitted a curriculum to his advisors for comment in 1811 when it was hoped work on the building would soon start. Another decade would pass, however, before that happened – in the meanwhile funds were slowly being gathered. What eventually brought all the Bishop's hopes and plans to fruition was a meeting and subsequent friendship with a wealthy Bristol business man, Thomas Scandrett Harford. They happened to be fellow guests in Gloucester in the spring of 1820 of Bishop Henry Ryder. Later that year Harford visited Burgess at Abergwili and, with the consent of his two brothers, offered the Bishop a site for the college at Lampeter in Cardiganshire. In addition to the land, he also gave £1,000 and through his father-in-law who was a close friend of Sir William Knighton, Keeper of the Privy Purse, won the support of George IV who made a donation of £1,000, half of it paid in November 1823 and the other half in May 1825. Donations also came from both universities.

On 9 August 1822 Burgess issued a printed prospectus for the college and three days later, on the King's birthday, the foundation stone was laid following a service in Lampeter Parish Church. It took nearly five years to complete the buildings. It was officially opened on St David's day, 1 March 1827, but the last payment for the works appears not to have been made until October 1829 by which time £22,500 had been expended [= £2,206,311]. By then Burgess had gone, having been translated to Salisbury in 1825. Lord Kenyon described the college in 1826 as 'one of the most blessed works of Christian piety and devotion to a Diocese from its Bishop, that hundreds of years have furnished, and as a Welshman I am most anxious that my countrymen should duly estimate their obligations to the good Bishop.' [BODLEIAN MS. Eng. lett. c137 quoted in a letter from G.W. Marriott to Burgess]

The project received support from Van Mildert in the neighbouring diocese of Llandaff and after his translation to Durham where in his 1827 *Charge* he commended Lampeter: 'an establishment which offers to the students many of the peculiar advantages of academical discipline'. Van Mildert, too, wanted to see higher standards in the 'religious, moral, and literary fitness' of the candidates offering themselves for ordination. Bruce Knight was his examining chaplain and given the particular task of examining every candidate's ability in the Welsh language. Van Mildert was translated to Durham in 1826 so did not see the new college open but his successor, C.R. Sumner, did and gave it his support.

Providing a training establishment was one thing, ensuring that only men with a real sense of vocation would be ordained was another. Burgess had a lifelong concern that only worthy candidates should be ordained and consequently he performed the functions of examining chaplain himself. Harford describes how he did it.

> The onerous duties which this office imposed upon him, so entirely engaged his thoughts and attention for the week preceding an ordination, that all other engagements were superseded, and he passed his time in the examining room, sedulously superintending the proceedings of the candidates, and satisfying himself as to their qualifications and attainments . . . Accurate Biblical knowledge, a competent acquaintance with the Greek Testament, and facility in English composition, were among the leading qualifications he required . . . But independently of the learned preparation which he thus required, he did his utmost to impress upon them the indispensable necessity of personal piety in order to a faithful and effectual discharge of the clerical functions. He would, in a kind but scrutinising manner, inquire into the motives of those who applied to him for orders; and unless they proved to be such as would stand the test of reason and of conscience, he gave them no encouragement. [HARFORD *op. cit.* p. 223f]

Burgess went on examining candidates himself long after his translation to Salisbury and almost till his death at the age of eighty-one. He wrote to his nephew in April 1835, 'I yesterday finished the labour of examination of candidates, who are to be ordained tomorrow. If I should live till this time next year, I shall probably devolve the greater part of the examination on the Archdeacon, after having been personally engaged in it just half a century. I became Bishop Barrington's chaplain early in 1785.' [*Ibid.* p. 464]

Initially, in his early years at St David's, he had been hostile to the use of the Welsh language and to Welsh culture but that changed and when in 1809 he drew up the earliest draft regulations for St David's College, he stated that the Principal and Lecturers should be *natives of the Principality* and in addition to being well-versed in Theology, Church History and Ecclesiastical Law, should be learned in Hebrew, Greek, Latin, English and *Welsh*.

John Banks Jenkinson, who succeeded Burgess as bishop, appointed an able staff: the Revd Llewelyn Lewellin of Jesus College Oxford as Principal and Professor of Greek and Senior Professor of Theology, the Revd Alfred Ollivant (a future Bishop of Llandaff), who was a Fellow of Trinity College Cambridge and a disciple of Charles Simeon, as Vice-Principal, Professor of Hebrew and second Professor of Theology, and Rice Rees, a twenty-five old as Professor of Welsh and College Librarian. On 30 January 1827, the Bishop issued a statement announcing the opening of the College on 1 March and estimating a student's total expenditure, excluding clothes and travel, would be not more than £55 a year. Two of the things he listed on the curriculum were 'The Welsh Language as a necessary and essential qualification in a country, in which it is the ordinary dialect of the people' and 'Theology in all its bearings, but most especially in its practical bearing upon an able, active and conscientious discharge of the sacred duties of a Parochial Minister'.

All looked fair for success and there was an initial surge of applicants beyond what had been expected but inevitably there were teething problems. In 1833 tuition fees were reduced as the number of applicants was dropping, and the death of Rice Rees in 1839 was a great loss. No one replaced him to teach Welsh. Because of its cost, the length of the course was reduced from four years to three and a half in 1841. The lack of endowment, paucity of scholarships, lacking the power to confer academic degrees (that was rectified in 1851) and the fact that some bishops in North Wales and England refused to accept candidates for ordination from St David's, all added to the college's difficulties. But it was producing many well trained candidates for ministry in South Wales.

In Copleston's diocese of Llandaff there were divinity classes at the grammar schools in Usk and Cowbridge where potential candidates for ordination were prepared. Soon after his arrival in 1828, he told Bruce Knight that he was minded to give preference to men trained at Lampeter.

> Dr Williams of Cowbridge does not seem to relish the plan of having recourse to Lampeter. My monition (at present a crude one) is that four years residence at Lampeter might be sufficient for a candidate from our Diocese in the way now required for Usk & Cowbridge, & that perhaps two years residence may be required to be passed there even for those who have studied two or three years with us. The system of lecturing at St David's must be superior to that of our seminaries, where the superintendence of the Divinity

> Students is an incidental & (in point of time & attention) a minor duty. Nor should I greatly respect a feeling of jealousy created by such a cause. [BROWN ed. *op. cit.* p. 65]

By 1840 Copleston was actively considering closing the two divinity schools in his diocese and relying on a supply of men from Lampeter. He told Bruce Knight 'Lampeter is so work conducted that I think we may require a residence there as a qualification, without providing a school nearer home. It always appeared to me as likely to be The Seminary for South Wales.' [*Ibid*. p. 249]

George Henry Law on his appointment to the huge diocese of Chester in 1812 experienced similar problems to those of Burgess a generation earlier in St David's. The sheer size of the 120 mile long diocese defeated even this energetic and conscientious bishop from exercising an effective oversight on his own. There was also great variety in the social geography of the diocese. On the one hand, there were the expanding industrial centres of Lancashire, the major port of Liverpool, the coal mining district of West Cumberland and the extensive shipping trade of Whitehaven and Workington. On the other, there was arable Cheshire, parts of the Yorkshire dales and of rugged, wild Cumberland and Westmorland. The problems he faced were many and acute but none more persistent than the shortage of educated clergy. Bishop after bishop in the previous century had singled out this problem for attention but none had succeeded in resolving it. Of the 133 men Law ordained in his first five years at Chester, 56 were graduates and 77 were non-graduates.

The story of how the 'Clerical Institution' in St Bees came to be founded at the end of 1816 and how over 2,000 men were trained there before its closure in 1895 has been told in my history of the college. [PARK *St Bees College: Pioneering Higher Education in Nineteenth Century Cumbria* 2nd edition 2008] The honour of founding the first modern theological college in the Church of England belongs to Law but the idea did not originate with him. The Headmaster of St Bees School, the Revd William Wilson MA, and acting incumbent of St Bees parish was in dispute with the Earl of Lonsdale whose family had grown rich on the coal of West Cumberland. Wilson was trying to have set aside as invalid a mineral lease obtained by the Earl's grandfather in 1742 which was meant to run for 837 years at an annual rent of only £3.10s.! The school was losing a lot of revenue each year, and the Court of Chancery ruled in the school's favour ten years later and made the Earl pay it £5,000 in compensation. The Earl had tried to get Wilson fired but the power of appointment and dismissal lay with the Provost of Queen's College Oxford who backed Wilson. In September 1815 Wilson wrote to the Committee of the Church Missionary Society stating the circumstances of St Bees School and proposing that a committee should be formed in London to attempt the recovery by law of its rights, 'in order it may become a Seminary or College for the training of Clergymen and Missionaries'. [CMS Committee Minutes G/C/1 Vol. 2 p.381] The CMS Committee wisely resolved not to get involved. Wilson appears then to have contacted Law in March 1816 with his idea of a clerical training establishment in the village. The bishop visited Whitehaven in July that year and stayed with the Earl at his castle in the town, and visited St Bees. The college did come into being but Wilson had no chance of becoming its first Principal. In October the Revd William Ainger MA, a Fellow of St John's College Cambridge, was appointed to the living by the Earl, at the Bishop's request, who also paid for the ruined chancel of St Bees Priory Church to be repaired in order to provide a lecture room and library. The Earl gave further financial support in the form of two and a half acres of land on the south and west sides of the church which he sold to Queen Anne's Bounty for the nominal sum of five shillings. This became the site of the new parsonage house and its grounds. Bishop Law gave £200 to procure a further £300 from the Bounty towards the cost of the house for Ainger. It was completed in 1820 at a cost of £1,085 [= £93,662].

Ainger preached at the ordination in Chester Cathedral in December 1816 and referred to the new foundation he headed as one 'designed to afford direction and assistance, in their presentation for Holy Orders, to those young men in the northern districts of the kingdom, who have it not in their power to seek the advantages of a regular academical education.' [AINGER *A Sermon at a General Ordination* p. iii] The Bishop had decided that there were to be no collegiate buildings providing the kind of corporate residential life enjoyed by students at the universities. The students were to board in private houses in the village and to meet for worship and tuition each morning at the Priory for which they paid Ainger a fee of £10 a year. These fees greatly augmented the stipend of the Principal-cum-Incumbent which was just £103 p.a. in 1816. The value of the living was never augmented until the college closed in 1895 and therein lay the seeds of its later demise. At the time, the financial arrangements must have seemed highly satisfactory to the Bishop who had acquired a training establishment for his diocese at negligible cost.

In 1817, Ainger was appointed by his Cambridge College to the living of Sunninghill in Berkshire which was worth £300 a year, so he became a pluralist in a modest way and, in his absence, Sunninghill was served by a curate. This preferment also provided him with the means to marry. He named his first born son George Henry after the Bishop who stood as one of the child's godparents. The boy would one day become the fourth Principal of the college.

Compared to the universities, the training at St Bees was very cheap – a man could live and study for less than £25 a term. There were two terms a year and initially students were expected to stay for two or three terms. In 1840, four terms, i.e. two years became the norm, and by then tuition fees had been doubled to pay the stipends of assistant lecturers. Students who were much older than normal university undergraduates were welcomed; the earliest extant college calendar (1851) states the age limits of the student body were twenty-one and thirty-five.

Whilst the college was intended for poor students who had attended local grammar schools, it quickly began to attract Oxbridge drop-outs, men such as Sir Richard le Fleming of Rydal Hall, Grasmere who had been sent down from Trinity Hall Cambridge and who entered St Bees in 1818. Nor were students restricted to the northern counties as Ainger had expected them to be. They came from the four corners of the kingdom. Founded as a diocesan institution to meet the pressing need for properly trained clergy to serve in the less well-endowed livings of the diocese of Chester, it at once began to furnish the needs of other dioceses and of the Church of England overseas. In the first five years of the college's existence, its students were ordained to serve in over twenty counties from Cornwall to Northumberland, and from the first student intakes of 1817 and 1818 men went to serve in the colonies and on foreign mission fields.

Bishop Law did get the ordinands he had hoped for. His Act Books record that of the eighteen Deacons he ordained in 1818 St Bees provided eight of them. In 1819 ten of the twenty-eight were from the college, and so it continued. One of the first men whom Law ordained from the college in 1817 was Jeremiah Walker. He had come from an isolated Lakeland settlement and he returned to minister in one as Curate of Seathwaite, becoming Perpetual Curate of the adjoining parish of Ulpha in 1821 where he stayed till 1866. Parkinson, the third Principal, wrote a short biography of Walker's grandfather whom he dubbed 'Wonderful Walker' having served as Curate of Seathwaite for 67 years.

By the time Ainger died in 1840, four hundred and seventy-eight students had attended the college. J.B. Sumner was now Bishop of Chester and he appointed a well-known Evangelical minister from Everton, the

Revd John Peddar Buddicom who was sixty years old. He brought with him his assistant curate, the Revd David Anderson, as Lecturer and Vice-Principal who would later become the first Bishop of Rupertsland in Canada. The number of applicants rose sharply – two hundred and seventy-three men were admitted in the six years Buddicom was there. The college would go on to even greater size under Parkinson, reaching its peak in 1851 when sixty-six were admitted and together with the previous year's intake, there were now one hundred and thirty-one theological students plus a staff of four classical and theological lecturers in the little village of St Bees. Law's modest diocesan initiative was now preparing more men for the ministry than the university colleges of Durham and Lampeter combined, was larger than many an Oxbridge college and with an academic staff the equal of any in Oxford or Cambridge. But by then it had lost its close links with Chester diocese and its bishop, and had become, in effect, a lucrative, private enterprise administered by the Vicar-cum-Principal.

Another serious defect in the whole process of selecting men for the ordained ministry, in addition to the absence of any professional training, was that some bishops were prepared to accept men after an extremely perfunctory examination carried out by a chaplain, or after what sometimes amounted to no examination at all. Few bishops were as conscientious in this matter as Burgess had been in St David's diocese. Even when St Bees was producing better trained men, old habits still prevailed. Ainger sent a man off to Chester in October 1821 at very short notice bearing a letter to the Bishop. He told the story in a letter to his friend H.H. Norris in London, who was one of the leading members of the innovative Hackney Phalanx. The student in question was from Somerset and his mother desperately wanted him back near her. Ainger agreed to help.

> Of course he did not wish to be fixed in the North: but I took the opportunity of introducing him to & stating his case to our Bishop when at St Bees, who said he should be ready to ordain him for any other diocese, in which he could obtain Letters Dimissory. They were not slow in acting on this information at Taunton. The curacy of that place of which he had an offer was the first object but the Bishop of Bath & Wells refused to admit a non-graduate as a candidate. The Bishop of Salisbury was next tried who allowed him to be his Uncle's curate at Hindon & Pestwood & granted him a Letter Dimissory to the Bishop of Chester whom he also requested to examine him. This important document did not reach St Bees until the time when he should have been at Chester to undergo his examination! He brought it to me in great tribulation. I ventured to send him off post haste with a letter in

his pocket to the Bishop, which I hoped might help him through. He reached Chester at 12 o'clock on Saturday night and called on the Bishop at an early hour the next morning who very kindly forthwith examined him *pro forma* & ordained him the same day! I have heard since from him & also from his father. They both seem very happy at this termination of the business, & his mother of course is delighted. [PARK *St Bees College* p. 37f]

The clerical old boys' network worked! But this young man had, at least, spent a year preparing himself for the ordained ministry.

The Clerical Institution at St Bees eased the problem of inadequately trained clergymen in the diocese of Chester but in no way did it solve it. Law's successor, Bishop Blomfield, who valued and supported the college, enumerated in his first *Charge*, delivered in the autumn of 1825, the evils with which the Church had to contend, amongst them he included the admission of unsuitable candidates to Holy Orders. The echoes of episcopal *Charges* throughout the previous century ring in his words.

> With regard to the admission of candidates for holy orders, I have already informed you, that I wish to have three months notice, at least, from every person who intends to present himself to me in that character. My object, in making this regulation, is, to obtain sufficient time for instituting a strict enquiry into the character and pursuits of those, who are desirous of entering the ministry; being persuaded that nothing more contributes to the purity and usefulness of our Church, than to secure, as far as is possible, the respectability of the clergy, by a careful scrutiny into the principles and habits of those who seek for admission into the sacred order, and by unyielding firmness in rejecting the unworthy. And here I most earnestly entreat you, my brethren, as you value the welfare of the Church, the interests of religion, and the ease of your own consciences, to exercise the greatest caution in signing testimonials for holy orders. They are almost the only formal security, as to moral character, which we have against the intrusion of improper persons into the ministry. [BLOMFIELD *Charge* 1825 pp. 28-30]

In a letter to his friend H.H. Norris dated 2 September 1824 Blomfield told him that Law had ordained too many clergy, implying that his predecessor had not been vigilant enough. He had rejected fifteen applicants before his first ordination 'schoolmasters, attorney's clerks, decayed merchants, etc who thought to take advantage of the peculiar circumstances of this diocese, which render it necessary to admit literates into the Church.' [BODLEIAN MS. Eng. lett. c.789, fol. 127]

We turn now to an institution which had strong episcopal support but it was not a diocesan one, namely King's College London. It was founded as a direct consequence of and almost in opposition to another newly founded academic institution in the city. London, a metropolis of over one million inhabitants, had no university until 1829. The vision for one came from the Scottish poet Thomas Campbell in 1825 who shared it with the Scottish lawyer-cum-politician Henry Brougham MP, the radical politician Joseph Hume MP, the utilitarian philosopher James Mill and many other liberal-minded public figures. Financial backing was given by the Jewish millionaire Isaac Lyon Goldsmid and other Jews and Dissenters. The Duke of Sussex laid the foundation stone of the Gower Street building on 30 April 1827 and eighteen months later classes in the faculties of Arts, Law and Medicine began. It was to be a secular institution open to men of all creeds or none. Officially Theology was not a taught subject but that did not preclude a few of the staff, led by Thomas Dale, the Professor of English Language and Literature, laying on theological lectures. Dale made it clear, however, that their aim was not to train future clergymen but to give laymen a grounding in the Christian Faith so that they could answer for their beliefs.

Almost inevitably, what Bishop Lloyd of Oxford called a 'rival college' came into being. The first firm proposal came from the Revd George D'Oyly, the Rector of Lambeth, who in 1828 addressed an open letter under the pseudonym of Christianus to Peel, the recently appointed Home Secretary, who was known to favour education with a religious bias. The heart of his attack on the Gower Street College was its 'entire omission of everything connected with Christianity among the topics of instruction . . . Professors are to be appointed on every branch of useful knowledge . . . but the topic of revealed religion is studiously, absolutely, and avowedly omitted.'

Action followed swiftly. On 21 June 1828 at the Freemason's Tavern in Westminster, the Prime Minister, the Duke of Wellington, chaired a great meeting to launch a Christian based college. With him on the platform were the Archbishops of York and Canterbury and the Primate of Ireland, seven other bishops and, according to press reports, 'the principal nobility'. The King had already signified his approbation, and he was requested to take it under his royal patronage and permit it to be called 'King's College, London'. The Archbishop of Canterbury was to be the Visitor to the college and the following were to be Governors by virtue of their office: the Lord Chancellor, the Archbishop of York, the Bishop of London, the Lord Chief Justice, the Home Secretary, the Speaker of the House of Commons, the Dean of St Paul's and the Dean of Westminster and the

Lord Mayor of London. With so many of the great and good supporting it, the venture could hardly fail. By 17 September £109,631 [= £10,646,857] had come in as donations and share money. £100 shares were sold which entitled the shareholder to preference in nominating students and a reduction in fees. The King donated a site next to Somerset House in the Strand. The College received its royal charter on 14 August 1829 and a College Council, whose foremost activists were Bishop Blomfield, who chaired it, and George D'Oyly, took over the administration from the Provisional Committee. D'Oyly's brother-in-law, the sixty-three year old William Otter who was the incumbent of St Mark's Kennington was appointed in June 1831 as the first Principal with a salary of £800 a year. He was required to have the particular charge of the religious and moral instruction of the students which he fulfilled by delivering theological lectures on the Evidences of Natural and Revealed Religion, and the Doctrines of Christianity, in conformity with the principles of the Established Church. On 8 October 1831, the college was formally opened by the Archbishop of Canterbury and Bishop Blomfield preached on the relationship of religion to education. The bishops attending the ceremony had come from an all-night sitting of the House of Lords at which they had helped vote down the second Reform Bill.

The College quickly attracted students despite it not yet having a charter to grant degrees. In 1834 the certificate known as AKC (Associate of King's College) was introduced for men who had completed three years study. Each day began with prayers in the chapel at 10 a.m. Principal Otter gave his Divinity lecture on a Monday and the class was examined in it on the following Friday. In 1835 he added 'some of the more important portions of Ecclesiastical History' to his lectures. The books used for this course were few – Butler, Paley and the Greek Testament. Every Sunday morning he preached in the college chapel and students were expected to attend unless they were going with their parents or guardians to some other place of Anglican worship. The students were receiving in effect as much theological instruction and attending worship as frequently as Oxbridge undergraduates but unlike them this was still not regarded as a preparation for ordination. The Council had also appointed a Chaplain from the outset.

Neither of the two London colleges was immediately given the right to confer degrees, largely, in the case of University College, because of strong opposition from the two ancient universities. Nockles explains why, 'The overwhelming conservative majority in Oxford insisted that a 'University' of London could not be chartered unless it taught the religion of the *Thirty-nine Articles*. Without teaching theology such an institution could not call itself a university . . . Oxford degrees were no mere badges of intellectual attainment or proof of knowledge, but the mark of a Christian, and specifically Church of England, education.' [P.B. NOCKLES 'The-Oxford movement and the university' in *The History of the University of Oxford* Vol. 6 Part 1 ed. by M.G. Brock and M.C. Curthoys].

The Whigs had hoped at first to make Oxbridge open to all and a Bill to abolish subscription to the *Thirty-nine Articles* was brought before Parliament in 1834 but it was defeated in the Lords. During the debate in the Commons, Sir Robert Inglis, the MP for Oxford University, attacked the notion that the universities were 'lecture-shops' – they were 'places of discipline and moral restraint . . . educating the rising generation of English gentlemen.' This education was founded on the basis of Anglican doctrinal religion. To admit dissenters ran the risk of causing partisan strife. The Chancellor of Cambridge, the Duke of Gloucester, argued that the university had been founded for 'the education of persons of the Church establishment and especially for the education of those who were destined to be the clergy of that establishment.' [quoted in BRENT *Liberal Anglican Politics* p. 193] Phillpotts of Exeter likewise claimed in the debate in the Lords that the universities were 'two great seminaries for instruction in the national religion.' If so, they had failed miserably in that regard.

Lord Radnor brought a similar Bill a year later. Again it was defeated at second reading in the Lords – that was on 14 July, three days later the Government announced the issue of a Charter establishing London University. The Charter, however, was given not to University College but to a new and separate metropolitan entity which would have the power to confer degrees to the secular University College and to the Anglican King's College and to such other colleges as would thereafter be created by Royal Charter. London would now become the centre of liberal, national higher education, not the two ancient universities.

In an attempt to christianize the secular college, Russell persuaded the Faculty of Arts in London in February 1838 to allow a *voluntary* theological examination to be instituted. Arnold, at Russell's request, had tried but failed to get the Faculty to support a proposal that 'as a general rule the candidates for the degrees of Bachelor of Arts shall pass an examination either in one of the four Gospels or the Acts of the Apostles in the original Greek; and also in Scripture History.' His proposal was supported by the Bishops of Chichester, Durham and Norwich but it failed to win sufficient support in the Faculty. Hence the compromise solution.

In August 1836, Otter tended his resignation on his appointment to the see of Chichester. Of the five years that he had presided over King's, Hearnshaw, the college's historian, wrote:

> Of the activities of Principal Otter in King's College, singularly little trace remains. His inaugural lecture, with all its ornaments of rhetoric, was never published. Of the weekly sermons that he preached in the college chapel on Sundays, and of the discourses in divinity that he delivered in the lecture theatre on Mondays, no record whatever survives. He was not a member of the governing body of the college ... He held a "situation" more eminent in degree, but identical in kind with that of the porter ... He certainly exercised no sort of control over the policy of the college.
> [HEARNSHAW *The Centenary History of King's College London* p. 123]

But all remembered him for his sweet reasonableness. F.D. Maurice said of him that 'by a courtesy which made itself felt in all his words and acts, and which evidently proceeded from a divine root within, he caused men of the most opposite opinions to understand that they were parts of the same family.' [*Ibid.* p. 85] An excellent quality which he continued to show in his new sphere of oversight in the diocese of Chichester.

Hugh James Rose, the Rector of Fairstead in Essex and very briefly Professor of Divinity at Durham, was appointed to succeed Otter but he died in Florence just two years later. Dr John Lonsdale, Rector of St George's Bloomsbury, succeeded him but five years later he became Bishop of Lichfield. His most notable act as Principal had been the appointment of F.D. Maurice as Professor of English Literature and History in 1840. Maurice would later be fired on account of his heterodox theological views by Lonsdale's successor, Richard William Jelf, a Canon of Christ Church Oxford. It was Jelf who proposed and brought into being a theological department in 1846. What he was, in effect, proposing was a *post-graduate* institution, for which there were by then two good precedents at Chichester and Wells. There was also the precedent of the Divinity Department at the University of Durham which admitted graduates. Equally influential on his thinking was his involvement in 1845 in the founding of yet another theological training establishment, St Augustine's College at Canterbury. Both he and Bishop Lonsdale, who still served on the Council at King's, were members of the 'Provisional Committee' for St Augustine's. The Archbishop of Canterbury and Bishop Blomfield were both active supporters of the Canterbury project, and without their support his proposals for a divinity department at King's could not have succeeded. It was not to be simply an additional faculty at King's. It was to be an Anglican institution whose members would be required to subscribe to the *Thirty-nine Articles* of the Church of England, a requirement not made of students in the College's Senior Department, What was coming into being was an establishment for training men professionally for the ordained ministry.

The 1846 College Calendar stated: 'The object in view in this Department . . . is to provide a system of sound Theological Instruction, essentially practical in its nature, for the large and important class of young men who propose to offer themselves as Candidates for Holy Orders'. Jelf reported to the Council on 13 February that both archbishops and twenty-one diocesan bishops had undertaken to receive as candidates for Holy Orders King's men who came with the college testimonial. The new department was immediately successful and grew steadily, and provided men to serve in the many new churches being built in the diocese of London and elsewhere. Blomfield showed his support and approval of Jelf in 1850 by discouraging a potential rival college from being established at Westminster, an idea being canvassed by Dr Wordsworth, one of the Canons. Blomfield wrote 'Now the fact is, that I have a sufficient supply of well-read Candidates from King's College where regular courses of theological lectures are delivered by able professors, under the care and direction of our excellent Principal, and where the Students are required to assist some of the Metropolitan Clergy in visiting and teaching the poor.' [BLOMFIELD Papers Vol. 49 ff.208-10]

The need for a university college in the north of England had been recognized for some years and York had been suggested as a possible site. The first firm proposal was made in a lecture given on 5 April 1831 by Thomas Greenhow, a surgeon in Newcastle, to found one in that town. His paper was subsequently published and news of his proposal was given to a wider audience through a report in the *Newcastle Courant*. Thomas Thorp, Vicar of Ryton and a Prebendary of Durham, reacted to the suggestion of a college in Newcastle by proposing one should be established in Durham attached to the cathedral. He wrote to Bishop Van Mildert on 11 June:

My Lord,
. . . I would fain bring before you the project of a University to be attached to our College [i.e. the Cathedral Chapter]. The slight extension of the establishments and a few Professorships founded by the body in the Cathedral would effect the object. It would give to the Dean and Chapter strength and character and usefulness – *preserving the Revenues to the Church and to the north* – and prevent the establishment of a very doubtful Academic institu-

tion which is now taking root in Newcastle. I trust you will not think me a projector beyond what the times require. [JENKYNS MSS IV A.6]

Van Mildert replied four days later. Events were to move fast, though at times the Bishop feared the scheme was stagnating. Fifteen weeks later, on 28 September 1831, the Cathedral Chapter formally voted the new institution into being. Those weeks had included much painful negotiation with the Dean (Bishop Jenkinson far away in St David's) and individual canons, some of whom were very reluctant to lose some of their income, and one of whom, Bishop Phillpotts, didn't approve of the scheme at all. He would have preferred a proper theological college for training men for the ordained ministry. Archbishop Howley's support was sought and gained, and it was he who first apprised the Prime Minister of the project on 4 October. Grey received a letter from Van Mildert next day giving more details, to which he replied immediately and positively. Grey, whose family home was in Northumberland, said that he had long been anxious for the establishment of an university in the north of England and assured the bishop 'that in whatever situation I may be placed, I shall be anxious to afford every assistance in my power to so useful and praiseworthy an undertaking'. The day his letter arrived, Van Mildert cast his vote by proxy in the Lords against the Earl's Reform Bill! It must have seemed to the Durham Chapter who had frequently been at loggerheads with three of the leading local Whig grandees that their plans for the university had been laid in the nick of time, for now the flood of abuse broke against the bishops and clergy with threats of violence raging.

The Durham Great Chapter was due to meet on 20 November and the bishop knew that the majority favoured funding the university from their successors' income rather than their own. It was only by applying pressure on senior members and by setting out in writing the full extent of his own generous financial support that they accepted the terms he was proposing. The Chapter resolved to proceed 'by the enfranchisement of property to the amount of £80,000 – equal to £3,000 per annum' from its estates in South Shields.

Whilst £3,000 a year would come from chapter revenues, it was the Bishop's personal generosity and persistent support for the scheme which ensured its success. In addition to offering to annex three stalls to the most senior members of staff, the Principal and the Professors of Divinity and Greek, he bought and gave three houses for staff use, made two single donations of £1,000 each and committed himself to an annual subsidy of £1,000. He was under pressure from Lord Grey and from Dissenters to allow people of any denomination to have all the privileges of the university without any religious test. In the end, the Cambridge practice was agreed which permitted non-Anglicans to be students but not to graduate. After some delays and set-backs, the Durham University Bill finally received the Royal Assent on 4 July 1832. It stated that the government of the university was vested in the Dean and Chapter with the Bishop as Visitor.

Thorp was appointed Principal but he was to prove a difficult and, at times, ineffective leader. H.J. Rose reluctantly accepted Van Mildert's invitation to come north and teach divinity but he was never happy in the post. He complained of being over-worked and was fearful about the financial security of the post. He did, however, draw up the regulations for the divinity class and expressed his hope in a letter to Joshua Watson that it would become 'a grand Theological School, where, even after the Universities [i.e. Oxbridge], they who could afford it might go for a year or two'. He hoped to attract Oxbridge graduates because his plan took account of three acknowledged weaknesses at the ancient universities: the Durham divinity curriculum offered something recognizable as a *professional* education, secondly students would be examined on the lectures they attended, and thirdly testimonials of moral character would be genuinely deserved.

Gaisford, the Dean of Christ Church Oxford and a former canon of Durham, was the man the Bishop wanted for the Professorship in Greek but he refused and recommended his brother-in-law Henry Jenkyns, a brilliant classicist and Fellow of Oriel who accepted. Jenkyns would become a very successful Professor of Divinity after Rose left in 1835. The range of his lectures may be judged from the list of subjects examined for the Licence in Theology, details of which were published in the *Durham University Calendar*. The 1837 edition lists them as being 'Ecclesiastical History of the first three centuries and of the Reformation, the Gospel of John, the Epistles to the Corinthians, Criticism of the N.T., the Church Catechism and English Composition'. Students who resided for two years were examined in the 'XXXIX Articles, Acts of the Apostles, Epistle to the Romans, Interpretation of the N.T., and the History of Liturgies'.

The first candidates for admission were examined on 28 October 1833; nineteen 'Students of the Foundation' and eighteen 'Students' for Arts were admitted plus five Divinity students, two of whom were already graduates. The question now was – would the bishops accept the degrees and testimonials of Durham men on the same footing with those of Oxford and Cambridge. Van Mildert, after consulting with Howley in

January 1834, wrote to all the bishops who all replied within a fortnight, generally in the affirmative as regards Arts graduates. But only York [Harcourt], Chester [J.B. Sumner] and Bath & Wells [Law], who all accepted St Bees men, welcomed the two year divinity class men. Bishop Phillpotts, despite holding a Durham prebend *in commendam* was only willing to take Oxbridge graduates with a Durham divinity certificate. Hereford [Grey] and Rochester [Murray] both declined to take Durham men, the former wanting more information, the latter saying he felt 'the market is already overstocked'. If he accepted ordinands from Durham, he would feel obliged to take them from Dublin, and St Bees and even from the University of London. Van Mildert sought to persuade him but in vain. The most encouraging reply came from Edward Maltby, the Whig Bishop of Chichester, who was soon to succeed Van Mildert at Durham. He wrote

> I am moreover persuaded that in accepting as candidates for Orders, those, who shall graduate in Arts at Durham, I have a chance of securing a better stock of really professional knowledge, than is at present supplied by our Universities to Students in Divinity.
> As I almost began my professional career as an Examining Chaplain forty years ago, this is a subject which has occupied a good deal of my attention. And I have long thought it desirable, not only that some specific time should be set apart, and some course of study pointed out, at the Universities for the acquirement of Sacred Knowledge; but that the Bishops also should lay down a set of rules, and prescribe a certain quantity of attainment, without which none should be admitted into Holy Orders. [THORP MSS 1. 167]

Durham needed a supplementary charter conferring the right to award academic degrees and applied for one in 1836. The Whig Government wanted to grant it conditional upon the university removing the subscription requirement. Maltby told Russell that Bishop Van Mildert had received an assurance from Lord Grey at the time of its founding that the government would not compel the admission of Dissenters. Lord Russell did, however, manage to make it a national, rather than a sectarian, institution when in 1840 the Senate agreed to issue certificates of attendance which the University of London then accepted as sufficient qualification for a London degree.

Van Mildert died on 21 February 1836 so he did not live to see his university flourish but right to the end of his life, he was still working to ensure its financial security. He wrote his last letter to his great friend Joshua Watson just three weeks before he died in which he reported,

I have written somewhat largely to the Archbishop on our Durham University concerns, and the arrangement of our prebendal stalls, which, I fear, will not go so smoothly as when Sir Robert Peel was an Ecclesiastical Commissioner. I have stirred up the Archbishop to do what he can for us; and, knowing his goodwill in the matter, I hope for the best.

[CHURTON *Memoir of Joshua Watson* Vol. 2 p. 48]

His biographer, Elizabeth Varley, summed up his achievement in these words:

He had built well, however. By his own vision, determination, perseverance and sacrificial generosity he had swept the Chapter in spite of themselves past the point of no returning. Van Mildert's University still had a hard passage ahead; but the life he had given it was too strong to fail.

[VARLEY *op. cit.* p. 179]

Edward Hughes, who did some early research in the Thorp Papers and subsequently wrote an article on *The Bishops and Reform 1831-33* published in the *English Historical Review* in 1941, was even louder in his praise: 'To have founded a University after the manner of a great medieval churchman would have been no mean achievement in any age; but to have done so in 1831-33 when the radical wolves "Hume & Co" were howling at the door of the ecclesiastical sheepfold was something of a miracle.'

As already indicated, Durham University offered a two year divinity course for 'literates' in addition to the three year Arts degree course, but it also became a post-graduate theological institution both for Durham Arts graduates who studied a further two years for the 'Licence in Theology' and for Oxbridge graduates who did just one year for the L.Th. Initially, there was just a handful of post-graduate students doing this – two BA graduates were among the first intake of five divinity students in October 1833. The first college designed *solely* for graduates wanting to prepare for ordination would be founded six years later in Chichester by Bishop William Otter.

There was one other educational institution which opened its doors in 1833 – King William's College on the Isle of Man. It was in effect a grammar school and not a theological college but it did include a few among its students who would be ordained to serve in the parishes on the island. The first principal was the Revd Edward Wilson MA, Fellow of St John's College, Cambridge, who had worked for the past seven years as the curate of St Michael's Church, Bath. The college owed its existence to Bishop William Ward. His granddaughter writes:

> King William gave his name to the College, but, alas! nothing more.
> The school, however, grew apace; in January, 1836, the Principal reported that there were about 170 pupils, of whom about 140 came from England, Scotland or Ireland and a few were sons of missionaries in India. Certain young men were in training for the Manx Ministry; and the chapel (built by the Bishop) offered two full services on Sunday – to which the neighbours had right of access with plenty of free seats. [WILSON *op. cit.* p. 135]

The need for a theological college where graduates could train had long been recognized. That Otter should have been involved in establishing the first one is not surprising given his life-long commitment to improving educational opportunities at all levels. One writer said of him in the *Educational Magazine* in 1840 that it was his 'conviction that the welfare and very salvation of England depended mainly – under divine providence – on the improvement of education.'

Some writers have wrongly ascribed the foundation of the college to Edward Manning, whom Otter had made a rural dean in 1837. He was certainly a key figure along with Dr George Chandler, the Dean of Chichester, but the initiative came from Otter We have Manning's own words to show this. In a letter to Newman at Oxford dated 2 March 1838, he wrote somewhat mockingly:

> I have got a case of the τοποσ αργυρόςταυροσ. My Bishop excessively wishes to establish in Chichester a college for candidates for Holy Orders – to take them for 6, or 12 months, and indoctrinate, and break them in. He has begged me to think of some scheme – I can only think of a lease of a house, and a few set of rooms, and some good Catholic who will live on £100 a year to poison them up to the crown of their heads. I have a promise from a friend of such a sum for 5 years. The Bishop is ready for any reasonable scheme – and would lend his best aid, and countenance, even to requiring candidates to attend, and having greater regard to them afterwards, if worthy, in the Diocese. [BODLEIAN MS. Eng. lett. c.654 fol. 19]

The role of the Dean and the cathedral were important in Otter's scheme as it unfolded. They figure in three of the eight paragraphs of the *Rules of the College* drawn up by the Bishop in 1840 in consultation with Chandler and Manning. No 1 begins 'Chichester Diocesan College is founded under the sanction of the Bishop, and in connection with the Cathedral . . .' The second stated that pupils would attend the service of the Cathedral once a day and partake of the Communion at least once a month; and the eighth listed the Dean, the Archdeacon, and the Prebendary in Residence as constituting a Council to assist the Bishop in the disposal of any property or funds which might accrue to the college, and in framing any new regulations which might be deemed requisite for its better government. Otter also consulted with the Dean about the appointment of a principal. The Dean's involvement extended to the provision of housing. When the college opened in 1839, the Principal and students were accommodated in a prebendal house provided by the Dean and Chapter. A year later, a further house was bought and some of the students moved into it. It seems from a letter Marriott wrote to Newman that it was the Dean and Chapter who put up the capital for it, and Chandler also contributed to the stipend of the Principal.

Roger Jupp in his paper *Nurseries of a Learned Clergy* says 'From its inception Chichester bore the imprint of Pusey's outline, and through Manning, a contributor to its founding, and Charles Marriott, its first principal, it bore the hallmark of Tractarian influence.' [BUTLER ed. *Pusey Rediscovered* p. 157] But Bishop Otter was no friend of the Tractarians, so he was never made aware of what Newman himself described as their 'illegitimate influence' on the advice that Manning tendered his bishop. Newman suggested names for a prospective principal four days after he received Manning's first letter about the college in March.

> Your college scheme is good. As to a head to it, Pusey suggests Ward the Bishop of the Isle of Man's son – which I do not fancy – as I told him. I suggested Seager, which he seems to think plausible. He also suggests your Dean himself, if you can trust him – what say you to this? It would be a means of strengthening cathedrals. [BODLEIAN MS. Eng. lett. c654 fol. 21]

It was just as well that the suggestion of Seager was not followed up as he converted to Rome in October 1843. On 15 March Manning wrote to Otter drawing his attention to a pamphlet written by G.A. Selwyn, a private tutor at Eton, entitled *Are Cathedral Institutions useless?* It was a powerful defence of cathedrals and contained detailed suggestions on how cathedral schools of theology for training clergy could operate. He saw them as a means of enabling the poorest men of merit, who could not afford a university education, to obtain a training, as well as being institutions to equip graduates for ordained ministry. In May Gladstone (an Oxford contemporary and friend) wrote to Manning offering him £50 for 'your Chichester scheme'. By June Manning wrote encouragingly to Otter, saying he would have 'the papers about the Clerical Education ready' shortly. At the end of June he was in Oxford and dined with Newman; he returned to Chichester with a name to put to Otter as Principal: Charles Marriott, a Fellow and Tutor of Oriel, just 28 years old and in Deacon's Orders, and a man much under the influence of Newman and Pusey. Otter took time over deciding even though he had liked Marriott when he met him. It was not till November that Marriott was offered the post but he did not take it up until February 1839; he spent Christmas with Manning in Rome who gave him 'a good lecture about what is to be done in Seminario'. He was also being advised by Wiseman about how Roman Catholic seminaries operated and was offered a letter of introduction to the head of one near Paris.

Marriott arrived in Chichester in February but did not have any students until Easter. Lectures commenced on Wednesday 10 April with three students in attendance. By the 25th he was writing in a depressed state to Newman and already saying he needed an assistant. He describes his situation,

> At present we read Acts four days a week, Catholic Epistles two days. This is our *primum mobile* – 12 to 1. Then every other day I ask a few questions in a part of *Pearson on the Creed*. We also read out Burton's smaller *Ecclesiastical History*, and the translation of *Eusebius* (parts of this must someday be read in Greek – I should like to contrive all through, but the men are not up to it at present so as to make the time bear it well). We read also Herbert's *Country Parson* by little bits, and now and then a scrap of poetry . . . Pray remember me most kindly to Pusey when you see him. I wonder whether they will do anything here in the end at all like his plan [i.e. in his 1833 pamphlet *Remarks on the Prospective and Past Benefits of Cathedral Institutions*]. There has been a little question raised about the degree of rule and discipline men are to be under. I expected that all to be settled for me, but it is not so entirely, and advice comes in forms not definite enough to make my way clear. As yet there is no institution properly so called, and one can hardly act as if there was. Applications are not so numerous as I once expected, and some are dropped off. I do not know whether this is my fault or the natural course of things. I could go on contentedly for myself with one or two, but it would not look very well without.
> [Pusey House OLLARD PAPERS XIII 25 April 1839]

By 11 May he was down to just one man but still expressing the wish for a Vice-Principal! He wrote appreciatively about Otter – 'The Bishop looks after me better than I was led to expect, he answers readily and gives very good and useful advice'. On Whitsunday he was ordained Priest by Otter. He wrote to Newman the same day – 'It is a comfort to feel myself invested with full powers for my work, which I seemed to be doing before as it were by stealth, and beyond my proper range. But that is rather the second thought than the first – which is more of fear.' [*Ibid*. 19 May 1839]

In Marriott's first year there were just six students and only two of them completed a full term under his supervision. The college register records of his second year:

> Lent Term 1840 – Lectures commenced Feb 4 with a general Introductory Lecture from the Principal on the Studies requisite for candidates for Holy Orders. This was printed, together with the Rules of the College drawn up by the Bishop, and a List of books approved by him for reading and reference, and a form of testimonial for admission. It was afterwards reprinted and published with slight alterations in the list of Books &c which were desired by the Bishop. The Rev. B. Foster occasionally assisted in the lectures, and the Rev. H. Browne lectured on the Book of Judges. Lectures closed on Tuesday April 14. During Lent a course of Lectures on the Mosaic Law were delivered by the Rev. H. Atkins in the Cathedral.
> [CHICHESTER COLLEGE REGISTER p. 2]

Marriott had taken a full part, lecturing on the State of the Jews and of the Heathen, on the Gospel History and on the Acts of the Apostles. In the Easter Term Browne continued to lecture on the OT and the Rev. J.L. Ross on *Pearson on the Creed*, and the Principal on the NT.

On 20 August Otter died at Broadstairs and was buried in the cathedral on the 28th – 'A great number of clergy attended, amongst others those who had been lately ordained by him from the College'. During 1840, seven Oxford men and three from Cambridge had spent some time at the college; of those ordained that year, two had completed two full terms and one a whole year, i.e. four terms. The Michaelmas Term ended on 20 December with an ordination at which two of the students were made Deacon. The college register then records: 'The Principal, before leaving residence, tendered his resignation to the Bishop, but afterwards received his Lordship's permission to absent himself for a time, and to appoint Ross his Deputy.' Ross and Browne ran the college from then on. In March, Marriott formally resigned and Bishop Shuttleworth appointed the Revd Henry Browne as his successor.

At the time of Otter's death, Marriott wrote to Newman

> I cannot tell you how we shall miss him. It will make my situation here quite a different thing, even should his successor be ever so favourable to the plan and kind to myself. But I hope that most of all works that have been begun

in this diocese will be in any case continued. [Pusey House OLLARD PAPERS XIII 24 August 1840]

Marriott's fears were justified as Otter's successor proved to be hostile to the Tractarians, and that may have been one reason why Marriott went on sick-leave before finally giving up and returning to Oriel College Oxford where he became Sub-Dean. He had not been a success but that is hardly surprising given his inexperience and his lack of self-confidence. Manning's scheming with Newman to get a sound Catholic appointed as principal had not been in the best interests of the college. Given that graduates were not required to attend any further training establishment after university by the bishops, and that six or twelve months at Chichester must inevitably involve them in further expense, it was essential to appoint a principal whose reputation would command respect and so attract young graduates who could anticipate that the additional expense and trouble would be worth it. The handful who came to study under Marriott is a judgement on their choice. The college still faced difficulties, not least in the person of an unsympathetic bishop who closed it down temporarily at Christmas 1845. By then just forty-six graduates had attended in the seven years of its existence, and of those only fifteen had been ordained in the diocese of Chichester. But Bishop Gilbert had a change of heart and lectures re-commenced in October 1846 under a new principal, the Revd Philip Freeman, Fellow and Tutor of St Peter's College Cambridge.

It was hardly a propitious start to the concept of having special theological colleges for graduates. The second one, founded at Wells in 1840, fared much better from the outset but neither enjoyed the approbation of Archbishop Howley who, in a letter to Gaisford at Oxford, expressed his fear of 'private Schools of Theology . . . in which peculiar systems of doctrine will be taught'. Written in October 1840, this must be seen as a veiled criticism of the two colleges so recently founded for graduates.

James Law, Chancellor of the diocese of Lichfield and the eldest son of the Bishop of Bath & Wells, wrote a pamphlet in 1844 on the subject of theological colleges which he was convinced were 'the fittest places for training Divinity Students'. He entitled it *A few Words respectfully addressed to the Bishops on the Preparation of Candidates for Holy Orders at the Universities and at the Diocesan Theological Colleges*, and in it he told how the college at Wells had come into being.

> In the Diocese of Bath and Wells, our Theological College was indebted for its existence to the liberality of two distinguished individuals connected with

the County and the Diocese, who tendered to their Bishop towards the first foundation of the College, each £100 a year for ten years. Under God, the College soon became self-supporting, or nearly so. But the above-mentioned gratuities were all-encouraging and invaluable at first. And to them, and to the Bishop's active lead and zealous co-operation, - not forgetting due thanks to our admirable Theological Professor, - are owing, under God, the existence and prosperity of the Institution. [J. LAW *A few Words* p. 10f]

The two benefactors were Archdeacon William Brymer and Francis Henry Dickinson MP for West Somerset 1841-47. In a letter written in 1890 at the time of the Golden Jubilee Dickinson gave some more details about the founding of the college:

Manning was really the author of our college. We copied his at Chichester . . He put it into Brymer's head and mine one day at Wells. Brymer said something about giving £100 for a Theological Library for the diocese and . . . went on, "But I would give £1,000 to put Pinder here with a college." I thought about it and a day or two after walked over to Charlton with my sister Sophie and told him that if he would give £100 a year for ten years I would do the same. We did so for about six and then as the college stood on its own better and we were neither of us so comfortable in our means as we had anticipated we left off. Ld J. Thynne and Acland gave I think £50 a year each . . . Lord John Thynne's assistance and advice were of very great value. The largest help came from James Law. I do not remember, I suppose, Brymer told him at once . . . What he spent I do not know. Assuming then he might have given the profits of the three ribs to his family, he gave us very largely indeed and besides that put the house and plan in order to unite and utilize the ribs. He must have given very much more than both of us together and should be considered the founder of the college. [Wells College Archives in Wiltshire County Record Office]

The 'ribs' referred to by Dickinson were houses which the Bishop had the power to grant to any prebendary whom he might desire to call into residence. One of these was made available to the Revd John Pinder as the residence of the Principal. Bishop Law was seventy-nine years old at the time and no longer the vigorous leader he had once been when he founded St Bees Clerical Institution. Although his son and Dickinson paid tribute to his support for the scheme, as the latter states it was really Chancellor Law acting on behalf of his father who became the driving force. In 1840 the Bishop had appointed his son commissary for the diocese.

The success of the college at Wells was assured because of the financial support provided from the outset and the availability of the essential buildings – a house for the principal, a chapel for worship, a meeting place for lectures and a library. They were also able to appoint an excellent, experienced priest as the first principal who stayed in post and gave the continuity and stability needed in the early years of the institution. Pinder was born in Barbados in 1794 but after education in England (Charterhouse and Caius College Cambridge) and ordination by the Bishop of London, he returned to serve as Chaplain at the Codrington Plantation 1818-27 and Principal of Codrington College 1830-35. After his return to England, he served for a while as Curate of St Mary's Lambeth 1837 and Principal of some almshouses styled 'Partis College' in Bath in 1839. Pinder was already known to be a Tractarian sympathiser, so Wells, like Chichester, appealed to Catholic-minded Oxford graduates in particular. It was he who determined the ethos of the college and its curriculum. Two extracts from his writings show his mind on these matters. First, from a sermon he preached at an ordination held in Wells Cathedral on 19 January 1840:

> Bear with me, my younger brethren in Christ, while I remind you that you are not entering into a *profession* (as it is sometimes termed) but that you are "called with an holy calling", as "ambassadors for Christ"; and henceforth pray that you be spiritually minded men of God, followers of the pattern of the Lord Jesus Christ. Live in the spirit of prayer. Never enter on your studies without prayer to the Fountain of all Wisdom. Approach the couch of the sick, and the school room, with prayer for a blessing of guidance.
> [PINDER *The Christian Ministry* p. 16]

An undated manuscript, written by Pinder and entitled *First Outline of Wells Theological College 1839*, provides details of his intentions:

> It is intended to open Wells Theological College on May 1st to all graduates at the Universities desirous of preparing herein for ordination (with the Divine permission) – the Students will attend Morning and Evening prayers of the Church daily.
> The Course of Study will consist of the Scriptures in the original. Selections from the early fathers and other standard Divines. The Evidences of Christianity. Ecclesiastical History in general and that of the C of E in particular with reference to Doctrine, Polity, Liturgy, Articles and Canon – the differences between the C of E and other Churches and Denominations in these respects. Jewish Antiquity. Practical and Pastoral Theology. The Plan of Instruction will embrace, in addition to the Lectures of the professor, daily

examination in some portion of the author in hand – as well as the interpretation and criticism of the Scriptures.

The time of lecturing will occupy daily not less than two hours. Sermons and plans of sermons are to be frequently prepared and read in Lecture room and submitted to the Principal.

The Students will read the Lesson, at the time of divine service, and be exercised at other times in the portions of the Book of Common Prayer with a view to correct enunciation. The Students with permission and under the guidance of the parochial clergy will be led and visit the sick and aged in their houses.

The Students will be required to make themselves acquainted with the National system of education in the Wells Diocesan Training School.

The time of residence will be not less than one twelve months, previously to Ordination.

The Students will provide for themselves in private lodgings.
[WTC Archives WTC/R/1]

He also drafted a document headed *Hints for the Statutes* which envisaged four terms in the year, a fee of £25 and students residing in lodgings chosen by the principal. Pinder's was the most comprehensive and detailed plan of all the colleges described in this chapter. The first term duly started, as planned, on 1 May 1840 with the names of three graduates entered in the register. By the end of September the number had risen to eleven and four men were ordained that month and a further three in December. The new term opened on 18 January 1841 with eight students present. Wells escaped the teething problems which Chichester experienced because it had in Pinder (from August 1840 also the Precentor of the Cathedral and a prebendary) a principal who had both a clear idea of the kind of training institution he wished to create and the ability to make it a reality. By the end of 1850, 213 students had matriculated at Wells, about a quarter of them graduates of Cambridge, with a single Dublin man, one non-graduate and all the rest were Oxonians.

Dickinson, Archdeacon Brymer, Chancellor Law and his father made the college possible; Canon Pinder made it a successful reality. They did not succeed, however, in associating the college formally or in practice with the cathedral chapter in the manner that Pusey in his 1833 pamphlet and others had hoped for. Dickinson had expressed just such a hope in a letter to Pinder in 1840 but it did not happen. Indeed in 1854, Pinder's fellow canons made it clear to HM's Commissioners looking into the state of cathedrals and collegiate churches that the chapter and the college were not connected and furthermore they opposed the widespread foundation of other theological colleges! This was probably because the Dean of Wells appointed in 1845 was Dr Richard Jenkyns, Master of Balliol, who was decidedly anti-Tractarian and not at all in favour of diocesan colleges. In evidence to the Oxford University Commissioners he wrote: 'If theological colleges, in connection with cathedral churches, were to be generally established throughout the kingdom, the effect, so far from being desirable, would in my judgement, check the advance of theological knowledge, and inflict a serious injury on the Church of England and the Universities.' [P.P. 1854 Vol. 25 *Report* pp. 105 and 603] It cannot have pleased him to have on his doorstep such a strong and successful theological college whose principal was a member of his chapter!

There were two other institutions which merit a mention. St Aidan's College in Birkenhead which dates from 1846 and St Augustine's at Canterbury 1848. J.B. Sumner gave the first of these his blessing, not that he expected it to last long, and he promised to ordain its alumni. That was the extent of his involvement as he moved to Canterbury in 1848. Its founder was Joseph Baylee, an energetic, evangelical Irish clergyman, who had completed the recently established theological course at Trinity College Dublin. After a spell as a missionary in a tiny coastal community in north west Ireland he came to Birkenhead in 1840 to assist another Irishman, the Revd Charles Maginess, albeit without the Bishop's licence. Birkenhead was a town experiencing rapid expansion with people flocking to it from all parts of the kingdom in search of work and prosperity. Soon after his arrival in the town, Baylee sought to meet the spiritual needs of the large number of Welsh workers who had settled in the district and he even taught himself Welsh in order to be able to minister to them personally. Sumner appointed him incumbent of Holy Trinity where he initiated many projects for the benefit of his parishioners: district visitors, meetings for female servants, Saturday Bible classes, separate meetings for gentlemen teachers and lady teachers connected with his Sunday school, missionary meetings, a lending library, a branch of the YMCA, a ragged school, many different funds to provide material help to the widows, orphans and poor, and to help the thousands of emigrants leaving for America. There was even a monthly breakfast meeting at which parishioners could share their ideas about parish life and make complaints, for example, if they felt too many collections were being taken at church!

He was conscious too of the far greater social and spiritual needs across the Mersey in the teeming slums of Liverpool, and he founded the Liverpool Parochial Assistant Association whose members would visit in the slums and try to help the poorest of the poor. These were all initiatives that Sumner would have approved of highly, hence his support for Baylee's latest idea – a theological college whose students would visit three afternoons a week in Liverpool's most needy districts. We have various accounts of the college's origins from the founder's own pen, and each of them makes mention of the needs of Liverpool. He also reckoned rightly that there was a need for many more clergy recruited from the ranks of those with ability but without the means to afford a university education. 1846 was a key year in this respect because the evangelical principal of St Bees College, R.P. Buddicom, died and a high churchman replaced him. Where could sound evangelicals with limited financial means go to be trained now? Birkenhead, of course! Here is an extract from one of Baylee's accounts.

> It seemed, at first, a very wild speculation, to provide for wants so vast, so overwhelming, as to be almost immeasurable. However, I determined to make the attempt, and I called upon the present Archbishop of Canterbury, who was then my diocesan. He was under the impression that I could not succeed, but he also thought that it would be a pity not to give me a chance of seeing what could be done, and in the year 1846 I got his permission to begin. I am not ashamed to say that I had not £5 with which to make my commencement, for, as I have not a mercantile character to maintain, I may proclaim my poverty without fear. The bishop of the diocese gave me his patronage, and promised to ordain such young men as I might present to him from time to time, efficiently and adequately instructed; and so we set about our work.
> [BAYLEE *Speech at the Inauguration of the new college* 1856 pp. 15-16]

Baylee put his plan for the Parochial Assistant Association to a meeting of the rectors of Liverpool who endorsed it. The plan was quite simple and consisted of employing young men of approved qualifications and character as parochial assistants to the respective incumbents of churches, while they received at the same time a theological education at the Birkenhead college. The rectors put forward his name to Sumner as the Theological Professor to the Association which the Bishop approved. On 24 June 1847 the college was opened with ten students in five large houses forming one block of building and capable of accommodating about forty boarders. The rent for the houses was guaranteed by four landed proprietors in Birkenhead. A decade later new buildings were erected to house what had become a very successful enterprise supported by evangelicals nationwide.

Royle claims that the founders of St Bees, St Aidan's Birkenhead and St

David's Lampeter 'were not so much concerned with increasing the learning of the clergy, as with providing non-graduate clergy in areas of shortage, and their status was low.' That is not entirely correct. There was, indeed, great need for more clergymen in Chester diocese and in south Wales but the bishops willing to ordain 'literates', and not all were, knew that these men needed to be both much more learned and better prepared professionally than literates had been in the past. The three named institutions all provided that. Their concern was with *quality* not simply quantity. Academically inadequate students who failed their exams were sent down and moral lapses, such as drinking in public houses, usually resulted in expulsion. The principals of St Bees and St Aidan's were very strict in this regard.

We turn now to a rather different institution in that it was designed for preparing men solely for ministry overseas in the colonies. St Augustine's was the brainchild of an Eton tutor, the Revd Edward Coleridge, and of William Grant Broughton, who was consecrated in the chapel at Lambeth Palace on 14 February 1836 as Australia's first bishop. Wellington had appointed him Archdeacon of New South Wales in 1828 which at that time came under the jurisdiction of the Bishop of Calcutta! Broughton campaigned vigorously to alert the Government and the Church in England to the spiritual needs of both the free and the convict inhabitants of the colony. SPG supported him in this, as did a number of individuals including Coleridge and Joshua Watson. When he returned to Australia as bishop, there were still less than twenty Anglican clergy and even fewer churches in a diocese the size of Europe. When the first four new clergy arrived in 1838, he wrote to SPG – 'Each of them may, I think, have the effect of adding a year to my life, or of preventing its being shortened by that interval through overwhelming anxiety and distractions.' In a letter to Coleridge in 1837, he wrote:

> I mentioned to the Bishop of London once, my persuasion that there was still wanting, within the Church of England, an Institution for rearing up clergymen for the Colonies. He gave me no encouragement to think that such a proposal could be brought to accomplishment, nor indeed could I very readily suggest whence the Funds were to be derived. But is it really impossible to find among the young graduates in the Universities some duly qualified and willing to engage in our service?
> [BAILEY *Twenty-five Years at St Augustine's College* p. 12]

The need for educated clergy was felt in other colonies too. A colleague of Coleridge's at Eton, the Revd George Augustus Selwyn, was consecrated the first Bishop of New Zealand in 1841. En route to his diocese, Selwyn called on Broughton in Sydney to discuss important topics of mutual concern, one of which inevitably was how to procure a supply of trained clergymen. Broughton sent an account of their meeting to Coleridge:

> It is this question which above all others has come home to the hearts of both of us . . . The conclusion at which we arrived was in favour erecting, under the immediate eye of each, a school of divinity in which promising young men, from eighteen to twenty-three, might be trained in the knowledge of the duties of their profession, as well as initiated into the practical discharge of them. The Bishop of New Zealand has already certain funds and resources applicable to that object.
> [WHITINGTON *William Grant Broughton* p. 125f]

Both men succeeded in establishing such a school – Selwyn at Waimate in 1842 which he called St John's College, and Broughton in a Sydney parsonage in 1846 which he called St James College. Meanwhile back in England both Marriott and Coleridge were raising funds for the Church in Australia and New Zealand, collecting theological books for their colleges and trying to establish an institution where clergy for the colonies could be trained. Various schemes were devised but none came to fruition until Mr Alexander Beresford Hope, a wealthy sympathiser of the Tractarians who had left Cambridge with a pass degree and a passion for antiquarian ecclesiastical architecture, bought the ruins of St Augustine's Abbey in Canterbury in June 1844. When Coleridge heard of this, he wrote to Hope asking him to give the site for a missionary college. Hope already knew of Coleridge's hopes and plans and had given him a generous donation. He wrote to Coleridge on 2 December 1844 saying it could be used for this purpose. The two men then approached the aged archbishop to gain his approval and support for an appeal to the public. Coleridge informed his friend Pusey in January 1845.

> God be praised for enabling me at last to say, that there is every reasonable chance of St Augustine's College at Canterbury being opened this year for the reception of Students. Alexander Hope has not only given the site, but has undertaken to have so much of the remains immediately restored by Webb and Butterfield, as to empower us to commence actual operations before the first Sunday of 1846 χαρισ τω θεω.
> The Archbishop meanwhile wishes me *privately* (though with his sanction) to ascertain promises to the amount of £25,000 [= £2,715,054] before he allows me to make a Public Appeal. I have already £11,000 from 32 persons.

Now will you first of all consider what you think it likely you may be able to contribute to the scheme; and secondly, will you send me drawn out fully on paper your views as to the *necessary* and *essential* Statutes . . .
                                                                    [Pusey House E. COLERIDGE MSS]

A Provisional Committee was set up consisting of Bishop Lonsdale of Lichfield, Bishop W.H. Coleridge (formerly Bishop of Barbados), Archdeacon Lyall of Maidstone, Dr Jelf of King's College London, the Revd Benjamin Harrison domestic chaplain to the Archbishop of Canterbury, Joshua Watson and Alexander Beresford Hope. Edward Coleridge served as Secretary. By December 1845 £50,000 [= £5,430,108] had been promised and the building work was well advanced. Bishop Coleridge accepted the archbishop's invitation to be the first Warden. The college staff was to consist of a Warden, a Sub-Warden, and six Fellows, all of whom were to be actively engaged in tuition. The two archbishops and the Bishop of London were to make the appointments. A three-year course of study was envisaged. There were some tensions over the arrangements for the college which Hope wanted to be a Catholic community in its ethos. An added complication was that Archbishop Howley died on 11 February 1848, a day short of his eighty-third birthday, and was replaced by the Evangelical Bishop of Chester who wanted the college to have a Council, something Hope resisted. Archbishop Sumner, however, agreed to consecrate and open the college on St Peter's Day, 29 June 1848. The apartments for fifty students were ready but as yet there were no students – the first six started on 28 November and by the end of the second year, there were twenty-one. There was also a new Warden, as Bishop Coleridge died in December 1849; he was the Revd Henry Bailey, Fellow and Hebrew Lecturer at St John's College Cambridge who was an enthusiastic supporter of SPG. He was interviewed by Bishop Blomfield in London on 4 February 1850 who offered him the post, and he was formally admitted by the archbishop a fortnight later. He would have a long and fruitful association with the college. This was the third theological college that Sumner had been associated with as a bishop: St Bees, St Aidan's Birkenhead and now St Augustine's Canterbury.

The majority of candidates for ordination continued to come from the colleges of Oxford and Cambridge where little had changed for the better. Bishop Charles Wordsworth, writing of the Oxford he knew in the late 1820s when an undergraduate at Christ Church, says that 'religious worship and instruction, however it might wear a fair appearance of formal routine, was essentially deficient, and in no sense satisfactory.'

[CHARLES WORDSWORTH *Annals of my Early Life* p. 36] Dean Hole recalling his years at Brasenose in the early 1840s wrote:

> It may be said you had constant services, sermons and divinity lectures. The services certainly were frequent; but they were also compulsory, and therefore attended grudgingly and as of necessity. They were said in a dreary edifice, and, as a rule, in a cold, monotonous, perfunctory tone, which did not invite devotion. I never heard a note of music in our college chapel; the University sermons (I do not remember that any were preached in college) failed to impress the undergraduate mind, except when Newman, or Pusey, or Claughton preached. No advantage was taken of lectures on the Greek Testament for exhortation, or reproof, or instruction in righteousness.
> [HOLE *op. cit.* p. 333]

This is a sorry picture of what ordinands were experiencing in some of the Oxford college chapels, and as Charles Wordsworth reflected, it was a wholly unsatisfactory preparation for future ministry. Some graduates, however, did benefit from Charles Lloyd's divinity classes but the number of men attending them was small. Kitson Clarke, nonetheless, saw signs of hope in this: 'the fact that men were coming to believe that it was necessary to provide a special training for the clergy seems not only to be a sign of the revival of life in the Church, but also a foretaste of a new conception of what the office of priest in the Established Church might be held to mean.' [KITSON CLARK *op. cit.* p. 50]

Cambridge evangelical students, as noted earlier, were better served thanks to Charles Simeon and his very able curates. Professor Monk had raised the issue of clerical education at Cambridge in 1822 but nothing was done. The need for serious reform was raised again later by three dons: Charles Perry in *Clerical Education* (1841) and James Hildyard in *Five Sermons*. Most influential was George Peacock (who had been appointed Dean of Ely in 1839) in his *Observations on the Statutes of the University of Cambridge* (1841). He recommended that systematic courses of lectures should be given annually to candidates for Holy Orders on the doctrine, liturgy and articles of the Anglican Church, on Hebrew, biblical criticism, ecclesiastical history, the Early Fathers, and moral philosophy. And, equally important, that they should be *examined* by the several theological professors who would issue a joint certificate to successful candidates. This would replace the one issued by the Norrisian professor which simply stated candidates had attended his lectures. [PEACOCK *Observations* ... pp. 168-170] Nothing came immediately of his recommendations but a *voluntary* theological examination for graduates was established in 1843. It rapidly became mandatory in effect as almost all bishops made it a requirement for candidates educated at Cambridge.

Cambridge poll men (the majority) were required to read Paley's *Evidences of Christianity* which provided them with a clear, logical and convincing compendium of the arguments for the truth of the Christian tradition. Likewise Paley's *Natural Theology* in which he argued that the whole of the natural world evidenced design and hence a Designer; that the fitness of organs to their purposes, the organisation and symmetry apparent in nature, the suitability of certain environments to the creatures which inhabit them testified to the existence of a divine plan and a divine Planner. His other work, *The Principles of Moral and Political Philosophy*, was also very popular, and was required reading by candidates for Classical Honours. Paley touched everybody. It was essentially a text book on Utilitarianism – the morality of an act can be tested in terms of its production of utility or happiness. But that was it. Undergraduates did not read theological books. Only professional theologians, such as Pusey at Oxford and Thirlwall at Cambridge, read the works on biblical criticism which were coming out of German universities in the early 19th century.

There were, of course, a few contemporary English theological writers, including some of the 'Reform Bishops', whose works would have been read by serious-minded graduates and clergy. Overton in his book *The English Church in the 19th Century (1800-1833)* singled out Kaye, Marsh and Van Mildert as being the most important:

> To Bishop Kaye, above all other men, the credit is due for having aroused a revival of interest in the study of the ancient Fathers, which was never more needed than in the early days of the 19th century. In 1826 Kaye, the Bishop of Bristol, published the first of his valuable patristic works, under the title of *The Ecclesiastical History of the Second and Third Centuries, illustrated from the Writings of Tertullian,* and in 1829 *An Account of the Writings and Opinions of Justin Martyr.* [OVERTON *op. cit.* p. 197f]

He held Van Mildert in similar high regard whom he regarded as the ablest theological writer of the early 19th century. The title of his Bampton Lectures given in 1814, when he was Regius Professor of Divinity, was *An Inquiry into the General Principles of Scriptural Interpretation.* In them 'he dwells upon what he considers "the essential doctrines of the Church" among which he includes "the ordinances of the Christian Sacraments and the Priesthood", and then he adds, "We are speaking now, it will be recollected, of what in ecclesiastical history is emphatically called THE CHURCH, that which has from age to age borne rule upon the grounds of its pretensions to Apostolical Succession."' [*Ibid*. p. 26] He likewise praised as 'a model of biographical skill' his *Life of Daniel Waterland* (1823) which was prefixed to an edition of Waterland's works in six volumes. Copleston did not share that view of his episcopal colleague. Commenting critically on an obituary he had read of him in the *Merthyr Guardian*, he wrote 'Van Mildert was rather a common place Divine – with little originality of thought, or power of illustration.' But having said that he added his estimation of him as a man – 'a good, charitable, pious man, generous, munificent, and laborious for the good of the Church & for the public good.' [BROWN ed. *op. cit.* p. 203]

Marsh's books on biblical criticism have already been listed (see p. 55f). J.B. Sumner was another influential writer though in his later years it was more as a pastor than as a theologian. None of the bishops, however, reached so many people or had the popular influence of Hannah More. Two million of her *Cheap Repository Tracts*, written primarily for children and the poor, were sold in a year. Sydney Smith was not a fan of her writing but millions of others were, including some of the bishops, who valued her as a source for good. She could certainly have taught candidates for Holy Orders and newly ordained clergy a thing or two about communicating with ordinary folk in simple, plain English.

We noted earlier how several bishops had voiced their opinions in their *Charges* about the need for candidates to have better theological training, and gave their recommendations for theological reading prior to being examined by their chaplain. Blomfield in his Primary Visitation *Charge* to the clergy of London in 1830 stated his view on the need for better provision of theological training:

> For my own part, I entertain a very strong opinion as to the necessity of one or more theological seminaries, in which, besides going through a prescribed course of study for one or two years, the candidates for Holy Orders might be exercised in reading the Liturgy of the Church and in the composition and delivery of sermons. [BLOMFIELD *Charge* 1830 p. 34]

He then stated his expectations of candidates, including their classical linguistic competence.

> If it be objected, that by thus raising the standard of clerical acquirements, we shall exclude some persons from the ministry, whose faculties are naturally less vigorous and active than those of others, we reply, that if a young man, with all the advantages of a good education, and knowing himself to be destined for this sacred and arduous calling, is unable to write Latin cor-

rectly, and to construe the Greek Testament, at the age of three and twenty, he is either greatly deficient in diligence and seriousness, or he is not qualified by natural endowments for the office of an expositor of God's Word.
[*Ibid*. p. 36]

Kaye also had strong views on ordination training. In 1819 he argued that all ordinands should undertake postgraduate study in divinity and be examined in it. At Lincoln he refused to ordain or license non-graduates, and was the first bishop to insist that all his Cambridge candidates for orders sit the postgraduate voluntary theological examination introduced in 1843. In his 1831 *Charge* Kaye had set out what he expected ordinands should be:

> thoroughly conversant with the Greek Testament; with the chronology of the Scriptures, and the connexion of profane with sacred history; with Jewish antiquities; with natural theology, or the arguments in proof of the existence and the attributes of the Deity, derived from the phenomena of the physical world; with the evidences of Christianity; and the with the doctrines of the Established Church, as propounded in the Articles and Liturgy.
> [KAYE *Charge* 1831 p. 66f]

Burgess in his *Charge* to the clergy of Salisbury in 1832 listed theological training as a priority in forthcoming Church reforms and provided a reading list. He was already doing what he could at that time by not only requiring candidates to have done some serious theological reading but also examining them on it. Harford describes his practice:

> He instituted preliminary examinations for the candidates for Deacons' Orders to take place at Salisbury about three months previously to the Ordination Week. At this they were to appear personally and to bring with them a written syllabus or abridgement of certain prescribed books, such as Pearson on the Creed, Butler's Analogy, Burnet's History of the Reformation and Pastoral Care, and they were required to give proof of their qualification for the performance of the public offices of the Church by reading aloud the Morning Service, in the Chapel, before the Bishop or his Chaplain, and a small congregation, consisting generally of the Dean and one or two Canons and Prebendaries of the Cathedral; and a sufficient competency in this very important part of clerical duty was an indispensable requisite for the candidate being permitted to proceed to his examination which subsequently embraced a thorough acquaintance with the Bible, Ecclesiastical History, the Evidences of Christianity, and the Thirty-nine Articles of Religion with their Scriptural Proofs; some proficiency in Hebrew was also required.
> [HARFORD *op. cit.* p. 406f]

Monk in his Primary Visitation *Charge* to the clergy of Gloucester in 1832 told them that he planned to hold ordinations twice a year and required all prospective candidates to communicate with him 'at least two months before Christmas day or Trinity Sunday'. He then set out what he was going to expect of candidates:

> In particular, a familiarity with the historical and doctrinal matters comprised in the whole of the Bible, an accurate and scholar-like acquaintance with the NT in the original language, with the Evidences of Natural and Revealed Religion, and with the Articles and some portion of the History of the Church, as well as such a knowledge of the Latin tongue as will enable its possessor to write or to translate correctly and classically, will be considered indispensable; nor can any person after this notice have the slightest ground to complain of hardship, if he offers himself while deficient in any one of these requisites, and experiences a rejection. To raise the standard of intellectual qualification among the Clergy is not only expedient, but necessary, with a view to the present condition of our country.
> [MONK *Charge* 1832 p. 23f]

J.B. Sumner has a very long appendix to the published version of his 1832 *Charge* which is devoted to his practice in respect of ordination. Part relates to the process of application:

> Those who desire to become candidates for Deacon's orders, must make application to me, at least three months before the time when they expect ordination, stating their age, College, academical degree, and usual place of residence; together with the names of three or more Clergymen, or other persons of respectability, to whom they are best known, and to whom reference may be made respecting their general character. On receiving a statement of these particulars, a time will be appointed for a personal interview with the applicants.
> It is not indispensably necessary that persons expecting to settle in the diocese, should defer their application till they are actually provided with a title, which may be sought afterwards, if they are permitted to become candidates. [J.B. SUMNER *Charge* 1832 Appendix p. xxxviii]

Jenkinson, in the hope of raising the standard of theological literacy in his diocese, has an extensive appendix with a 'List of Books recommended to the Clergy of the Diocese of St David's' in his 1836 *Charge*. It includes books written by some of his episcopal colleagues at that time: Van Mildert's Bampton lectures on *Scriptural Interpretation*, Gray's *Key to the OT*, J.B. Sumner's *Evidences of Christianity, Apostolical Preaching,* and *Records of the Creation*, Marsh's *Comparative View of the Churches of*

England and Rome and his translation of Michaelis's *Introduction*, as well as some by other contemporary English theologians such as Burton, Ollivant and Thomas Turton, and many from earlier generations such as Butler, Hooker, Paley and Pearson. He provides a much shorter list of what he expects candidates for Deacon's orders to have read.

An earlier publication compiled by the Revd W.J. Hall MA and printed privately for a group of friends was a *List of Books recommended to students in divinity by different Bishops and other Eminent Divines, together with Directions for the Formation of a Theological Library*. Of the nineteen authorities he quotes, seven were bishops: Blomfield, Burgess, Huntingford, Jenkinson, Lloyd, Ryder and Van Mildert. The lists vary greatly in length – Huntingford lists just ten books, Lloyd's runs to ten pages. The works of Paley, Butler, Pearson, Hooker and Horne are most frequently listed; Marsh, J.B. Sumner and Van Mildert are also recommended. It seems that just twenty-five copies of this compilation were printed – the British Library's copy has Hartwell Horne's name inscribed in it, one of the writers whose works are recommended.

Joseph Allen preached on *The Necessary Preparation for Holy Orders* at his first ordination in Ely Cathedral on 27 November 1836, taking as his text *2 Timothy 3. 17*. The sermon was later published. In it he repeated things he had said earlier in his *Charge* in Bristol about what he expected of candidates – 'seriousness and diligence' especially in their undergraduate years.

> The skill acquired in the language of the sacred volume, especially in that of the NT, will enable the student in divinity rightly to understand the word of God; and his proficiency in reasoning will lead him to make those just deductions from it, which are necessary for the right comprehension of its various precepts and doctrines. Such is the result of time well-spent at the University. [ALLEN *The Necessary Preparation – A Sermon* p. 6]

In closing, he recommended three authors: 'the most celebrated work, and corner-stone of our Established Church, Bishop Pearson *On the Creed*', the lectures of the late Dr Hey and the lectures of Bishop Herbert Marsh delivered in Cambridge University 'who has condensed so much information in so small a compass, and has reasoned so clearly upon subjects of great difficulty and importance, that the labours of the student in divinity are greatly diminished since the publication of these most learned and useful lectures'. [*Ibid.* p. 16]

Maltby reproduced in the appendix to his Primary Visitation *Charge* in Durham in 1837 a list of required reading for ordinands which had first appeared in his first *Charge* to the clergy of Chichester. They cover the usual areas of natural and revealed theology, OT history and geography, the critical study of the Greek NT, and the *Thirty-nine Articles*. He reminds all candidates of the requirements of the 34th Canon that they shall 'be able to yield an account of their faith *in Latin*'.

The anonymous series of *Letters to a newly created Prelate* published in 1841 by W.C. Taylor has one dealing with the selection and examination of candidates for holy orders and the bishop's responsibilities pre- and post-ordination. The writer, who was well-informed about the Church, approved of the theological colleges at Chichester and Wells (he quotes the prospectus for Wells) and urged his episcopal friend to found one in his diocese. Prospective clergymen, he argued, needed professional and practical training every bit as much as lawyers and medics:

> I may have dwelt too long upon this subject, but I feel very deeply that clerical education, training expressly directed to the profession which young men are to pursue through an arduous career, at the peril of salvation and the hazard of immortal souls, has been strangely neglected at a time when every other profession is showing itself more and more eager to have special and practical instruction for probationers. It is painful to think that the clerical profession may, from this cause, in a very short time find itself below the level of all the other professions in this country; for the world will not estimate its value by general scholarship, even though the church may long possess more than its average share; it will judge clergymen, as it does lawyers and physicians, by professional activity, and by nothing else. And the world is right in so doing; a church is not established to be an ornament only, it is a means to an end. If a clergyman knows not how to lead his flock in the right way, it is no compensation for those who go astray that he knows more Hebrew than a Jewish rabbi, or can solve mathematical problems which would have perplexed Newton.
>
> [TAYLOR op. cit. p. 237f]

Much had been achieved in regard to clerical education between the founding of St Bees in 1816 and of Wells in 1840 but Archbishop Howley was not satisfied. Understandably so, because eighty percent of all ordinands were still coming from Oxford and Cambridge with varying degrees of competence in Greek, Latin and mathematics but still lacking any substantial knowledge of theology or pastoralia. He expressed his concerns to Gaisford, who was also concerned about the matter, in a letter dated 9 October 1840:

> I entirely agree with you in respect of the necessity of providing a more dis-

tinct and professional education for clerical students than is now obtained in the Universities. I can see no other mode of qualifying the clergy in general for the discharge of their professional duties. Many of them at present enter the Church with very little knowledge of what they are required to do, very little of the nature of their office, or the truths which they are required to teach, and hardly any power of composition or elocution. Some years ago I formed a plan for the remedy of this evil, and I communicated my notions to several persons but at the time when I was on the point of proposing it, my proceedings were stopped by the death of Dr Burton [d. 1836], who, I believe, would have been ready to cooperate in the promotion of my views. My general idea was taken from the practice of the Navy, in which no one can receive a lieutenant's commission without passing an examination before a regular board and being reported fit. My proposal went to the establishment of similar boards composed of members of the two Universities without whose certificate of fitness, confirmed by a quasi-degree of the University no one would be entitled to appear before the Bishop as a candidate for Holy Orders. [OXFORD UNIVERSITY ARCHIVES NW/21/5]

Howley and Gaisford batted various ideas back and forth in their correspondence that autumn. Backing for the provision of better theological education came from the Government which accepted proposals made in the Second Report of the Ecclesiastical Commissioners and incorporated in the Dean and Chapters Bill of 1840. Christ Church Oxford was allowed to retain six stalls to which two new professorships of ecclesiastical history and biblical criticism would be attached. Howley told Gaisford that he wanted a 'Professorship for the instruction of the young men in their professional duties as parish priests' and the second stall was eventually attached to a chair in pastoral theology. By the late Spring of 1842 the two new chairs were finally established. Two stalls in Ely Cathedral were also to be given for the promotion of 'religious education and instruction.' Here, at last, were grounds for hope that an improvement in the provision of theological education at the two ancient universities was under way.

Episcopal Family Life

At home

Given their high public profile, it is easy to forget that bishops did also have a private life and a place or two or three they could call home! But quite how private that could actually be when they all had a dozen or more servants in the house, listening and observing, is open to question. Even when out travelling on vacation, staying with relatives or friends in their country houses, servants accompanied them. They were rarely, if ever, alone as a family.

In addition to the see house, where one existed for not all dioceses had one, they needed a London house. Some chose to rent a house for the duration of the parliamentary session, others bought one. Unlike today when see houses are maintained by the Church Commissioners and bishops are spared any personal outlay on bricks and mortar, that was not the case during the period under review. Just as an incumbent was expected to maintain a parsonage out of his income, or even build a new one if necessary, so too bishops had to find the funds for their house(s) either from the revenues of the see or from any private means they might have inherited.

The *Morning Herald* coined a new word in this respect: *re-edificator* in its obituary notice for Archbishop William Howley on 12 February 1848.

> Probably no Prelate since the Reformation has been so eminent a *re-edificator* . . . London House was built by him; - Lambeth Palace was re-built; and Canterbury Cathedral has scarcely known the absence of the restorer's hand, since Dr Howley took his seat upon its throne. In these great works, we should say, on a very rough estimate, that more than £200,000 [= c £20 million today] must have been expended. This sort of munificence is becoming fashionable now, but the late Archbishop began the work when no other person in the kingdom besides himself dreamt of such things.

Howley was, in fact, following the example of his predecessor at Canterbury, Manners-Sutton, who purchased Addington with a twelve hundred acre estate as a country seat for archbishops, the previous one at Croydon having been sold in 1780. Howley commissioned a report from Edward Blore, a Gothic revivalist architect, which led to considerable demolition of much of the old palace at Lambeth in 1829 and its replacement by a great new west wing completed four years later.

Other bishops too laid out large sums on the houses they regarded as a family home, as well as it being an official residence. Blomfield, for example, spent an estimated £10,000 on Fulham Palace and its grounds. Edward Venables-Vernon made many repairs and alterations to the fabric of Rose Castle and to its gardens when he was Bishop of Carlisle between the years 1791-1807. Ten of his sixteen children were born there and he wanted it to be a real family home. Hugh Percy also spent a fortune on Rose Castle. Bouch writes:

> In the years 1829-31 he carried through extensive alterations at Rose which completely changed the appearance of the fabric. The incongruous mixture of architectural styles, caused by successive bishops having introduced their own ideas, gave way to a uniform plan under a scheme prepared by the Quaker architect Thomas Rickman. Inside the magnificent oak staircase ornamented by the bishop's arms, the famous Chinese wall paper, and the carved mantelpieces in the drawing room were erected ... To complete his plans the bishop employed Sir Joseph Paxton to lay out the gardens. In all he is said to have spent £40,000 on these improvements, of which £10,000 was borrowed from the see.
> [BOUCH *Prelates and People of the Lake Counties* p. 385f]

Despite all this, it must have been an uncomfortable place to live in for much of the year as there was no adequate heating. Huntingford too had to carry out major renovations when he moved from Gloucester to Hereford in 1815 but he did have the means as he still enjoyed the emoluments of being the Warden of Winchester College.

Before moving to the stately see house of Farnham Castle in 1828 on his appointment to Winchester, Charles Sumner and his young family lived for a year in a much more modest house in Llansanfraed five miles from Abergavenny in Wales which his wife Jennie loved – she called it 'my little Switzerland' and would have been content to live there all her life.

Copleston, who was a bachelor, rented the same well-furnished country gentleman's house that the Sumners had lived in for which he paid £200 a year when he was appointed to Llandaff in 1828. His first impressions of the house, he said, were very agreeable. 'The house I have hired is admirably situated in a large lawn, at a good distance from the road, and very convenient.' [W.J.COPLESTON *Memoir of Edward Copleston DD* p. 125f] Seven years later, he moved to Llandough Castle which he sublet from a military man who had gone abroad. The house was more convenient for visiting his diocese but some people did not like his being based there. Later still he was able to set his mark on his own see house and grounds which he bought at Hardwick near Chepstow. His only criticism of it was that it was not quite as roomy as he wished 'especially in regard to visitors' servants'. The *Gentleman's Magazine* described it as 'a cheerful and convenient mansion, with a well-situated garden, the improvement of which, and of a walk through a copse on a steep cliff hanging over the Wye, was to the Bishop the source of constant interest and amusement.' [*GM* 1849 p. 301] He had the satisfaction of seeing the 1st prize for grapes being awarded at the Chepstow horticultural show to his gardener – with 2nd prize for dahlias. He said of him, 'He is a most valuable servant – fond of his art, as all gardeners are, & never so happy as when employed in it – but he is also active, strong, skilful in all departments - & what is still more extraordinary, not conceited.' [BROWN ed. *op. cit.* p. 247]

Another bishop who moved three times was John Kaye whose episcopal palace was in Buckden Huntingdonshire at the time of his appointment to Lincon in 1827. Changes in diocesan boundary caused a move to Willingham House, near Market Rasen, in November 1838, and then to Riseholme Hall, two and half miles north of Lincoln four years later. The Hall had been enlarged by the Ecclesiastical Commissioners to serve as the episcopal palace at a cost of £52,185 [= about £6.5 million today].

Big houses required lots of staff with rooms for them too and they cost big sums to run. Van Mildert had two residences in his diocese, Durham Castle which he gave to the newly created University of Durham, and his castle in Bishop Auckland which dated from 1183, set in 800 acres of parkland. The see house of the Bishop of Winchester, Farnham Palace was another Norman castle and had thirty-two bedrooms, and soon after his appointment Charles Sumner bought a large mansion on St James's Square as a London residence with the proceeds of another London property. He had a third residence, Wolvesey Palace (another Norman Castle), at Winchester which he used when visiting his cathedral city.

Some official residences were not only excessively large and damp, they were also very difficult to heat in winter such as Bathurst's palace in Norwich which he was always glad to leave for a warmer, dryer house in London, Cheltenham or Malvern. Though that had not been his first impression when he wrote to his wife from London waiting for the King to sign the *congé d'élire* and to kiss his hands, 'The more I hear of Norwich, the more I am convinced that we shall like it, especially the garden and the ground about the house, not to mention that the house itself is (I am told) very convenient.' [THISTLETHWAYTE *op, cit.* p. 132] Bathurst decided to cut back on staff as he neither had the means of his predecessor,

Manners-Sutton, nor was he willing to take up loans from bankers to pay for a lavish lifestyle as his predecessor had done. He wrote to his wife from London after his appointment,

> We shall, I trust, enjoy ourselves many years at Norwich – as many, I mean, as a man at my time of life has a right to look forward to. I am anxious to set out, with accommodations for ourselves and our friends, and the more so, as the line we are taking, in getting rid very wisely of my predecessor's attendants, and of limiting our expenses, compared with his, may have the appearance of parsimony, which I wish to avoid, as much as I do its opposite extreme. Hitherto we have seen little company; hereafter we shall enlarge our circle of acquaintance, - which your hospitable temper will not dislike.
> [*Ibid.* p. 136]

Winters in Abergwili, too, were avoided as the house was so damp until Jenkinson spent lavishly on improving it during his episcopate. The *Gentleman's Magazine* said that 'the greatest part of his income was applied to improvements in his palace at Abergwilly and the grounds, for the purpose of employing the poor.' [*GM* 1840 p. 321] Jenkinson was also Dean of Durham so he spent three months of the year there – the *Durham Advertiser* is quoted in the *GM*'s obituary of him and it is presumably referring to his Durham residence when it says 'His knowledge of books was extensive. He lived mostly in his well-chosen library, to which he was principally devoted.' That sounds like an implied criticism of the episcopal dean's priorities rather than a positive comment on a room in his house.

We get a glimpse inside another residence from a sermon preached by Henry Moore in Eccleshall parish church shortly after the death of Samuel Butler. The preacher had known the Bishop and his house well – 'with a love of literature and research, which displayed itself in an almost princely collection of choice books, beautiful works of art, and rarest antiquities, so that his house at its very threshold told tales of other times.' [MOORE *A Sermon on the Death of the Rt Rev Samuel Butler* p. 19] This abundance of costly artefacts must have been bought during the years when Butler was the highly successful Headmaster of Shrewsbury School.

Phillpotts's first letter to his secretary Ralph Barnes requested details of the palace in Exeter and about a school out of the city where his young sons could be educated. He then turned to another of his immediate priorities: wine. 'I fear the present Bishop may not leave me any old wine. If you have an opportunity at any sale to purchase for me some dozens of port, claret or *sherry* (the latter is the only wine I myself drink) really old and good, I shall be much obliged. Madeira I shall bring with me. I have enough of wine in casks.' [DAVIES op. cit. p. 89f] Ten days later he wrote that he was

> delighted to find that the garden and pleasure grounds are such as to justify the constant employment of a gardener and labourer. No expense is more to my taste than making *home* comfortable for myself and my daughters. I have resolved to transport my wine, and some furniture from home in a small collier, which I shall freight myself, in order to have full control. I should suppose that there will be 60 or 70 tons of coal. Is there safe storage in the premises at Exeter for so much under lock and key? Or could it be easily *made* safe? [*Ibid.* p. 90]

Phillpotts visited his diocese for three weeks in the New Year, following his consecration on 2 January, and sent this homely request to Barnes: 'Will you be so obliging as to give orders that my bed be thoroughly well-aired. I suffer extremely from cold, and am now somewhat of an invalid.' [*Ibid*. p. 98]

Spouses + families

The choice of a spouse is always one of the most important decisions any human being makes but for a young clergyman in the late 18th and early 19th centuries it could have additional, even immense, significance for his future career. We have seen several examples of this already: Percy's marriage to an Archbishop's daughter, Phillpotts marrying the niece of the Lord Chancellor's wife, Longley's preferment came via his wife's family, even Otter owed his first living to his father-in-law.

All but four of the forty-five bishops in this study were married – the bachelors were Bethell, Copleston, Huntingford and Thirlwall. Though Huntingford, at the request of his dying brother Thomas, took his widow (whom he always referred to as 'sister') and seven young children into his home and became a surrogate father to them. His biographer writes: 'Henry was his Uncle's most rewarding nephew, and upon him the Warden lavished every care and an endless stream of advice and the fruits of his knowledge. Indeed the Warden was indefatigable in his concern for the happiness and well-being of his charges.' [STOWELL op. cit. p.16] Both boys were educated at Winchester and four of the five girls he also sent away to school, the fifth being deemed too weak. Copleston, too, took on the role of surrogate father to the children of his brother who died in 1841. The *GM* says that 'he virtually adopted his ten sons and daughters'.

Four of the married ones had no children: Burgess, Carey, Musgrave and Van Mildert, though the last named had two foster daughters, the nieces of his wife Jane. The norm at the time was to have large families and many of the bishops complied – Phillpotts heads the list with eighteen, followed by Blomfield and Grey with seventeen, Harcourt fifteen, Ryder and Majendie thirteen apiece, Bathurst, Murray and Percy eleven each, and J.B. Sumner had ten. Sometimes, a new baby was an annual event – poor wife! Lloyd and his wife married in August 1822 and within four years had a family of one son and three daughters. Coincidentally, both Kaye and Monk also had one son and three daughters.

Blomfield lost his first wife, Anna Maria Heath in child birth in 1818. Five of their six children had died by 1822; only Maria (1817-1840) survived. A year later he married Dorothy Kent, a widow with one son. They produced a steady stream of children: seven sons and four daughters – Charles James (1820), Mary Frances (1821), Frederick George (1823), Isabella (1824), Henry John (1825), Francis (1827), Arthur William (1829), Lucy Elizabeth (1830), Charles James (1831), Alfred (1833) and Dorothy Hester (1836). Four of his sons were christened Charles James, as three of them died in infancy in 1813, 1818, and 1822.

He wrote to his friend Monk on 14 August 1822 with the news of the death of another child. The letter reflects the current view held by most Christians that such suffering was God-sent.

> You will, I am sure, sympathize with me under the additional calamity with which I have been visited in the loss of my only remaining little boy, who died last Friday, after a few days' illness, of the same fatal malady which has already deprived me of four of my children, water in the head. For my own part, I cannot but perceive that this is the particular kind of trial with which God is pleased to visit me, amid much prosperity. This loss revives the recollection of others, and especially of the last. [A. BLOMFIELD *op. cit.* p. 81]

He felt the loss of his mother equally keenly in 1844 who had died just ten minutes before his arrival in Bury St Edmund's. She was buried in the same vault as his father, two sisters and his five year old son, Edward Thomas. After the funeral he wrote to his wife

> The loss of one dear friend makes us value those who are left more highly, and cling to them more closely. It is a great consolation to me to reflect upon your great and unvarying kindness to my dearest mother; to whom, from the first day of your connexion with her, you were in all respects, as a daughter, and who loved you in return as a mother. [*Ibid.* Vol. 2 p. 70]

His sons achieved a measure of fame: Alfred became Bishop of Colchester and wrote a biography of his father, (Sir) Arthur William as a popular architect, Henry became an admiral, and Fred, the eldest, who was a great friend of Matthew Arnold, became a rector in the city.

George Ryder wrote part of a biography of his father, which was then finished by his brother, Admiral of the Fleet Sir Alfred Ryder, in which he gives some of his own impressions of growing up in a vicarage and then a palace. If the clergy of Gloucester were not initially happy at the prospect of an Evangelical bishop coming to them, Ryder's children were equally unhappy at the family having to go! His son wrote about Lutterworth and having to leave it, 'They were so happy there, surrounded by all that love, friendship, and esteem can confer, and must I say it, they could not get over the short-cropped powdered wigs that then disfigured Bishops; and then Wells was such a bright, lively change to them, whereas Gloucester was all stateliness and gloom.' [A.F.RYDER ed. *A Memoir of Henry Ryder* p. 52] The family suffered a bereavement in 1825 which George described as 'a severe blow to our father and mother'. It was the death by drowning of their son, Charles Dudley, a midshipman on HMS Naiad off the mouth of the Tiber.

George Sumner regarded his early childhood spent in Wales as one of unalloyed joy.

> The pattern of life was simple. The family met the household staff every morning for family prayers. After that the bishop worked in his study or on diocesan business. He spent the afternoon in visiting incumbents or schools. Sometimes both he and his wife went together to call on neighbours. The evening was free and he read aloud to her and to the children; poetry, reviews, essays or novels of a serious kind. George Sumner always claimed that he learned from the example of his father how to regulate his life. Charles was an early riser, punctual and diligent in his episcopal duties.
>
> [COOMBS *op. cit.* p. 24]

Blomfield, like Sumner, gathered his family and all the servants for daily prayers – he believed that 'family prayers brought them all to a proper sense of equality and fellowship'. Originally this practice was most commonly associated with evangelical 'methodistical' homes but later was done in most middle and upper class Christian homes. He wrote a *Manual of Family Prayers* in 1824 which went through seven editions, and was widely used in America as well as in Britain. It had prayers for morning and evening devotions, as well as special prayers for use in times of sickness and bereavement. There was a growing market for such books later in the century.

Blomfield was not alone in having to bury a wife – J.B. Sumner's died at the comparatively early age of forty-six, and they lost Caroline, their third daughter, at the age of two months. Infant mortality and death through accidents or infections such as measles, scarlet fever, diphtheria, typhus and cholera was an accepted fact of life in most homes. Robert Gray lost several daughters to consumption. Bathurst, too, suffered this way – his favourite son, Charles, a highly gifted child, died aged nine in 1795 of measles. His wife was awaiting the birth of a new child and knew nothing of the boy's death until her husband wrote to her – he could not bear to give her the news face to face. He wrote,

> It is also very painful to me to act a part to you, and to suppress any longer what you must so soon know. The sweet boy was given over the day you were brought to bed, and died a few days after. I need not point out to you what I suffered. My affection for you, and the mercy and goodness of God, carried me through this severe trial. Since his death, my spirits have been far more composed, and my mind more easy. It will be a satisfaction to you to know that he died easily, and had every possible attention paid to him.
>
> I have only one thing to add, and that is my earnest request that you will (with your usual delicacy and kindness to me) refrain from talking of him to me, unless, hereafter, my spirits should be strong enough to begin the subject myself; and, what is of more consequence than all, that you will keep up yourself, because I am more interested in your comfort and happiness than in anything else in the world. [THISTLETHWAYTE *op. cit.* p. 74f]

That last sentence rings hollow and suggests that he little understood a mother's grief when he would not let her share it openly with him. Later they had the double tragedy of losing their son, Benjamin, in mysterious circumstances (probably murdered) in 1809 in Austria whilst on a secret diplomatic mission, and then fifteen years later that son's seventeen year old daughter, Rosa, who drowned in the Tiber. Another son, Robert, who had two livings in Norwich diocese, also died prematurely in December 1828.

Grey of Hereford had three wives, having lost the first two in childbirth. He married in 1809 and had ten children by his first wife who died in 1821 (so, she had given birth almost every year); he married again in 1824 and had four more, and lastly in 1831 to whom three were born. Of the seventeen, four were dead by the time of his own death in 1837.

The Wards lost three of their seven children, the first was a two year old daughter to whooping cough, the other two had grown to adulthood but both died in the same year that Ward was consecrated Bishop of Sodor and Man. The first was their daughter Charlotte, who died six months after giving birth to her first child. A few months later, Tom their eldest son, who was a promising student at Trinity College Cambridge about to sit the examination for a scholarship, died. It was Holy Week 1829 'when a sudden seizure deprived him of speech and mental power, and the doctor gave no hope of recovery.' The Bishop reached his son in time and wrote to his wife back home at Bishop's Court on the Isle of Man:

> Our Son still lives but will be entered on life everlasting before this can reach you. It is a heavy blow . . . All our Children will be gifts to Heaven that the Angels will rejoice over, and to their Mother Heaven will be indebted for this, under God our Saviour, not to their father. You instituted our Tom in the knowledge of the Saviour with the earliest dawn of infant reason: you will join your Tom again, and receive your reward in his sweet company never more to part. [WILSON *op. cit.* p. 114]

Tom died on Good Friday morning. In his next letter to his wife, Ward writes,

> He died at the hour when our Saviour stood before Pontius Pilate. I can never doubt but [that] that love with which he melted Peter by a look, and which on this day carried the thief from the cross into Paradise, has received the spirit of my beloved son into rest and glory. . . Would God I knew how you were . . . I am better than I could expect . . . Kind friends stick by me – several young friends of my dear Tom, who will attend him to the tomb.
> [*Ibid*. p. 115]

Despite the devastation of losing his eldest and much loved son, Ward was almost immediately back at work. On the evening following the funeral, he writes, 'So now my anxieties for this angel son being at rest I shall turn my mind to duties' and he details his objects in going to London the next week. [*Ibid*. p. 116] He must have been made of stern stuff for a few days later he tells her he is to have an interview with Peel about getting some financial help for his diocese. Bereavement was not going to deter him from doing his duty by his tiny diocese: 'If I cannot obtain church room for the poor, and bread for my clergy, what can I do? But those objects attained, and education for the future race of the clergy, and our little Isle will be converted into a garden of the Lord, and I shall lay down my head and depart in peace.' [*Ibid*. p. 117] He would later have the joy of ordaining his surviving son, William, whom he priested along with five other candidates on Palm Sunday 1836.

There were, of course, many other happy family events to celebrate, not least, making a good marital match. Bathurst's daughter, Tryphena, recalled one from the early weeks of her father's episcopate when the whole family was gathered in London.

> The only circumstance I can recollect to have made much impression upon me during our six weeks' residence in London, was the marriage of my third brother, Benjamin to Miss Call, the eldest sister of Sir William Call, of Whiteford House, Cornwall. The engagement was formed at Vienna, when he was I believe only nineteen. The marriage took place in my father's house in Manchester Square, before my brother had reached the age of one-and-twenty. Soon after his marriage he went out with his wife to Stockholm, as Secretary of Legation. [THISTLETHWAYTE *op. cit.* p. 135]

One of his joys was officiating at the weddings of his children. His favourite daughter, Tryphena whom he called Tiny, was married late in life on 16 January 1827 when her father was eighty-three. She had been constantly caring for him for four years following the death of her mother:

> My father performed the ceremony, by special licence, in his drawing room at Cheltenham. I had several times witnessed the marriage ceremony performed by my father, as well for his sons and daughters as for other friends, and I never remember a single occasion on which he was not considerably affected in the course of the service, I felt therefore some apprehensions on his account; but he was singularly cheerful, and so perfectly composed that, far from evincing even the lightest tremor or hesitation in his voice or manner, he on the contrary appeared to have imparted to me a composure almost equal to his own. I had the satisfaction of leaving my father under the care of my eldest sister, and he was never without the society of some part of his family, after my departure from home. [*Ibid.* p. 310]

Finding suitable, and preferably wealthy, spouses for daughters was an issue most bishops faced. Otter did well. His eldest daughter, Sophia, married the Revd Henry Malthus, son of Otter's close friend, the political philosopher Thomas Robert Malthus. He became Vicar of Effingham in Surrey in 1835 which he held till 1882 and Otter appointed him to the living of Donnington in Sussex two years later. His second daughter, Caroline, married John (later the first Lord) Romilly; the fourth, Maria, married Lord Justice Sir William Milbourne James; and the fifth, Emily, married Edward Strutt, the first Lord Belper.

John Sutterton, who became Charles Sumner's colleague as the first Suffragan Bishop of Guildford in 1874 (having previously served as his archdeacon for many years), preached an *In Memoriam* sermon in St Andrew's Farnham on the death of his diocesan. In it he offers some insightful, personal comments on family life in the episcopal palace as he had observed it.

> It boots little what a man is to those without, in his intercourse with the world and the discharge of public functions, if he is not found to fulfil his relationships to those who have the first claims upon him. It is what he is as a father, a husband, a master, a brother, that denotes his character. The home is the nursery of all true, social and public virtues. There we see what a man's real temper, disposition and character are, and there they are gradually developed and formed . . . It was in the bosom of his family, and amidst his children, and children's children – so bright, so loving, so gentle, so thoughtful, so sympathetic, so playful, so winning to the youngest infant, so kind and considerate to his domestics, so cordial and affable to his intimate friends – it was there he appeared to the greatest advantage, and those who saw it knew the fountain from whence his large hearted diffusive charity welled forth.' [UTTERTON *In Memoriam* p. 8]

An earlier anonymous writer in a series of letters, published in 1841, to a friend who had been appointed a bishop offered him some sensible but sobering advice about bringing up his children and what lay in store for them:

> The younger children of the less wealthy peers, and all the children of a bishop, are brought up in a style from which they must expect in after life to descend. Your station imposes upon you the necessity of living in a lordly mansion, keeping a rich table, supporting an extensive equipage and establishment of servants, procuring such masters for your children as consist with your dignity, and mixing with the company suited to your rank. These things end with your life; the change is a great trial, and feeling that it awaits your children, you should carefully train them so that these externals should sit loose upon their minds, and that they should feel within themselves internal resources, both oral and intellectual, of which no change can deprive them . . .
> A bishop ought strenuously to exert himself to leave his children comfortably settled in the ranks of the gentry, but he must remember himself, and he must impress upon their minds, that after his death they will cease to have anything to do with the nobility. In effecting the mental discipline necessary to fortify them for this trial, you will derive great assistance from

associating with those who have won their way to distinction in other professions by their merits and their exertions. [TAYLOR ed. *op. cit.* 320f]

The writer, who repeatedly encourages his episcopal friend to show independence in his thinking and actions, has much good advice to offer to any newly preferred bishop but his publication came too late to be of benefit to the forty-five men who figure in this study.

Providing for sons and other family members
Bathurst was already thinking of how he might further his sons' careers just days after his appointment as bishop. In a letter to his eldest daughter, Henrietta, he wrote:

> Benjamin's appointment is not worth more than 20s. a day, but it is a material point to have obtained at so early an age an independent situation. James is made, without any solicitation, Commissary to the German Legion. For Henry, if I live a few years, I shall be able to provide, and I will do the best I can for dear mama, you, Try, Caroline, Robert and Coote – to all of whom give my kind love, and accept the same yourself. [THISTLETHWAYTE *op. cit.* p. 132f]

He was constantly seeking to use his contacts at Westminster to promote the careers of his sons, particularly the eldest, Henry, whom he appointed Archdeacon of Norwich as well as to the richest livings in his gift – he had hoped to secure an Irish bishopric for him, but without success. The son died in 1844, bitterly disappointed at not succeeding his father as Bishop of Norwich – an appointment he had expected, having run the diocese for so many years on his aged father's behalf. In a fit of pique he wrote *An Easter Offering for the Whigs from Archdeacon Bathurst* in which he lifted the lid on nepotistic practices. Biber, in his biography of Blomfield, is scathing about Bishop Bathurst's nepotism and about his eldest son, citing it as an example of the bad old days before men of Blomfield's character were appointed. {BIBER *Bishop Blomfield and his Times* pp. 15-18] The truth, however, is that Blomfield was little different. He appointed his son, Frederick, to the very wealthy living of St Andrew Undershaft with St Mary-a-Axe in the City and made him a prebendary of St Paul's, and to his son, Alfred, he gave the living of St Philip, Stepney.

Just as fathers desired to promote the interests of their sons, so too did their sons and other close relatives expect older family members to use their influence to advance their prospects and careers. The young Thomas Huntingford fell in love at an age when he realized he could not afford to marry but as he put it 'Speaking in a worldly sense it was a very rash measure, my only prospect of ever being able to marry was from the circumstance of my having my Uncle a Bishop and the Warden of Winchester. I persuaded myself I should soon get either a living or a fellowship at Winchester.' [STOWELL op. cit. p. 29] Fortunately his uncle approved of the young lady though warning them they would have to wait several years which they did. In the meantime he used his connections to get his nephew appointed as private tutor to the son of a Duke. Later he ordained him and appointed him to the valuable living of Kempsford worth between £500 and £600 which was in his gift; a prebendal stall in Hereford cathedral followed in due course. His care for Thomas did not end there:

> They were often at Hereford for weeks at a time, especially during the musical meetings. The Bishop made useful gifts of money to them from time to time and saw to it that by modest advancement, Thomas's income gradually increased. He appointed him Precentor of Hereford which was worth £100 a year in tithes besides having the patronage of the living of Walford. In 1825 he offered him the living of Whitborne, near Worcester. . . The Bishop had already provided the other nephew Henry with a living at Hampton Bishop worth £400 a year with an "excellent house". [*Ibid.* p.42]

An even richer living came later for Thomas. The Bishop also showed a similar care for his foster daughters who all married well.

One of Phillpotts's earliest acts as a bishop was to ordain his eldest son, William John, privately as a Deacon to a curacy of just £50 a year which is what the previous curate had received. Recognizing that this small sum which was below the recommended minimum might cause adverse comment, he told his secretary 'It may be well not to let it be known unnecessarily what his salary is.' [DAVIES op. cit.p. 102] He had told Barnes three weeks earlier that he would accept no *title* with a smaller salary than £70 a year unless in very peculiar cases, the circumstances of which had been stated to him. Eighteen months later in October 1831, his son was ordained Priest at Phillpotts's first ordination held at Exeter when there were fifteen candidates for the diaconate and sixteen for the priesthood. The ordination, incidentally, was performed outside the Embertide season, which provoked some adverse criticism. Twelve days later, the Bishop presented his son with the living of Uny Lelant with Towednack in west Cornwall. When The Revd Thomas Hill Lowe was appointed precentor of Exeter cathedral in October 1832, he vacated the vicarage of Grimley in the diocese of Worcester (described by Reginald Shutte as 'a comfortable piece of preferment' which was worth £1,200 a year) the young man was collated to it on vacating the living of Uny. Other preferment came in due course, including a prebendal stall, the office of Archdeacon of Cornwall and the Chancellorship of the diocese. He appointed his son, Thomas, Vicar of St Feock, Truro and his son, Henry John, Vicar of Lannerton, Tavistock.

Whilst deploring letters begging him to use his influence on behalf of particular candidates, Phillpotts was not above doing just that for his own sons. He wrote to Sir Robert Peel in 1843 soliciting his help for a son returned home on grounds of ill-health from service in the East India Company but the bishop was courteously side-lined to applying to the Secretary of State for the Colonies. He met with no better response when applying to Lord Hardwicke on behalf of another son discharged from the army on grounds of ill-health.

Archbishop Harcourt had eleven sons, one of whom died young. Of the remaining ten, the eldest became an MP, two became Captains in the Royal Navy and two Lieutenant-Colonels in the Army. The remaining five all enjoyed ecclesiastical preferment, four in the diocese of York and the fifth as a prebendary of Southwell.

C.R. Sumner gave his son George Henry the living of Old Alfresford in Hampshire, who was later appointed Suffragan Bishop of Guildford and whose wife, Mary, is famous as the founder of the Mothers' Union.

Kaye had just one son, William Frederick, whom he appointed Perpetual Curate of South Carlton and Rector of Riseholme. The son married the eldest daughter of his father's successor, John Jackson, and then served as Archdeacon of Lincoln from 1863 until his death in 1913.

Law made his third son, Henry, Archdeacon of Wells and a canon of the cathedral, but before then he had appointed him Vicar of Childwall on his ordination in 1821, then Vicar of St Anne's Manchester a year later, and in 1824 Archdeacon of Richmond. His fourth son, Robert, whom he ordained in Chester in 1823, he immediately appointed Vicar of Weaverlea and two years later Rector of Wallasy, followed by a canonry in 1826. On the bishop's translation to Bath & Wells, Robert was made a prebendary and then the Treasurer of Wells Cathedral. His eldest son, James Thomas, who was ordained priest in 1815, enjoyed three livings and a prebendal stall in Chester diocese before becoming a prebendary of Lichfield in 1818 and then its Chancellor. He was also Vicar of Harborne 1825-45, and became a Special Commissary of the Diocese of Bath & Wells in 1840. The family preferment didn't stop there – George Henry Law Jr was ordained by his grandfather in 1845 and was immediately appointed to a Somerset curacy, and then became Principal Surrogate in the Diocese of Lichfield in 1847 (presumably through his uncle's influence).

In comparison to Law, Davys's nepotism was modest - he provided for his family by appointing his brother Owen Archdeacon of Northampton in 1842 with a canonry in his cathedral and the living of Fiskerton in Lincolnshire. Chadwick states that he also steadily promoted his relatives to be canons of the cathedral. [CHADWICK *op. cit.* p. 161]

Otter's eldest son, William Bruère, was appointed Vicar of Kinlet in 1837 which he held until 1847 and then, in addition, Vicar of Cowfold in West Sussex six miles from Horsham. His father also appointed him prebendary of Somerley in Chichester Cathedral in 1839. He eventually became Archdeacon of Lewes but that happened long after his father's death.

Burgess had no children but he did have two nieces whom he treated with paternal affection. One died of tuberculosis, the other added greatly to his comfort by her 'sedulous attentions'. She married in 1833 the Dean of Salisbury's eldest son, the Revd C.B. Pearson, to whom Burgess gave the valuable prebend of Fordington. The couple had a son born the following year. Harford gives a rare glimpse of family life in the episcopal palace: The infant son 'attracted much of the Bishop's notice and affection. He delighted in having it brought to see him, and in making his musical boxes play for its gratification.' [HARFORD *op. cit.* p. 449]

Howley who as archbishop had immense patronage to bestow was not able to use it for the benefit of his sons as they all died young before he could promote them. Van Mildert, likewise, had no immediate family to prefer though he did, exceptionally, give a living to his nephew, William Ives, whom he ordained Priest privately in St Paul's in 1825. His biographer claims that 'as in other branches of his life, Van Mildert put the needs of the Church above all else. He never gave preferment to anyone, family or not, whom he thought unsuited to it; and in general, none of his protégés let him down.' [VARLEY *op. cit.* p. 109]

Copleston, too, put a man's ability first when making appointments. Despite having three nephews in holy orders, the only living, and it was one of little money value, he gave to a family member, his eldest nephew, was that of Lamyat in Somerset which had been placed at his disposal when he presented the incumbent there with a living in his gift in Gloucestershire. It had, however, the attraction of being near the Copleston family home of Offwell.

It is a small rectory £250 a year – in an excellent neighbourhood, about 40 miles from Offwell (whereas before he was living in Buckinghamshire on a benefice of the same value but in point of vicinity very disagreeable) and all the circumstances of the parish such as a quiet country clergyman would desire – an excellent little church in good repair & a nice new-built parochial school, & a rural population of between 200 & 300 without dissenters.

[BROWN ed. *op. cit.* p. 143]

When the bishop's brother died in July 1842, his eldest son vacated Lamyat to take over Offwell, and Copleston then appointed a young clergyman who was engaged to his niece Catherine, to Lamyat thereby keeping both livings in the family. By the standards of the time, this was a very modest personal exercise of the preferment in his gift.

Sparke of Ely (*q.v.* p. 142f) and John Luxmoore of St Asaph were the two worst nepotists. The latter ensured his eldest son had a rapid and increasingly well-rewarded rise in the Church. Venn notes that as Dean of St Asaph from 1826-54 he had £1,200 a year, the rectory of Crudly brought him another £1,000, Darwen £200, a sinecure rectory at Brownyard another £200, and then there were additional emoluments as Chancellor of the cathedral and from a canonry at Hereford. His second son, who married a daughter of Pusey, was given a perpetual curacy and two sinecure rectories which he held from the time of his ordination in 1823 until his death in 1860 – two more livings and a canonry at St Asaph came later.

Of course, not all sons followed in their episcopal father's footsteps. The army and the navy claimed several of them. Ryder's son, as noted earlier, became an admiral and one of the Bathurst's sons became a general but when in semi-retirement his father again came to his aid pestering friends at Westminster to appoint him to a sinecure post – eventually Governor of Berwick upon Tweed.

Entertainment

An episcopal palace was both a family home and a place of work, just as vicarages were and still are. Fulfilling the second role could easily impinge on the first, especially when it came to offering hospitality. A few bishops entertained on a grand scale. Archbishop Howley still kept up public banquets at Lambeth and anyone could come as long as they wore court dress. The guests, in effect, invited themselves and the domestics of the Prelate 'stood with swords and bag-wigs round pig, and turkey, and venison'. He also enjoyed giving private dinner parties at which Southey and other literary men were sometimes his guest. It is said of him that he was good at 'guiding the conversation into a channel which would call forth the literary powers of his guests . . . and how he designedly avoided topics of public agitation'. [DARK *Seven Archbishops* p. 188] Despite all the pomp of his lifestyle, Joshua Watson, who frequently enjoyed these grand social occasions, reckoned the Archbishop remained a simple and gentle man.

When Blomfield was appointed to London, he visited Fulham Palace before the Howleys had moved out and learned from his predecessor's wife something of what she had done by way of entertainment and the cost thereof.

> Mrs Howley was an hospitable hostess who had entertained 970 people to dinner during the previous year, 1827. She told him her annual housekeeping bill which included coal, linen and washing was only £1,600 and that she had spent £800 on staff wages. The family's clothes bill amounted to £1,000.
> [JOHNSON *op. cit.* p. 30]

That is a total of £3,400 [= £ 320,935]. Most households in Britain in 1827 existed on £50 a year or less, so one can see the vast gulf between the lifestyle of the bishop's family and that of the average citizen. She had also spent £900 [= £84,953] on carriages – Johnson reckons that meant the bishop kept two coaches and several coachmen. Blomfield went on to visit another of his residences in the capital, London House at No 32 St James' Square which he deemed to be inferior to St Botolph rectory in Devonshire Square despite it having seventeen bedrooms and several grand reception rooms. The Bishop of Winchester, Charles Sumner, was his neighbour at No 21 St James' Square but Blomfield preferred to live at Fulham Palace with its famous gardens stretching along the banks of the Thames.

Generous hospitality at Auckland Castle was a required element in the Bishop of Durham's life in the Palatinate. Canon Ilderton, the Rector of Ingram, recalled half a century after the event his ordination by Van Mildert in 1834 and the hospitality shown to the newly ordained by the bishop.

> The newly ordained clergy were invited to dinner at Auckland Castle; and on presenting ourselves we were ushered into a large apartment, where we awaited the coming of the bishop. Presently the door opened, and he entered – a slight and graceful figure – followed by his chaplains . . . He went round the circle which we made to receive him, bowing to each in turn, and addressing a few words to those with whom he was personally acquainted.

> We were entertained with becoming splendour, and while partaking of his lordship's venison, & c., I saw that his own repast consisted of a basin of broth or gruel, which he sipped occasionally. At the same time, his conversation with those near him was as animated as if the beverage had been of a much more exhilarating description. [VARLEY *op. cit.* p. 205]

Some, but not all, bishops entertained ordination candidates to lunch or dinner on the eve of their ordination, or following it, as in the case just quoted. Hospitality at the episcopal palace was a natural and frequent part of a bishop's care for his clergy. Skinner in his diary records numerous occasions when Bishop Law invited him to meals and to stay as a guest at his palace in Wells. Skinner who was widowed early and left with the care of three children had a difficult time in his parish despite being a caring pastor to his people. The bishop was aware of his problems and sought to give him the personal encouragement and support he needed. On one of his stays with the bishop in 1828 he wrote, 'Nothing could exceed the real benevolence and kindness of the worthy Bishop; he has quite won my heart and attached me to him.' [COOMBS. H. & P. ed. *op. cit.* p. 363] Hospitality was reciprocated – he records on Monday 6 September 1829,

> We had nearly done breakfast when a servant of the Bishop's arrived at the Parsonage, saying his Master would soon be with us to breakfast and with a party of ladies; and by nine he arrived with the three Miss Laws and their brother, the family of the late Lord Ellenborough. The two elder ladies seemed to be well-informed women and have made proper observations during their travels abroad ... I have engaged to visit the Bishop at Weston-Super-Mare. [*Ibid*. p. 416]

Law had written in advance but the letter didn't arrive till the day after his family party had made their unexpected visit. Skinner commented 'he is indeed a kind-hearted man, and if only he had been a brother Clergyman residing in the neighbourhood, it would have given me pleasure always to have received him; but as a superior from whom I have received so many proofs of kindness and hospitality, it is a delight to me to make any return in my power.' [*Ibid.*]

Lloyd was another who exercised a ministry of hospitality. An historian of the diocese tells of the bishop's 'wish to cultivate the friendship of his clergy, and to find opportunities of intercourse with them in other than formal and official manner, was shown by his practice of holding public days at which they might be present with the ladies of their families without an invitation from himself.' [MARSHALL *Diocesan Histories, OXFORD* p. 176] And adds that it was a custom which ceased under his successor (Richard Bagot) who chose not to live at Cuddesdon.

Leisure activities and vacations
Tryphena Bathurst tells of family holidays several weeks long spent at Great Malvern – the four girls riding or walking all day when the weather permitted with their parents 'pacing soberly, with wandering steps and slow, across the beautiful fields' which surrounded the town. Her parents removed to Cheltenham for the winter, chiefly for the benefit of her mother's health. In a letter to her written by her mother, there is a description of how they spent their time:

> Your dear father continues charmingly well, and enjoying his leisure walk and game of whist, twice a week now, always in a quiet way. . . We are getting on with Sully, [Sully's *Memoirs* of Henry IV which the bishop read, or was read to, four nights in the week] and now pitying Henry's weakness and passion for the fair Gabrielle, whom he would have married, had Sully been a less sincere friend. [THISTLETHWAYTE *op. cit.* p. 246]

Copleston's favourite recreational pastime seems to have been walking which he frequently enjoyed whilst travelling round his diocese. His diary entry for 15 September 1832 reads:

> Viewed Lanfoist church and parsonage; the church admirably repaired and furnished. The parsonage in a sadly dilapidated state. After this, ascended the Blorenge by the tram-road with Captain Nares; one hour took us to the top. After enjoying the noble prospect towards Brecon, and in every other direction, descended to Llanellen, where my carriage met us and took us home. The weather was beautiful, and the walk, though fatiguing, by no means unpleasant. [W.J. COPLESTON *op. cit.* p. 153]

Twelve days later, the entry reads: 'Confirmed in Abergavenny church about two hundred and forty. After church ascended the great Skerrid with Dr Macbride; a fine cloudless day. Returned to friends staying with me at Llansanfraed.' [*Ibid.*]

He also enjoyed a close loving relationship with his parents and his brother and was never happier than when he could return to visit them for his summer holidays at Offwell two miles from Honiton in Devon. These few lines written in November 1828 give some indication of how much the place and his family meant to him.

> I am now in my native place, my Father in his 80th & my Mother in her 82nd year, both well and cheerful, arrived from Exeter to meet me under my brother's roof, where most of his ten children are also assembled. Yesterday the duty of the Church was done by my Father & his Grandson, in the Evening by my brother & myself. My father came to this living in 1774 which he resigned to my brother about 28 years ago, and the parsonage as well as the village having undergone all sorts of improvements, the place is full of interesting recollections. [BROWN ed. *op. cit.* p. 65f]

Not surprisingly, he built a retirement home for himself there in 1839.

George Sumner recollects the summer holiday of 1832 which was typical of many he enjoyed with his parents:

> As soon as the confirmations were over the Bishop took Mrs Sumner and his family to Bonchurch, in the Isle of Wight, where he thoroughly enjoyed change of air and scene. It was usually his habit in the autumn to take a month or six weeks' rest, and no one enjoyed a holiday more than he did. Mrs Sumner writing from Bonchurch to a friend, says, "We are greatly enjoying ourselves here by walking and rambling over the rocks, inhaling the sea air, admiring the exquisite views, and still more by being alone with our children, and permitted to enjoy their society as we can never do at home. To be so much with my husband, and see him thus surrounded with his children, and delighting to hear them converse freely, are sources of happiness which you, my dear friend, will be able to appreciate."
> [G.H. SUMNER *op. cit.* p. 220]

But that one became, in part, a working holiday as he took the services at Brighstone on some Sundays in the absence of the vicar, Samuel Wilberforce, whom he would later appoint Archdeacon of Surrey.

Blomfield in his Chester days chose the Lake District for his family holidays and sought the advice of William Wordsworth when planning his first visit there, informing the poet that he would be accompanied by his wife, four children and eight servants. They stayed in Rydal, of course. After his move back to London, Blomfield, by way of relaxation at home, enjoyed music and attending concerts but not the theatre which he did not consider to be conducive 'to the ends of piety and morality'. His chief interest was gardening and he introduced many new and rare trees to the already famous gardens of Fulham Palace which he enjoyed guiding friends and visitors around.

Visiting members of one's extended family or friends in their large houses and country estates was a normal part of life for men of their station and class. Bishop Stanley died on one such family holiday. In August

1849, he and his wife accompanied by three of their adult children, Arthur, Mary and Catherine set off from Norwich on a tour of Scotland. The Bishop died at Brahan Castle near Dingwall on 5 September. His body was taken by boat from Invergordon to Yarmouth, and transported to Norwich for interment in the Cathedral. The family had to vacate the palace and Kitty Stanley and her daughters moved to 6 Grosvenor Crescent in London. Tragedy hit the family again soon afterwards. In December news came that their son Charlie had died suddenly at Hobart of gastroentiritis, and in March 1850 their firstborn son, Owen, died of epilepsy on board his ship HMS Rattlesnake in Sydney Harbour. News of his death did not arrive in London until 4 July – three months after Catherine had married C.J. Vaughan, the Headmaster of Harrow, who had been her brother Arthur's closest friend since their days together at Rugby under Arnold.

The aristocratic Hugh Percy at Carlisle was remembered as 'a great farmer; he was reputed to be the best judge of a horse in all the district and Sunday afternoons were usually spent looking round his farm and giving an opinion on any neighbours' horses which were being bought or sold. He used to drive his own four horses all the way to London.' [BOUCH op. cit. p. 387]

John Bird Sumner had a more leisurely form of relaxation, namely painting landscapes in water colours. Lambeth Palace Library has two albums of his work, dating from his years as archbishop. The one is entitled 'Sketches from Nature' and contains twenty-one views of the parkland surrounding Addington Palace; the other is a similar collection with thirteen landscapes. He had presumably honed his skills as a painter in his earlier years at Mapledurham and Chester.

Sickness and old age
Old age almost invariably entailed a measure of serious ill-health. Sometimes it was the wife who became gravely ill and this adversely affected her partner too. Van Mildert is a case in point. The last three years of his life were overshadowed by his wife's ill health. In the autumn of 1833, his wife Jane suffered a stroke which affected her personality. By February next year she was near to death. There were rallies and relapses, hopes raised only to be dashed. By March the bishop was 'much broken by his domestic distress.' She was no longer able to accompany him on his journeys south and he dreaded having to leave her. 'I am very anxious to return to Mrs V.M., whose distress at my absence is exceedingly painful to me', he wrote to Thorp in March 1835 during one of his brief visits to London. She did, however, manage to outlive her husband.

Charles Sumner lost his beloved wife Jennie when they were both just fifty-nine. She was buried at Hale, the church built by the bishop and funded largely by him. Coombs says that after her death he rarely spoke of her again, and he took over a scantily furnished servant's bedroom. His son George and his young family moved to Farnham so that he could act as his father's chaplain – probably more importantly so that the old bishop could derive solace in having loved ones with him. Emily, his youngest daughter took over her mother's role as châtelaine. He gave instruction in his will that his own funeral was to be as private as possible and that his mortal remains were not to be buried in the cathedral but alongside those of his wife 'who was all in all to him for over thirty years'. He was a widower for twenty-five years.

Phillpotts lost his wife in 1863 after fifty-nine years of marriage when he was eighty-five. A Thank You letter, written to Pusey in reply to one from him, reveals a gentler and tender side to this old warrior:

> It is indeed a sad desolation. But I humbly thank God that He has left the stronger to encounter it. She, the most tender and affectionate of human beings whom I have ever known, would have been (without most special support from above) absolutely overcome. Thank God she is at rest! The wrench which I have experienced is, through God's mercy, made more tolerable by memory of her whom I have lost. It is wonderful to myself that memory should be thus soothing, but so it is. Earlier in life this would not have been. Now I seem to be permitted to enjoy in portraits, and in the colloquy with most affectionate daughters, formed by her blessed example, a continual intercourse with her. May I derive all the blessedness of the trial, which it is mercifully designed to bring with it. [DAVIES *op. cit.* p. 397f]

Copleston, who had no wife to support him in his troubles, suffered for many years from stomach disorders which could be so severe that he was put out of action for weeks. The state of his health figures frequently in his correspondence. He wrote, for example, in May 1834:

> The very distressing symptoms I continued to feel drove me from London. I am persuaded that I should not have recovered there, notwithstanding some fluctuations in the disorder. The whole nervous system was affected - & life was becoming quite a burden. The journey hither has been beneficial. The air, the quiet, the rural rambles & the domestic society of this place, are all admirably adapted to a restoration of that tone which had been relaxed. After a few days I confidently expect to be refitted for my London duties - & as soon as ever that is the case, I shall repair to my post.
> [BROWN ed. *op. cit.* p. 167]

In September 1837 he wrote from Bath:

> In addition to the malady which has harassed me for the last five weeks, [a disorder of the liver and stomach] I have had the misfortune to lose an apparatus of false teeth by the failure of one of its supports - & this accident has driven me to Bath. In a case of dyspepsia mastication is more especially indispensable - & the means of this I am now endeavouring to provide by the help of Parkinson the Dentist.
> My general health is so much affected that I almost doubt my ability to perform any episcopal duties this year. [*Ibid*. p. 242]

Things didn't get any better and by mid-November, when he was back home in Hardwick House, he was complaining

> This has been the most dismal year of my life. After two months severe indisposition in May & June, I came here perfectly well early in August - hoping to enjoy my new residence, to see yourself & many other friends here, and to engage in all the duties of my Diocese – but on the 12th of August a return of that impracticable dyspeptic malady, which poisons life, & unfits me for all duties & all pleasures, came on. I struggle in vain against it, & had the benefit of the daily attendance of Mr Watkins, a very sensible & skilful medical man of Chepstow. The disorder wore off in about two months – but was succeeded by one of another kind – a large abscess in the back of my neck – extremely painful, & slow in arriving at maturity. About a week ago it became safe to use the lancet, & then an immense discharge of matter gave me relief, I have now a seton inserted, which will prevent the accumulation by a continual drain. It has weakened & relaxed me. I still live the life of an invalid, & am preparing for my migration to St Paul's in December. [*Ibid*.]

One feels for this poor man but his afflictions were of a temporary nature. Bishop Monk spent his closing years almost blind, and Bishop Marsh became senile. Bagot was unable to minister as his mind, too, was affected but that was not all. The *Gentleman's Magazine* records that in addition to a 'painful mental aberration' he also suffered heart disease, lost the use of one hand and had to have it amputated. Phillpotts, too, ended his days in a sorry state. Butler lived with pain during the two years he served as a bishop. As Henry Moore put it 'It was a fiery trial wherewith he was tried. In early life he had struggled with great difficulties; his whole course had been a course of labour; the prize was now gained [i.e. a bishopric] but the hour of victory was the beginnings of sorrow; pain and suffering were his daily portion'. [MOORE *op. cit.* p. 11]

In 1836 just a month after publishing his proposals for a Metropolis Churches Fund, Blomfield became almost totally incapacitated. Biber describes it as 'a severe inflammatory attack, attributable to the excessive fatigue and exhaustion to which he subjected himself in the performance of his arduous duties. For some time his life was seriously endangered.' [BIBER *op. cit.* p. 202] He was out of action for most of that year. Eleven years later, now aged sixty, he had an accident on a visit to the Queen at Osborne House. He slipped on the polished floor, bruising his right eye and temple. Soon afterwards he suffered what sounds like a stroke – his face was paralysed and his speech became slurred. It was so bad that he could not speak in public for several months and never recovered completely. He was the front runner to succeed Howley when the archbishop died a year later but Lord Russell rightly judged he was no longer fit enough to take on the duties of that office.

When not nursing ailments and no longer seriously engaged on diocesan business, what did aged bishops do? Bathurst, as we know, played whist. His son defended this activity on mental health grounds – 'it may be admitted,' he wrote, 'that a less frequent employment of evenings in a rubber of whist might have been more dignified and suited to his station; though, on the other hand, latterly this amusement appeared to those about him to contribute very much towards the keeping his faculties together, and therefore to be not only excusable, but positively advisable.'

Burgess wrote Latin verses and continued to be engaged in scholarly reading and writing. He came under some criticism in his later years at Salisbury for dereliction of duty. Harford wrote:

> His fondness for professional study and literary retirement did, indeed, induce a life of comparative seclusion; and hence, perhaps, many persons less acquainted with his general habits were inconsiderate, not to add uncharitable enough, to place to the account of indolence or negligence the gradually increasing infirmities of almost octogenarian age.
>
> [HARFORD *op. cit.* p.396]

More particularly as one of his clergy recalled - 'some slight deficiencies; for a letter occasionally unanswered, or an official paper mislaid; for some well-devised plan for the good of the Diocese imperfectly carried out, some salutary regulation only casually enforced'. [*Ibid.* p. 393] His interests lay elsewhere:

> On his library table, to the close of his life, were sure to be found the newest

and most accredited works on Theology and Biblical Criticism, both English and Latin, with the contents of which, in spite of his defect of vision, he made himself master to the full extent required by his own special objects of pursuit and research . . . He amused himself with writing Latin verse to the last, and composed a few lines in this language, expressive of the devout tendency of his affections, within a month of his death. English poetry, which had been one of the delights of his youth, lost none of its charms after he grew old. To store his memory with its choicest beauties was a practice that never forsook him. [*Ibid*. p. 444f]

His last deliberate act on his deathbed was to check the printed proofs of a scholarly letter he had written to Dr Scholz defending his own views on a controverted verse in 1 John – Harford records 'With the aid of his man-servant and of Mrs Burgess, he at length accomplished his object, though with great difficulty. With this effort the Bishop resigned every earthly anxiety, and his thoughts became wholly absorbed by religious meditation and prayer.' [*Ibid*. p. 490] It was his last publication: *Three Letters to the Rev. Dr Scholz on the Contents of his Note, on 1 John v. 7, in his Edition of the Greek Testament* which went on sale later that year. What an entirely appropriate way for a Greek scholar to die!

Bathurst marked his 80th birthday by going shooting and bagging a pheasant. His daughter Tryphena described the event and commented on his mental alertness too at that time:

> He was at the time on a visit to his friend, Mr. Coke, at Holkham [a landowning Whig MP]. During a walk he was taking on his birthday with my brother, the General, who had his gun under his arm, my father seeing a fine cock pheasant, could not resist the impulse of the moment, and seizing the gun, he shot the bird dead on the spot – an extraordinary instance of the elasticity of his spirits, as well as of the vigour and strength of his constitution, at that advanced period of his life. On my return to Norwich, a few days after, I had the pheasant stuffed, in order to preserve it as a memorial, I should think unprecedented, of the activity of a Bishop of the age of eighty. His faculties likewise in every respect, and his uncommon memory, he still retained to perfection. You might quote a passage from almost any of the celebrated poets, ancient or modern, and he would not only repeat from memory several lines in continuation, but often whole pages. This may seem like exaggeration, but it is a fact, well known to his family and most intimate friends. [THISTLETHWAYTE *op. cit.* p. 293]

At the age of 83, he was still prepared to travel in winter the long journey to London to cast his vote in the House of Lords or as he termed it 'the

Hospital of Incurables'. In January 1832, aged eighty-eight, he slipped on the step outside his home in Bryanstone Square and fell with great violence against the pavement cutting his head badly and bleeding profusely. Before the surgeon could arrive, he was given a glass of brandy, to which he later said he owed his life. His daughter describes the scene:

> The cut on the temple was very severe, and the side of his head was considerably swollen. One eye was completely closed for several days; and his face was covered with bruises and greatly disfigured. Yet such was his spirit, that no one could persuade him from sitting up that evening and playing his usual rubber of whist, in defiance of the positive injunctions of the medical attendants. [*Ibid.* p. 393]

Later that year, after leaving his proxy vote to be cast in favour of the Reform Bill, he hastened back to Norwich – a three day journey – to ordain fifty candidates! He carried out his last ordination in June 1834, aged ninety. The previous year, Bishop Kaye of Lincoln held confirmations for him in Lynn and Norwich, and Bishop Sumner of Winchester and Blomfield of London also took services on his behalf. Towards the close of July 1835, he made his last appearance in the Lords. Supported by Lord Plunkett, he tottered up to the table and took the oaths, to enable him to leave his proxy in favour of the Government of Lord Melbourne who duly appreciated this 'gallant and spirited act'. [*Ibid.* p. 431]

He lost an old servant who had been in his service for thirty years as butler and valet, the only person he had ever allowed to assist him in dressing, or during the night. Thereafter he refused assistance from anyone much to the alarm of his family and friends. His daughter, Tryphena, describes his closing months in these words:

> For some months before his death he used to say, he would rather go to bed in his clothes than be helped by anybody. For the last year or two of his life, indeed, he would say to any friend who called to see him, "I wish you may be as well as I am, at my age; I am free from pain of body and uneasiness of mind, and I am quite prepared to go, whenever it shall please God, and the sooner the better, though I am very thankful. Now my friend, I must shake hands with you, I am too weak to talk." There were very few with whom he entered into any further conversation, for the last year or two of his life.
>
> [*Ibid.* p. 445]

Given that the average lifespan of a man in England in the early 19th century was probably under sixty, the bishops were exceptionally long-lived.

Bathurst tops the list at 93 followed by Phillpotts at ninety-one, then Harcourt at ninety, nine lived to be octogenarians: Maltby 89, Bethell 86, Howley and Davys 84, Huntingford and Law 83, JB Sumner and Marsh 82, and Burgess 81. A few died comparatively young: Bowstead was just forty-two, Lloyd forty-five, Denison fifty-three and Grey fifty-five.

The death scenes are known of a few of the 'Reform bishops'. Here are a couple of interest. Hilda Stowell, drawing on Thomas Huntingford's autobiography has recorded the death scene of her episcopal forebear. Thomas and his family were making their customary visit to Uncle George in the spring of 1832. The bishop, though unwell (he was nearing eighty-three) was still following his daily routine at Winchester where he had retained his post as Warden in addition to his bishopric.

> After four days of weakness, spending some of the time in bed, he rose up at midday on the Sunday. "He was assisted in putting on his clothes, but washed his head and face himself. His mind was still firm, he knew it was Sunday and put on his usual Sunday dress and wig. After a while he was placed in a chair and carried downstairs to be in the dining room with a nephew on each side of him. He attempted a little episcopal business and finally, he raised himself upright in his chair, his eyes closed; breathed very short, quick and with great effort, for about a minute; and then without more struggle: and I verily believe with no pain whatever, sunk back into the easy composed posture and placid appearance of one calmly sleeping!"
> [STOWELL *op. cit.* p.53]

Bathurst's son, James, the retired general, was at his father's bedside when Henry, the archdeacon son, administered the sacrament to their father for the last time. Henry later recorded this final theological and pastoral exchange between father and son. 'The General asked him more than once, "Do you not believe that we shall meet again, and know each other again in another world?" The Bishop said, "I do; and if I did not feel so, I think I could not be happy."' [BATHURST *Memoir* Vol. 2 chapter 6]

The *Gentleman's Magazine* in its obituary of James Bowstead, the Bishop of Sodor and Man, gave expression to the bizarre belief, held at that time, that the God of love revealed in the life of Jesus deliberately inflicted suffering on faithful Christians – even on bishops – who were then expected to just accept it in obedience to His will!

> In the midst of his usefulness, it pleased God suddenly to visit him with severe bodily affliction, which for the last two years of his life prevented him taking any active part in the administration of his diocese. The closing scene

of the Bishop's life was attended by severe suffering which was borne with the greatest patience and resignation to the Divine will. [*GM* 1842 p. 649]

No retirement

There were no proper arrangements in place to allow a man to retire on a pension, so bishops had to stay on in office long after their 'use by' date. Bathurst had proposed, but without effect, that a coadjutor bishop should be appointed when a diocesan bishop reached the age of seventy. Carey, the Bishop of St Asaph, was in poor health for several years and spent the last two before his death in 1846 at his London home, never visiting his diocese. His essential episcopal duties such as ministering confirmations and ordinations were carried out on his behalf by Thomas Vowler Short, the Bishop of Sodor and Man, who, as a boy, had been at Westminster when Carey was the headmaster. The Bishop of Bangor also helped out with a few confirmations in 1845.

Bathurst spent his closing years mostly in semi-retirement in Great Malvern where his wife was buried, leaving the diocese to be administered by his oldest son, the archdeacon. The son was to experience bitter disappointment when he was not allowed to succeed his father as bishop. Bishop Murray commiserated with him – "That is how the Government rewards its supporters." Law's eldest son likewise acted for his father at Wells but he neither expected to nor did succeed him.

Vernon Harcourt continued in office as archbishop into his ninety-second year when he had an accident whilst out walking with his chaplain in the grounds of Bishopthorpe. As they were crossing a wooden bridge over an ornamental pond, it collapsed plunging both men into the water up to their necks. 'Well Dixon', said the Archbishop, 'I think we've frightened the frogs.' It proved to be his last walk as he died next day.

Blomfield suffered an attack of hemiplegia in the autumn of 1853; eighteen months later his eyesight began to fail and he sought help from a specialist in Grafrath near Düsseldorf who recommended a less stressful life. "Not possible" replied the Bishop. He suffered another stroke in October 1855 which affected his left side and his speech. He recognised that he was no longer able to bear the heavy responsibilities of leading the Church in the most populated diocese in the country. He wished to retire but said he could not afford to do so as he had provided for every needy cause he could during his episcopate and had not accumulated wealth. In effect, he needed a substantial pension. There was an outcry as no clergy were provided with pensions, so why should he be given one? Fortunately, the Prime Minister was sympathetic to his plight and he was allowed by an Act of Parliament to resign his bishopric in 1856, and was permitted to retain Fulham Palace as his residence and given a pension of £6,000 a year! [= £577,143] Maltby had offered to retire in 1855, aged eighty-five and nearly blind, on a £4,500 annuity from the Durham revenues. They were the first bishops permitted to retire since the Reformation. Blomfield died shortly after retirement; his widow lived on for a further thirteen years, dying in 1870 at Richmond. Maltby lived on till 1859, dying at his London residence.

For the last six years of his life, Phillpotts was physically infirm though, as Bishop Samuel Wilberforce, who visited him in 1867, noted 'in full force intellectually'. He was planning to resign the year he died. It was worse for Charles Sumner who was paralysed in speech for six years and 'stricken down by weakness and brought, in various ways, into a painful experience of bodily tribulation. He lost his power of writing, and could only sign his name by copying it from a piece of paper in front of him.' [G.H. SUMNER *op. cit.* p. 478] Wilberforce succeeded him in 1869 but died four years later, a year before Sumner.

When Bishop Bagot was no longer capable of ministering in the diocese of Bath & Wells, the Bishop of Gloucester & Bristol took responsibility for it too, after parliament had passed an Act to that effect.

Wealth + wills

Many of the bishops had substantial financial assets when they died – far more than any twenty-first century bishop or archbishop is ever likely to have. G.W.E. Russell wrote in the DNB that Howley had 'used, without abusing, a princely revenue,' and left £120,000 [= nearly £13 million] in personal bequests when he died in 1848. Davys' estate was put at 'under £80,000', that is about £9,000,000 today. C.R. Sumner left £80,000 and his brother, the archbishop, 'under £60,000'. Archbishop Harcourt left £66,000, Percy £67,000 and Pepys £50,000. Several were noted for their generosity to charitable causes; the ODNB lists Denison, Ryder and C.R. Sumner among them. There were others too.

Blomfield's son says that the average income of the see of London was £15,000 to £16,000 a year, and of this his father 'set apart £5,000 annually to be bestowed in public and private charity, so that during his tenure of the see, he must have given away not much less than £150,000'. That is more than fifteen million pounds sterling in today's terms. One of his clergy said of him, 'Not only was his hand ever open to give largely, his heart was open also to give considerately and feelingly'. [R.BLOMFIELD *op. cit.* p. 85]

Van Mildert poured his episcopal revenues into church-building, parsonage-building, stipend augmentation, and public education. Varley states that 'his correspondence shows many unostentatious gifts to people he considered deserving, even some he considered undeserving. Thorp estimated his private giving at £1,400 per annum, with subscriptions and other known charities accounting for a further £2,600.' [VARLEY *op. cit.* p. 121] Four thousand a year then equates to about £400,000 now. Unfortunately, Van Mildert's servants missed out on legacies intended for them because he had not signed a codicil to his will.

Burgess left his library of 8,000 volumes to St David's College, Lampeter, and sufficient money to build an extension to the library to house them. Howley, too, left his library to his long-serving chaplain, Benjamin Harrison, to assist in the theological studies of the clergy of Canterbury. It formed the nucleus of the Howley-Harrison Library at the cathedral after 1887. Maltby left his library to Durham University.

Carey left £20,000 for the better maintenance of such bachelor students of Christ Church, duly elected from Westminster School, as, 'having their own way to make in the world', shall attend the divinity lectures and prepare themselves for holy orders.

Phillpotts gave £10,000 in 1862 to set up a fund for the augmentation of small livings. In his will he left his books to form the nucleus of a theological library for the clergy of Cornwall and clearly hoped that the diocese of Exeter would be divided at his death and Cornwall would form a new one. That didn't happen until 1877.

Ward, who had one of the poorest sees, still managed to give generously to re-building several churches and chapels on the island, and to the building and establishing of King William's College, claiming thereby in his own words 'I have been able to promote the future prosperity of religion and learning'. He once said that he was the only bishop who would depart his diocese poorer than when he arrived, and that was probably true and a distinction worth noting.

On the other hand, a critic of bishops who amassed wealth, writing in 1836, tells of an Irish bishop who had died in 1826 leaving £120,000 to his children and 'a *poor* Welsh bishop died very recently [presumably Luxmoore], leaving upwards of £100,000 to his heirs.'

One thing is clear from this – whilst some bishops did undoubtedly accrue very large sums of money, not all of them accumulated wealth on earth in preference to treasure in heaven.

An Assessment

This biographical study of the forty-five men who held episcopal office in the Church of England between 1828 and 1840 has, I believe, shown two popular beliefs to be mistaken. The first was the widely held contemporary notion that all the bishops of that time were wealthy, nepotistic, self-indulgent and generally unworthy of the high office they enjoyed, as the comments quoted at the start of the book illustrate. And secondly, the view held by some later historians that there were no good, active, conscientious, reforming bishops before Samuel Wilberforce. It is clear that the qualities and abilities which he displayed as a hardworking, reforming bishop were already to be seen in a good number of the men who held episcopal office in the period under review. And he too, good and great as he was, shared some of the less attractive sides to be seen in some of his predecessors, such as worldly ambition. Arthur Burns argues in his study of *The Diocesan Revival in the Church of England c1800-1870* 'significant diocesan reform had commenced long before Wilberforce's episcopate and formed the context for his own achievement'. [BURNS p. 13] This book provides evidence to support that view.

There were various kinds of more or less contemporary assessments made about the life and ministry of individual bishops. There were the critical ones found in books such as William Carpenter's *A Peerage for the People* published in 1841, the solicitous ones found in the sermons preached at or after their funerals, and the more formally worded ones in some newspapers, which often simply gave the details of their academic achievements and their Church preferments, and those in the pages of the *Gentleman's Magazine*. The latter usually included a comprehensive list of the prelate's publications and some comments on his scholarship and amiable disposition – so even Sparke of Ely is a 'worthy and learned prelate'. Though it is noticeable in Sparke's case that whilst no explicit reference is made to his shameless nepotism, the writer does list the extensive preferments the bishop had bestowed on his two sons. And then there were the uncritical, laudatory ones written often by a son or daughter, such as Dean Stanley's *Memoirs* of his parents and Tryphena Thistlethwaite's of her father, Henry Bathurst. We can make our own assessment based on the accessible evidence of the times.

The best were, in my judgement, and I list them alphabetically: Blomfield, Burgess, Copleston, Kaye, Law, Van Mildert, Otter, Ryder, Stanley, and the two Sumner brothers. **Blomfield** stands head and shoulders above the rest in his ability as an administrator and for his leadership of the Ecclesiastical Commission. The *Gentleman's Magazine* describes him as 'the most conspicuous member of the English prelacy'. He was also probably the most able and fluent public speaker on the bench and made weighty contributions to debates in the Lords. Copleston, who was often a bit critical of his episcopal colleagues, had held Blomfield in high regard ever since first hearing him in the Lords. He wrote in March 1829:

> In my opinion he is decidedly the best speaker there – I think the best *speaker* I ever heard. No preparation – no effort – no declamation – no passion – yet spirited, natural, unfailing in thought or in word – without any distension of period, or embarrassment of language or grammatical inaccuracy. There is a consciousness of power & resources in his manner – a calm intrepidity – and a commanding tone in his delivery which at once marks him as a leader & a champion. [BROWN ed. *op. cit.* p. 68]

On the occasion of his promotion to London, Copleston said of him,

> He is by far the ablest man on the Bench, the only very good speaker, quite a man of business, and as candid, upright, fearless and conscientious a person as I know. He has also a noble spirit as to money . . . He is distinguished by ability, learning, disinterestedness, independence of mind, and an habitual sense of duty, beyond any man I ever met with.
> [A. BLOMFIELD *op. cit.* p. 141]

His first biographer, G.E. Biber, said with justification that no one could possibly deny 'that the history of the Church for the last quarter of a century bears the impress of his character'. B.W. Richardson, writing in 1887, described him as 'a great layman as well as a bishop, and had he, by fate, entered the House of Commons instead of the Church, he would perchance have given England such a Prime Minister as she had never seen before.' [quoted in BROSE *Church and Parliament* p. 95] The *Lincolnshire Herald* in its obituary of him on 11 August 1857 wrote of his unbounded liberality and munificent gifts and then focussed on the huge load of work he had got through daily.

> He was always at work in his study for two hours before breakfast; and day by day would see him occupied with his enormous correspondence, his Clergy, his Committees, his Diocesan and Parliamentary duties, till late in the evening. He was always punctual, laborious, self-denying, and without great method and regularity it would have been impossible for him to perform a third part of the duties he achieved.

The *Morning Post* in its obituary of him on 7 August 1857 stated 'He was one of those who make their way to the highest ecclesiastical dignity, not by private interest or the influence of aristocratic connections, but by sheer hard and persevering labour . . . it is not too much to say that few prelates ever discharged them [i.e. episcopal duties] with equal, and none with superior zeal and earnestness.'

Not all, of course, held him in such esteem. The Unitarian writer, Harriet Martineau, didn't know quite where to place him theologically. She felt that he should have divested himself of some of his wealth and patronage and she mocked his sabbatarianism.

> The Oxford party advocated popular amusements, and on Sundays, after service, as much as other days; and the Bishop of London proclaimed in the Lords the number of boats that went under Putney-bridge on Sundays. This was never forgotten nor forgiven; and the image of the Prelate, in his purple, sitting in his palace at Fulham, counting the people who came for fresh air on their only day of the seven, was often brought forward years after the Bishop himself was suspected of Tractarianism.
> [MARTINEAU *Biographical Sketches* p. 171]

Malcolm Johnson quotes a number of obituary notices in his Life of Blomfield which are inevitably somewhat mixed in their assessment of him. One passage, however, reproduces the views of the three men who had worked most closely with him in the diocese of London and knew him as well as anyone:

> All praised his energy and ability. Archdeacon Sinclair said that an abruptness of manner hid a kind-hearted sensibility, which probably accounts for the popular error of supposing him to be a harsh, stern man. Archdeacon Hale called him 'one of the most simple-hearted of mankind, one of the firmest of friends', and likened him to St Paul, somewhat to the disadvantage of the saint. Both, he said, were scholars and founders of churches, both were pious, charitable, fearless and affectionate but St Paul, unlike Charles James, was a poor speaker. [JOHNSON *op. cit.* p. 150]

Sinclair in a sermon he preached in St Mary Abbots Kensington on the Sunday after Blomfield's death recalled visiting the bishop when he was ill and at a time when he was under attack for the decisions of the Ecclesiastical Commission.

> He explained to me his reasons, and then, suddenly raising himself on his bed, exclaimed with strong emotion, "They now blame me for these meas-

ures. They call these dangerous compromises; but they will hereafter confess that these very measures have been the saving of the Church."
[SINCLAIR *A Sermon: 'He being dead yet speaketh'* p. 16]

Thanks to Blomfield, his successor came into a goodly inheritance – a reorganised and reformed diocese with many more places of worship and many more clergy to minister in them, and many more schools. And all the bishops enjoyed one not insignificant personal blessing thanks to him. On a very hot summer's day in Brighton he let the King know what 'a serious encumbrance' wearing an episcopal wig was. William sent a messenger, 'Tell the bishop that he is not to wear a wig on my account; I dislike it as much as he does, and shall be glad to see the whole bench wear their own hair.' [CHADWICK *op. cit.* p. 134]

Burgess is best remembered for all that he achieved in his twenty-two years in the diocese of St David's, where he made a number of reforms, raising clerical standards and, most notably, founding a clerical training institution which still exists today in the form of St David's University College. The *Gentleman's Magazine* described it as 'an imperishable monument to the activity and munificence of Bishop Burgess in the Principality'. On his translation to Salisbury, clergy and laity in the Archdeaconry of Carmarthen wrote him a letter of appreciation for his ministry, of which the following few lines are a part:

> Your Lordship found the diocese of St David's, in the year 1803, in a most dilapidated state in every view. The churches and ecclesiastical buildings were generally in a ruinous condition; many of the clergy were incompetently educated, and disgraced their profession by ebriety and other degrading vices; but your Lordship, by requiring a strict attention to duty from the Commissaries General and rural Deans, succeeded in restoring the churches in some districts to a state of exemplary neatness; and by submitting to become your own examining chaplain and requiring superior learning and theological knowledge from the candidates for Holy Orders, by enforcing the law against irregularities, and by withholding institution from all who were not competently skilled in the language of their parishioners, your Lordship has gradually furnished the diocese with a body of clergy much superior to that which we ever possessed before. [HARFORD *op. cit.* p. 336f]

It is a worthy assessment of what a bishop, whose first love was classical literature and not national Church affairs or diocesan business, could and did effect in a diocese. Others, however, saw him differently. On his death, Lord Holland described him in his diary as 'that voluminous but obscure pamphleteer and polemick'. Copleston too was critical of Burgess's scholarship but that is not how his Welsh clergy remembered him. Their letter of thanksgiving included these lines about his scholarly writings:

> But this is not all. While your Lordship was occupied in these laborious undertakings, and in attending to the detail of the various minor, yet harassing duties of this too extensive diocese, you were engaged in composing learned works, in answer to the heretical cavils of the enemies of our Church Establishment; and though possessed of deep learning, which qualified you to figure in the first ranks of literature, you wrote numerous familiar religious tracts and catechisms for the instruction of the youth of your diocese.
> [HARFORD op. cit. p. 337]

An historian of Salisbury diocese tactfully noted that Burgess was 'well-stricken in years when he came to us', so past his best but still endowed 'with far-seeing wisdom and open-hearted charity' and active enough to show an especial 'care for his poorer clergy, and those associated with them in the care of the more slenderly-endowed parishes.' He did this by founding and endowing the Salisbury Church Union Society, one of whose objects was 'to help them when in sickness or in trouble, and by grants towards building houses to enable them the more constantly to live in their parishes.' [JONES *Diocesan Histories, SALISBURY* p. 273]

Copleston was generally recognized to have exceptional intellectual ability though he wrote and published little. Roger Lee Brown, who probably knows him best from having transcribed and edited his correspondence, rates him very highly for his pastoral ministry. First noting his willingness to delegate authority to men who were his equals in leadership and ability and his remaining within the diocese over a significant period of time, Brown comments:

> It is clear he made it his business to develop this acquaintance with his clergy, which he seems to have done through his visitations and confirmation tours, his hospitality in his local residences and at London, and his excursions into his diocese. Peter Virgin's comment that 'bishops and incumbents . . . were simply unknown to each other' is untrue for Copleston; not only for incumbents but also for curates. His was an intimate care.
> It is this picture we can see in these letters to Knight and Traherne . . Copleston's leadership of men, his good working relationships with his senior colleagues as well as with his junior clergy, his ability to forge an *esprit de corps* amongst them (as Ollivant, his successor, noted), his courtesy, modesty, encouragement of good clerical practice, linked with his sense of humour, his willingness to set aside the strict interpretation of the law if it was in

the public interest, and a deep concern for each individual, helped erode his paternalism and his antipathy to the Welsh language, and ensured that his achievement in the diocese of Llandaff was as substantial as his more widely recognized achievements at Oriel College. [BROWN ed. *op. cit.* p. 47]

The *Bristol Mercury* in its short obituary of him on 20 October 1859 singled out just one aspect of his ministry for approbation, which it said other bishops could well copy.

> Whenever a living in his gift fell vacant, his lordship invariably made inquiries for the most hard-working and deserving curate under his episcopal jurisdiction, and to him, on due investigation, he made a practice of presenting the living. This circumstance endeared his lordship to the poorer clergy of his diocese, and rendered him extremely popular with the laity also.

Kaye had borne a huge burden with the oversight of the largest number of parishes and clergy of any bishop in the Church of England. At his death in 1853, his obituaries paid tribute to his personal, moral and intellectual qualities, his 'piety, his mild virtues, his gentle manners, his meek and humble deportment' as well as his 'pleasantness of disposition'. His work as a bishop was, however, a more contested area. [AMBLER ed. *op. cit.* p. xvi] A letter from 'A Lincolnshire Man' appeared in the *Morning Chronicle* three days after his death calling for the appointment of 'a *working* bishop' as his successor, someone in the mould of William Broughton, the Bishop of Sydney Australia. He likened Kaye to Lincoln Cathedral 'of the past', 'monumental rather than practical', 'an excellent specimen of a school of bishop of which we do not mind saying that . . . has passed away'. [*Ibid.*] Richard Smith who had been Kaye's legal secretary and joint principal registrar of the diocese since the 1820s leapt to his defence, citing the many improvements during Kaye's episcopate. Clerical non-residence had been reduced by two thirds, aided by the building or rebuilding of 214 parsonage houses, church schools had been built, candidates were better prepared for ordination (those from Cambridge had been required to pass the university's voluntary theological examination), the number of confirmations had been increased and made 'a most solemn and impressive rite', and much more. It may be that the 'Lincolnshire Man' who was so critical was reflecting on Kaye's ministry in his closing years, for the bishop admitted in his last *Charge* in 1852 that he felt he was becoming 'daily less competent' and had greater need of the 'indulgence' of his mistakes by his clergy as well as their support to his 'weakness'. [*Ibid.*] His published parish correspondence shows a bishop much involved in trying to do what was right and best for his clergy in the many difficult pastoral situations brought to his notice. One criticism, however, which may well have been true was that whilst he was good at telling his clergy what they should be doing, he was less good at ensuring they actually did it. Clerical practice did not always follow episcopal precept. But that was probably true in every diocese. Another of his critics, Sydney Smith who was so opposed to the Ecclesiastical Commission, of which Kaye had been a foundation member, said of him unkindly, 'He has the art of saying nothing in many words beyond any man that ever existed.' The *Gentleman's Magazine*, however, praised him for something quite different.

> In the distribution of his patronage, if he had any fault, it is a fault which many in these days will willingly forgive, but which, it is hoped, the friends of the departed prelate will not willingly forget – that, in his impartial and disinterested anxiety to reward what he believed to be the merits of others, he omitted the opportunity of rewarding an exemplary minister whom he most deeply loved, and to whose claims there was but one objection – that he was his own son. [*GM* 1853 p.429]

Law will always be remembered as the founder of the first modern theological college in the Church of England when he was Bishop of Chester. He strove tirelessly to serve and visit even the furthermost and smallest parishes in his vast diocese. Local newspapers, such as the *Whitehaven Gazette*, reported on his daily itinerary when visiting Cumberland and the many practical problems he identified and tackled – from advising on drainage round church buildings to improving the appallingly low stipends of some of the rural clergy he met. What the news reports illustrate is a 'hands-on', engaged, caring bishop. The quotations given earlier from Skinner's journal, which date from his later period as Bishop of Bath & Wells, indicate he remained a deeply caring pastor to his clergy. The *Gentleman's Magazine* described him as being in Church matters a staunch Conservative, as regards the State a Liberal, and, highlighting a not uncommon problem in episcopal old age, said of his later years

> As long as his health lasted, he always performed his episcopal functions with much zeal and assiduity but during his later years at Bath & Wells was unequal to the discharge of his duties and his son, Chancellor Law of Lichfield, was appointed his Special Commissary – when he resigned that the Bishop of Salisbury exercised the full responsibility of both sees. [*GM* 1845]

Otter's achievements as a gentle reformer in such a short episcopate were exceptional. The theological college he helped found was training ordination candidates until 1994 when it was closed. His teacher training college moved into new buildings in 1850 when it was named the 'Bishop Otter College'. Those buildings now form the historical core of the newly established University of Chichester. He is not forgotten locally.

Archdeacon Julius Hare in the introduction to the published edition of his 1840 *Charge* describes it as 'an unintentional panegyric on Bishop Otter'.

> For to him, under God, it is mainly owing, that I have been enabled to talk so hopefully of the prospects of the Church in this Diocese. The new institutions which have risen up amongst us have been his work, and if a new spirit has been kindled in any of us, it will have proceeded in no small measure from him. [HARE *Charge* p. iv]

Earlier on the same page, Hare describes Otter as 'a true Father in his Church. It was a day of sorrow through the Diocese, when tidings reacht [sic] us: many mourned as for a domestic affliction: many felt almost as though they had indeed lost a father.' [*Ibid*.] The *Gentleman's Magazine* noted his achievements but chose to major on his character,

> He had a largeness of hand that was never straightened by a selfish carelessness . . . the same nice regard of the feelings of others rendered easy the most difficult functions of the episcopate. His admonitions were weighty, because they were gentle. He disarmed opposition by forbearance, and won the reluctant by the fairness and equity of his injunctions. There was always about him the true dignity of goodness, which put him above every kind of self-elation . . . to the young, especially of his clergy, he was a father . . . In his whole temper of mind he was a man of peace, and above all things he yearned for the unity of the Church. [*GM* 1840 p. 540]

Ryder is remembered as being the first openly Evangelical cleric to be made a bishop. CMS was in his debt for his willingness to do what no other bishop would do at the time, namely ordain its candidates for holy orders directly for service on the mission field, but his support reached far wider than just Evangelical societies. He was also in his own way an evangelist, frequently setting an example by taking services and preaching in ordinary churches and chapels in order to assist his parochial clergy, and not restricting himself to the big occasions such as confirmations, ordinations and preaching charity sermons. He retained much of the spirit of the diligent parish priest which he had been prior to his preferment.

The *Gentleman's Magazine* praised him for this in particular and commented approvingly on his ministry for twelve years as a parish priest at Lutterworth. Likewise, he discharged his duties of a Christian bishop 'with unwearied zeal and exemplary fidelity. In his pastoral exhortations, as well to the clergy as to all within his charge, "he determined to know nothing among them save Jesus Christ and him crucified".' [*GM* 1836]

Davies in his Tyndale Church History Lecture on Ryder says of him:

> No great scholar or profound theologian, he succeeded in gaining the confidence and affection of his clergy and people to a remarkable degree. Perhaps one of the finest tributes paid to him was from an anonymous writer [in *The Church of England Magazine*] shortly after his death. 'In Christ was all his hope; he was anxious that others should find in Him everlasting peace and security. He had experienced in his own heart the transforming efficacy of the grace of God; he feared that any should mistake amiability of character for real conversion. Prelates there may have been more deeply versed in theology as a science, or who may have shone more brightly in the walks of literary acquirements; but it would be difficult to name one whose heart appeared to be more entirely under the sanctifying influence of divine grace, or who was more anxious to set forth in all their purity, the great fundamental doctrines of the Gospel.
>
> [DAVIES *The First Evangelical Bishop* p. 18]

Stanley had the longest parochial experience of all the bishops and had been an exemplary and much loved pastor. He is a man I warm to. The two letters sent to all his former parishioners in Cheshire after his death (see Appendix 3) show what a care of souls he had exercised there. Following the lethargic Bathurst, he brought new life to the diocese of Norwich – he could hardly fail to do otherwise. One of his chief concerns had always been the education of poor children and he supported it generously and in every other way he could. Even as a bishop he made time to visit in local schools and encourage both teachers and pupils. Coincidentally, shortly before his death he had requested that as large a number of schoolchildren of the poorer classes as possible should attend his funeral – eleven hundred did! The *Gentleman's Magazine* quoted from a sermon Dean Pellew had preached in Norwich Cathedral the Sunday after the bishop's funeral, 'I doubt not that all who were of an age to appreciate his exertions in the cause of education gratefully and feelingly lament the loss of their benevolent friend and benefactor. In the expenditure of his income, the rule to which he adhered was to give away and spend in his diocese all the emoluments he derived from it.' It also noted that the bishop's most popular publication was his *Familiar History of Birds* published in two volumes in 1835. [*GM* 1849 p. 535]

Charles Richard Sumner may have risen to the top simply because of royal favour, but once in office he proved to be an exceptionally hard-working prelate. His son wrote about him and the reforming episcopal movement of which his father was such a prominent member:

> It is not too much to say that, during the term of his tenure of the see, a revolution was effected in the episcopal office. Prelates with wigs, great state, and corresponding haughtiness of manner gave place to real over-seers of the clergy, sympathising in the pastors' struggles, cheering them in their disappointments, counselling them in their difficulties. Bishops Blomfield, Kaye, and the two Sumners were in the van of this movement. The perfunctory discharge of customary duties was felt to be no longer the ideal of perfection to be aimed at. Real hard work was the order of the day.
> [G.H. SUMNER *op. cit.* p. 135]

John Bird Sumner went on to become Archbishop of Canterbury but in the years under review he showed himself to be a hardworking, reforming diocesan bishop with the drive and imagination to encourage new ways of reaching out to the unchurched in the growing industrial centres of Chester diocese. His practice of getting up early each morning in order to pray and study, and lighting his own fires rather than require a servant to do it, suggests he really does deserve his reputation as a simple, humble man of God. Scotland puts it nicely in his biography of Sumner:

> Although he was an able academic, a competent administrator, a lucid writer and a gifted preacher whose sonorous voice and easy manner was eagerly sought after, he was remembered by all, and particularly those in his own diocese, as a saintly, dignified man whose simple lifestyle and gracious manner commended him to everyone of whatever party or station in life.
> [SCOTLAND *op. cit.* p. 127f]

Van Mildert had no sons to educate and set up in life, so he poured his vast episcopal revenues into church-building, parsonage-building, stipend augmentation, and public education. The *Gentleman's Magazine* said of him 'As a theological writer the late Bishop of Durham stands in the first class' and then chose to comment on how he had spent his considerable wealth.

> To his unbounded charity, public and private, every corner of his diocese can bear its testimony. The University of Durham was chiefly formed by his

munificent support. His private charities were supplied with promptitude and delicacy. Princely almost as was his income, his Lordship has died, comparatively speaking, a poor man; and provision for his amiable widow arises chiefly from her beneficial interest in a life policy, now to be realized by his Lordship's demise. [*GM* 1836 p. 426]

Of those who had notable strengths but equally notable flaws, **Phillpotts** is the most obvious one. Opinions about him varied enormously. The *Morning Chronicle* had once referred to him as 'that obscene renegade' and Prime Minister Melbourne described him in a letter to Lord John Russell in 1839 as 'that devil of a bishop, who inspired more terror than ever did Satan'. In that same year an anonymous writer, probably an evangelical churchman, published a short critique of him under the title *The Bishop of Exeter as he is and as he ought to be.* It seems to have been sparked off by a public dispute between Phillpotts and one of his clergy. He wrote,

> I care little upon what particular dogma of church government you have agreed to differ with your rector – but I do come forward to tell you that cause of offence, and just cause too, has been *again* given to the thinking portion of the community, by your Lordship's acts and deeds, in your capacity as a professional minister of the Gospel . . .
> When I come to consider the exalted station your Lordship holds in society – the fearful responsibility you incur, the professional servant of God, the extensive revenues you claim as the reward of your services, I am wholly at a loss to conceive how you can suffer yourself to be carried away by that spirit of worldly pride and intolerant bigotry which has ever characterized your daily walk and conversation. [ANON *The Bishop of Exeter* pp. 3 & 7]

W.J. Conybeare, in an article about Phillpotts published in the *Edinburgh Review* in January 1852, damned him as 'a shrewd and worldly churchman, violent by calculation, intemperate by policy, selfish in his ends, and unscrupulous in his means'. At the other extreme, Baron Bunsen recorded in his *Memoirs*, 'November 20, 1838. Yesterday, was the great day to visit the Bishop of Exeter . . . it is a great delight to talk with a man of such eminent talent.' [DAVIES *op. cit.* p. 154] Davies rates him very highly: 'Loyal and even tender in family relationships; staunch in friendships; violent in controversy; brilliant in debate, he certainly deserves to be commemorated as one of the outstanding figures on the Bench during the nineteenth century.' [*Ibid*. p. 399]

T.S. Evans, a preacher in Durham Cathedral on the Sunday after Phillpotts' funeral paid an eloquent tribute to him, describing him as 'ever zealous for the faith once delivered to us . . . a champion of our beloved church in her catholicity and simplicity . . . He was a master in controversy; and, if wielding this spiritual weapon he encountered much opposition and achieved some unpopularity, surely, if there was blame anywhere, it was often rather the fault of his adversaries than his own.' [quoted in WOLFFE *op. cit.* p. 110]

A later writer summed him up rather neatly in these words:

> The subject of countless stories, always amusing, not always edifying; restlessly active in enforcing discipline; in lawsuits innumerable; a prolific writer of letters and pamphlets; a constant astonishment to onlookers; compelling an unwilling admiration from those who liked him least by the vigour of his utterances and actions; exasperating more often than winning over his foes; and not seldom embarrassing his friends by utterances which they could scarcely defend, and by his championship of causes which had been better left alone. [E.C.S. Gibson *Henry Phillpotts* in COLLINS ed. *Typical English Churchmen from Parker to Maurice* p. 308]

Another controversial bishop was **Marsh**, who was regarded by his old college as 'the foremost man of letters and divine in Cambridge' in his time, 'and the most learned bishop on the bench.' It is sad that he is best remembered for his persistent efforts to prevent Calvinistic evangelicals from serving in his diocese. Carnell says of him, 'Marsh could be dictatorial, legalistic, and short tempered, but he was sensitive to the practical needs of his clergy, especially those whose stipends were hit by the economic recession that followed the Napoleonic wars.' [CARNELL *op. cit.* p. 60] He adds some personal details which make Marsh sound a more attractive man than the 'intolerable bigot' that the *London Magazine* once called him.

> Alongside his conservative Churchmanship co-existed an openness of mind in biblical studies. He would have welcomed the advances in biblical criticism which have been made since his day. His brilliance as a conversationalist, and his skill as a chess player, complemented each other. He liked his pipe too; and if the cathedral sexton, reported in the *Stamford Mercury* of 24 May 1839, is to be believed, 'many hours of the day were thus spent in inhaling Greek and tobacco'. [*Ibid.*]

The *Gentleman's Magazine* said of him, 'As a Bishop he ever showed the greatest attention to his clergy over whom he was placed, and was most prompt and exact in the dispatch of business. As a man, he was liberal in all his views, of great benevolence and remarkable for his friendliness of disposition.' [*GM* 1839] That is not a view that Calvinist clergy and ordinands who wished to minister in his diocese would have shared.

As the two archbishops held the highest office, they deserve mention but the fact that **Howley**, who died in 1848, has had to wait until 2015 for even a modest sized *Life* of him to be published, and **Vernon Harcourt** is still without a biographer is surely a sign of their mediocrity. Howley was Archbishop of Canterbury for twenty years but was accorded little praise, except for his gentleness and attractive character, either by his contemporaries or by later writers. Burgon in his *Lives of Twelve Good Men*, written in 1888, is the exception. There, in his chapter on Hugh James Rose, he describes Howley as 'one of the wisest prelates who ever graced the throne of Augustine . . . His calm and admirable judgement, - clear understanding, - fine tact, never forsook him . . . a great discerner and rewarder of merit: he instinctively attracted to himself good and learned men . . . His special claim to the Church's gratitude is founded on the fact that he presided wisely at the helm during a season of extraordinary trial to the Church, and under the Divine blessing piloted the good ship safely through the storm.' [BURGON *Lives* . . p. 189f] As archbishop, he was certainly by the helm but it was the Bishop of London who was steering the ship. Sir Reginald Blomfield described Howley as 'a pious amiable man, but timid and more anxious to avoid trouble than reform abuses'. [R. BLOMFIELD *op. cit.* p. 52] Not everyone was convinced by his apparent amiability; one observer wrote 'Under the mildest and most conciliatory exterior, it is said by those who know him best, he conceals much of the haughtiness arising from conscious superiority of birth and station'. [GRANT R*andom Recollections of the House of Lords* p. 375f] *The Times* in its obituary said quite bluntly of him 'It can scarcely be said that what fell from his lips ever deserved to be called a speech'. His biographer, James Garrard, however, argues that whilst he was a poor public speaker, he was an effective leader behind the scenes and made a considerable contribution to the reform of the Church in the 1830s. 'When Grey described him as a "poor miserable creature", he was doing an impressive hatchet job on his Reform legislation'. [GARRARD *Archbishop Howley* p. 108] The *Gentleman's Magazine* has a lengthy but muted obituary – this brief extract reflects its diffident tone: 'Generally speaking, he performed the duties of his high office with perfect propriety – not backward to assist public charities, not lukewarm in promoting the efficiency of our ecclesiastical system. Of a gracious, temperate spirit, he neglected few, if any, of the obligations appertaining to his office, and supported its dignity with decent splendour.' [*GM* 1848 p. 427]

A similar assessment is given of Vernon-Harcourt, his fellow archbishop, at York who is damned by faint praise.

> Without using the language of panegyric, it may be said that the deceased prelate bore his high dignities with meekness, exercised the large powers with which the law invested him with as much usefulness and justice as might fairly be expected from a man of moderate learning and average intellect, and dispensed the great patronage with which a long episcopal life furnished him in a manner which, if it calls for no extraordinary applause, ought certainly to escape from any kind of censure beyond that which attaches to a little more nepotism than in modern times is sanctioned by the practice of men in high places. [*GM* 1848 p. 82]

Greville described him as 'the most prosperous of men, full of professional dignities and endowments . . . he lived in the exercise of magnificent hospitality and surrounded with social enjoyments' – to which Sir Reginald Blomfield adds 'the very last man to reform anything.' [R. BLOMFIELD *op. cit.* p.70] Tindall Hart in his history of the Archbishops of York says, 'It has generally been accepted that he was a sweet-tempered, gentle person; but some nineteenth century memoirs suggest other less desirable characteristics: a quarrelsome temper, and the development of an awe-inspiring, not to say terrifying presence, in his old age.' [TINDALL HART *op. cit.* p. 160]

George Davys was another episcopal mediocrity. He merits few words of praise from anyone. Melbourne had not wished to confer a bishopric on him. He is variously described as 'a simple, safe parson' [Johnson], 'plain, honourable, good-hearted, unintelligent, undistinguished' [Chadwick] yet the fact remains, that as Victoria's chief tutor for fifteen years when she was a child, he had a life-long influence on her religiously. And when Victoria's mother asked Bishops Blomfield and Kaye in 1831 to assess whether she was being given an education fit for a future queen, they reported very positively after examining her. 'The Princess displayed an accurate knowledge of the most important features of Scripture, History, and of the leading truths and precepts of the Christian Religion as taught by the Church of England.' [JOHNSON *op. cit.* p. 40f] Chadwick has more to say on Davys's preferment and record as a bishop:

> But when newspapers used the neglect of Davys as evidence of Melbourne's atheistical influence, it became even Melbourne's interest to prefer him. On these dubious grounds Davys became Bishop of Peterborough, where he was universally liked, where he steadily promoted his relatives to be canons

of the cathedrals, and where his record of votes was not what Whig ministers could wish. He lived a long time, peacefully and thriftily and without exertion, and when at last he died the *Times* remarked ambiguously: 'His ambition through life was rather to be good than great. Higher praise it is impossible to bestow.' [CHADWICK *op. cit.* p. 161]

Carnell observes, 'No controversies, like those that enlivened Herbert Marsh's episcopate, ruffled the calm of George Davys' twenty-five years as bishop.' His ministry was not without good effect for he had a simple style of writing and some of his educational tracts and two books of *Village Conversations* proved to be very popular and went through several editions. The *Gentleman's Magazine* was less positive in its assessment of them – 'His Lordship took no active part in religious controversy, and never evinced warm interest in political questions . . . He was an elegant and useful but unambitious writer and compiled various educational works.' [*GM* 1864]

Given his poor start in life, **Ward** rose high but not as high as the House of Lords as the Bishop of Sodor and Man did not have a seat there. The Principal of King William's College, Douglas gave a brief assessment of his late bishop in a letter of condolence he wrote to Mrs Ward: 'Poor Mona! [i.e. Isle of Man] She has lost in her late Bishop such a hearty and active friend, she will not soon look upon his like again. There can be no doubt, under God, he saved her Bishoprick, and in that saved her no one can tell what future blessings'. [WILSON *op. cit.* p. 211] This is a fair assessment for it was whilst suffering from cataracts in both eyes, near blind, and dependent on an amanuensis that he rallied support across the country to reverse the decision of the Ecclesiastical Commission to merge the diocese with Carlisle after his death. He succeeded, and it still exists today as does King William's College which he founded. The *Gentleman's Magazine* also praised him for this - 'How he learnt to perform his duty, and how his labours have been blessed, that Island, formerly so miserably poor in its consecrated buildings, but now studded with beautiful and even stately Churches, can but tell.' [*GM* 1838]

Bishops were not always kind in their judgements about one another – Copleston in particular was sharply critical about several of his colleagues in his private correspondence, as BROWN's transcriptions have revealed. Burgess, he said, had 'a total absence of critical acumen & discrimination, joined to childish credulity'; Van Mildert, in his judgement, 'was rather a common place Divine – with little originality of thought, or power of illustration'; of Thirlwall, he wrote, 'I remember reading his introduction to Schleiermacher's St Luke - & that certainly left no impression on your mind that he was a Believer in our sense of the word. I hope, like many other rationalists, he has seen his error long ago.'

Bathurst was awarded a kinder account by Lord Holland as he had 'left little property, a pure and unblemished name for disinterested benevolence and liberality' but he had also left 'two or three mad and unreasonable sons'. Presumably a reference in particular to Archdeacon Bathurst's bitter and public disappointment at not succeeding his father. That same son was not uncritical in his assessment of his father's episcopate:

> It could also have been wished, that in his society he had mixed more with the clergy, and especially if of an evening he had had conversation parties of the city clergy instead of a game of whist; and if he had, like Bishop Burnett, made it his business to visit among the county clergy, many of whom, being in easy circumstances, would have been pleased and delighted to receive him; and by means of which visiting he might have become more particularly acquainted with most things as connected with the diocese; from which it must be also admitted, that it will be wished he had kept his oft repeated resolutions not more to absent himself. [BATHURST *Memoir* vol. 2]

Among the less prominent members of the bench was **Hugh Percy**. His obituary notice in the *Carlisle Patriot* on 9 February 1856 reveals two quite different sides to the man. Not unexpectedly given his aristocratic background, he was not remembered as having been an approachable pastoral figure:

> His manner was polished and courteous, but far removed from familiarity. Few of the clergy were admitted to his society, most of them only met him on public occasions, yet no one had reason to complain of a mere want of polite reception... In some things he may have been deemed hard to deal with and dictatorial, especially by those who did not know him well and had not studied his manner. [BOUCH *op. cit.* p. 387]

On the other hand, the same writer considered him an example of what a parish priest should be:

> He frequently officiated most unostentatiously for the neighbouring Clergy when necessarily absent . . . and even within a few days of his death visited the sick in the parish of Dalston [a couple of miles from Rose Castle] and in the absence of the vicar had administered the Sacrament to the old and infirm. He was of the High Church, but no Tractarian and set not his affection on medieval frippery; he stood aloof from that and equally so from the disorganised portion of the Church, who descend so low in the case of discipline as to be indistinguishable from dissenters. [*Ibid.*]

The Percy papers in the Cumbria Archvives Centre include an obsequious letter written to him which may illustrate the tone of address that an aristocratic bishop expected from his inferiors. It begins 'We the Dean and Chapter of the Cathedral Church of Carlisle, deeply sensible of the many advantages we especially enjoy under your Lordship's mild and paternal superintendence, are anxious to present to your Lordship our heartfelt congratulations on the second merciful interposition of Providence in shielding you from the danger of a most severe and alarming illness, and restoring you once more to the blessings of renewed health and strength.' [CUMBRIA ARCHIVES DX 1398/4]

There were others who, by the standards of the late eighteenth/early nineteenth centuries, did a reasonable job: Joseph Allen of Bristol then Ely, Robert Gray of Bristol, J.H. Monk of Gloucester and Edward Maltby of Chichester and then Durham are examples of this kind. The first three were old fashioned, conservative high churchmen and not overly keen to see reforms. The *Gentleman's Magazine* says of **Allen**

> He was not a man of showy talents, or remarkably ambitious of literary distinction, nor did he place himself in the front ranks of any party, either in Church or State, but he was never backward in the performance of the duties of his Station, whenever the progress of legislation in matters ecclesiastical called for his active interference. . . Recently when two Fellowships, one at St John's, the other at Jesus College, became vacant, his Lordship showed his desire of rewarding academical merit by throwing them open as prizes for general competition; and in the disposal of his Church patronage, he was manifestly influenced by the same disinterested and honourable motives. [*GM* 1845]

Gray's earlier ministry at Bishopwearmouth was commended by the same journal - 'He made the poor of the district his peculiar care, and many who had seen better times had reason to rejoice in his well-timed bounty.' And the writer rated him highly as a bishop:

> His death is a serious blow to the Established Church. Of all the bishops, the Bishop of Bristol, was perhaps the most distinguished for his high and unshaken principles, his cool and immoveable courage. His conduct at the burning of his palace has immortalised his name . . . on the very day when the city of Bristol was in flames around him, the Bishop preached a sermon of singular excellence . . . Unmoved amid the madness of the people, and of the tempest which was bursting around him, he regarded his life less valuable than the duty he owed God. [*GM* 1834 p. 646]

It also noted that there was no mitre on the bishop's coffin as it had been kept in the palace and consequently destroyed in the fire caused by the rioting mob.

About **Monk**, the *Gentleman's Magazine* declared 'In fact, though a clear thinker and fluent writer, he was but a second-rate orator at the best.' It did have some positive things to say too.

> In religious matters, though a sound and attached Churchman, he observed a safe and cautious line, as his easy and open nature probably inclined him; his favour, however, was generally shewn to the High Church rather than the Evangelical party . . . [he] regularly devoted a tithe of his income to the augmentation of small livings in his diocese. He contributed also considerable sums towards the restoration of churches, the building of parsonages, and of parochial and diocesan schools. [*GM* 1856]

The writer noted too that Monk had suffered from partial blindness for many years which the bishop felt impeded him in carrying out his episcopal duties.

The *Gentleman's Magazine* claimed that **Maltby** belonged to the Evangelical school, though that is a questionable statement, and regarded him as 'one of the greatest scholars of the age' and 'a zealous friend of Durham University' where he had instituted prizes to be competed for. It said that he had arranged with his family for the transfer of his own most valuable library to the university as a memorial of his regard, and especially to encourage and assist students of classical literature.

So much for the best of the bench – sadly, others are remembered for the wrong reasons, among them Sparke of Ely and John Luxmoore of St Asaph. Both proved to be highly successful simply at enriching their sons.

A couple of assessments about the period illustrate, on the one hand, the good work done by individual bishops; and, on the other, the challenge that bishops in rural dioceses faced but with varying degrees of success. First, Professor Gash notes that the *essentials* of the Establishment had survived all the threats and challenges of the 1830s: the *Anglican* Monarchy created by the Act of Settlement; the participation of bishops in the House of Lords; the inalienable claim of the Church to its ecclesiastical property – all these criteria were still in existence at the end of the decade. [GASH *op. cit.* p. 116] It is not too much to claim that Blomfield among the bishops and Peel among the politicians were the saviours of Church establishment. Secondly, W.R. Ward wrote in a paper published in the *Journal of Ecclesiastical History* in 1965: 'The real tragedy for the Church in this period, it may be argued, was not that industrialisation concentrated people where her endowments, manpower and accommodation were thinly spread, but that things went so badly where her resources were concentrated.' [WARD *op. cit.* p. 67] This 'tragedy' has been amply illustrated in this book – rural parishes without a resident incumbent or a curate as there was no fit parsonage or because the incumbent was a pluralist and lived elsewhere, or poorly paid temporary curates leading a single service on a Sunday and then rushing off to take another elsewhere, and rarely visiting the parishioners to get to know them. The almost inevitable consequence was that parishioners either abandoned their church and joined the Dissenters in their chapels or ceased to attend worship anywhere. We have seen how some bishops tried to enforce residence and assisted in the building or repair of parsonages, and insisted on two services with a sermon each Sunday, and thereby in some places the decline in church membership was reversed.

Though the Church of England was in far better shape by 1840 than it had been in 1828 thanks to the reforms of that period, much still needed to be done as is evident from a letter Hook wrote to Archdeacon Samuel Wilberforce in July 1843. The latter was intending to make a speech about the education of factory children and wrote asking for Hook's advice about any points he thought might be useful. The reply he got must have given him quite a shock. Hook did not think it was right for the Church to be asking the State for financial support 'when the money is to be supplied by Dissenters and infidels and all classes of the people.' In his view the Church should be entirely responsible for the education of the people and should pay for it itself. For Wilberforce, soon to become a bishop, Hook's words must have come as something of a cold shower:

> If we are to educate the people in Church principles, the education must be out of church funds. I would not have the State take away the funds of the Church, but I would have the Church make an offer of them. We want not proud Lords, haughty Spiritual Peers, to be our Bishops. Offer four thousand out of their five thousand a year for the education of the people, and call upon the more wealthy of the other clergy to do the same, and a fund is at once provided. Let Farnham Castle and Winchester House and Ripon Palace be sold, and we shall have funds to establish other Bishoprics. Let the Church do something like this, and *then* the Church will live in the hearts of the people who now detest her...
>
> You see I am almost a Radical, for I do not see why our Bishops should not become poor as Ambrose or Augustine, &c., &c., that they may make the people truly rich. [STRANKS *op. cit.* p. 75f]

In Hook's judgement, the bishops were not living up to his high ideal of episcopacy but, on the other hand, most of them were clearly not as bad as their radical critics and the enemies of the Establishment had made them out to be.

Bishop John Utterton, preaching in 1874 on the death of Charles Sumner, contrasted the state of the Church when Sumner had been called to the Episcopate in 1824.

> God forbid that I shall exalt one good man at the expense of others . . . but still I say, that the name of CHARLES RICHARD SUMNER with that of his noble hearted, unaffected, pious and able brother will ever stand out in the annals of our Church as of those who were among the first to rise up to a true sense of their opportunities, to the duties and responsibilities of their positions as chief fathers of the Church of God. [UTTERTON *op. cit.* p. 10]

This is true but the Sumner brothers were just two of many bishops in their generation who rightly deserve such praise.

Appendix 1
Episcopal Stipends

The details are taken from the 1st Report of the Ecclesiastical Commission dated 16 June 1835 and give an average figure for the three years 1829-31. Using the Bank of England's Inflation Calculator, the equivalent purchasing value in 2014 of these stipends is noted in brackets.

Details of the *in commendam* posts held by eleven bishops are given on the next page.

		In commendam income
Canterbury	£19,182 (= £ 1,777,415)	
Durham	19,066 (= £ 1,766,666)	
London	13,989 (= £ 1,296,228)	
York	12,629 (= £ 1,170,210)	
Winchester	11,151 (= £1,033,258)	
Ely	11,105 (= £ 1,028,995)	
Worcester	6,569 (= £ 608,667)	
St Asaph	6,301 (= £ 583,854)	
Bath & Wells	5,946 (= £ 550,960)	
Norwich	5,395 (= £ 499,904)	
Lincoln	4,542 (= £ 420,864)	
Bangor	4,464 (= £ 413,637)	
Chichester	4,229 (= £ 391,861)	
Salisbury	3,989 (= £ 369,623)	
Lichfield	3,923 (= £ 363,507)	£1,500 (= £138,991)
Chester	3,261 (= £ 302,166)	£813 (= £75,333)
Peterborough	3,103 (= £ 287,526)	
Exeter	2,713 (= £ 251,388)	£565 (= £ 52,353)
Oxford	2,648 (= £ 245,365)	£6,036 (= £599,299)
Sodor & Man	2,555 (= £ 236,748)	£978 (= £90,622)
Hereford	2,516 (= £ 233,134)	
Bristol	2,351 (= £ 217,845)	£687 (= £63,6658)
Gloucester	2,282 (= £ 211,451)	£2,125 (= £196,904)
Carlisle	2,213 (= £ 205,058)	£1,027 (= £95,162)
St David's	1,897 (= £ 175,777)	£3,266 = (£302,629)
Rochester	1,459 (= £137,972)	£2,840 (= £263,156)
Llandaff	924 (= £ 85,618)	£2,965 (= £274,739)

Several Bishops received income from other offices which they held *in commendam* but which were not permanently annexed to their sees:

Bristol held a Canonry at Durham worth £687 p.a. (= £ 63,658)
Carlisle held the Chancellorship of Salisbury Cathedral £1,027 p.a. (= £ 95,162)
Chester held a Canonry at Durham £813 p.a. (= £ 75,333)
St David's held the Deanery of Durham £3,266 p.a. (= £ 302,629)
Exeter held a Canonry at Durham £565 p.a. (= £ 52,353)
Gloucester held a Prebend at Westminster £1.500 p.a. (= £ 138,991) and the benefice of Peakirk £625 p.a. (= £ 57,913)
Lichfield held a Prebend at Westminster £1,500 (= £ 138,991)
Llandaff held the Deanery of St Paul's £2,965 p.a. (= £ 274,739)
Oxford held the Deanery of Canterbury £2,000 p.a. (= £ 185,321), plus the benefice of Blithfield £3,288 p.a. (= £ 304,668) and the benefice of Leigh £748 p.a. (= £ 69,310)
Rochester held the Deanery of Worcester £1,600 p.a. (= £ 148,257) and the benefice of Bishopsbourne £1,240 (= £ 114,899)
Sodor & Man held a Prebend at Salisbury £12 p.a. (= £ 1,112), plus the benefice of Great Horkesley £609 p.a. (= £ 56,430), and the benefice of Alphamstone £357 (= £ 33,080)

The Established Church Act of 1836 set episcopal stipends at new levels on the death of the current holders –
Archbishop of Canterbury	£15,000 [= £1,530,300]
Archbishop of York	£10,000
Bishop of London	£10,000
Bishop of Durham	£ 8,000
Bishop of Winchester	£ 7,000

A fund was established to set the incomes of other bishops at not less than £4,000 nor more than £5,000.

Appendix 2
Population & Benefices of the Dioceses taken from the Returns of 1831

These details were published as an Appendix in J.H. Newman's pamphlet on *The Restoration of Suffragan Bishops Recommended* 1835

Diocese	Population	Benefices
Chester	1,883,958	616
London	1,722,685	577
York	1,496,538	828
Lichfield	1,045,481	623
Lincoln	899,468	1,273
Exeter	795,416	607
Winchester	729,607	389
Norwich	690,138	1,076
Durham	469,933	175
Canterbury	405,272	343
Bath and Wells	403,795	440
Salisbury	384,683	408
St David's	358,451	451
Gloucester	315,512	283
Worcester	272,687	232
Chichester	254,460	266
Bristol	232,026	255
Hereford	206, 327	326
Peterborough	194,339	305
Rochester	191,875	93
St Asaph	191,156	160
Llandaff	181,244	194
Bangor	163,712	131
Oxford	140,700	208
Carlisle	135,062	128
Ely	133,722	156

Lord Henley's pamphlet *A Plan for a new arrangement and increase in number of the dioceses in England & Wales* published in 1834 provides a slightly different set of diocesan statistics but also based on information available in 1831. Neither Henley nor Newman lists Sodor and Man.

Appendix 3
Bishop Edward Stanley
ADDRESS TO MY PARISHIONERS

The God in whose presence I now stand knows how deeply I was interested in your welfare, and how earnestly I sought to bring everyone who heard me to a knowledge of the Gospel. While life was granted, such was my desire; in the hour of death, it will still be my wish. Accept then, from the grave, the last Address you will ever receive from a Minister who would meet you again in a better world. The time will shortly arrive (you know not how soon) when you will be called upon to follow me. Are you prepared? Have you endeavoured to prepare, with due earnestness, for your eternal summons? It is an awful thing to depart from life – to be separated, in a moment, from all that occupied or interested us here below. What is the world now to me? My days are past like a dream – the eternal world is now before me. And soon shall it be thus with you. Your life is as a vapour, and quickly it passeth away. But the record of your good or evil shall appear again, for or against you. From the grave I put the question: What has been your life? Have I been the instrumental means of increasing your faith, and preparing those committed to my charge for the great change which I have undergone? Or, heedless of the advice it was my wish and duty to give, have you lived from hour to hour, from day to day, indifferent to the future, and thoughtless as to the things that shall come hereafter? If such has been your course, let me not speak from the grave in vain. I speak for your eternal good – for the salvation of your souls – while time and opportunity are still within your reach. But if some were indifferent, all were not. Some amongst you were steady and faithful followers of that Saviour who, in life, was my hope, and in the grave is my dependence. If, as a departed spirit, I am permitted to look upon the scenes in which so great a portion of my mortal course was spent, with what pleasure shall I behold you going on to that perfection which awaits the true Christian in heaven! In life I knew and loved you; in death I would not be divided. My dear parishioners, may we meet again to commence a closer and dearer connexion, as angels of God, in the world of blessed spirits.

Farewell!

EDWARD STANLEY

ADDRESS TO THE SCHOOL CHILDREN

MY DEAREST CHILDREN

When I lived, I loved you as a parent, and I spared no pains to make you good and happy. Now I am gone down to the grave, and you will see me, you will hear me, no more. But, though dead, I would yet speak. Forget not then the parting words of one who so earnestly wished for your present and eternal welfare. When I lived, I spoke to you often of God and of your Saviour. You will soon be called from the world to follow me, and then you will, I hope, feel how blessed a thing it was to have known and served them. In life you can see them only with the eye of Faith – in death you will behold them as they really are. So live, then, that you may look forward to the hour of your departure as to an hour which shall place you in a state of everlasting happiness. If you would thank me for the pains I bestowed upon you when on earth, show that thankfulness by the purity of your lives. Attend to the following short rules, and God grant we may meet again in heaven, where you may rejoice in having done so.

Pray to God morning and evening. Prayer, like a ministering angel, if rightly offered, will guard you from sin in the hour of temptation.

Watch over your words and actions; for God is a witness to all you say and do.

Reverence the Sabbath; keep it as a Christian ought to keep it. A holy Sabbath is the parent of a holy week; and holy weeks shall end in a holy immortality.

EDWARD STANLEY

Bishop Stanley wrote these two letters about a year before his removal from the parish of Alderley to the see of Norwich. He countersigned them about seven years afterwards, with a request that a copy of each might be sent after his death to every house in the parish and to each of his former school-children.

Bibliography

Principal Manuscript Sources
Bodleian Libraries: Correspondence of Bishops Copleston, Shuttleworth, Burgess, Bagot, and Lloyd.
British Library: Liverpool Papers, Peel Papers, Bishop Samuel Butler Papers.
Trinity College Cambridge Library: Several letters of Bishops Allen, Bathurst, Blomfield, Burgess, Kaye, Maltby, Marsh, Otter, Stanley and C.R. Sumner.
Cumbria Record Office: Bishop Percy Papers
Durham University Library: Bishop Van Mildert and Thorp Papers
Exeter Cathedral Library: Bishop Phillpotts papers
Lambeth Palace Library: Bishop Blomfield Papers and Archbishop Howley Papers.
Llandaff Cathedral Archives: Bishop Copleston Papers

Hansard's Parliamentary Debates 3rd Series
Vol. XXXII of Accounts and Papers, 1854 contains General Index to Bills 1801-1852 pp.104ff Ecclesiastical Affairs, and General Index to Reports of Select Committees, 1801-1852, pp. 95ff
First Report of H.M.'s Commissioners appointed to consider the state of the Established Church, June 16 1835
Second Report March 10 1836
Third Report May 20 1836
Fourth Report June 30 1836
Fifth Report March 6 1837

Periodicals
The British Critic and Quarterly Theological Review 1827-43
The British Magazine and Monthly Register of Religious and Ecclesiastical Information 1832-49;
Christian Remembrancer 1819-1840
The Gentleman's Magazine 1828-1875
The Record 1828 onwards

Biographies & Memoirs of Bishops (in alphabetical order)

Bathurst H.	Memoirs of the late Dr Henry Bathurst	1837
Card H.	A Sermon on the occasion of the Death of Henry, Lord Bishop of Norwich	1837
Thistlethwayte T.	Memoirs & Correspondence of Dr Henry Bathurst	1853
Linnell C.	Some East Anglian Clergy (chapter 8 deals with Bishop Bathurst and his eldest son)	1961
Hanekamp J.C.	An Appeal for Life: the Life of Dr Henry Bathurst	1992
Biber G.E.	Bishop Blomfield and his Times	1857
Sinclair J.	"He being dead yet speaketh" A Sermon on the Death of Charles James Blomfield	1857
Blomfield A.F.	A Memoir of C.J. Blomfield 2 vols.	1863
Martineau H.	Biographical Sketches pp. 167-174	1869
Blomfield R.T.	Memoir of C.J. Blomfield: Bishop of London 1828-56	1935
Johnson M.	Bustling Intermeddler? The Life & Work of C.J. Blomfield	2001
Harford J.S.	Life of Thomas Burgess	1840
Price D.T.W.	Bishop Burgess and Lampeter College	1987
Moore H.	A sermon on the death of Samuel Butler	1839
Bather E.	A sermon . . . Samuel Butler	1840
Butler S.	Life & Letters of Dr Samuel Butler, Head-Master of Shrewsbury School 1798-1836, and afterwards Bishop of Lichfield 2 vols.	1896
Percival A.C.	Very Superior Men (ch 4 is about Samuel Butler of Shrewsbury)	1973
Copleston W.J.	Memoir of Edward Copleston with Selections from his Diary and Correspondence	1851
Whately R.	Remains of the late Edward Copleston . . . containing some Reminiscences of his Life	1854
Tuckwell W.	Pre-Tractarian Oxford: a reminiscence of the Oriel "Noetics" (Ch 2 is about Copleston)	1909
Brown R.L. ed.	The Letters of Edward Copleston, Bishop of Llandaff, 1828-1849	2003
Dark S.	Seven Archbishops (Howley pp.185-191)	1944
Carpenter E.	Cantuar: The Archbishops in their Office (William Howley pp. 290-99)	1971
Stephenson A.M.G.	The Victorian Archbishops of Canterbury	1991

Bellenger D.A. & Fletcher S.	The Mitre and the Crown: A History of the Archbishops of Canterbury	2005
Garrard J.	Archbishop Howley 1828-48	2015
Stowell H.M.	George Isaac Huntingford	1970
Kaye J.	Works. (With a memoir of the author)	1888
Ambler R.W. ed.	Lincolnshire Parish Correspondence of John Kaye Bishop of Lincoln 1827-53	2006
Baker W.J.	Beyond Port & Prejudice: Charles Lloyd of Oxford	1981
Ives C.	Sermons on several Occasions and Charges, to which is prefixed a Memoir of William Van Mildert	1838
Varley E.A.	The last of the Prince Bishops: William Van Mildert	1992
Holtby R.T.	Bishop William Otter	1989
Anon	The Bishop of Exeter [Phillpotts] as he is and as he ought to be	1839
Shutte R.N.	The Life, Times and Writings of the Rt Rev Henry Phillpotts, Lord Bishop of Exeter	1863
Davies G.C.B.	Henry Phillpotts, Bishop of Exeter 1778-1869	1954
Ryder T.D. ed.	A Memoir of Henry Ryder	1886
Davies G.C.B.	The first Evangelical Bishop: Some Aspects of the Life of Henry Ryder	1958
Stanley A.P.	Addresses & Charges of the Rt Revd Edward Stanley with a Memoir	1851
Stanley A.P. ed.	Memoirs of Edward and Catherine Stanley 2nd ed.	1879
Utterton J.S.	In Memoriam. Charles Richard Sumner	1874
Sumner G.H.	Life of Charles Richard Sumner, Bishop of Winchester	1876
Coombs J.	George & Mary Sumner: Their Life and Times	1965
Scotland N.	The Life & Work of John Bird Sumner	1995
Thirlwall J.C.	Connop Thirlwall, Historian and Theologian	1936
C of E Diocese of Sodor & Man	Sixty Years ago: an Eventful Episcopate. How the Diocese of Sodor & Man was saved [An Account of the last Days of Bishop William Ward]	1896
Wilson E.C.	An Island Bishop: Memorials of William Ward, Bishop of Sodor & Man 1828-1838	1931
Watson R.	Anecdotes of the Life of Richard Watson	1817

Carnell G.	The Bishops of Peterborough 1541-1991	1993
Fitzpatrick W.J.	Memoirs of Richard Whately with a glance at his Contemporaries and times 2 vols.	1866
Collins W.E. ed.	Typical English Churchmen. From Parker to Maurice pp. 299-327 are about Phillpotts	1902
Bouch M.L.	Prelates and People of the Lake Counties	1948
Tindal Hart A.	EBOR: A History of the Archbishops of York	1986
Scotland N.	'Good and Proper Men': Lord Palmerston & the Bench of Bishops	2000
Brown R.L.	In Pursuit of a Welsh Episcopate	2005

Charges 1828-1840

Allen J.	A Charge delivered to the Clergy of the Diocese of Bristol at the Primary Visitation	1835
	A Charge delivered to the Clergy of the Diocese of Ely	1837
Bagot R.	A Charge addressed to the Clergy of the Diocese of Oxford	1834
	A Charge addressed to the Clergy of the Diocese of Oxford	1838
Bethell C.	A Charge delivered at the Triennial Visitation of the Diocese of Gloucester	1828
	A Charge delivered to the Clergy of the Diocese of Bangor in September 1834	1834
Blomfield C.J.	A Charge delivered to the Clergy of the Diocese of Chester	1825
	A Charge addressed to the Clergy of the Diocese of London	1830
	A Charge addressed to the Clergy of the Diocese of London	1834
	A Charge addressed to the Clergy of the Diocese of London	1838
Burgess T.	Primary Principles of the Christianity and the Church: A Charge addressed to the Clergy of the Diocese of Salisbury	1829
	A Charge addressed to the Clergy of the Diocese of Salisbury	1832
Butler S. (Archdeacon)	Charges delivered to the Archdeaconry of Derby in 1827,29,30,31,33,34,35	

Butler S.	A Charge delivered to the Clergy of the Diocese of Lichfield & Coventry, at his Primary Visitation	1836
Chandler G. (Dean)	A Charge to the Clergy of the Deanery of Chichester	1832
Copleston E.	A Primary Visitation Charge to the Clergy of the Diocese of Llandaff	1830
	Charge to the Clergy of the Diocese of Llandaff	1833
	Charge to the Clergy of the Diocese of Llandaff	1836
	Church Discipline and National Education. Charge to the clergy of the Diocese of Llandaff	1839
Dealtry W. (Chancellor of Winchester)	The Church and its Endowments: a Charge	1831
	A Charge delivered in the Autumn of 1834 at the Visitation in Hampshere	1835
	Obligations of a National Church: a Charge	1838
Denison E.	A Charge delivered to the Clergy of the Diocese of Salisbury, at his primary visitation	1839
Gray R. A	Charge delivered to the Clergy of the Diocese of Bristol in June-July 1831	1831
Hare J.C. (Archdeacon)	The Better Prospects of the Church: a Charge to the Clergy of the Archdeaconry of Lewes, delivered at the Visitation in 1840	1840
Howley W.	A Charge delivered to the Clergy of the Diocese of Canterbury at his Primary Visitation	1832
	A Charge delivered to the Clergy of the Diocese of Canterbury	1840
Jenkinson J. B.	A Charge to the Clergy of the Diocese of St. David's at the primary visitation	1828
	A Charge delivered to the Clergy of the Diocese of St. David's, at the visitation ... in 1836	1836
Kaye J.	A Charge delivered at the Primary Visitation to the Clergy of the Diocese of Lincoln	1828
	A Charge delivered at the Triennial Visitation	1831
	A Charge delivered at the Triennial Visitation	1834
	A Charge delivered at the Triennial Visitation	1837
	A Charge delivered at the Triennial Visitation	1840
Law G. H.	The spiritual duties of a Christian Minister. A charge delivered to the Clergy of the Diocese of Bath and Wells in July	1828
	A Charge delivered to the Clergy of the Diocese	

	of Bath and Wells in May and June 1831	1831
	A Charge delivered to the Clergy of the Diocese of Bath and Wells	1837
Longley C.	A Charge delivered to the Clergy of the Diocese of Ripon, at the primary visitation	1838
Lyall W. (Archdeacon)	The Nature & true Value of Church Property examined, in a Charge delivered to the Clergy of the Archdeaconry of Colchester	1831
	Sentiments of the Clergy on the Question of Church Reform briefly stated. A Charge delivered to the Clergy of the Archdeaconry of Colchester	1833
	A Charge delivered to the Clergy of the Archdeaconry of Colchecter.	1837
Maltby E.	A Charge delivered to the Clergy of the Archdeaconry of Chichester at the Primary Visitation . . . to which are added, directions for candidates for Holy Orders in that Diocese	1834
	A Charge delivered to the Clergy of the Diocese of Durham at the Primary Visitation	1837
Marsh H.	A Charge delivered to the Clergy of the Diocese of Peterborough, on the influence of the Roman Catholic question on the Established Church	1827
	A Charge in July, 1831 ... to the Clergy of the Diocese of Peterborough	1831
Mildert W. Van	A Charge delivered to the Clergy of the Diocese of Durham in 1827	1828
	A Charge delivered to the Clergy of the Diocese of Durham	1831
	A Charge delivered to the Clergy of the Diocese of Durham 2nd ed.	1832
	Sermons on several occasions, and Charges	1838
Monk J.H.	A Charge to the Clergy of the Diocese of Gloucester, ... at the primary visitation	1832
	A Charge delivered to the Clergy of the Diocese of Gloucester	1835
	A Charge delivered to the Clergy of the Diocese of Gloucester	1838
Otter W.	A Charge delivered to the Clergy of the Diocese of Chichester . . . at his Primary Visitation	1838

Phillpotts H.	A Charge delivered to the clergy of the Diocese of Exeter at his primary visitation	1834
	A Charge delivered to the Clergy of the Diocese of Exeter at his triennial Visitation	1836
	A Charge delivered to the Clergy of the Diocese of Exeter at his triennial Visitation	1839
Ryder H.	A Charge to the Clergy of Lichfield & Coventry at his Second visitation	1828
	A Charge to the Clergy of Lichfield & Coventry at his third visitation	1832
Stanley E.	A Charge delivered to the Clergy of the Diocese of Norwich, at the primary Visitation	1838
Sumner C.J.	A Charge delivered to the Clergy of the Diocese of Llandaff in September 1827	1828
	A Charge delivered to the Clergy of the Diocese of Winchester at his primary visitation	1829
	A Charge delivered to the Clergy of the Diocese of Winchester	1833
	A Charge delivered to the Clergy of the Diocese of Winchester at his third visitation	1837
Sumner J.B.	A Charge to the clergy of the Diocese of Chester at the primary visitation	1829
	A Charge delivered to the Clergy of the Diocese of Chester at the triennial visitation	1832
	A Charge delivered to the Clergy of the Diocese of Chester at the triennial visitation	1835
	A Charge delivered to the Clergy of the Diocese of Chester at the triennial visitation	1838
Thorp C. (Archdeacon)	A Charge to the Clergy of the Archdeaconry of Durham	1830
	A Charge to the Clergy of the Archdeaconry of Durham	1832
	A Charge to the Clergy of the Archdeaconry of Durham	1836
Wilberforce S. (Archdeacon)	A charge delivered to the Archdeaconry of Surrey	1840
Wilkins G. (Archdeacon)	A Charge delivered at the visitations at Nottingham, Retford and Newark	1832
	A Charge	1834
	A Charge	1835

| Wilkins G. | The National Church Re-adjusted. A Charge to the Clergy of the County of Nottingham | 1836 |

Other Episcopal Publications relating to Reforms

Allen J.	The Necessary Preparation for Holy Orders, A Sermon	1836
	The Correspondence between the Eccl Commissioners and the Bishop of Ely	1837
Blomfield C.J.	A letter on the present neglect of the Lord's Day	1830
	Speech in the House of Lords on the Irish Church Bill 24 August 1835	1835
	Speech on National Education 28 May 1839	1839
	A Letter to his Grace the Lord Archbishop of Canterbury, upon the Formation of a Fund for endowing Additional Bishoprics in the Colonies.	1840
Burgess T.	The Bishop of Salisbury's Letters to the Duke of Wellington, on the Catholic Question.	1829
	A Letter to the Bishop of Norwich from the Bishop of Salisbury in reply to a letter by Henry Bathurst published in the *St James's Chronicle* Concerning Catholic Emancipation	1830
Butler S.	Thoughts on Church Dignities	1833
Kaye J.	A Letter to his Grace the Archbishop of Canterbury on the Recommendations of the Ecclesiastical Commission	1836
Law G.H.	Remarks on the Present Distresses of the Poor	1830
	A Pastoral Letter on the present aspect of the times addressed to the Clergy ... and inhabitants of the Diocese of Bath & Wells.	1831
Otter W.	A Vindication of Churchmen who become members of the British & Foreign Bible Society	1812
Stanley E.	A Few Words in favour of our Roman Catholic brethren 3rd edition	1829
Sumner J.B.	A letter to the clergy of the diocese of Chester, occasioned by the act of the legislature granting	

	relief to his Majesty's Roman Catholic subjects	1829
Thirlwall C.	A Letter to Thomas Turton DD	1834
Ward W.	A Statement in reference to the proposed suppression of the Bishopric of Sodor and Mann . . . . By the Bishop and the Laity of the Isle of Mann	1837

Church Reform   Books are listed in order by year of publication

Watson R.	A Letter to his Grace the Archbp of Canterbury	1783
Arnold T.	The Christian duty of granting the claims of the Roman Catholics ...	1829
Berens E.	Church-Reform (by a Churchman)	1830
Beverley R.M.	A Letter to His Grace, the Archbishop of York on the Present Corrupt State of the Church of England	1831
Burton E.	Thoughts upon the Demand for Church Reform	1831
Wade J.	The Extraordinary Black Book new edition	1832
Henley, Lord Robert	A Plan of Church Reform 2nd ed.	1832
Henley, Lord R.	Union of Dr Burton's & Lord Henley's Plans	1832
Dealtry W.	The Importance of the Established Church	1832
Beverley R.M.	A Second Letter to His Grace, the Archbishop of York on the Present Corrupt State of the Church of England	1832
'A Clergyman of the C of E'	Safe & easy steps towards an efficient reform: one more efficient than that of Lord Henley.	1832
'A Layman'	Church Reform : A letter to his Grace the Archbishop of Canterbury	1832
Wilkins G.	A letter to Earl Grey on the subject of ecclesiastical reform.	1832
Tiptaft W.	Two Letters addressed to the Bishop of Salisbury	1832
Berens E.	Remarks on Lord Henley and Dr Burton on Church Reform: in a Letter to a Member of Parliament	1833
Arnold T.	Principles of Church Reform	1833
	Postscript to Principles of Church Reform	1833
Bloomfield, S.T.	Analytical View of the Principal Plans of Church Reform	1833
Pusey E.B.	Remarks on the Prospective and Past Benefits of Cathedral Institutions	1833

Fletcher W.	Church Reform	1833
Gleig G.R.	Letter to the Lord Bishop of London, on the subject of Church Reform	1833
Price U.	Reform without Reconstruction, being an Enquiry into the Advantages of a safe & practicable Arrangement for removing to a great Extent, Inequalities in the Temporalities of the Established Church, without Legislative Interference	1833
D'Oyly G.	A Letter to the Rt Hon Earl Grey on the Subject of Church Rates	1834
'A Layman'	Thoughts on the Church Establishment	1834
Henley, Lord R.	A Plan for a new arrangement and increase in number of the dioceses in England & Wales	1834
Gisborne T.	Considerations on Objections current against Ecclesiastical establishments	1835
Johnes A.J.	A Letter to Lord John Russell, on the Operation of the Established Church Bill, with reference to the Interests of the Principality of Wales	1835
Noel B.W.	The State of the Metropolis Considered in a Letter to the Lord Bishop of London	1835
Newman J.H.	On the Restoration of Suffragan Bishops	1835
Clericus Anglicanus	Three Letters to His Grace the Lord Archbishop of Canterbury. On Church Property, Episcopacy, Cathedrals, & the Clergy	1836
Bowles W.L.	The Patronage of the English Bishops	1836
	Further observations on the last report of the Church Commissioners, particularly as respects the patronage of deans and chapters and cathedral music	1836
Anon	Statistics of the Church of England, as developed in the Reports of the Ecclesiastical Commissioners	1836
Best S.	The Case of the Deans and Chapters considered	1837
Smith S.	A letter to Archdeacon Singleton, on the Ecclesiastical Commission	1837
Benson C.	On the Proceedings of the Ecclesiastical Commission: a Letter to the Bp of Lincoln	1837
Wordswotth C.	The Ecclesiastical Commission and the Universities	1837

Selwyn W.	The Substance of an Argument . . . against those Clauses of the Benefices Pluralities Bill . . . to the great Prejudice of the Bishops of England & Wales	1838
Smith S.	A Letter to Lord John Russell on the Church Bills	1838
Alford F. ed.	Life, Journal & Letters of Henry Alford	1873
Overton J.	The English Church in the 19th Century 1800-33	1894
Dibden L.T. & Downing S.E.	Ecclesiastical Commission	1919
Balleine G.R.	A History of the Evangelical Party in the Church of England	1933
Mathieson W.L.	English Church Reform 1815-1840	1923
Cnattingius H.	Bishops & Societies: and a study of Anglican colonial missionary expansion, 1698-1850	1952
Wand J.W.C.	The Second Reform	1953
Wymer N.	Dr Arnold of Rugby	1953
Brown C.K.F.	A History of the English Clergy 1800-1900	1953
Webster A.B.	Joshua Watson	1954
Brose O.J.	Church & Parliament . The Reshaping of the Church of England 1828-1860	1959
Vidler A.R.	The Church in an Age of Revolution	1961
Henriques U.	Religious Toleration in England 1787-1833	1961
Best G.F.A.	Temporal Pillars. Queen Anne's Bounty, the Ecclesiastical Commissioners, and the Church of England	1964
Bowen D.	The Idea of the Victorian Church	1968
Thompson K.A.	Bureaucracy and Church Reform: The Organisational Response of the Church of England to Social Change 1800-1965	1970
Chadwick O.	The Victorian Church Part 1 3rd edition	1971
Flindall R.P. ed.	The Church of England 1815-1948	1972
Hylson-Smith K.	Evangelicals in the Church of England 1734-1984	1988
Virgin P.	The Church in an Age of Negligence	1989
Rowlands J.H.L.	Church, State & Society 1827-1845	1989
Barrett P.	Barchester. English Cathedral Life in the Nineteenth Century	1993
Knight F.	The 19th Century Church & English Society	1995
Wolffe J. ed.	Evangelical Faith and Public Zeal	1995
Dewey C.	The Passing of Barchester	1991

Burns A.	The Diocesan Revival in the Church of England c.1800-1870	1999
Parry J.P. & Taylor S.	Parliament and the Church	2000
Brown S.J.	The National Churches of England, Ireland and Scotland 1801-46	2001
Jacob W.M.	The Clerical profession in the long 18th century, 1780-1840	2007

Political Biographies & Letters

Grant James	Random Recollections of the House of Lords from 1830 to 1836	1836
Carpenter W.	A Peerage for the People	1837
Greville C.C.F.	The Greville Memoirs Vol. 1 A Journal of the Reigns of King George IV and King William III	1874
Jennings L.J. ed.	The Croker Papers 3 vols.	1884
Reid S.J.	Lord John Russell	1895
Maxwell H. ed.	The Creevey Papers	1904
Trevelyan G.M.	Lord Grey of the Reform Bill	1920
Gore J. ed.	Creevey	1948
Aspinall A. ed.	Three Early 19th Century Diaries	1952
Cecil D.	Lord M	1954
Turberville A.S.	The House of Lords in the Age of Reform	1958
Longford E.	Wellington Pillar of State	1972
Gash N.	Peel	1976
Kriegel A.D. ed.	The Holland House Diaries 1831-1840	1977
Gash N.	Lord Liverpool	1990
Smith E.A.	Lord Grey	1990
MacDonagh O.	The Life of Daniel O'Connell 1775-1847	1991
Palmer B.	High & Mitred: Prime Ministers as Bishop-Makers 1837-1977	1992
Hibbert C.	Wellington A Personal History	1997
Pearce E. ed.	The Diaries of Charles Greville	2005
Hurd D.	Robert Peel	2007

Political Reform

Gladstone W.E.	The State in its Relations with the Church	1834
Clayton J.	Bishops as Legislators: a record of votes and speeches delivered by the bishops ...	1906
Davis H.W.C.	The Age of Peel & Grey	1926
Sykes N.	Church and State in England in the 18th century	1934

Trevelyan G.M.	British History in the 19th Century and after New edition	1937
Gill J.C.	The Ten Hours Parson: Christian Social Action in the 1830s	1959
Ward J.T.	The Factory Movement 1830-55	1962
Gill J.C.	Parson Bull of Byerley	1963
Derry J.W.	1793-1868 Reaction & Reform	1963
Machin G.I.T.	The Catholic Question in English Politics 1820-1830	1964
Gash N.	Reaction and Reconstruction in English Politics 1832-1852	1965
Soloway R.A.	Prelates & People. Ecclesiastical Social Thought in England 1783-1852	1969
Finlayson G.B.A.M.	Decade of Reform. England in the 1830s	1970
Llewellyn A.	The Decade of Reform – the 1830s	1972
Hunt J.W.	Reaction and Reform 1815-1841	1972
Kitson Clark G.S.R.	Churchmen and the Condition of England 1832-1885	1973
Brock M.	The Great Reform Act	1973
Norman E.R.	Church and society in England 1770-1970	1976
Machin G.I.T.	Politics and the Churches 1832-1868	1977
Salbstein M.C.N.	The Emancipation of the Jews in Britain: The Question of the Admission of the Jews to Parliament, 1828-1860	1982
Brent R.	Liberal Anglican Politics 1830-1841	1987
Smith E.A.	Reform or Revolution? A Diary of Reform in England 1830-32	1992
Evans E.J.	The Great Reform Act of 1832 2nd ed.	1994
LoPatin N.D.	Political Unions, Popular Politics and the Great Reform Act of 1832	1999
Burns A. & Innes J. ed.	Rethinking the Age of Reform: Britain 1780-1850	2003
Fraser A.	Perilous Question: The Drama of the Great Reform Bill 1832	2013

Other works

Hall W.J.	Lists of Books recommended to Students In Divinity	1830
Taylor W.C.	The Bishop: a Series of Letters to a newly created Prelate	1841
Foster J.	Alumni Oxonienses 1715-1886 4 volumes	1888

Hole S.R.	The memories of Dean Hole	1893
Ellman E.B.	Recollections of a Sussex Parson 2008 reprint	1912
Venn J.A.	Alumni Cantabrigienses part 2	1940
Winstanley D.A.	Unreformed Cambridge	1935
Stranks C.J.	Dean Hook	1954
Chadwick O.	Victorian Miniature	1960
Witts F.E.	The Diary of a Cotswold Parson: Reverend F.E. Witts 1783-1854 ed. David Verey	1978
Garland M.M.	Cambridge before Darwin	1980
Butler P. ed.	Pusey Rediscovered	1983
Coombs H. & P. ed.	Journal of a Somerset Rector 1803-1834 John Skinner	1984
Miller J.	Religion and the Popular Print 1600-1832	1986
Brock M.G. & Curthoys M. (eds)	The History of the University of Oxford Vol VI Part 1	1997
Dowland D.A.	19th Century Anglican Theological Training: the Redbrick challenge	1997
Carter G.	Anglican Evangelicals - Protestant Secessions from the Via Media	2006
Park T.	St Bees College: Pioneering Higher Education in 19th Century Cumbria 2nd ed.	2008
Thompson D.M.	Cambridge Theology in the 19th century (Chapter 2 is on Herbert Marsh and the rise of Biblical Criticism)	2008
Stone M.	The Diary of John Longe 1765-1834	2008
Shenton C	The Day Parliament burned down	2012

Articles

Turberville A.S.	The Episcopal Bench, 1783-1837 in *Church Quarterly Review* vol. CXXIII pp. 261-285	1937
Hughes E.	The Bishops & Reform 1831-32: Some Fresh Correspondence in *English Historical Review* 56 pp. 459-90	1941
McDowell R.B.	The Anglican Episcopate, 1780-1945 in *Theology* Vol. L No 384 pp.202-209	1947
Welch P.J.	Contemporary Views on the Proposals for the Alienation of Capitular Property in England 1832-40 in *Journal of Ecclesiastical History* Vol. 5 pp 184-195	1954

Brose O.J.	The Irish Precedent for English Church Reform: the Church Temporalities Act of 1833 in *Journal of Ecclesiastical History*, Vol. 7 no 2 pp. 204-225	1956
Lewis C. J.	The Disintegration of the Tory-Anglican Alliance In the Struggle for Catholic Emancipation in *Church History* Vol. 29, no 1 pp. 25-43	1960
Pollard A.F.	A Trap to catch Calvinists (or Bishop Marsh's Eighty-seven Questions) *Church Quarterly Review* 162 pp.447-54	1961
Best W.J.	The Life and Times of William Van Mildert. *Journal of Theological Studies* 14. pp. 355-70	1963
Smith W.G.	The Bishops and Reform in *The Historical Magazine of the Protestant Episcopal Church* Vol. 32, No 4 pp. 361-370	1963
Roberts D.	How Cruel was the Victorian Poor Law? in *The Historical Journal* Vol 6 pp. 97-107	1963
Ward W.R.	The Tithe Question in England in the Early Nineteenth Century in *Journal of Ecclesiastical History* Vol. 16 pp.67-81	1965
Cullen M.J.	The making of the Civil Registration Act of 1836. *Journal of Ecclesiastical History* Vol. 25 pp. 39-59	1974
Wolffe J.R.	Bishop Henry Phillpotts and the Administration of the Diocese of Exeter 1830-1865 in the *Devonshire Association Report & Transactions* Vol, 114	1982
Knight F	Ministering to the Ministers: the Discipline of Recalcitrant Clergy in the Diocese of Lincoln 1830-1845 in *Studies in Church History* Vol 26 pp. 357-366	1989
Gibson W.T.	The Professionalisation of an Elite: the Nineteenth Century Episcopate in *Albion* Vol 23 no 3	1991
Smith M. ed.	Henry Ryder: A Charge . . . in *C of E Record Society* Vol 12 pp. 51-107	2004
Burns A. & Stray, C.	The Greek-Play Bishop: Polemic, Prosopography, and Nineteenth Century Prelates in *The Historical Journal* Vol. 54 pp. 1013-1038	2011

Academic Theses

Welch P.J.	Bishop Blomfield	London PhD	1952

Foskett R.	John Kaye & the Diocese of Lincoln Nottingham PhD		1957
Stephenson A.M.G.	The Formation of the See of Ripon and the Episcopate of C.T. Longley.	Oxford B.Litt	1960
Moore E.R.	John Bird Sumner, Bishop of Chester 1828-48	Manchester University MA	1976
Virgin P.N.	Church and State in Late Georgian England, 1800-1840	Cambridge PhD	1979
Fealey, M.S.	Of Bishops and Bastards: the Blomfield : Phillpotts Debate on the Illegitimacy Clauses of 1834	Oxford Master of Studies	1988
Braine R.K.	The Life & Writings of Herbert Marsh 1757-1839	Cambridge PhD	1989
Knight F.M.R.	Bishop, clergy and people: John Kaye and the diocese of Lincoln 1827-1853	Cambridge PhD	1990
Park T.	Theological Education and Ministerial Training in the Church of England 1800-1850	Open PhD	1991
Garrard J.	Archbishop William Howley	Oxford DPhil	1992

INDEX OF PEOPLE

Abercorn, Marquess of 68,74
Acland, Sir Thomas 137,300
Adeane, Jane 66
Addington, Henry 60,82,89
Ainger, G.H. 283
Ainger, William 282-284
Albert, Prince 73
Alexander, Bp. N. 15,
Alford, Dean Henry 194,195
Allen, Bp Joseph 14,36,77,84,93, 154, 252,253,260,313,362
Althorp, Viscount 77,119,191
Ambler, R.W. 135,161,351
Anderson, David 284
Andrew, W.W. 192,193
Apthorp, Harriet 59
Arbuthnot, Bp. A. 15
Arbuthnot, Charles 71,
Arbuthnot, Harriet 108
Arnold, Mathew 322
Arnold, Thomas 25,32,72,93,98, 120,124,150,288
Ashley, Lord 122,124,137,
Aspinall, A. 77,116,117,145, 148
Atholl, Duke of 48,89,93,116
Atkins. H. 298
Attwood, Thomas 107

Babington, John 46,
Bagot, Lord 49,87
Bagot, Bp. R. 14,37,87,111,162, 207,249,250,263,264,334,338,344
Bailey, Henry 305,307
Baines, Edward 132
Baker, W.J. 28,36,54,87,214
Balleine, G.R. 92
Barnes, Ralph 319,320,328
Barrett, Philip 155
Barrington, Bp Shute 50,54,55,58, 63,64,76,80,89,90,92,197,218,279

Bath, Marquis of 153
Bathurst, Benjamin 323,325,327
Bathurst, Caroline 327
Bathurst, Charles 323
Bathurst, Henry 2nd Earl 50,85,211
Bathurst, Archdn Henry 98,327, 342
Bathurst, Bp H. 14,17,19,24,26, 38,39,50,66,85,86,97,98,105,177, 182-185,189,190,192,193,195,196, 210,241,250,318,321,323,327,331, 339-343,346,354,361
Bathurst, Henrietta 327
Bathurst, General James 98,327, 342
Bathurst, Robert 38,39,323,327
Bathurst, Rosa 323
Bathurst, Tryphena (see Thistlethwayte)
Baylee, Joseph 303,304
Beaufort, Duke of 153
Bedford, 6th Duke of 73
Belli, Mary Frances 68
Benson, Christopher 158
Bentley, R. 57
Bentham, Jeremy 126,
Bethell, Bp C. 14,15,21,71,81,94, 111,145,186,202,203,221,222,249, 320,342
Beverley, Earl of 68
Beverley, R.M. 2,111,115,142
Beynon, Archdn T. 278
Biber, G.E. 115,133,206,327 339,347
Bishop, S. 20
Blakesley, Dean 161
Blomfield, Bp. Alfred 44,321,322, 327,347
Blomfield, Sir Arthur 321,322
Blomfield, Bp C.J. 6,8,14.15,17,23, 36,44,45,56,60-62,70,71,74,114-

115,118,124,126,127,129-132,134,
137,138,141,147,148,151,156,157,
164,166-168,171,176,180,188,190,
196,206,207,209, 210,214-217,221,
229,238,244-247,260,261,273,285,
287,289,290.307,310, 313,317,
321-323,325,327,332,335,339,
341,343,344,346-349,355.359,363
Blomfield, Edward 61
Blomfield, E.T. 321
Blomfield, F.G. 321,322,327
Blomfield, Admiral Henry 321,322
Blomfield, Sir Reginald 17,344
358,359
Bloomfield, S.T. 151,152
Blore, Edward 316
Bouch, C.M.L. 317,336,361
Bowen, D. 123,124,212,218,
219
Bowles, W.L. 164
Bowstead, Bp. J. 15,35,36,93,342
Brancker, Thomas 59
Brent, R. 79,288
Bright, Margery 55
Brinkley, Bp. J. 15,111
Bristol, Lord 61,62,74,
Brock, M. 82,109,288
Brodrick, G.C. 28,
Brose, Olive 238,239,347
Brougham, Lord 60,66,77,83,84,
117,147,286
Broughton, Bp W.G. 167,305,306,
351
Brown, Abner 45,46
Brown, R.L. 8,96,105,112,129,
132,174,177,178,189,191,195,201,
203,204,212,213,251,281,310,318,3
31, 335,337,338,347,350,351,360
Browne, Henry 298
Browne, Sir William 33
Bruere, Nancy S. 67
Brymer, Archdn Wm. 300,302
Buccleugh, Duke of
Buddicom, R.P. 284,304

Bull, Parson 121-124
Bunsen, Baron 65,356
Burdett, Sir Francis 101
Burdon, Rev 190
Burgess, Bp Thomas 6,14,16,24,
25,37,39,40,54,55,70,71,89,90,95,
102,103,111, 172,181,187, 211,217,
218,228,239,277,278,280,284,311,
313,321,339,342,345, 346,349,
350,360
Burgess, Mrs 340
Burgon, J.W. 358
Burnett, Bp 361
Burney, Charles 43
Burns, Arthur 140,165,177,178,
206-208,220,346
Burton, Edward 131,148,149,313,
315
Burton, J. 40,
Bute, Lord 213
Butler, Charles 63
Butler, Bp Joseph 313
Butler, Perry 296
Butler, Bp Samuel 14,59,71-73,83,
84,178,228,229,243-245,319,338
Butler, Samuel Jr 83
Butterfield, William 306
Buxton, Fowell 121

Call, Sir William 325
Campbell, Thomas 286
Canning, George 64,92,101,107
Card, T . 22
Carey, Bp W. 14,15,37,79,80,
84,111,202,203,321,343,345
Carnell, G. 89,357,360
Caroline, Queen 63,74
Carpenter, W. 2,73,74,76-82,
84,85,87-95,346
Carr, Bp Robert 14,37,77,78,
194,207,
Carter, Grayson 211
Carus, William 46
Carwithin, Dr 191

Cecil, Lord David 96,134
Chad, Sir George 182
Chadwick, Edwin 126,
Chadwick, Owen 34,86,120,192,
193,330,349,359
Chandler, Dean George 207,
238,295,296
Charlotte, Queen 97
Chesterfield, Lord 60
Chichester, Earl of 137
Christiansen, O.J. 4
Churchward, W. 195
Churton, 294
Clarges, Sir Thomas 76
Clark, G.S.R. Kitson 115,199,210,
308
Clarke, E.D. 33,
Clarke, James S. 67
Clarke, M.L. 172
Claughton, T. 308
Clayton, Joseph 99,100,115
Close, Francis 46,
Cnattingius, H. 168
Cobbett, William 73,75,210
Coke, Mr 185,340
Coleridge, Edward 305-307
Coleridge, John T. 66
Coleridge, Samuel T. 18
Coleridge, Bp W.H. 307
Collinson, Septimus 20
Colman, 59
Conybeare, W.J. 356
Conyngham, Lady 75
Conyngham, Lord Albert 66
Conyngham, Lord F.N. 66
Conyngham, Lord Mount-Charles
66,75
Conyngham, Marquess 66,67,75
Coombs H. & P. 126,223,333
Coombs, J. 75,76,322,337
Copleston, Catherine 331
Copleston, Bp E. 8,15,20,29,32,35,
37,40,41,52,53,69,87,94,103,105,
111,112,115,129,173,176-178,180,
188,189-191,195,201-203,212,213,
226,230,239,241-244,251,255-257,
270,271,280,281,310,317,320,330,
331,334,335,337,346,347,349,350
Copleston, W.J. 317,334,335
Cornewall, Bp F.H.W. 14,90
Corrie, Bp Daniel 46
Cottenham, Earl of 94
Croker, J. W. 109,204,205
Crooll, Rabbi Joseph 120
Crow, James 2
Crowe, Mr. 41
Cullen, M.J. 134
Cumberland, Duke of 117
Curthoys, M.C. 288

Dale, Thomas 286
Dark, 332
Daubeny, Rev 143
Davies, G.C.B. 174,175,195,320,
328,337,354,356
Davys, Bp George 14,16,36,70,
88,89,330,342,344,359,360
Davys, Archdn Owen 330
Dawes, Richard 40
Dealtry, William 269,270
Denison, Bp E. 14,17,18,37,54,
90,129,162,271-273,342,344
Denison, Archdc G. 17,18
Derry, 74
Dewey, C. 188
Dickinson, F.H. 300,302
Dobree, P.P. 61
Douglas, Jane 51
Douglas, Henry 111
D'Oyly, George 67,78,286,287
Drake, Rev 193,194
Dudley, Charles 48,322
Dudley, Sir H. Bate 143
Durham, Lord 63,116,117

Eldon, Lady 42,80,
Eldon, Lord 42,62,64,80
Elgin, Lord 42

Ellman, E.B.   78,79,181,193, 194
Elrington, Bp T.   15,111
Engel, .   31
Evans, Rev. A   20
Evans, Eric   106,113
Evans, T.S.   356
Everleigh, J.   32

Fardell, Henry   143,144
Fealey, M.S.   127
Finlayson, G.   119,128
Fleming, Sir R. le   283
Fortescue, Lord   174
Foster, B.   298
Fox, Charles James   16
Fox, Charles Richard   79
Freeman, Philip   299
Froude, R.H.   54

Gaisford, Dean Thomas   61,292, 299,314,315
Gardiner, Bp Stephen   116
Garland, M.M.   33
Garrard, James   8,358
Gash, N.   70,71,135,138, 139,363
George III   73,82,90,91,101
George IV   67,70,74,75,78, 82,93,104,278,286,287
Gibbon, Edward   53
Gibson, E.C.S.   357
Gilbert, Bp   299
Gill, J.C.   122,123
Gisborne, Thomas   153
Gladstone, W.E.   59,137,161,169, 200,296,
Gloucester, Duke of   288
Goderich, Viscount   93,97,116,
Goldsmid, Isaac L.   286
Goodenough, Dean   84
Gould, Baring   194
Gower, Earl   90
Grant, Charles   120

Grant, James   358
Grant, Robert   120
Gratton, (Lord)   101
Gray, Bp Robert   14,37,76,87,111, 233,312,323,362
Greenhow, Thomas   290
Grenville, Lord   34,52,94,
Greville, C.C.F.   75-77,109,113, 116,117,359
Grey, Charles 2nd Earl   10,12,20,30, 63,72,78,82,98,107-109,115,116, 119,122,126, 132,146,147,149, 150,152,237,291,293,358
Grey, Bp Edward   14,16,17,37, 70, 72,82,83,129,134,157,180,293,321, 323,342
Grey, Sir George   331
Gronow, Rees   58
Grosvenor, Lord   214
Grote, G.   19

Hale, Archdn   348
Halévy, Élie   101
Hall, W.J.   313
Hamilton, Sir William   33
Hampden, Bp   72,
Harcourt, Archbp E.V.V.   15,24,38, 68, 90,91,115,123,130,158, 181, 194,218,286,293,317,321,329, 342-344,358,359
Hardwicke, Lord   329
Hare, Archdn. J.C.   19,65,353
Harford, J.S.   25,39,40,55,89, 181,182,188,217,218,278,279,311, 330,339,340,349,350
Harrison, Benjamin   258,307,345
Harrowby, Earl of   83
Hart, Tindall   194,359
Hawkins, Edward   32,
Hawtrey, Stephen   21,59
Headlam, Stewart   99
Hearnshaw, F.J.C.   289
Heath, Anne M.   61,321
Heathcote, G.   60

Henley, Lord   1,131,148,149, 151,238,
Hervey, Lord   61
Hey, Dr   313
Hildyard, James   308
Hill, William   51
Hobhouse, John   71,133,
Hole, Dean S.R.   181,192,308
Holland, Lady   79
Holland, Lord   71,72,77,79,82, 86,118,134,136,141,146,349,360
Hollis, C.   22
Hook, Dean W.F.   98,198,364,365
Hooker, Richard   205,313
Hope, A. Beresford   306,307
Horne, Hartwell   313
Horsley, Bp Samuel   19
Howley, Archbp W.   6,8,14,24,37, 62, 68,71,74,87,95,101,110,111, 114-116,120,121,137,138,141, 146-148,152,155,156,162,163, 166-168,175,188,190,202,207,217, 218,234,272,273,286,289,291,292, 299,306,307,314-316,330,331, 342,344,345,358
Hughes, Edward   294
Hughes, Jane S.   58
Hughes, T.S.   191
Hume, Joseph   109,286,294
Hunt, Henry   107
Huntingford, Bp G.I.   14,24,25,37, 39, 60,70,71,82,313,317,320, 328,342
Huntingford, Henry   320,328
Huntingford, Mary   60
Huntingford, Thomas Sr   320
Huntingford, Thomas Jr   327, 328,342
Hurd, Bp Richard   180
Hurd, Douglas   133
Huskisson, W.   53

Ilderton, Canon   332
Inglis, Sir Robert   258,288

Ives, Cornelius   37,51,102,117
Ives, William   320

Jackson, Cyril   32,36,42,79,
Jackson, Bp John   329
Jacob, W.M.   29,64,90,177
James, Sir William M.J.   325
Jelf, R.W.   288,290,307
Jenkins, Rev   173,174
Jenkinson, Bp J.B.   15,24,38,71, 95,173,203,204,221,225,227, 253,280,291,312,313, 319,
Jenkyns, Charles   144
Jenkyns, Henry   292
Jenkyns, Dean Richard   303
Jeremie, J.A.   188
Johnes, A.J.   1,155,201,
Johnson, Malcolm   216,332,348,359
Jones, O.W.   277
Jones, John   173,174
Jones,   350
Jupp, Roger   296

Kaye, Bp John   14,29,35,43,47, 56,57,71,72,84,101,111,135,157, 158,160,162-164,173,184,185,188, 192,196,207,221,224, 231,232,244, 247,248,259,260,273,274,309,311, 318,321,329,341,346,351,352,355, 359
Kaye, W.F.   329
Keate, John   84
Keble, John   32,130
Kennedy, B.H.   59
Kent, Dorothy   61,321
Kent, Duchess of   88
Kenyon, Lord   278
King, Lord   147
Kitson, Mr   196
Knight, Bruce   96,112,132,173, 188-190,195,198,226,239,243, 251,256,279-281,350
Knight, Frances   166,188,224
Knight, R.   212,213

Knighton, Sir Wm 278
Kriegel, A.D. 72,77,82,86,118, 136,141,146

Lancaster, J. 56
Lauderdale, Lord 93
Law, Edward (Lord Ellenborough) 16,76,110,117,333
Law, Bp G.H. 6,14,16,35,36,66, 71,76,111,112,124,125,176,223,229-231,281-285,293,300,329,330,333, 342,343,346,352
Law, G.H. Jr 329
Law, Chancellor James 299,300, 302, 329,352
Law, Archdn Henry 329
Law, Bp John 16
Law, Robert 329
Lawrence, Bp T.St. 15,111
Lecarriere, Marianne 55
Leeds, Duke of 174
Lewellin, Llewelyn 280
Lewis, C.J. 105
Lingard, John 63
Linnell, Charles 19,182,183,190,
Liverpool, Lord 52,53,57,62,63, 67,70,71,74,75,80,81,83,84,86,91, 95,205
Lloyd, Bp Charles 14,16,23,30,36, 37,42,53,69,70,86,87,94,103,104, 214,286,308,313, 333,342
Longe, Henry 195,196
Longe, John 195,196
Longe, Robert 196
Longley, Bp C.T. 15,37,72,92,93, 198,266,267,320
Lonsdale, Earl of 281,282
Lonsdale, Bp John 67,289,307
Lopartin, N.T. 111
Lowe, T.H. 328
Lunn, Bp David 8
Lushington, Charles 135
Luxmoore, Bp J. 15,17,94,331, 345,363

Lyall, Archdn W. 119,188,233, 234,243,307

Maber, Rev 174
Macbride, Dr 334
Machin, G.I.T. 132,138,151
Maginess, Charles 303
Majendie, Bp. H.W. 15,70,94,321
Maltby, Bp E. 14,15,24,36, 43,44,60,61,70-72,77,78,84,105, 134,145,148,157, 172,244,247, 257,258,293,313,342,344,345,362, 363
Maltby, Elizabeth 78
Malthus, Henry 126,325
Malthus, T.R. 67,325
Mann, Horace 179,
Manning, Edward 295,296,299,300
Mansell, Bp W.L. 45,60
Mant, Bp Richard 15,41
Marchant, D. le 77,117,145,147
Marriott, Charles 296-299,306
Marriott, G.W. 278
Marsh, Bp H. 14,30,35,36,42, 43,55,56,70,71,88,111,159,186, 187,197,207,208,220,221,232,244, 309,310,312,313,338,342,357,360
Marshall, 334
Martineau, Hariet 348
Martyn, Henry 46
Mary I, Queen 116
Mathieson, W.L. 113,114,147, 152,153
Maunoir, Jennie de 66,75,317,337
Maunoir, J.P. de 66
Maurice, F.D. 289
Melbourne, Lord 1,12,13,15,71, 72,79,83,84,86,88,90,92-96,132-135,154,155,159,160,162,250, 341,356,359
Melville, Lord 109
Merivale, Charles 195,
Metcalfe, Charles 22
Michaelis, J.D. 55

Middleton, Bp T.F. 167
Milbourne, Sir Henry
Mildert, Jane   336
Mildert, Bp W. Van 6,8,15,19,37, 51,52,71,80,91,100,101,103,104, 110,111,115,117,123,130,173,179, 198,221,222,232,233,244,257,258, 278,279,290-294,309,310,312,313, 318,321,330,332,336,345,346,355, 360
Mill, James   286
Milner, Isaac   88,
Monk, Bp J.H.   14,36,56-58,61, 81,110,111,116,126,157,162,164, 172,183,184,196,197,207,208,235, 250,251,261,262,308,312,321,338, 362,363
Monk, Mrs   197
Moore, Archbp   51
Moore, Henry   319,338
More, Hannah   49,54,197, 198,310,
Morpeth, Viscount   119
Mortlock, Eliza   57
Murray, Bp G.   14,15,16,38,48, 89,103,111,116,118,145,184,212, 250,272,293,321,343
Murray, Bp Lord George 16,89
Musgrave, Bp. T.   14,36,83,321

Nares, Captain   334
Newcastle, Duke of 33
Newdigate, Sir Roger 67
Newman, John Henry 28,53,54, 104,151-153,169,212,295-299,308,
Newton, Isaac   33
Niebuhr, B.G.   65,
Nockles, P.B.   287,288
Noel, Baptist   209
Norfolk, Duke of 171
Norman, E.R.   101,104,166,176, 348
Norris, H.H.   284,285
North, Lord   50,82

Northumberland, Duke of 68,81

Oakeley, Frederick 54,66
Oastler, Richard   121,123,
O'Connell, Daniel 102,
Ollivant, Alfred   280,313,350
Ongley, 3rd Lord 67
Orange, Prince of 68,74
Otter, Caroline   325
Otter, Emily   325
Otter, Maria   325
Otter, Sophia   325
Otter, W.B.   330
Otter, Bp. W.   6,14,33,36,56, 67,72,78,79,169,207,262,263,287, 289,294-299,320,325,346,353
Overton J.   186,201,309

Paine, Thomas   106,123,
Paley, William   28,309,313
Park, Ben   144
Park, Trevor   281,285
Parkinson, Richard 283,284
Parr, Samuel   83
Parsons, John   32
Paxton, Sir Joseph 317
Peacock, Dean George 308
Pearson, C.B.   330
Pearson, Bp John 313
Peel, Sir Robert   12,16,34,37,42, 53,64,69,72,79,86,94,100,103,108, 132,133,146-148,151-154,158,201, 250,286,294,324,329,363
Pellew, Dean   354
Pepys, Bp. H.   15,94,344
Percival, Spencer 52,91,
Percy, Bp Hugh   15,68,92,111,112, 184,317,320,321,336,344,361,362
Perry, Charles   308
Phillipps, Sophia 48
Phillpotts, Bp H.   6,14,20,37,41,42, 62-64,70,80,95,110-112,114,116, 117,127,131,132,137,147,153,157,

159,165,174,175,191,194,195,204,
211,212,217,239,240,253,254,256,
263,271,288,291,293,319-321,328,
329,337,338,342,344,356
Phillpotts, Henry John 329
Phillpotts, Thomas 329
Phillpotts, William 328
Pinder, J.H.   300-302
Pitt, William   70,73,85,88,90,
101, 140,141
Plunkett, Lord   341
Pollard, Arthur   186
Porson, Richard   45,56,57,61,81
Porteus, Bp   93.140
Portland, Duke of 41
Powis, Earl of   157
Prowett, John   210
Pusey, E.B.   54,151,206, 209,
296,297,302,306,308,309,331,337

Queensbury, Duke of 52

Radnor, Lord   93,288
Raikes, Henry   200
Raikes, Robert   199
Randolph, Bp John 98
Rashdall, John   188,192
Rees, Rice   280
Reeve, A.   8
Regent, Prince   76-78,168
Reimarus, H.S.   55
Richards, Rev   195
Richardson, B.W.   347
Richmond, Duke of 176
Rickman, Thomas   317
Rippon, Cuthbert   135
Roberts, David   128,129
Robinson, Thomas   49
Rolle, Lord   114
Romilly, Lord John 325
Romilly, Sir Samuel 67
Rose, H.J.   289,292,358
Ross, J.l.   298
Routh, Martin   42,62,63,80

Rowell, Bp. G.   8
Royle, Edward   198,304
Russell, G.W.E.   344
Russell, Lord John 1,73,78,79,101,
132,135,137,146,153,155,161,164,
288,293,339,356
Russell, Lord Wriothesley 73
Rutland, 3rd Duke of 73
Rutland 5th Duke of 79
Ryder, Admiral Sir Arthur 322
Ryder, Charles Dudley 48,322
Ryder, George Dudley 212,322
Ryder, Bp Henry   14,36,47,48,49,
83,111,123,130,182,197,198,206,
212,220-222,237,278,313,321,322,
344,346,353,354

St Aubin, Sir John 67
Sadler, M.T.   121,122
Salbstein, M.C.N. 120
Sandon, Lord   137
Schleiermacher, F. 65,93
Scholefield, J.   46
Scholz, Dr J.M.A. 340
Scotland, N.   8,173,200,355
Scott, Robert   59,
Seager,   296
Sedgwick, Adam   72,
Selwyn, Bp G.A.   296,305,306
Senior, Nassau   126,
Sharp, John   194
Sheepshanks, Archdn 174
Shelburne, Lord   140
Shenton, C.   130
Shore, James   211,212
Short, Bp T.V.   92
Shrewsbury, Earl of 196
Shutte, Reginald 42,329
Shuttleworth, Bp P.N. 14,15,24,
26,37,72,79,298
Simeon, Charles   43,45-47,56.62,
88,280,308
Sinclair, Sir J.   41
Sinclair, Archdn John 348,349

394

Skinner, John   125,223,333,352
Smith, Canon Dr   155
Smith, E.A.   82,109,112,119
Smith Richard   351
Smith, Robert   33
Smith, Sydney   1,24,53,72,88,98,
157,161,164,165,187,215,310,352
Smith, Walter G.   118
Soloway, R.A.   85,123,205,209,
210,233,266
Somerset, Duke of 211
Southey, Robert   331
Sowerby, Thomas   46
Sparke, Bp Bowyer E. 11,14,36,
79,143-145,155,331,346,363
Sparke, Edward   144
Sparke, John Henry 143,144
Spencer, 2nd Earl 53,61,77,93,
94,191,
Spencer, Hon George 61,191
Spencer, Lady   74
Stanley, Dean A. P. 27,43,50,51,
86,172,186,207,218,336,346
Stanley, Catherine 27,336
Stanley, Charles   336
Stanley, Bp Edward 14,27,36,43,
47,50,64,85,86,138,171,172,177,
183,185,186,199,207,209,218,268,
269,335,336,346,354,369,370
Stanley, Sir John 27,50,85,86
Stanley, Kitty   336
Stanley, Mary   336
Stanley, Owen   336
Stapleton, Mary H. 54
Steel, John   224
Stone, L.   31
Stone, M.   196
Stowell, H.M.   320,328,342
Stranks, Archdn C.J. 98,199,364
Strutt, Edward   325
Styleman, Mr   182
Suffield, Lord   147
Sumner, Caroline   323

Sumner, Bp C.R.   14,15,18,20,34,
43,46,66,70,75,76,98,104,111,113,
130,138,162,176,177,180,191,192,
207,220,221,227,230,241,258,259,
279,317,318,322,326,329,332,335,
337,341,344,346,355,365
Sumner, Emily   337
Sumner, G.H.   18,34,67,75,98,
104,113,138,322,329,335,337,344,
355
Sumner, Hannah   19
Sumner, Humphrey   20
Sumner, Bp J.B.   6,15,18,20,43,46,
47,58,76,92,98,126,130,145,169,
173,200,205,206,219,226,235,236,
244,252,264,265,283,293,303,304,
307,310,312,321,323,336,342,346,
355, 365
Sumner, Mary   329
Surtees, Deborah M. 42,62
Surtees, William   42
Sussex, Duke of   286
Sutton, Archbp Charles Manners
14,36,49,52,70,73,83,86,91,92,143,
144,155,168,220,316
Sutton, Charles Manners Jr 74
Sutton, Thomas Manners 73
Sykes, Norman   179,180

Taylor, Sir Herbert 116
Taylor, W.C.   172
Thirlwall, Bp. C. 15,19,36,64-66,
72,95,96,124,201,309,320,360
Thistlethwayte, T. 85,97,98,185,
190,211,318,323,325,327,334,340,
341
Thomas, D.R.   17
Thomas, Rev (of Pentyrch) 195
Thomason, Thomas   46
Thompson, W.H.   66
Thorp, Archdn Thomas 237,257,
290,292,336,345
Thynne, Lord J.   300
Thynne, Viscount Thomas 60

395

Tieck, J.L. 65
Tiptaft, W. 211
Tomline, Bp George Pretyman- 45,61,73,78,155,
Townsend, Lt-Gen Samuel 26
Traherne, J.M. 105,189,350
Trench, Archbp P le Poer 15,111
Trevelyan, G.M. 21
Tuckwell, William 26
Turberville, A.S. 77,135,
Turton, Thomas 65,313
Tyrwhitt, Thomas 40,

Utterton, Bp. John 326,365

Varley, Elizabeth 8,91,294,330, 333,345
Vaughan, C.J. 8,336
Venn, John 93,331
Victoria, Queen 16,70,88,139, 209,359
Vidler, Alec 170
Virgin, Peter 148,191,208, 217,350
Voltaire 123

Wade, John 10,11,141-144,
Walker, Jeremiah 283
Ward, Charlotte 324
Ward, J.T. 123,124,276
Ward, Thomas 324
Ward, Bp William 15,26,27,35,93, 97,156,295,323,324,345,360
Ward, Mrs 360
Ward, William 296
Ward, W.R. 159,363,364
Waterland, Daniel 310
Watson, Joshua 138,292,293,305, 307,332
Watson, Bp Richard 44,140,141, 171,180,258,
Webb, 306
Webster, A.B. 206,210,258
Welch, P.J. 163

Wellington, Duke of 10,12,64,80-82,87,92,102,104,108-110,112, 114,138,141,286,305
West, H. 193
Westmorland, Lord 1,71
Wetherell, Sir Charles 111,117
Wharton, Joseph 39,
Whately, Archbp R. 29,30,32,53, 69,72,120,130,173,216,
Whewell, W. 65,
White, Joseph B. 90
Whitington, 306
Wieland, C.M. 55
Wilberforce, Bp Samuel 124,200, 201,335,344,346,364
Wilberforce, William 19,83,
Wilkins, Archdn George 150,245, 256,
William IV 70,77,86,94,113,116, 132,135,174,209,349
Williams, Archdn John 96
Williams, Dr (of Cowbridge) 280
Williams, Wm. 212,213
Wilson, Edith 97,295,324,360
Wilson, Edward 294
Wilson, William 281,282
Winchilsea, Lord 10,137
Wiseman, Nicholas 297
Witts, F.E. 183,184,196,197
Wolffe, J.R. 174,175,198,357
Woollcombe, Mr 41
Wordsworth, Bp Charles 290,307, 308
Wordsworth, Christopher 65,95, 161
Wordsworth, William 18,335
Wykeham, William of 23,24,60,
Wymer, N. 25

York, Duke of 80
Yorke, Bp. James 66

St Bees Theological College
Pioneering Higher Education in 19th Century Cumbria

The year is 1816. The Church of England is facing immense problems and is beset by many ills of its own making, among them the lack of properly trained clergy. A northern Bishop founds a college to meet the needs of his vast diocese which includes all the new industrial towns of Lancashire. He chooses St Bees, a small village on the coast of Cumberland. It is a village with deep Christian roots: the site of a pre-Viking Christian community, a Norman Benedictine Priory and an Elizabethan Grammar School. A village which had produced two Archbishops in the reign of Elizabeth I. At its peak in 1850-51, the college had over 120 students, many more than the younger foundations of St David's College Lampeter (1827) or Durham University (1833), and it had hopes of being granted a Charter like theirs to award academic degrees. The petition, however, was rejected. In 1895, after having trained over two and a half thousand men, it suddenly closed.

Dr Trevor Park, a former Vicar of St Bees, drawing on many contemporary sources tells the story of this pioneering institution of higher education whose students frequently came out top in the examinations that bishops held prior to ordination, beating graduates of Oxford and Cambridge. This revised edition of his short history of the college, first published in 1982, draws on much new material, including a collection of letters from the early 19th century discovered in a St Bees attic in 2007.

ISBN 978-0-9508325-1-0   **UK £8.00**

"Nolo Episcopari"
A Life of C.J. Vaughan

"No living man has laid the Church of England under greater obligations" wrote Archbishop Benson about Charles Vaughan.

Schooled under Thomas Arnold at Rugby, Vaughan became a Scholar of Trinity College Cambridge where he graduated in 1838 as 1st Classicist and Chancellor's Medallist, and was elected a Fellow. Appointed Headmaster of Harrow at the age of twenty-eight, he restored its reputation over the next fifteen years as one of the greatest schools in the country. In 1860 he was offered the bishopric of Rochester which he refused. Other bishoprics were offered later. He declined all of them.

Instead of becoming a bishop in the south, Vaughan went north to work for nine years as a parish priest in Doncaster where he enjoyed enormouse success. It was there he began his life's greatest work: helping young Oxbridge graduates prepare themselves for Ordination. Over 430 men, who were given the nickname 'Vaughan's doves', trained with him. Eighteen of them became bishops, two of them archbishops. He was also a preacher and writer of national renown, publishing over 130 volumes – mostly sermons and NT commentaries. In 1872 *Vanity Fair* alluded to this when he was included in its series 'Men of the Day'. He was pictured in the pulpit of the Temple Church in London, whose Master he was by then, and the caricature was given the title *"Nolo Episcopari"*. Randall Davidson, a future Archbishop of Canterbury, who was one of his 'doves' at that time, called him "A worker in the foremost rank of living Englishmen."

His reputation, however, was tarnished in 1964 when Phylis Grosskurth revealed in her biography of J.A. Symonds, who had been at Harrow under Vaughan, that Symonds in his private *Memoirs*, written 30 years after the events, had accused the Head of sexual misconduct with another pupil. An accusation accepted uncritically in the 1960s by many who were all too ready to see the story as a Victorian scandal which had been covered up. Trevor Park, drawing on the private journals and letters of a school friend of Symonds which throw serious doubt on the truth of Symonds's story, argues convincingly that Vaughan was innocent of the charge.

Charles John Vaughan was an inspirational figure in the Victorian Church. His life story deserves to be made known.

ISBN 978-0-9508325-4-8   **UK £14.00**